HANAKO 花子
AND THE TERROR OF ALLEGORY

VOLUME 1

BY SAKAE ESUNO

HAMBURG // LONDON // LOS ANGELES // TOKYO

Hanako and the Terror of Allegory 1
Created by Sakae Esuno

Translation - Satsuki Yamashita
English Adaptation - Bryce P. Coleman
Copy Edit - Jill Bentley
Retouch and Lettering - Star Print Brokers
Production Artist - Michael Paolilli
Graphic Designer - Al-Insan Lashley

Editor - Cindy Suzuki
Print Production Manager - Lucas Rivera
Managing Editor - Vy Nguyen
Senior Designer - Louis Csontos
Art Director - Al-Insan Lashley
Director of Sales and Manufacturing - Allyson De Simone
Associate Publisher - Marco F. Pavia
President and C.O.O. - John Parker
C.E.O. and Chief Creative Officer - Stu Levy

A TOKYOPOP® Manga

TOKYOPOP and are trademarks or registered trademarks of TOKYOPOP Inc.

TOKYOPOP Inc.
5900 Wilshire Blvd. Suite 2000
Los Angeles, CA 90036

E-mail: info@TOKYOPOP.com
Come visit us online at www.TOKYOPOP.com

HANAKO TO GUUWA NO TELLER Volume 1
© Sakae ESUNO 2004
First published in Japan in 2004 by KADOKAWA
SHOTEN PUBLISHING CO., LTD., Tokyo.
English translation rights arranged with KADOKAWA
SHOTEN PUBLISHING CO., LTD., Tokyo
through TUTTLE-MORI AGENCY, INC., Tokyo.
English text copyright © 2010 TOKYOPOP Inc.

ISBN: 978-1-4278-1608-5

First TOKYOPOP printing: March 2010
10 9 8 7 6 5 4 3 2 1
Printed in the USA

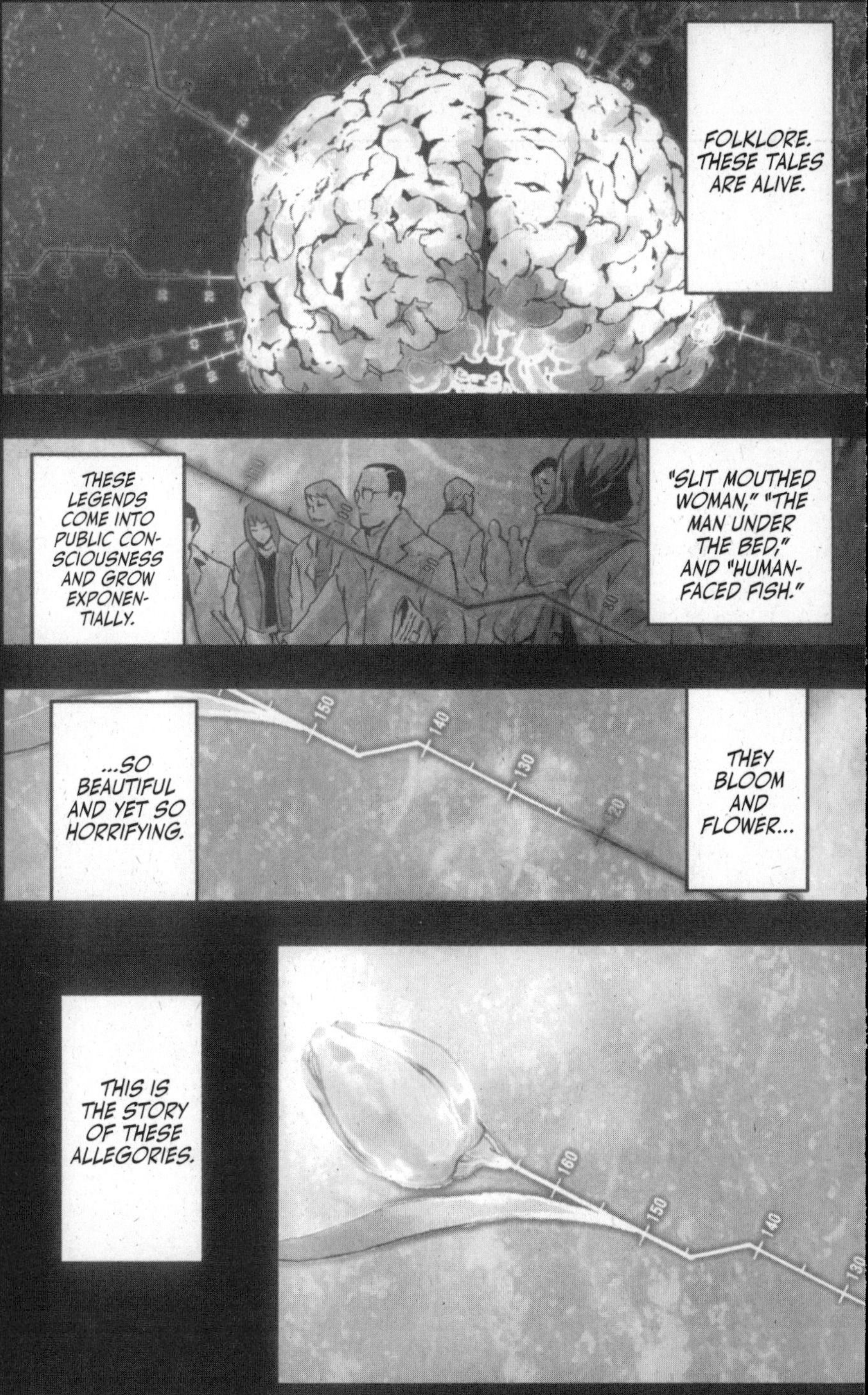
FOLKLORE. THESE TALES ARE ALIVE.
"SLIT MOUTHED WOMAN," "THE MAN UNDER THE BED," AND "HUMAN-FACED FISH."
THESE LEGENDS COME INTO PUBLIC CONSCIOUSNESS AND GROW EXPONENTIALLY.
THEY BLOOM AND FLOWER...
...SO BEAUTIFUL AND YET SO HORRIFYING.
THIS IS THE STORY OF THESE ALLEGORIES.

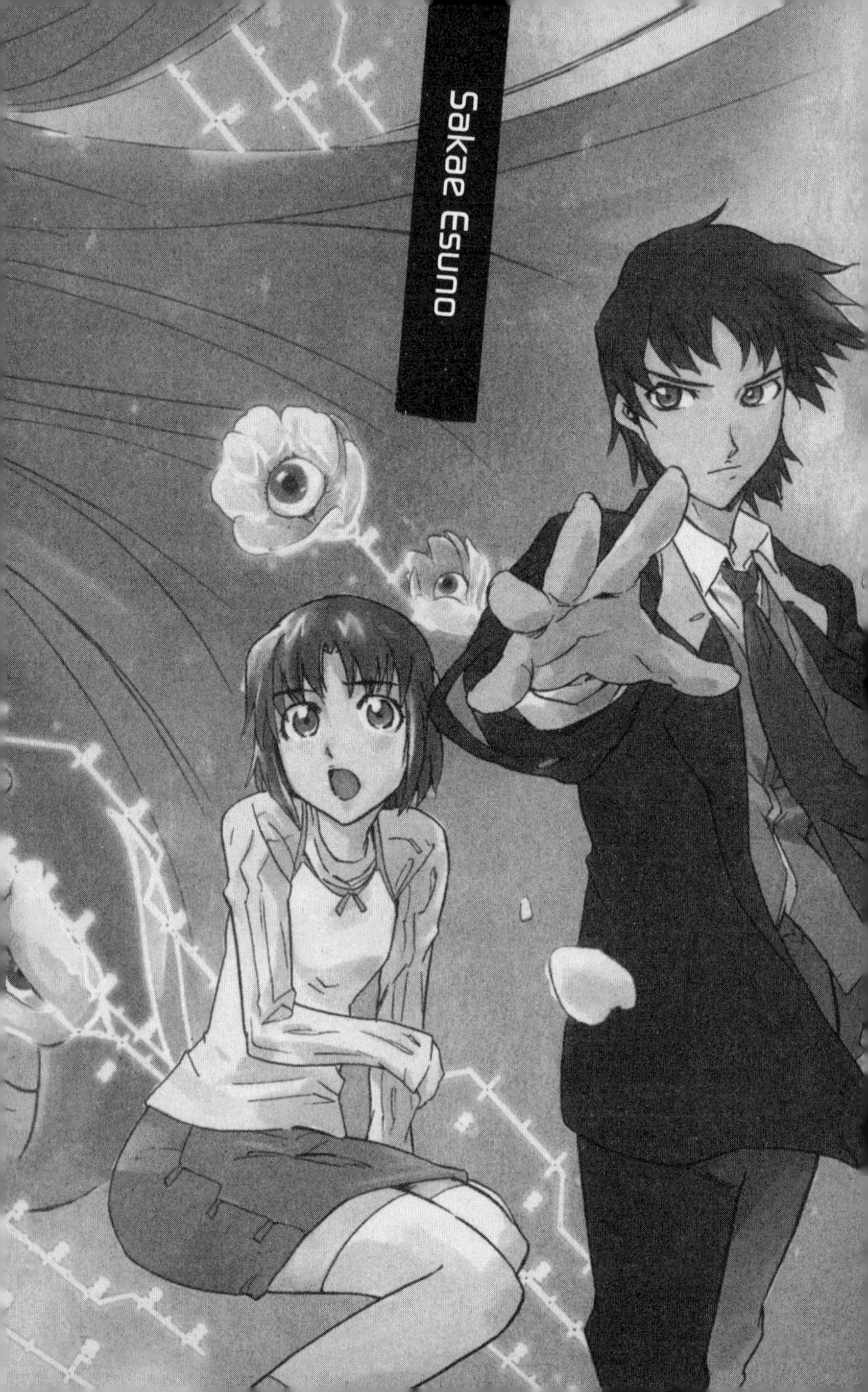
Sakae Esuno

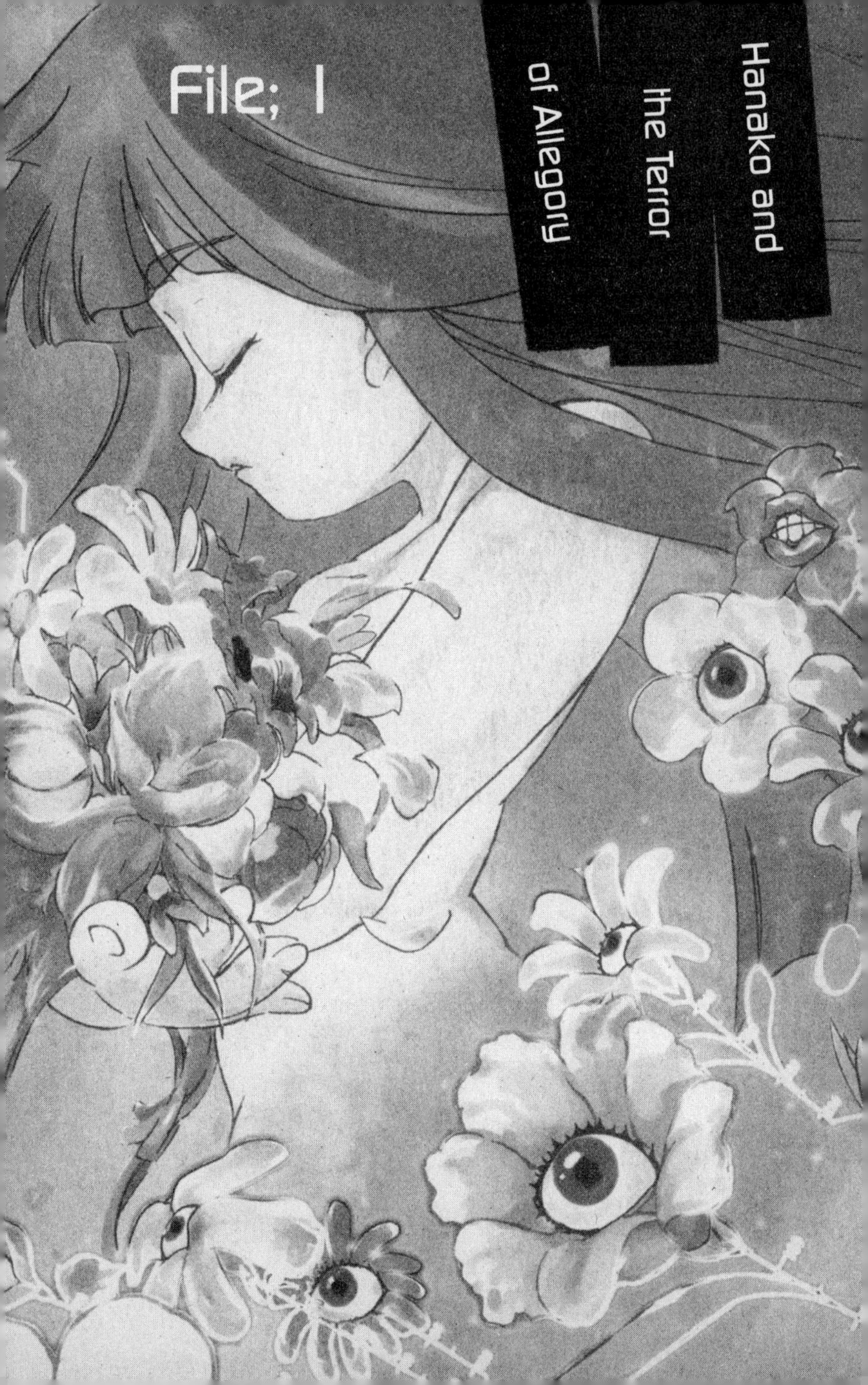
File; 1
Hanako and
the Terror
of Allegory

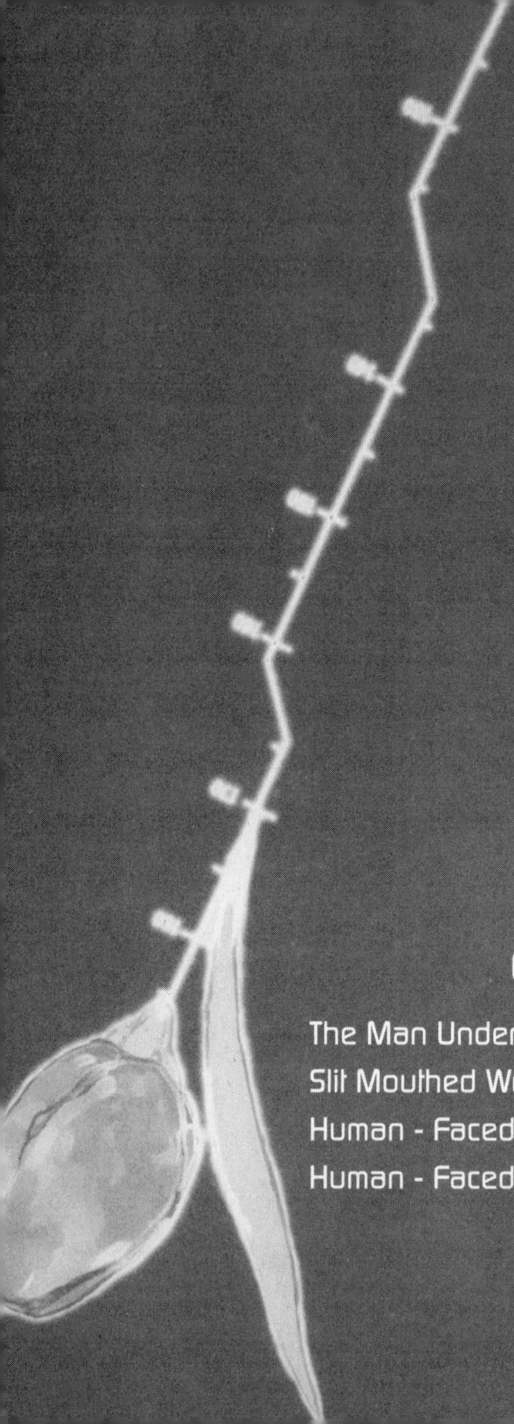

Hanako and the Terror of Allegory

File; 1

Contents

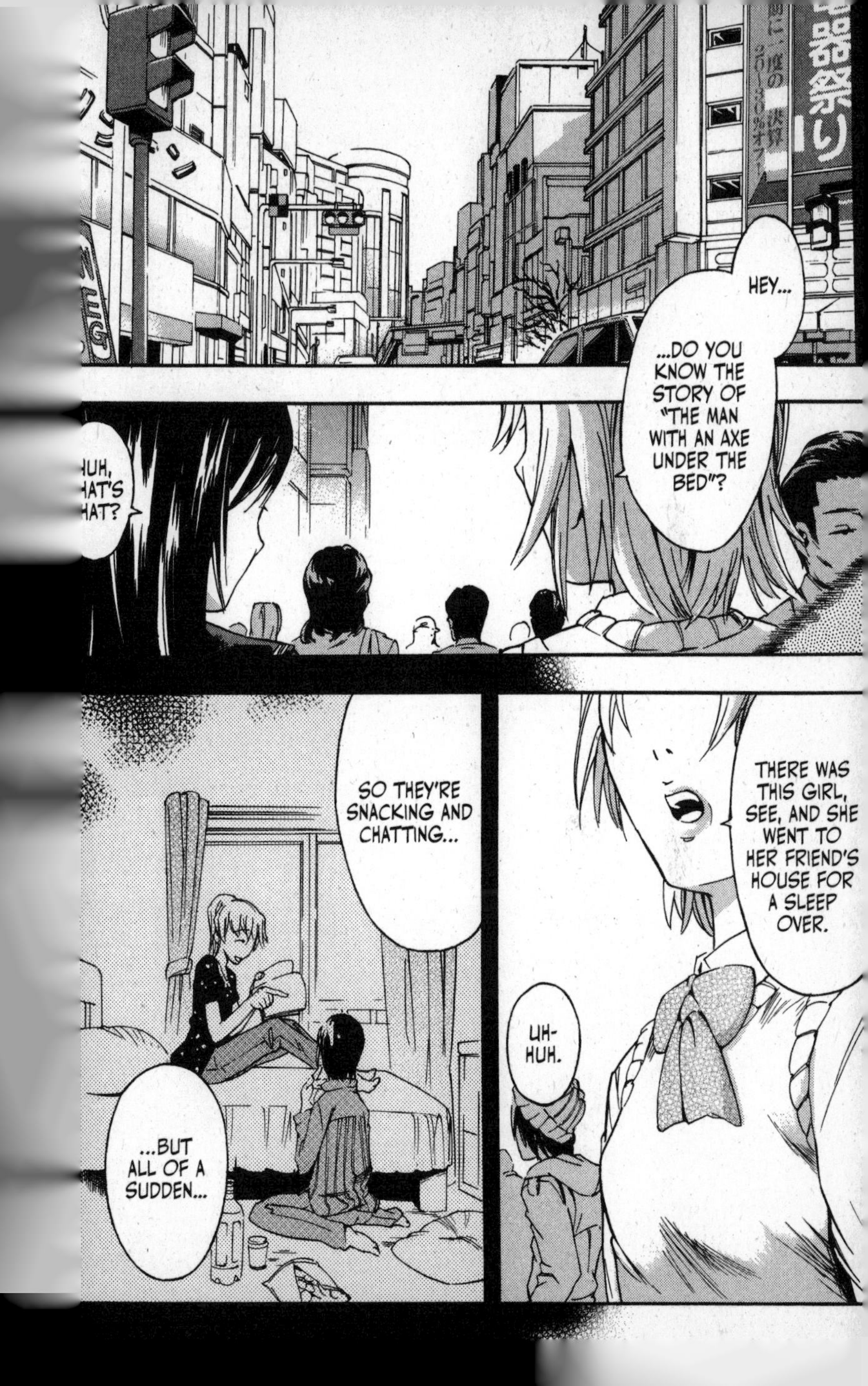
器祭り
HEY...
...DO YOU KNOW THE STORY OF "THE MAN WITH AN AXE UNDER THE BED"?
HUH, HAT'S HAT?
THERE WAS THIS GIRL, SEE, AND SHE WENT TO HER FRIEND'S HOUSE FOR A SLEEP OVER.
UH-HUH.
SO THEY'RE SNACKING AND CHATTING...
...BUT ALL OF A SUDDEN...

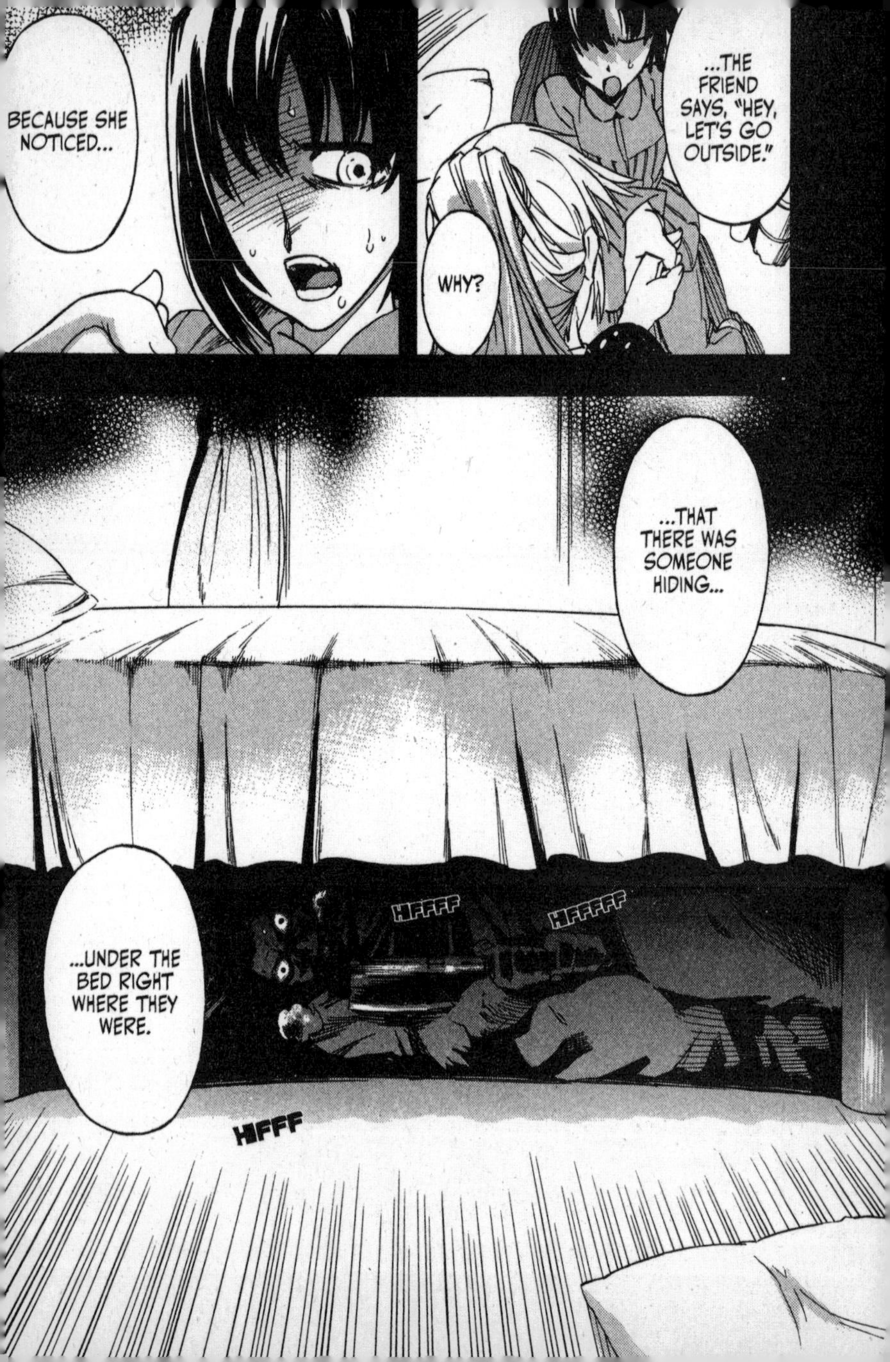
...THE FRIEND SAYS, "HEY, LET'S GO OUTSIDE."
WHY?
BECAUSE SHE NOTICED...
...THAT THERE WAS SOMEONE HIDING...
HFFFFF
HFFFF
...UNDER THE BED RIGHT WHERE THEY WERE.
HFFF

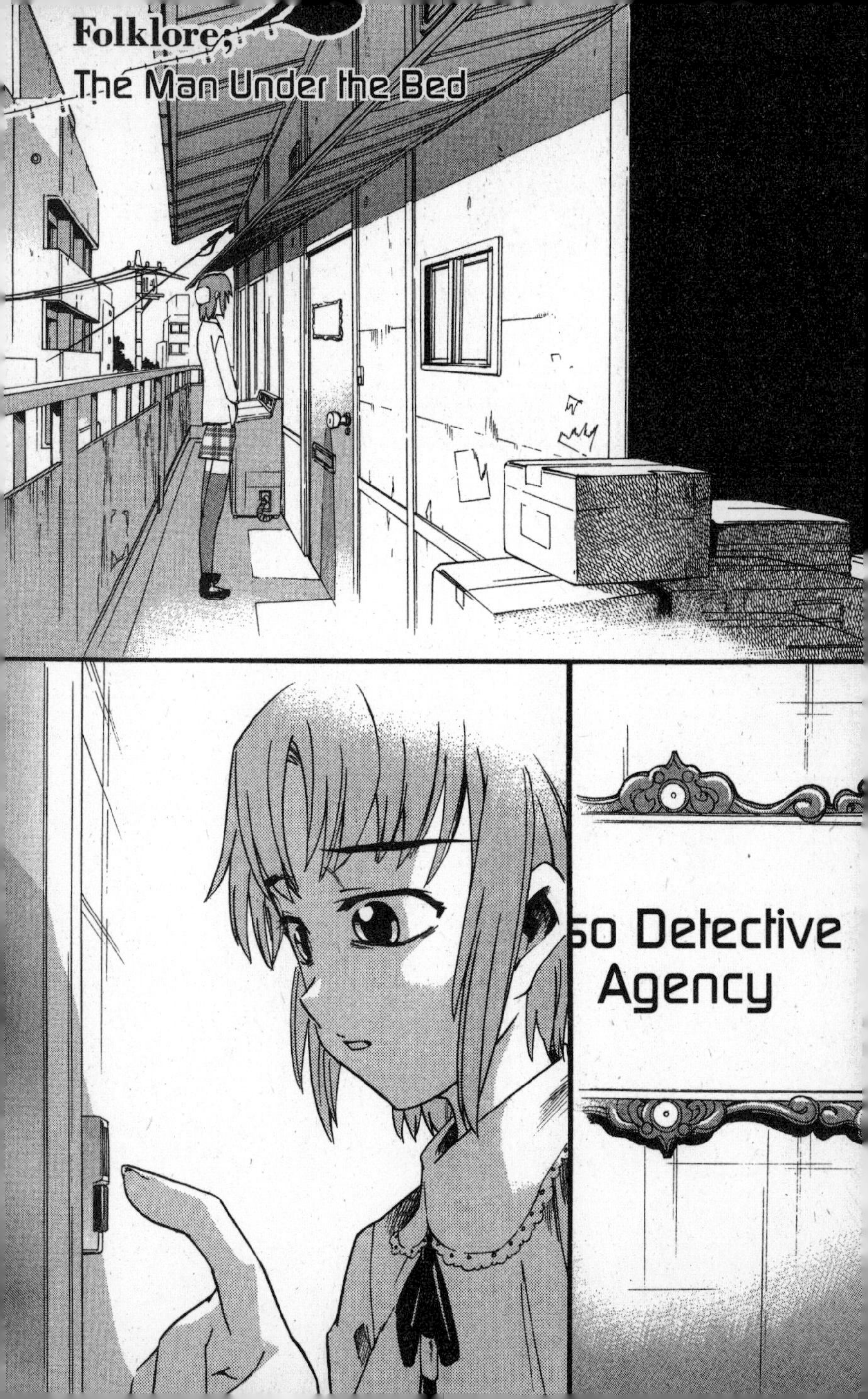
Folklore;
The Man Under the Bed
so Detective
Agency

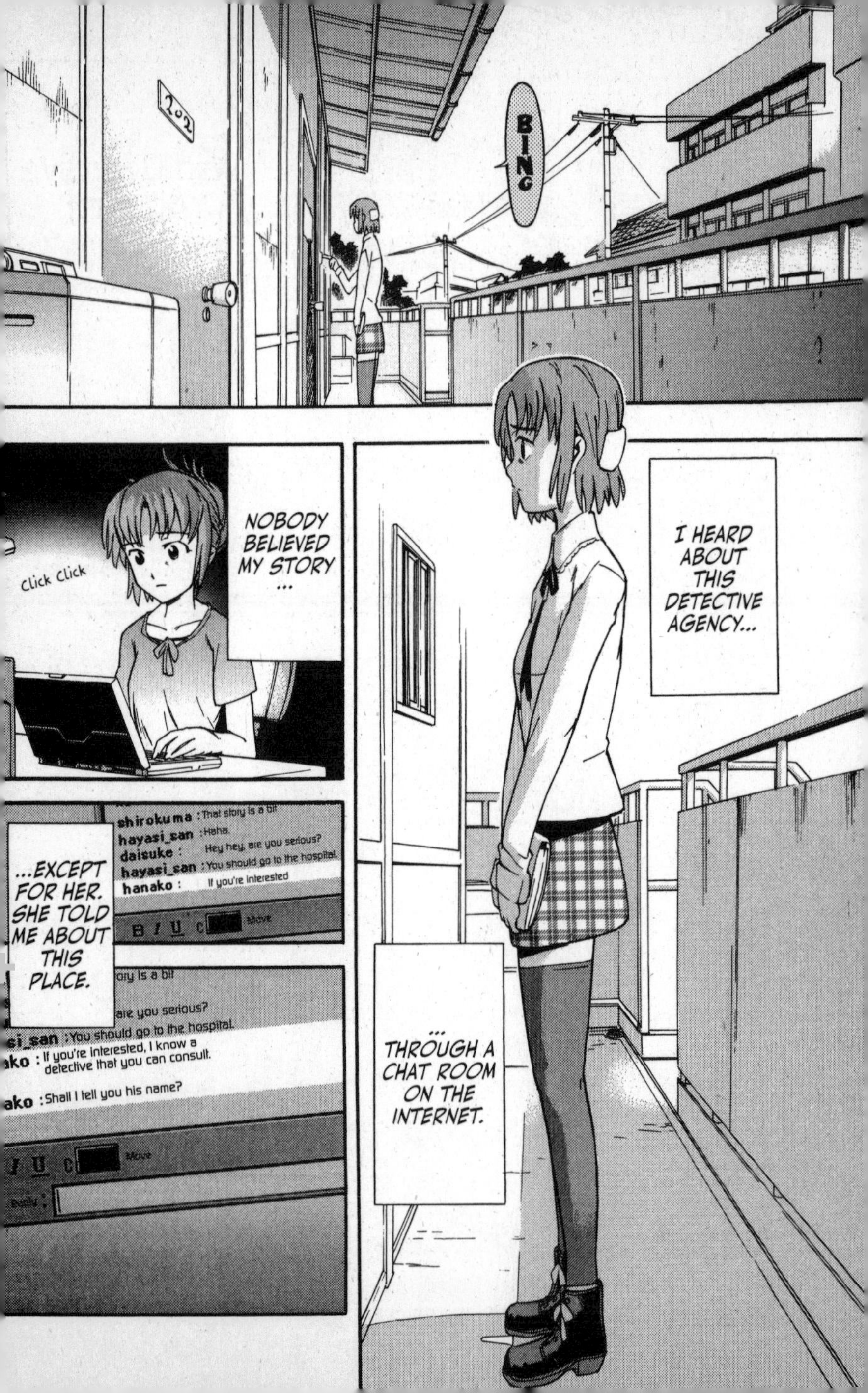
202
BING
I HEARD ABOUT THIS DETECTIVE AGENCY...
...THROUGH A CHAT ROOM ON THE INTERNET.
NOBODY BELIEVED MY STORY...
Click Click
shirokuma : That story is a bit
hayasi_san : Haha.
daisuke : Hey hey, are you serious?
hayasi_san : You should go to the hospital.
hanako : If you're interested
B I U C Move
...EXCEPT FOR HER. SHE TOLD ME ABOUT THIS PLACE.
ory is a bit
are you serious?
si_san : You should go to the hospital.
ako : If you're interested, I know a detective that you can consult.
ako : Shall I tell you his name?
I U C Move

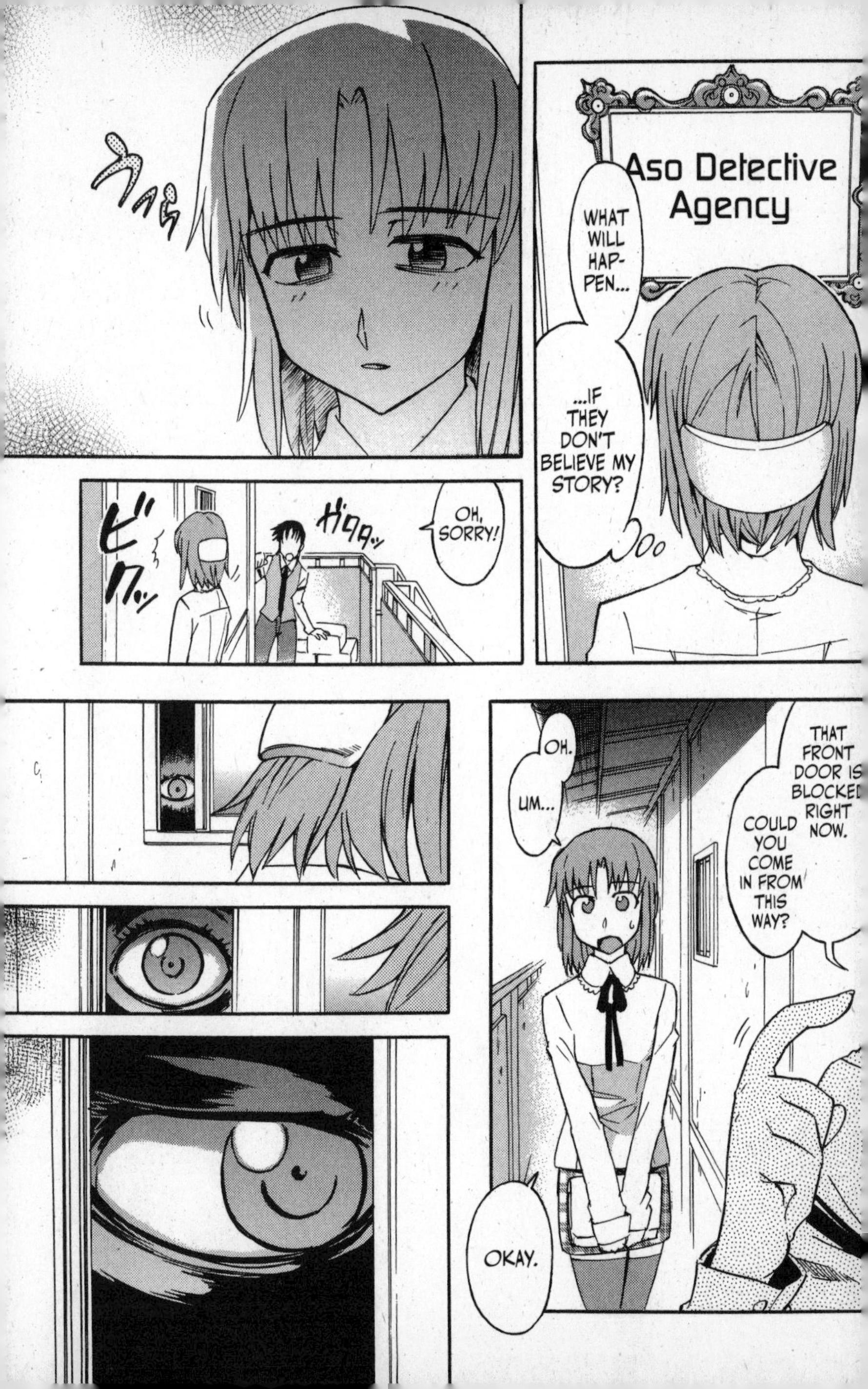
Aso Detective Agency
WHAT WILL HAP-PEN...
...IF THEY DON'T BELIEVE MY STORY?
OH, SORRY!
THAT FRONT DOOR IS BLOCKED RIGHT NOW.
COULD YOU COME IN FROM THIS WAY?
OH.
UM...
OKAY.

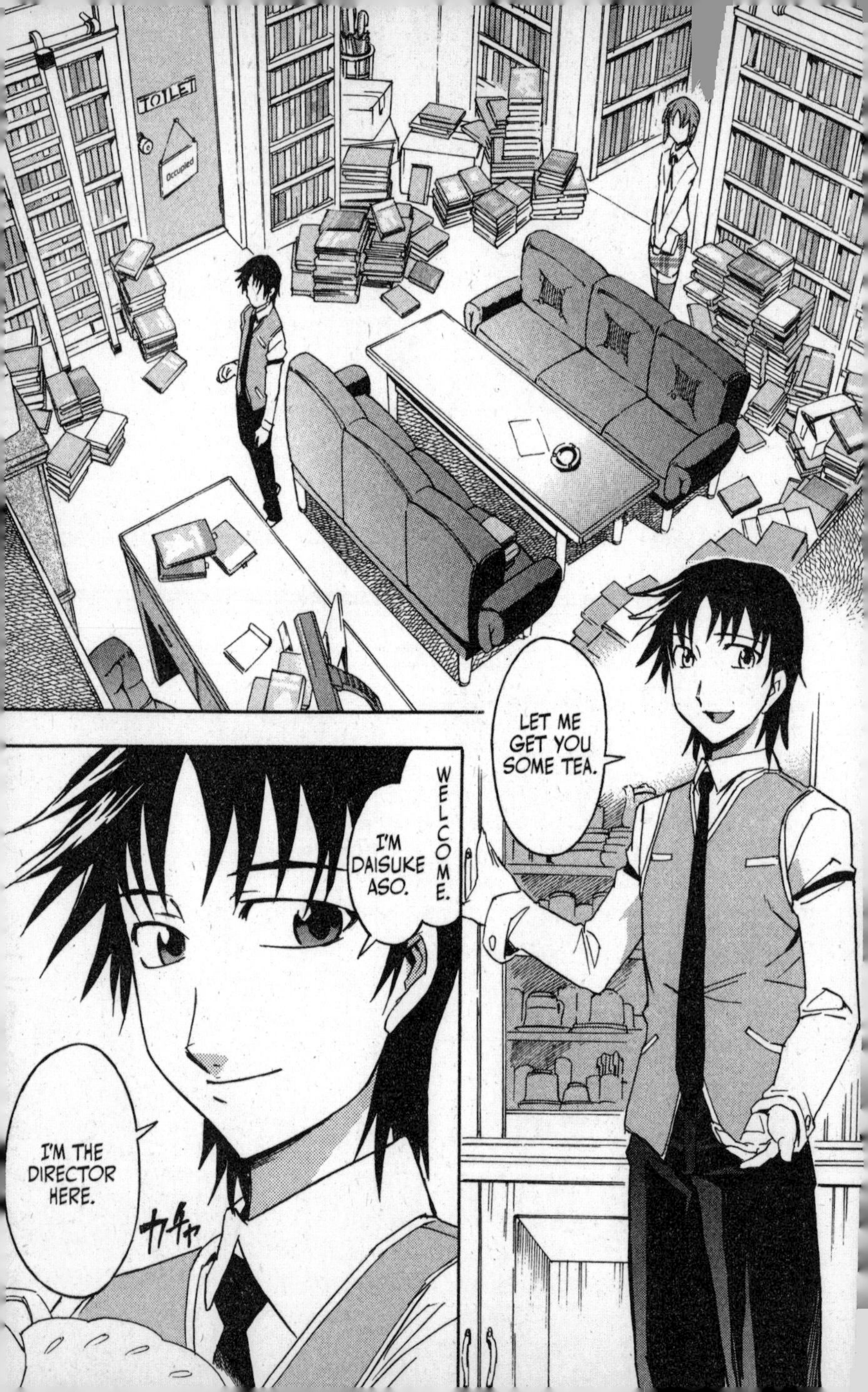
TOILET
Occupied
LET ME GET YOU SOME TEA.
WELCOME.
I'M DAISUKE ASO.
I'M THE DIRECTOR HERE.
カチャ

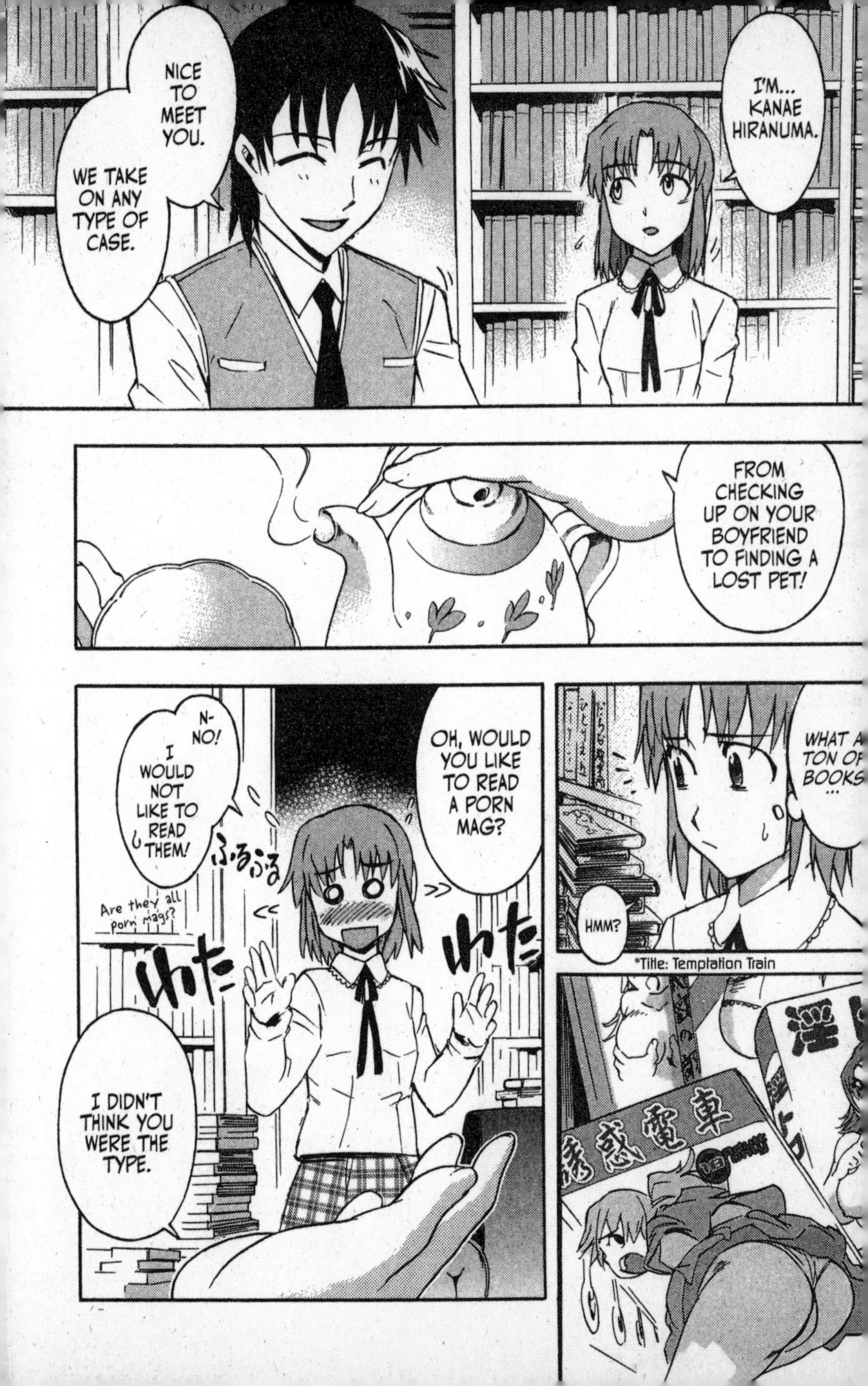
I'M... KANAE HIRANUMA.
NICE TO MEET YOU.
WE TAKE ON ANY TYPE OF CASE.
FROM CHECKING UP ON YOUR BOYFRIEND TO FINDING A LOST PET!
WHAT A TON OF BOOKS...
HMM?
*Title: Temptation Train
誘惑電車
OH, WOULD YOU LIKE TO READ A PORN MAG?
N-NO! I WOULD NOT LIKE TO READ THEM!
ふるふる
Are they all porn mags?
わた
わた
I DIDN'T THINK YOU WERE THE TYPE.

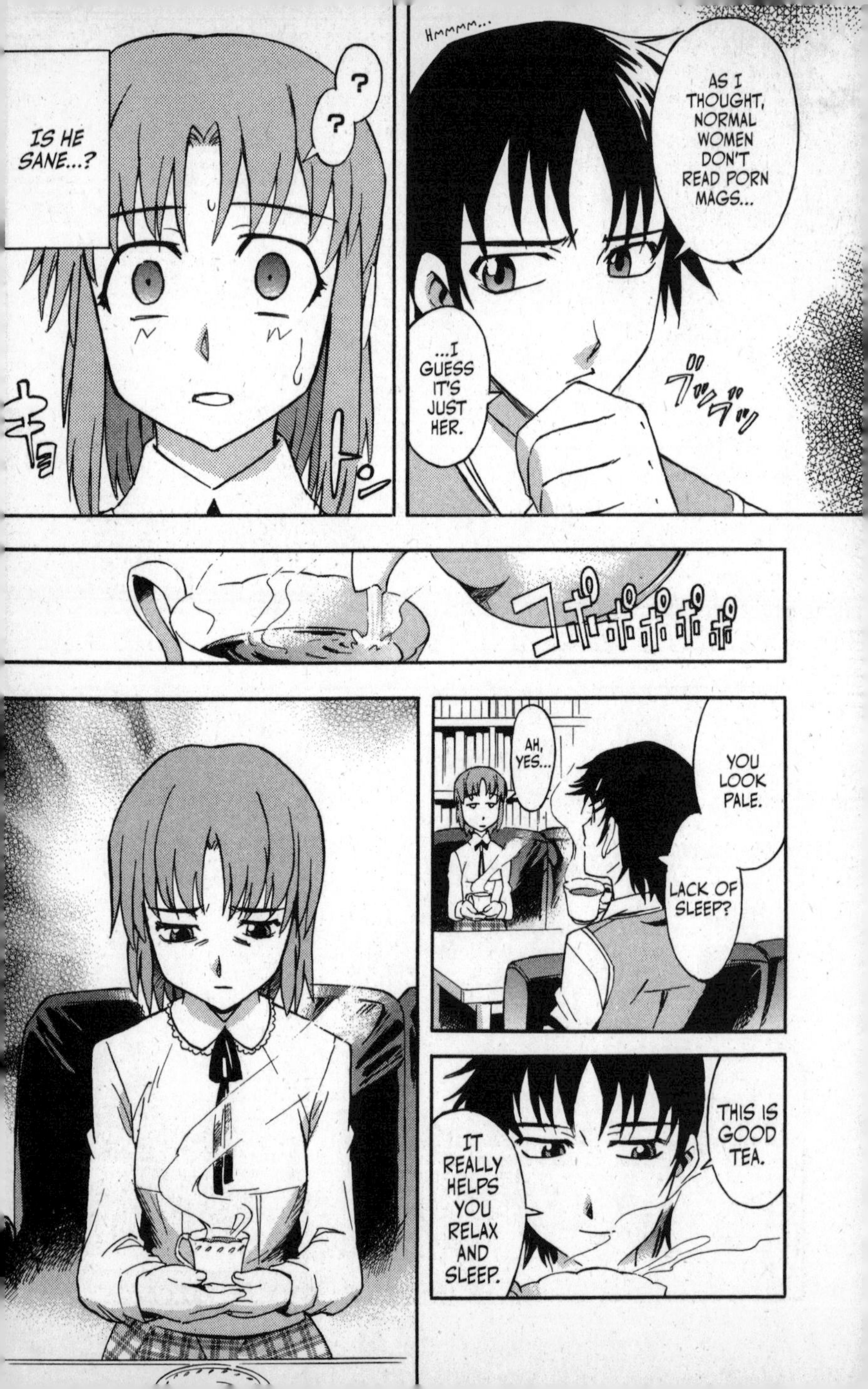
HMMMM...
AS I THOUGHT, NORMAL WOMEN DON'T READ PORN MAGS...
...I GUESS IT'S JUST HER.
ブツブツ
?
?
IS HE SANE...?
キョトン
コポポポポポ
YOU LOOK PALE.
LACK OF SLEEP?
AH, YES...
THIS IS GOOD TEA.
IT REALLY HELPS YOU RELAX AND SLEEP.

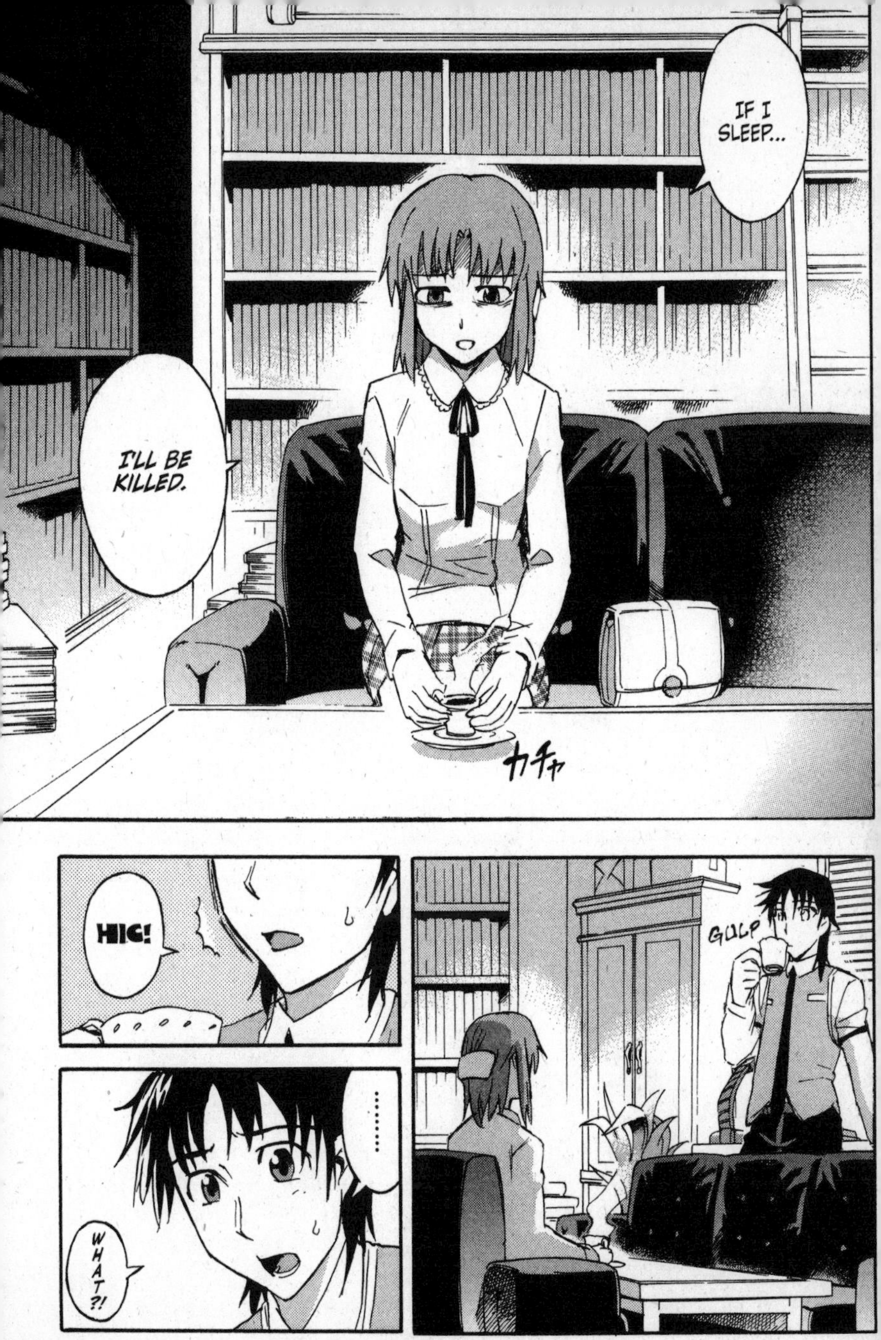
IF I SLEEP...
I'LL BE KILLED.
カチャ
GULP
HIC!
......
WHAT?!

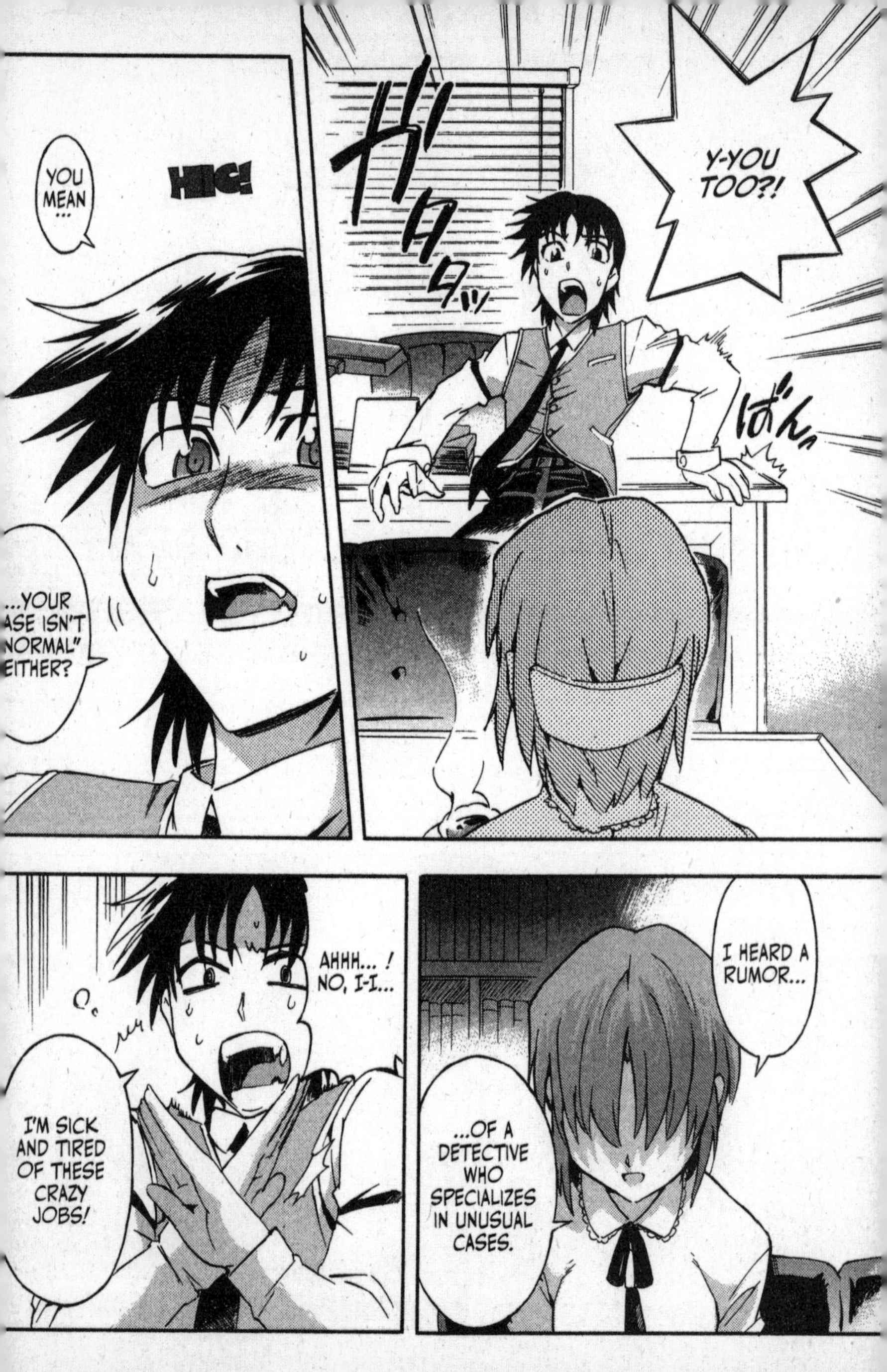
Y-YOU TOO?!
ガタタッ
ばんっ
YOU MEAN ...
HIC!
...YOUR ASE ISN'T NORMAL" EITHER?
I HEARD A RUMOR...
...OF A DETECTIVE WHO SPECIALIZES IN UNUSUAL CASES.
AHHH... ! NO, I-I...
I'M SICK AND TIRED OF THESE CRAZY JOBS!

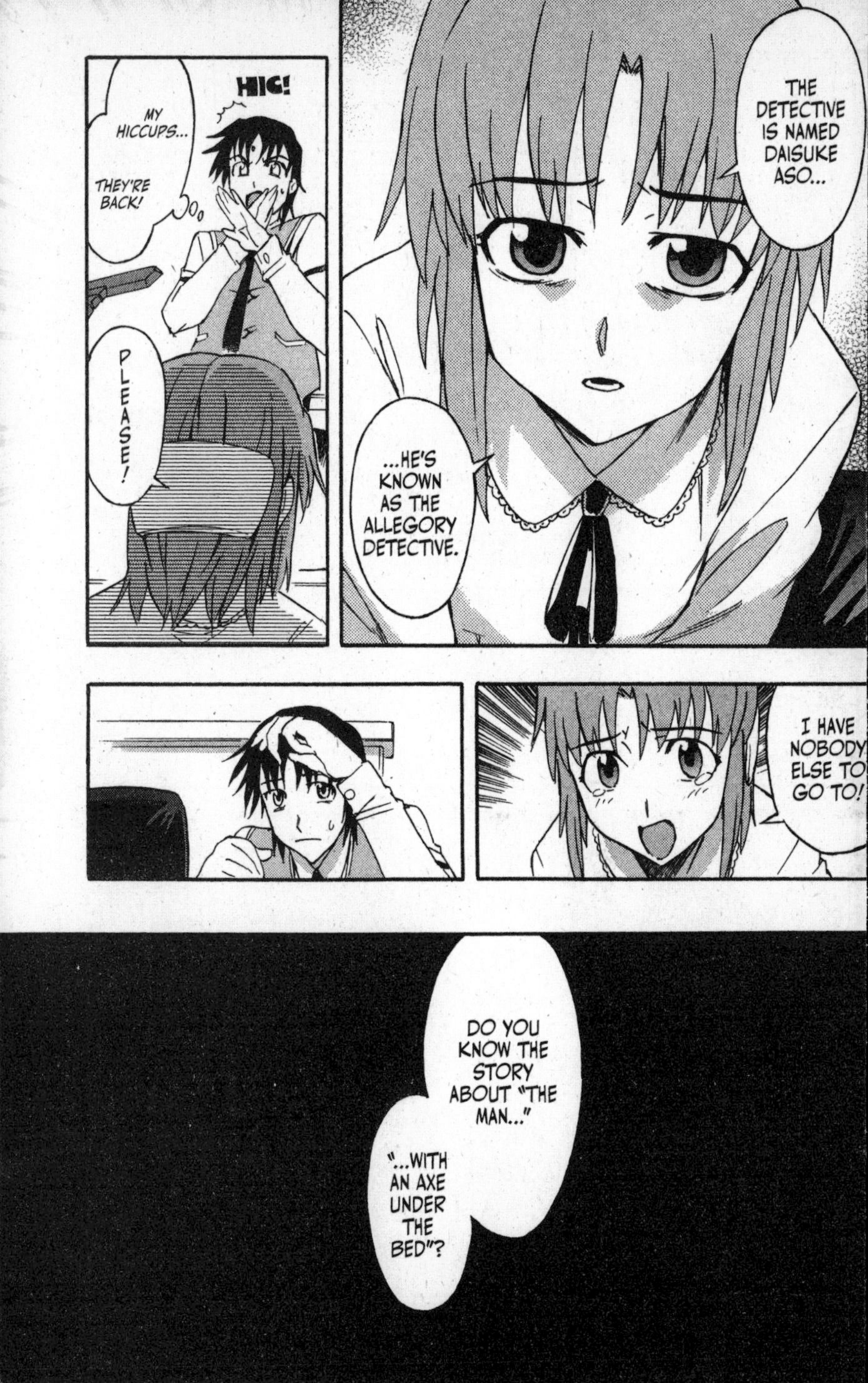
THE DETECTIVE IS NAMED DAISUKE ASO...
...HE'S KNOWN AS THE ALLEGORY DETECTIVE.
HIG!
MY HICCUPS... THEY'RE BACK!
PLEASE!
I HAVE NOBODY ELSE TO GO TO!
DO YOU KNOW THE STORY ABOUT "THE MAN..."
"...WITH AN AXE UNDER THE BED"?

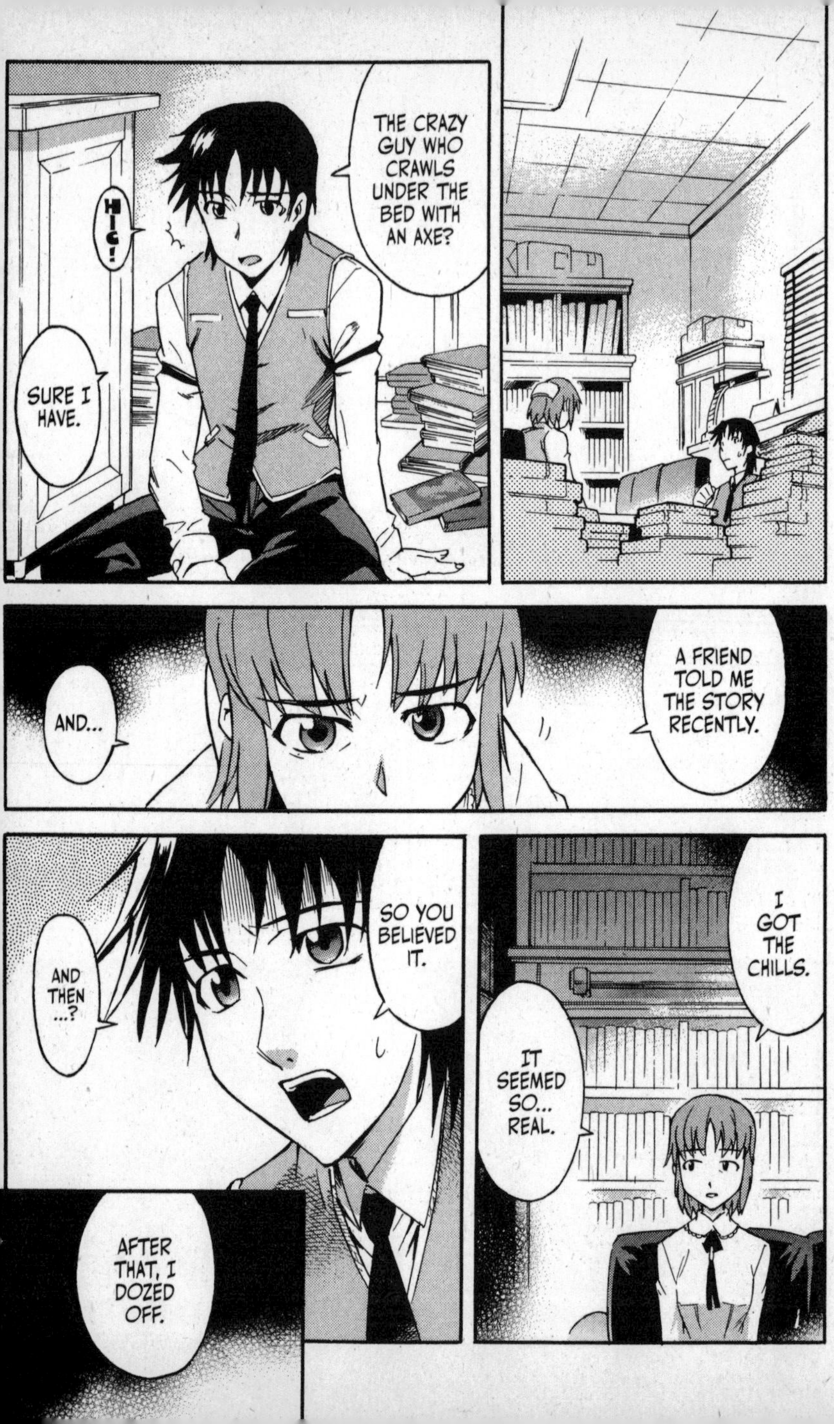
THE CRAZY GUY WHO CRAWLS UNDER THE BED WITH AN AXE?
HIC!
SURE I HAVE.
A FRIEND TOLD ME THE STORY RECENTLY.
AND...
I GOT THE CHILLS.
IT SEEMED SO... REAL.
SO YOU BELIEVED IT.
AND THEN ...?
AFTER THAT, I DOZED OFF.

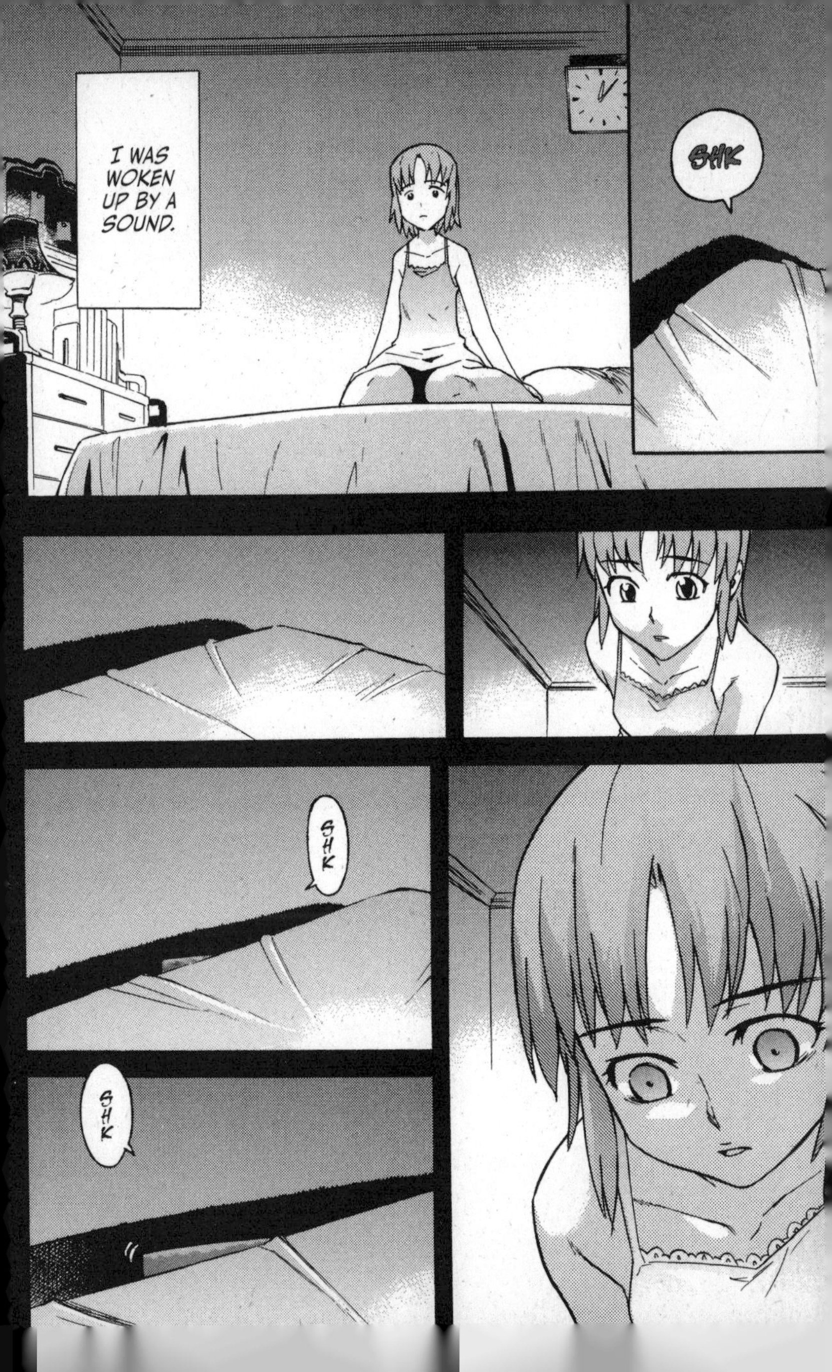
SHK
I WAS WOKEN UP BY A SOUND.
SHK
SHK

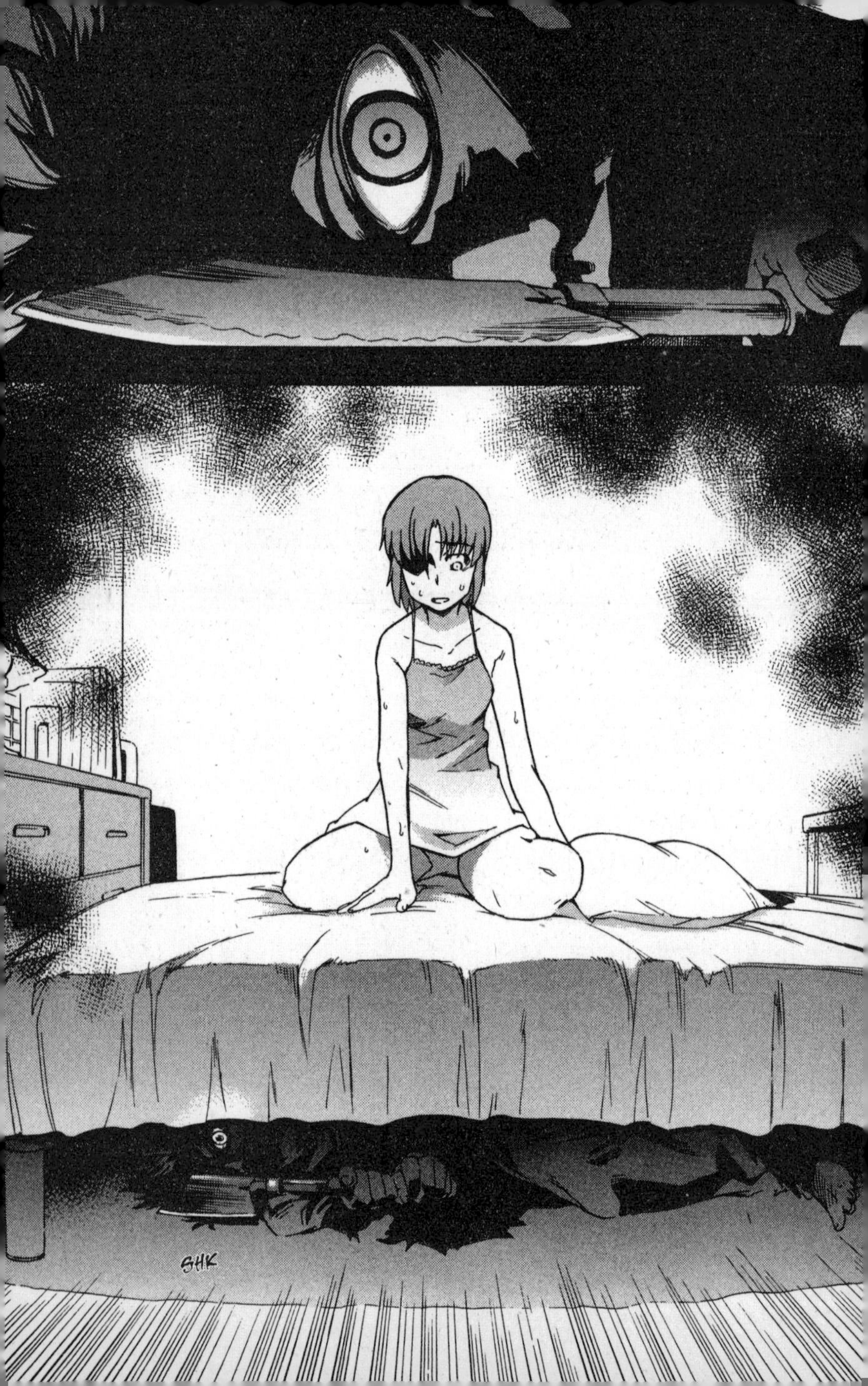
SHK

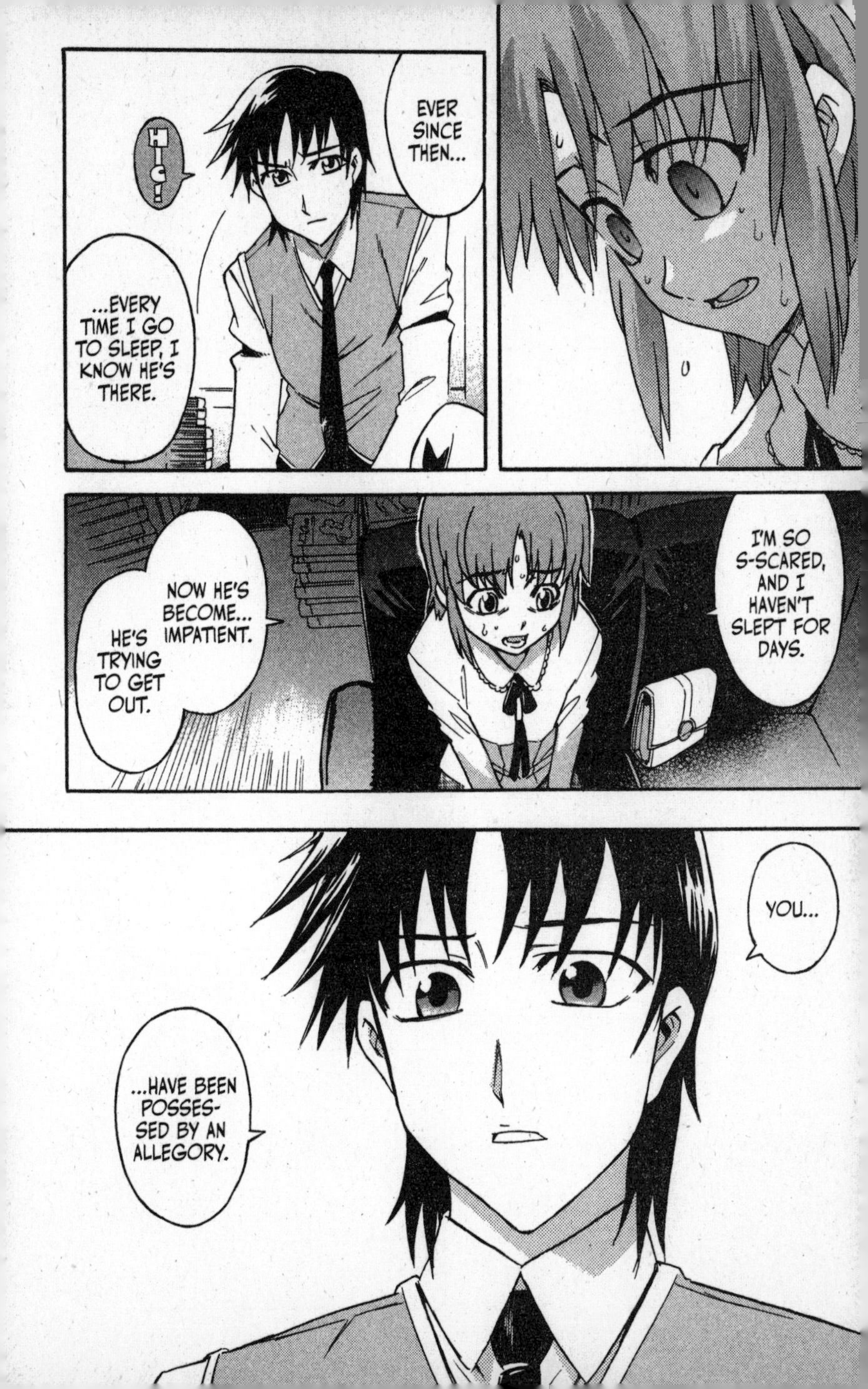
EVER SINCE THEN...
HIC!
...EVERY TIME I GO TO SLEEP, I KNOW HE'S THERE.
I'M SO S-SCARED, AND I HAVEN'T SLEPT FOR DAYS.
NOW HE'S BECOME... IMPATIENT.
HE'S TRYING TO GET OUT.
YOU...
...HAVE BEEN POSSES-SED BY AN ALLEGORY.

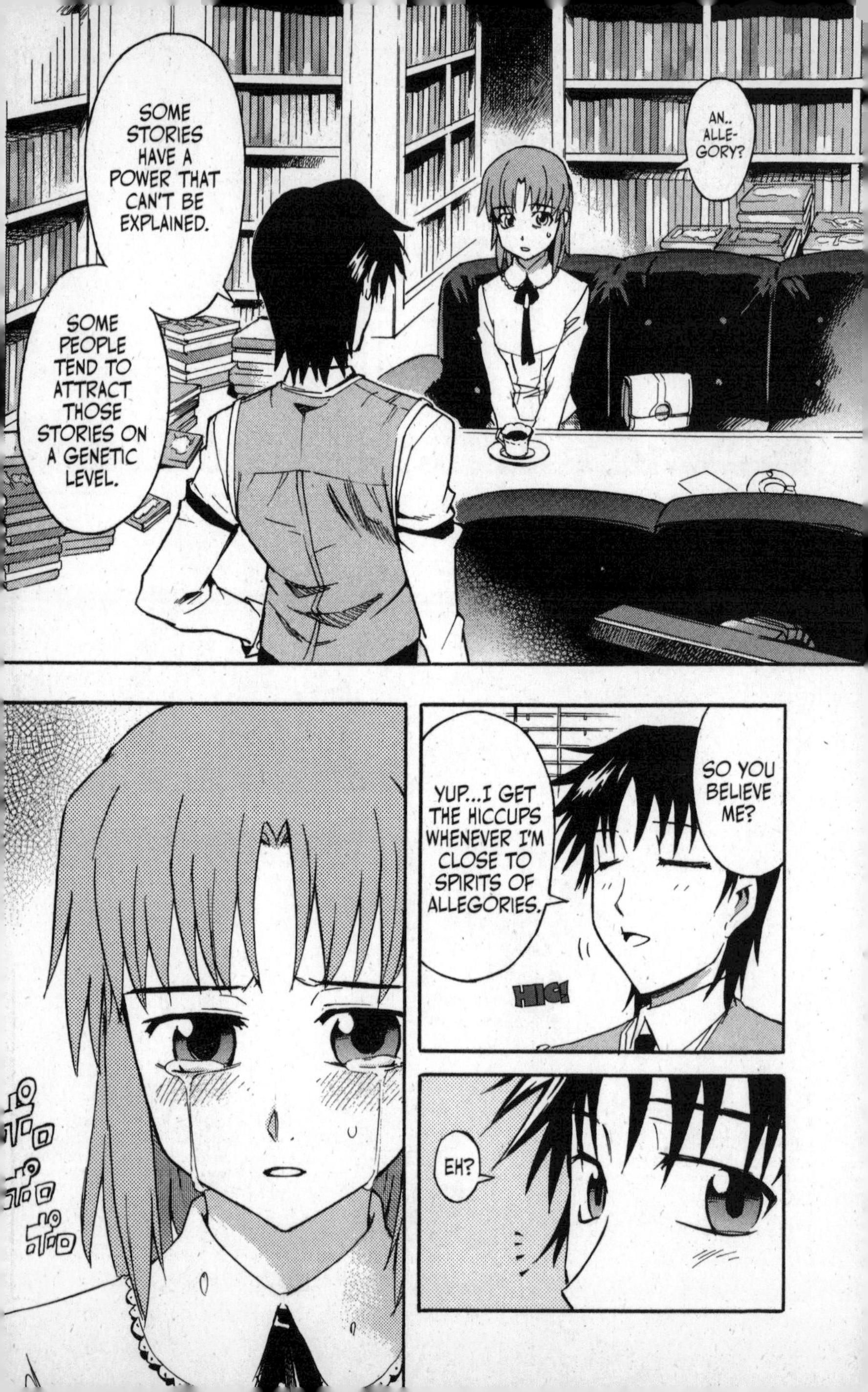

AN.. ALLE-GORY?
SOME STORIES HAVE A POWER THAT CAN'T BE EXPLAINED.
SOME PEOPLE TEND TO ATTRACT THOSE STORIES ON A GENETIC LEVEL.
SO YOU BELIEVE ME?
YUP...I GET THE HICCUPS WHENEVER I'M CLOSE TO SPIRITS OF ALLEGORIES.
HIC!
EH?
ポロ
ポロ
ポロ

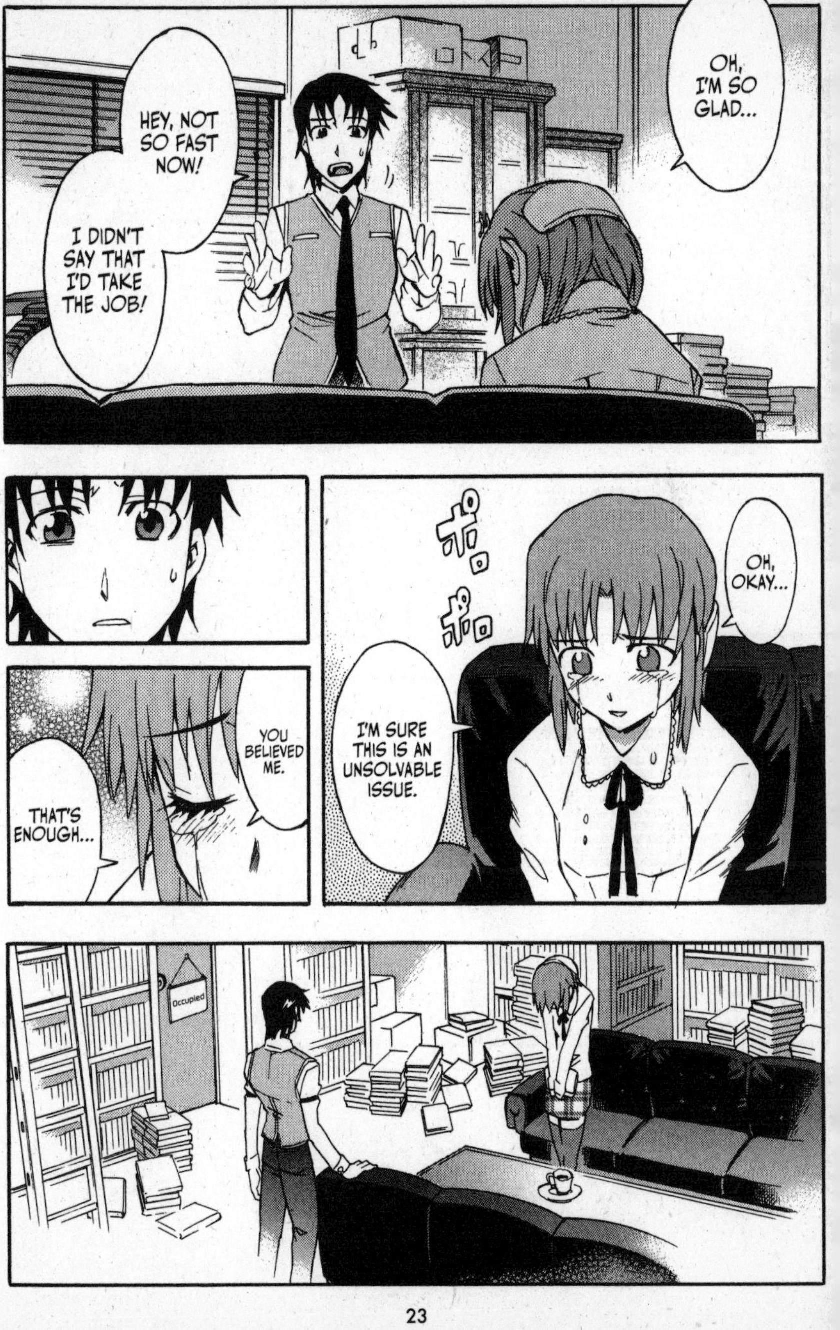
OH, I'M SO GLAD...
HEY, NOT SO FAST NOW!
I DIDN'T SAY THAT I'D TAKE THE JOB!
OH, OKAY...
ポロ
ポロ
I'M SURE THIS IS AN UNSOLVABLE ISSUE.
YOU BELIEVED ME.
THAT'S ENOUGH...
Occupied

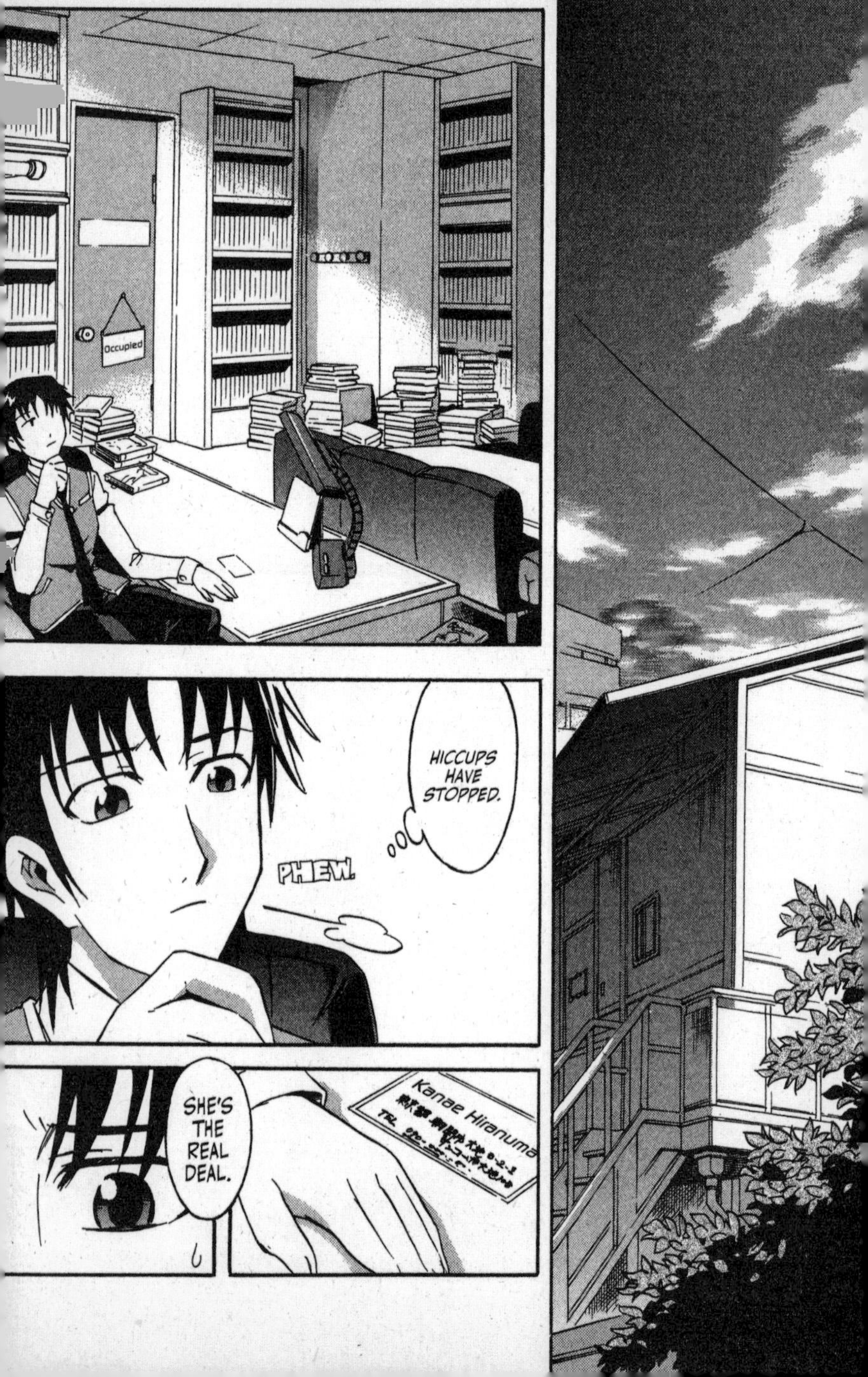
Occupied
HICCUPS HAVE STOPPED.
PHEW.
Kanae Hiranuma
SHE'S THE REAL DEAL.

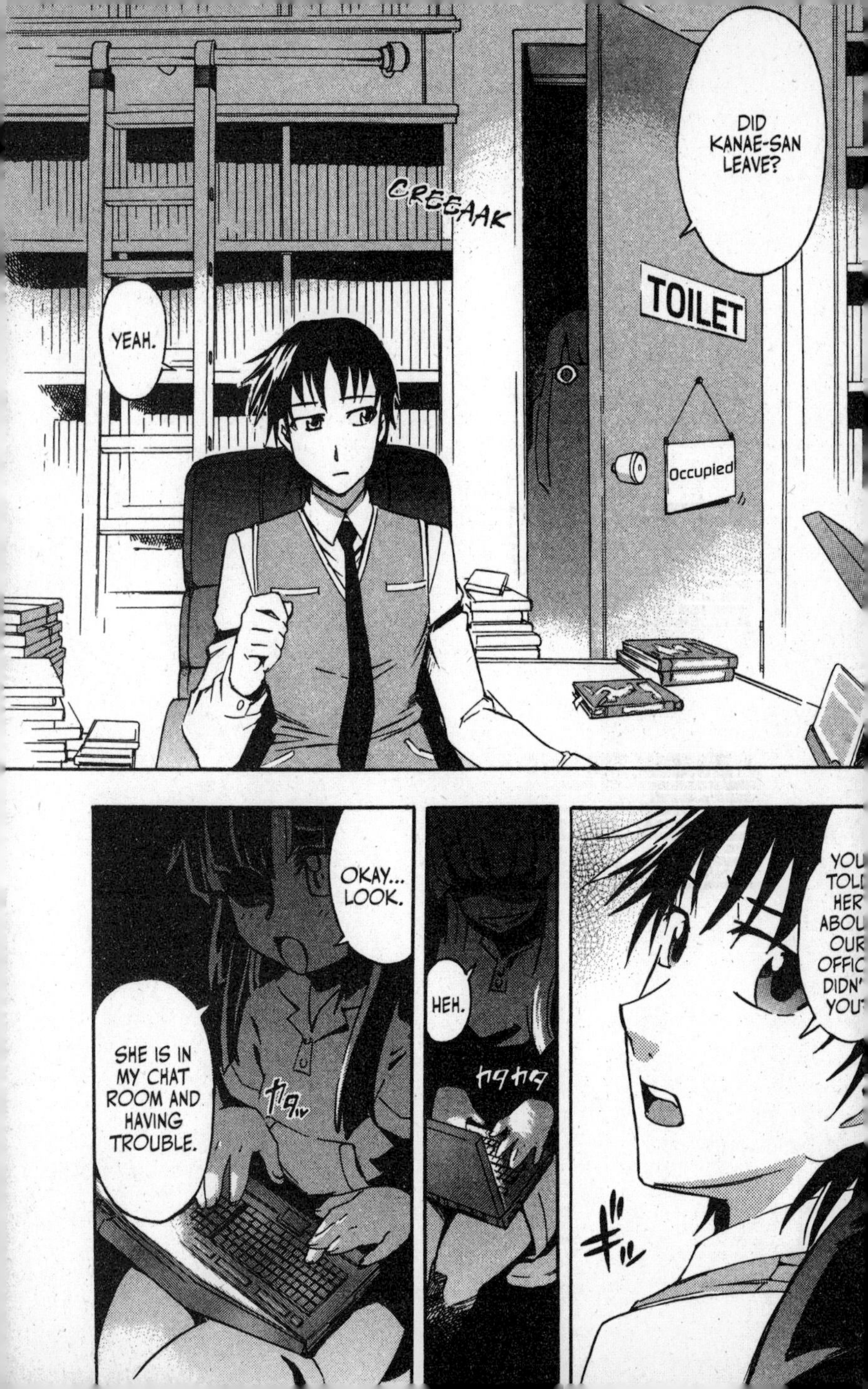

DID KANAE-SAN LEAVE?
CREEAAK
TOILET
Occupied
YEAH.
YOU TOLD HER ABOU OUR OFFIC DIDN' YOU
ギュ
HEH.
カタカタ
OKAY... LOOK.
SHE IS IN MY CHAT ROOM AND HAVING TROUBLE.
カタッ

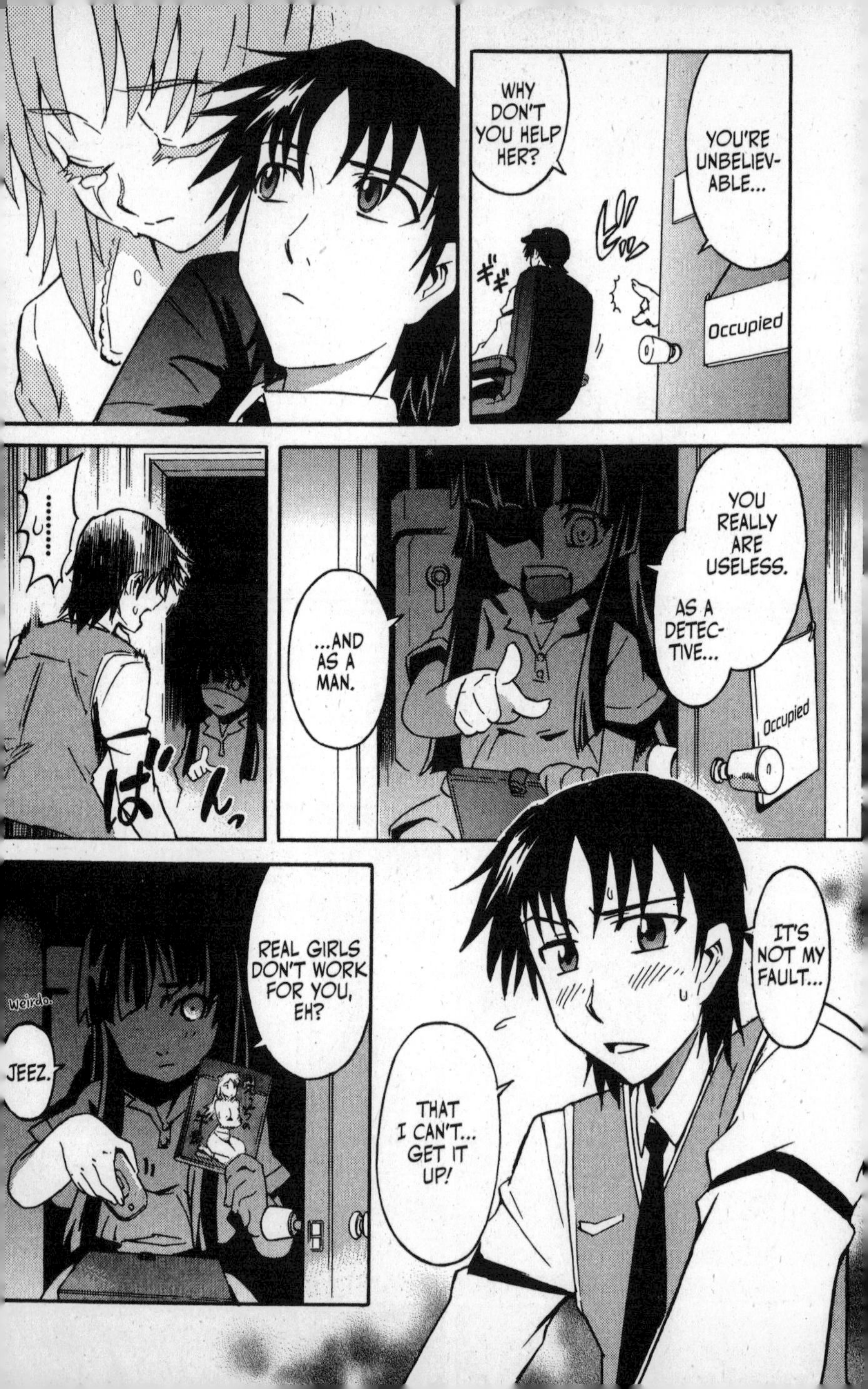
YOU'RE UNBELIEV-ABLE...
WHY DON'T YOU HELP HER?
Occupied
YOU REALLY ARE USELESS.
AS A DETEC-TIVE...
...AND AS A MAN.
Occupied
......!
ばんっ
IT'S NOT MY FAULT...
THAT I CAN'T... GET IT UP!
REAL GIRLS DON'T WORK FOR YOU, EH?
weirdo.
JEEZ.

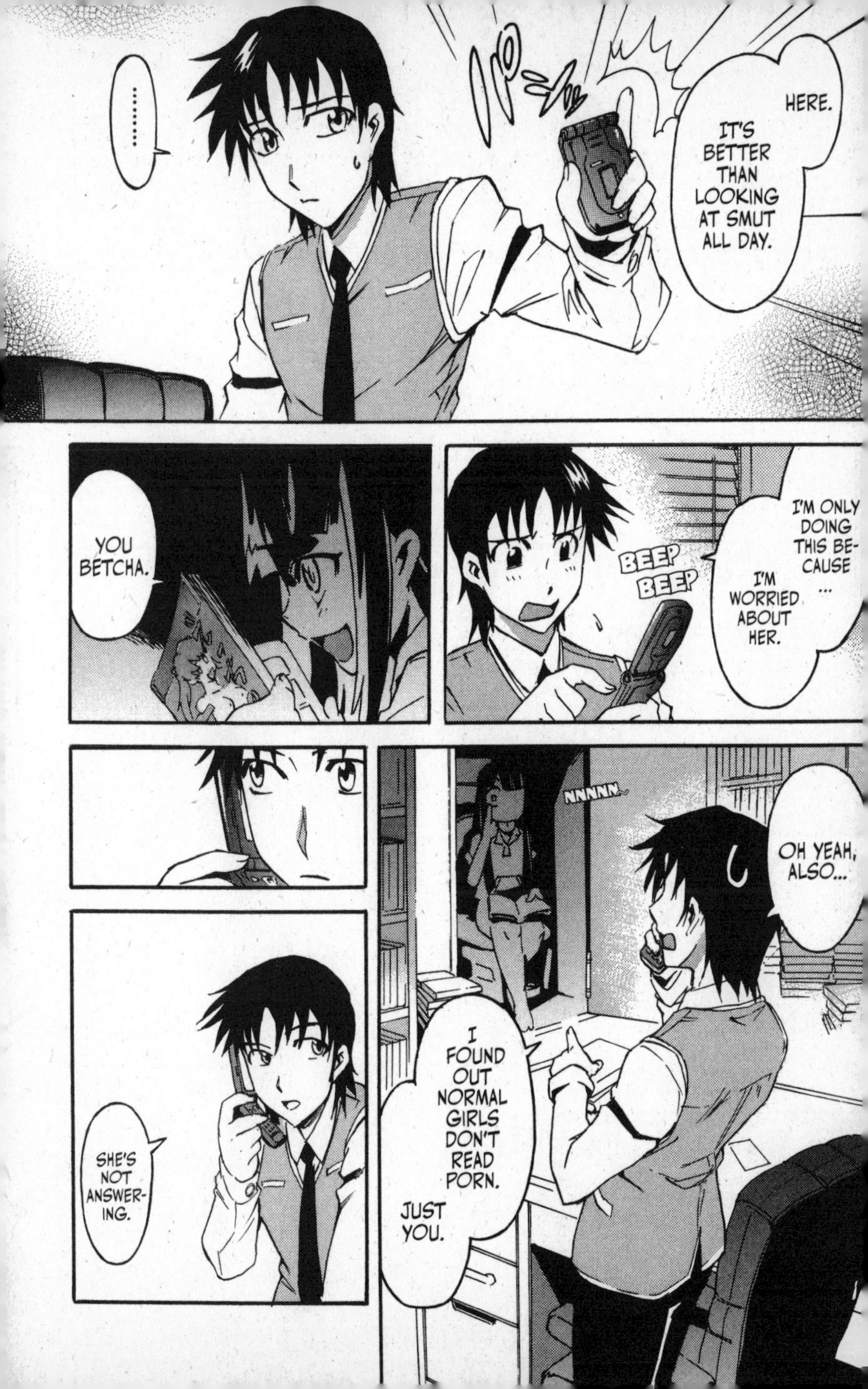
HERE.
IT'S BETTER THAN LOOKING AT SMUT ALL DAY.
......
I'M ONLY DOING THIS BE-CAUSE ...
I'M WORRIED ABOUT HER.
BEEP BEEP
YOU BETCHA.
NNNNN
OH YEAH, ALSO...
I FOUND OUT NORMAL GIRLS DON'T READ PORN.
JUST YOU.
SHE'S NOT ANSWER-ING.

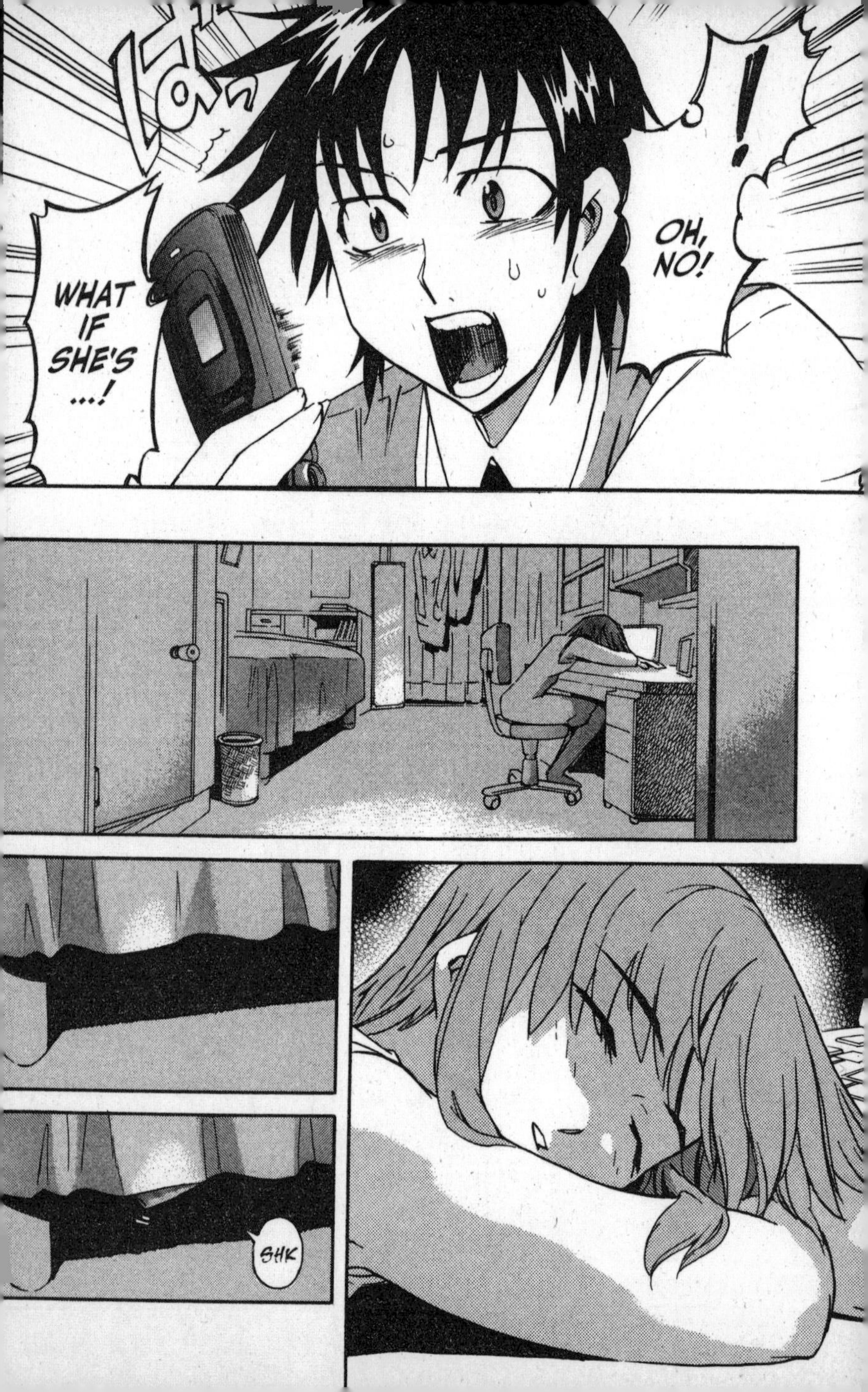
!
OH, NO!
ぱっ
WHAT IF SHE'S ....!
SHK

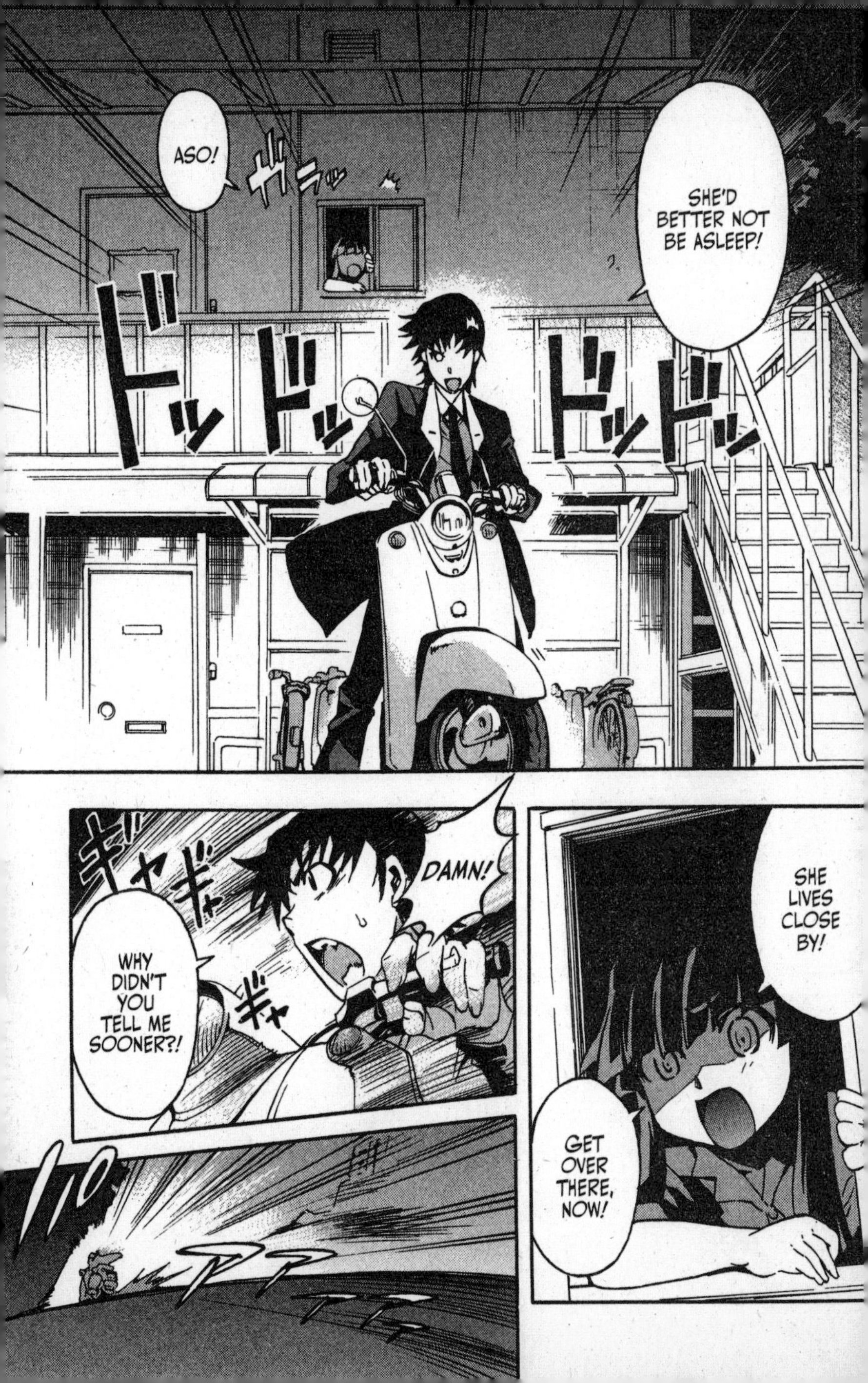
SHE'D BETTER NOT BE ASLEEP!
ASO!
SHE LIVES CLOSE BY!
GET OVER THERE, NOW!
DAMN!
WHY DIDN'T YOU TELL ME SOONER?!

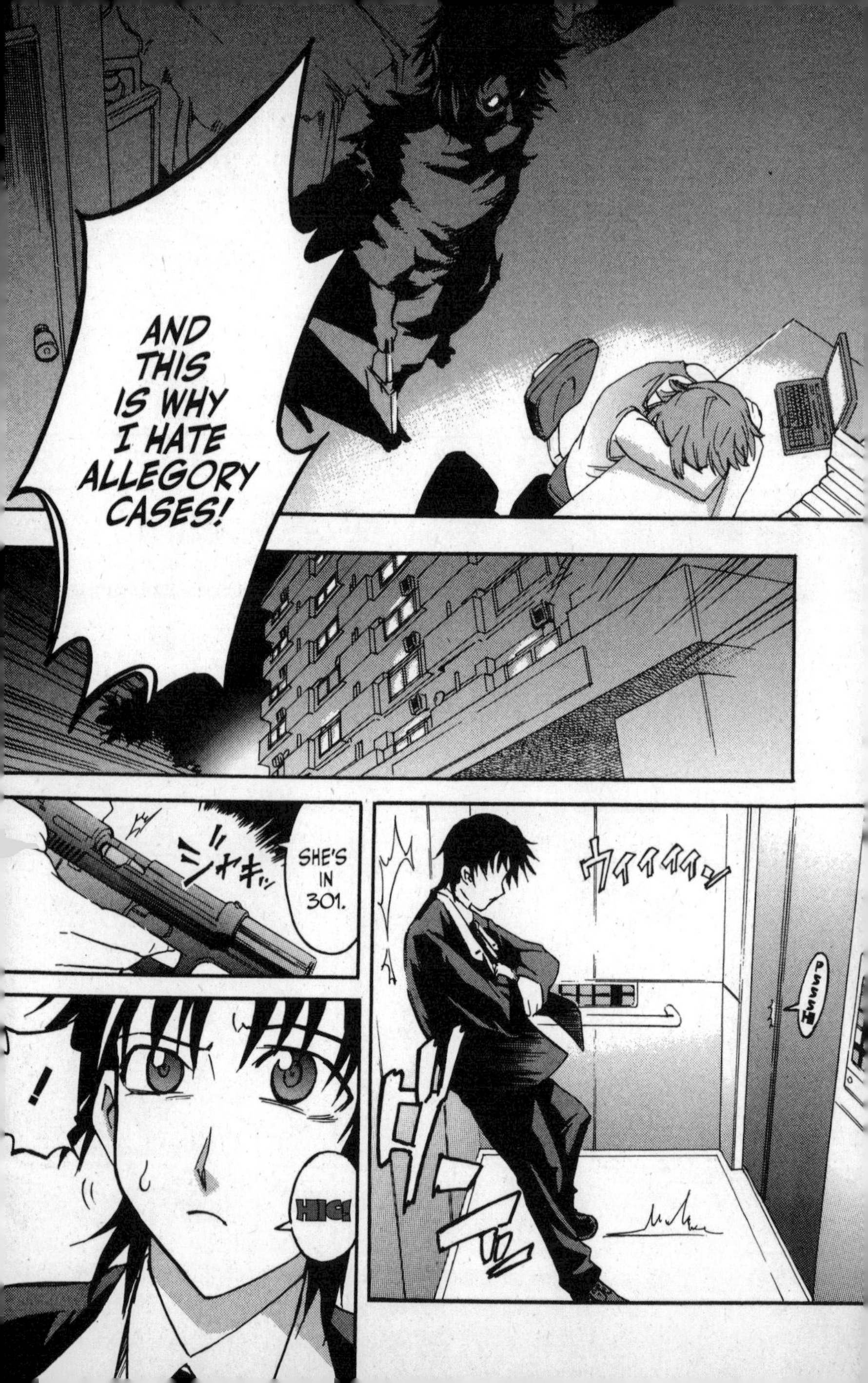
AND THIS IS WHY I HATE ALLEGORY CASES!
ウィイイイン
PSSSH
SHE'S IN 301.
ジャキッ
!
HIC!

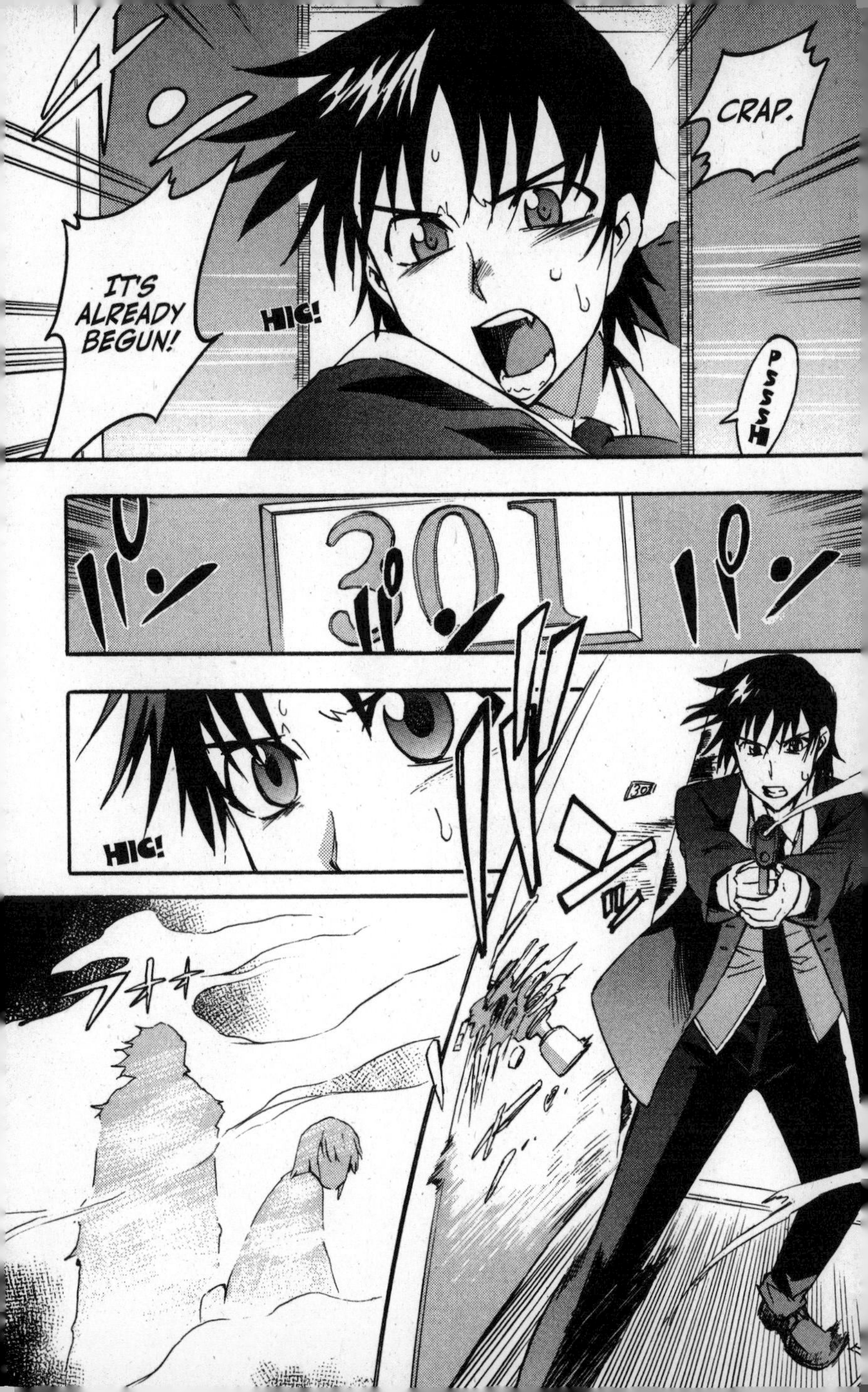
CRAP.
IT'S ALREADY BEGUN!
HIC!
PSSSSH
301
HIC!

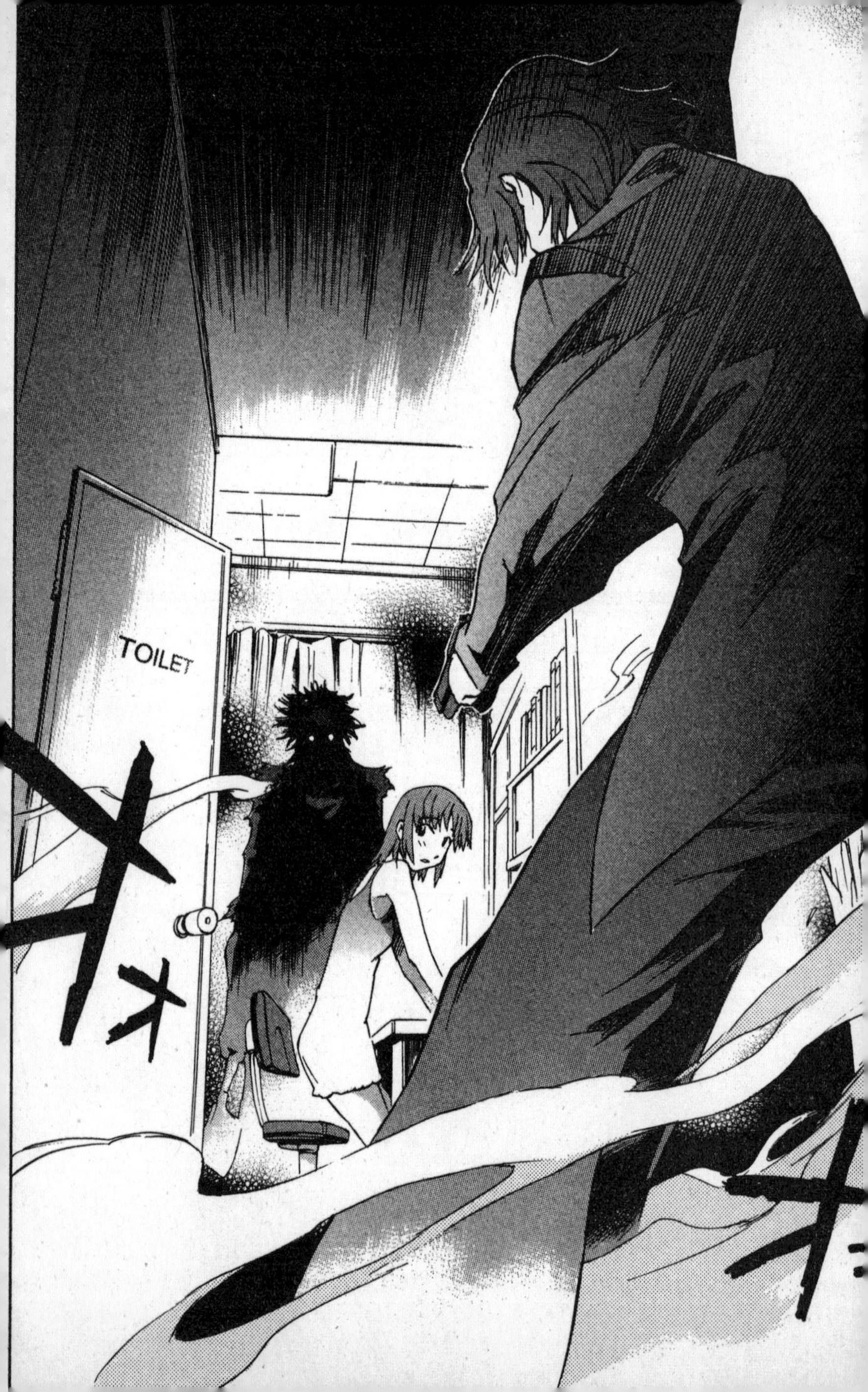
TOILET
オオ
オ

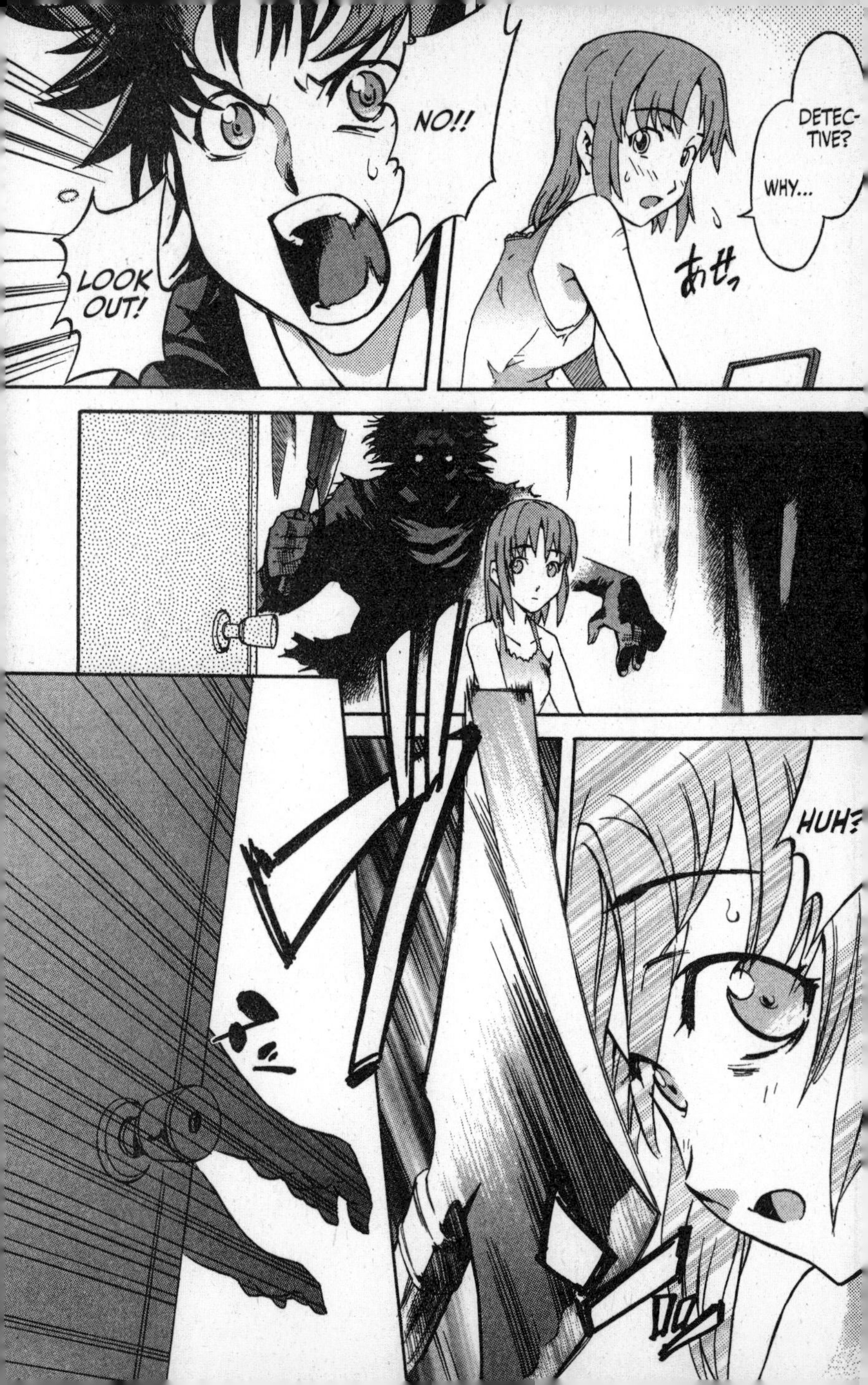
DETECTIVE?
WHY...
あせっ
NO!!
LOOK OUT!
HUH!?

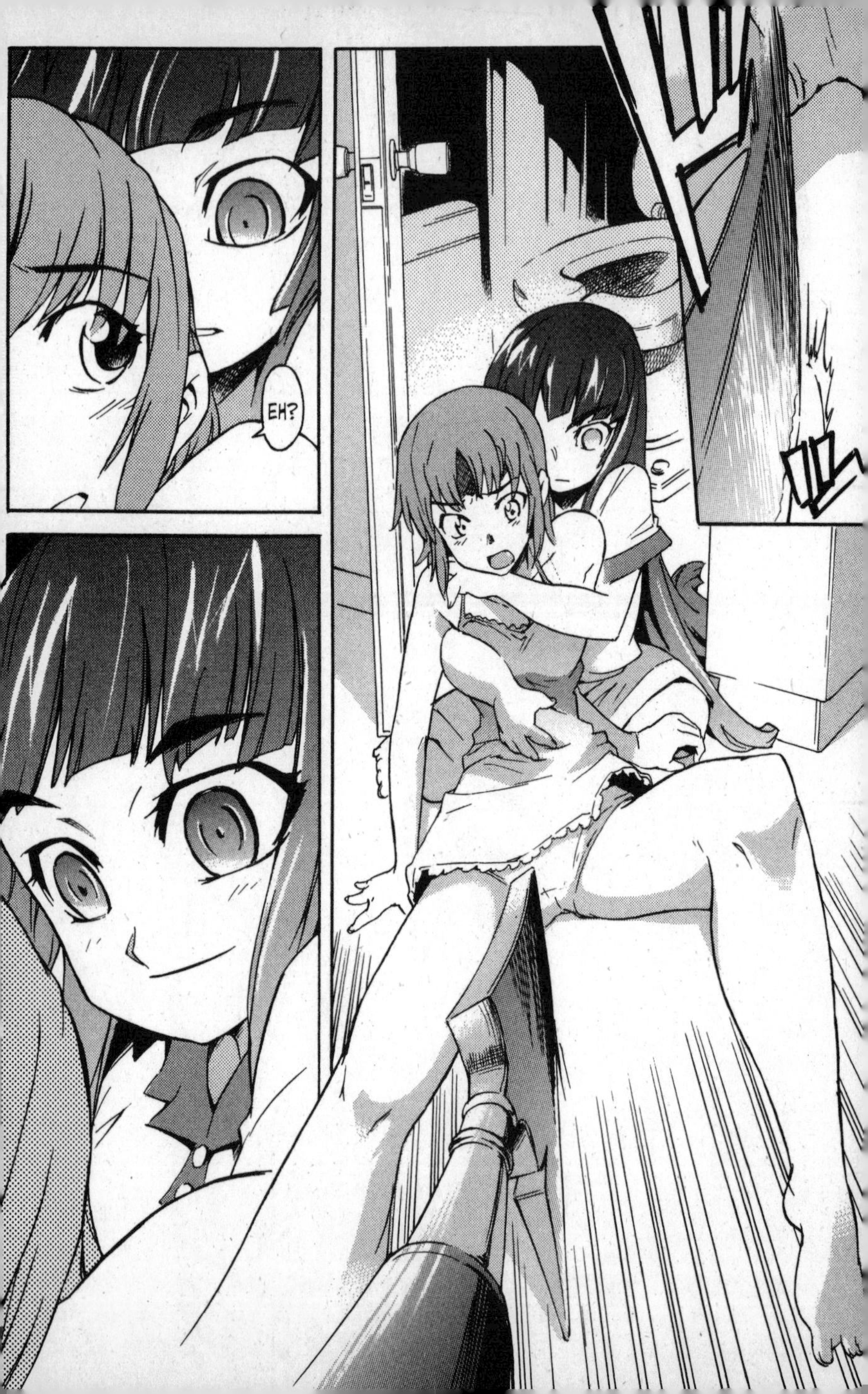
EH?

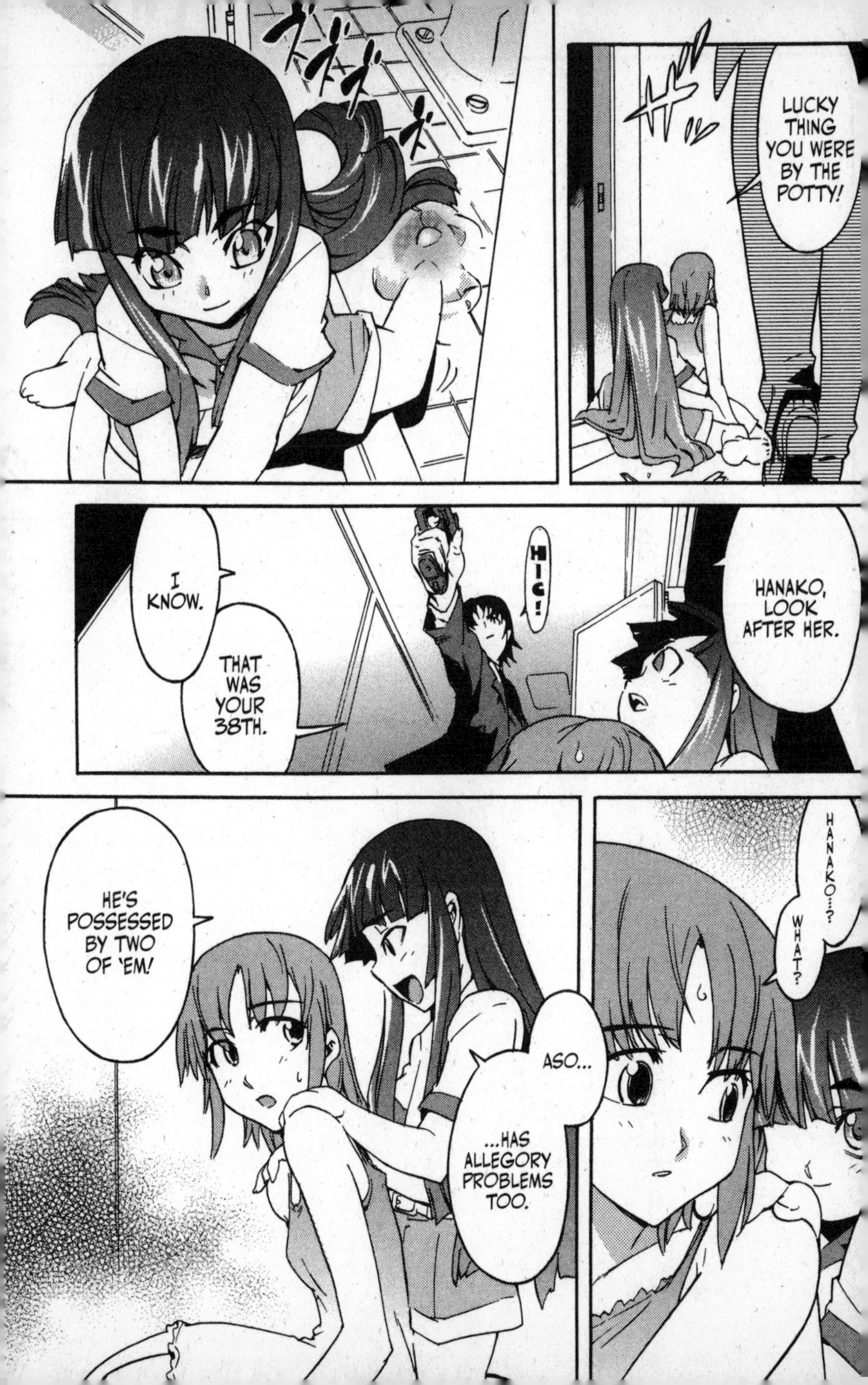
LUCKY THING YOU WERE BY THE POTTY!
HANAKO, LOOK AFTER HER.
HIC!
I KNOW.
THAT WAS YOUR 38TH.
HANAKO...?
WHAT?
ASO...
...HAS ALLEGORY PROBLEMS TOO.
HE'S POSSESSED BY TWO OF 'EM!

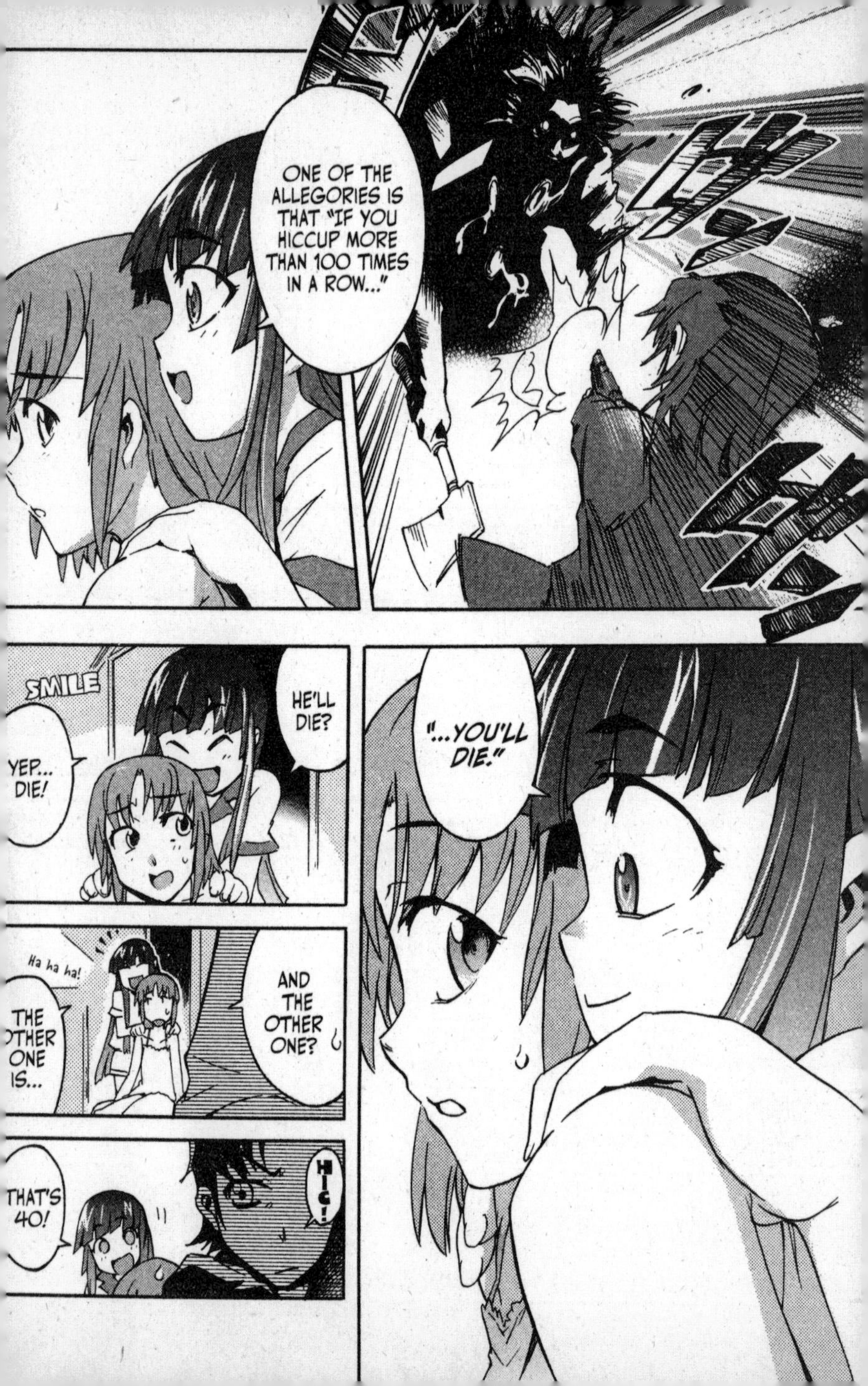
ONE OF THE ALLEGORIES IS THAT "IF YOU HICCUP MORE THAN 100 TIMES IN A ROW..."
"...YOU'LL DIE."
HE'LL DIE?
SMILE
YEP... DIE!
AND THE OTHER ONE?
Ha ha ha!
THE OTHER ONE IS...
HIC!
THAT'S 40!

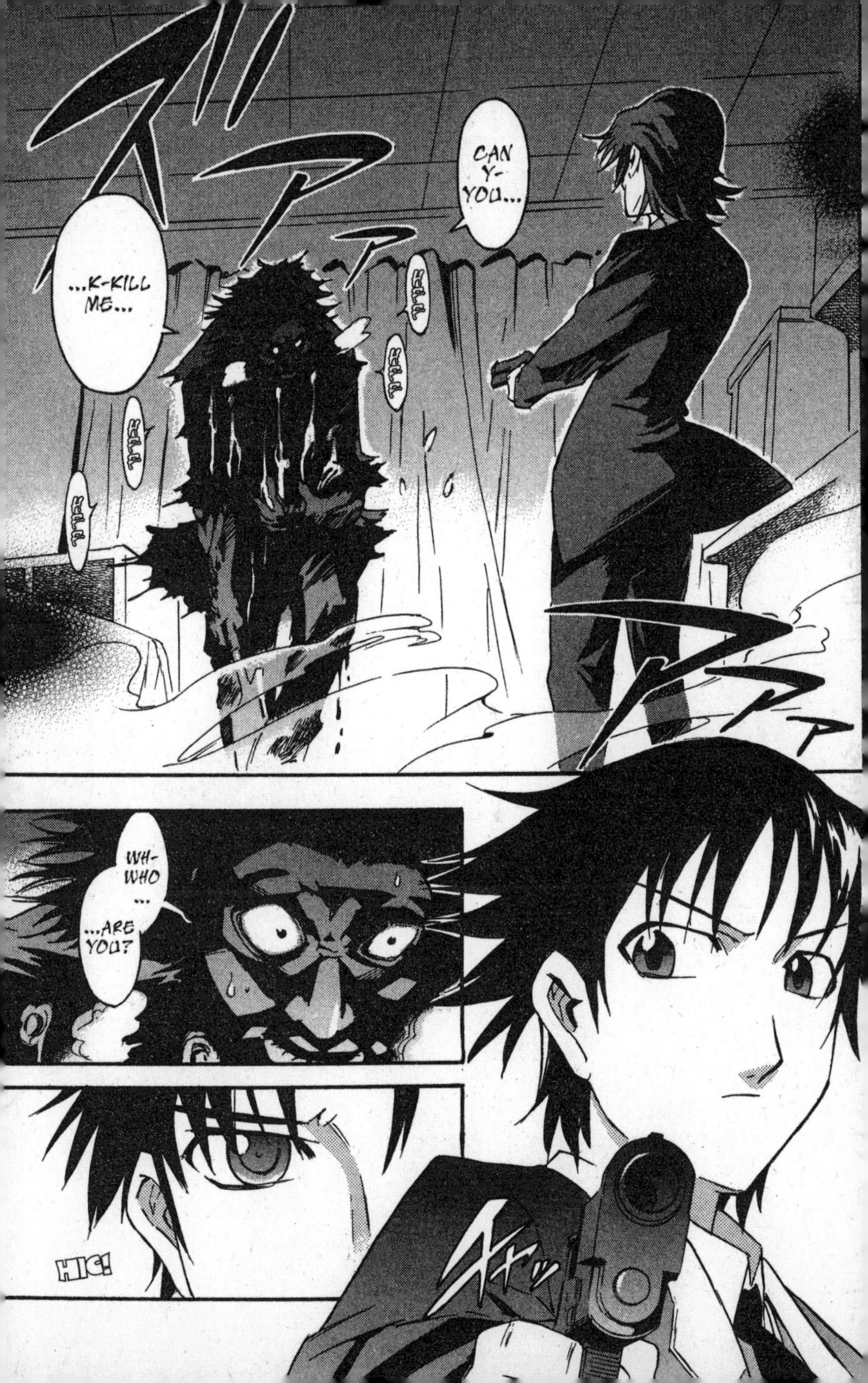
CAN Y- YOU...
...K-KILL ME...
WH- WHO ...
...ARE YOU?
HIC!

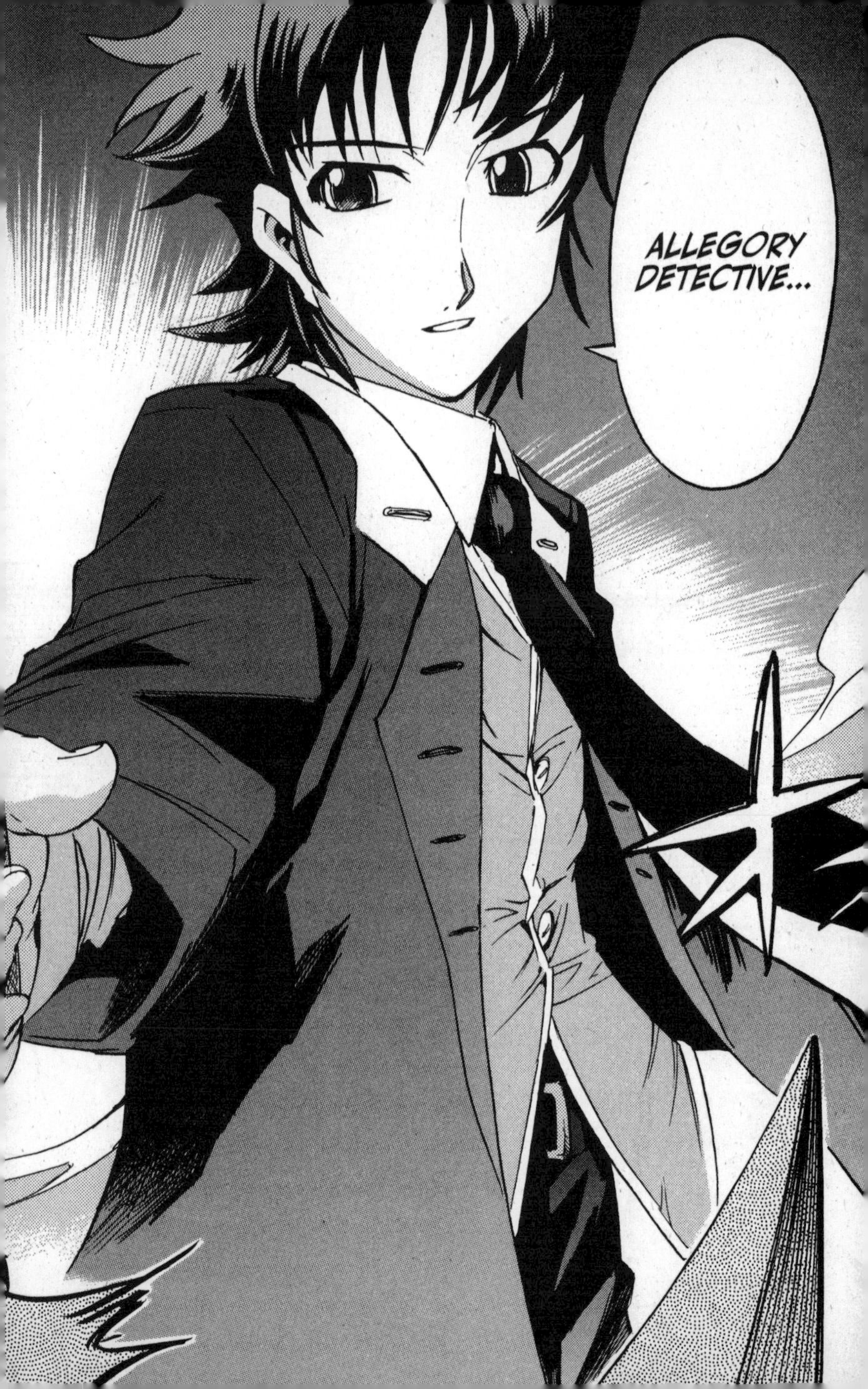
ALLEGORY DETECTIVE...

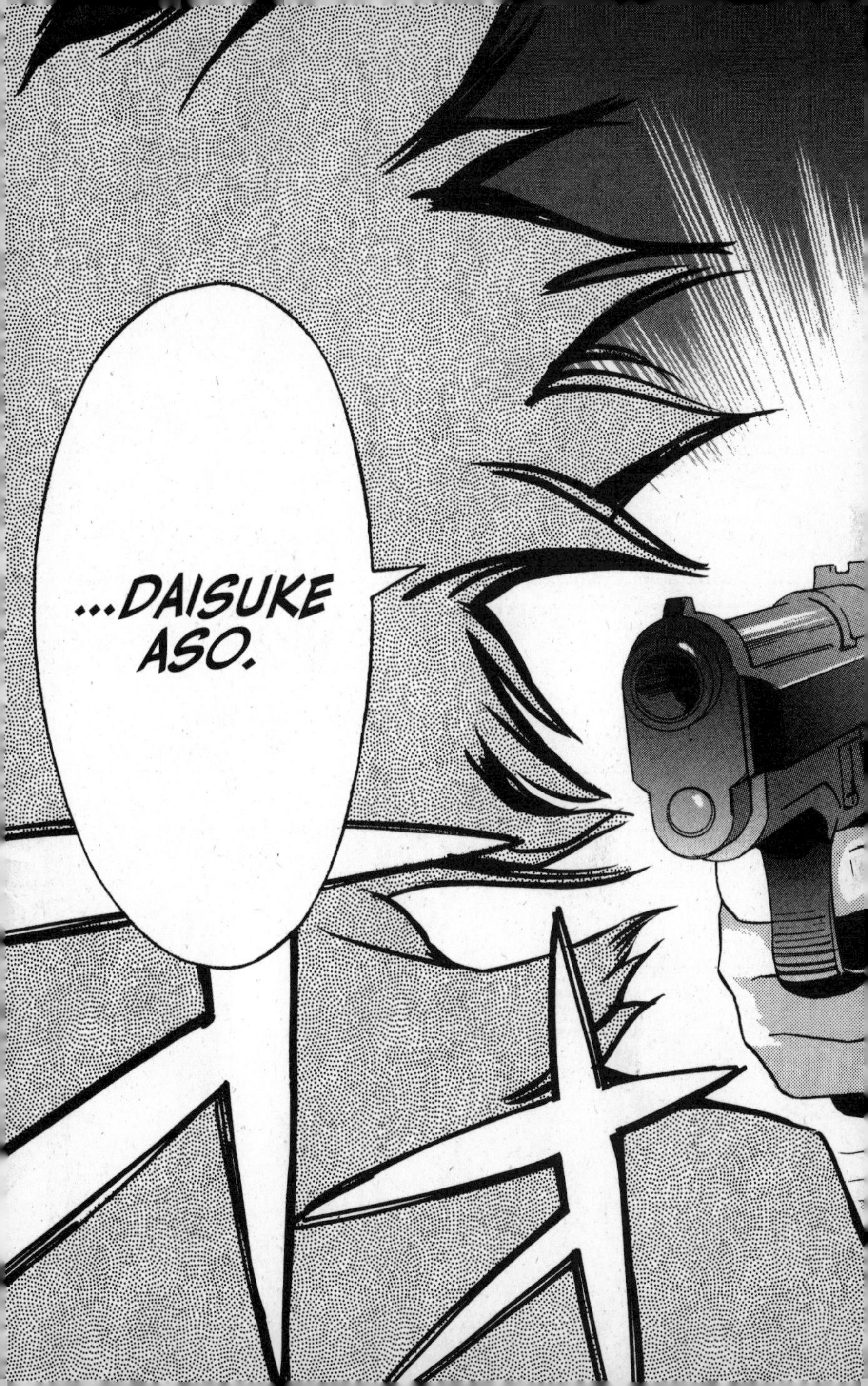
...DAISUKE ASO.

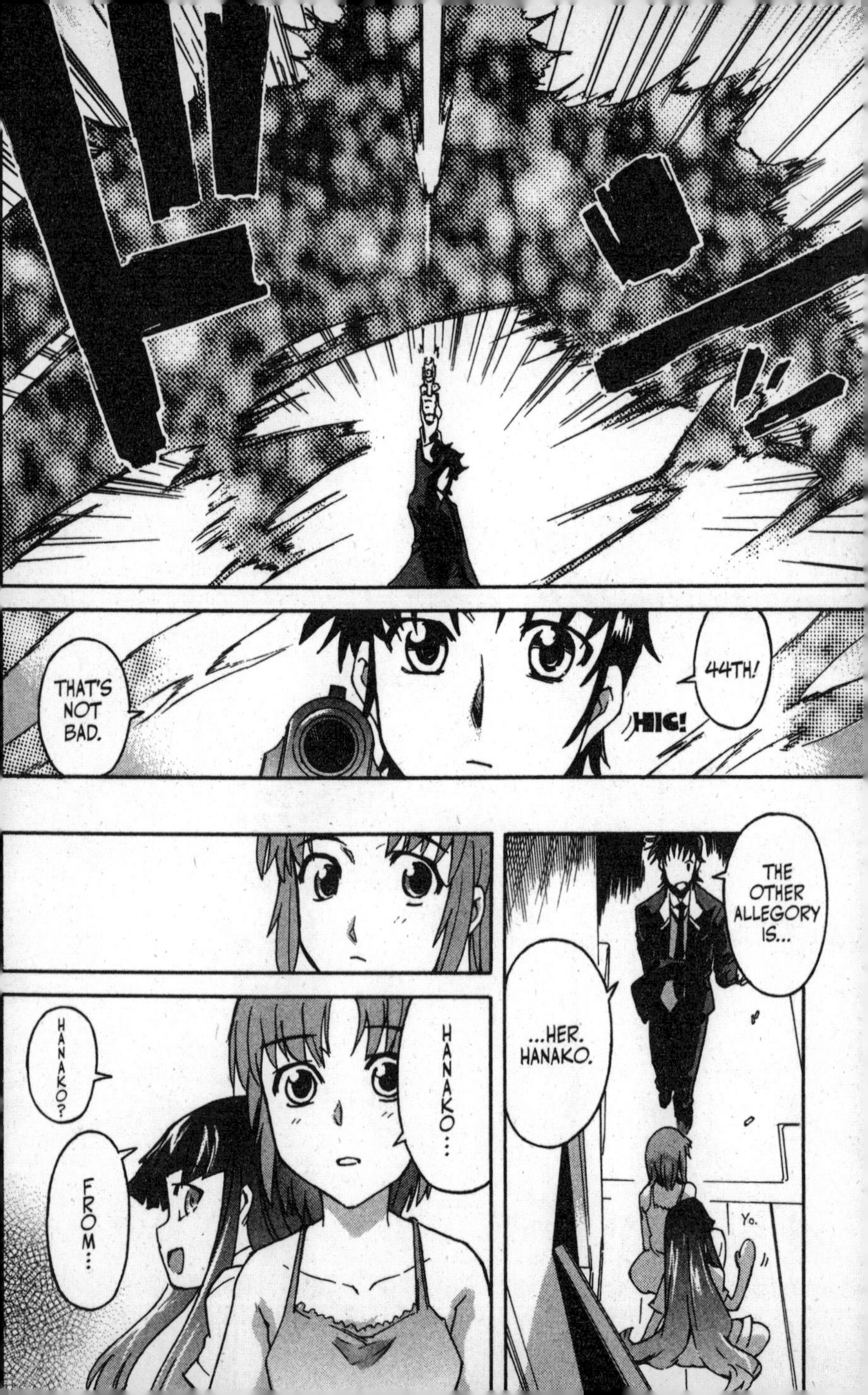
44TH!
HIG!
THAT'S NOT BAD.
THE OTHER ALLEGORY IS...
...HER. HANAKO.
Yo.
HANAKO...
HANAKO?
FROM...

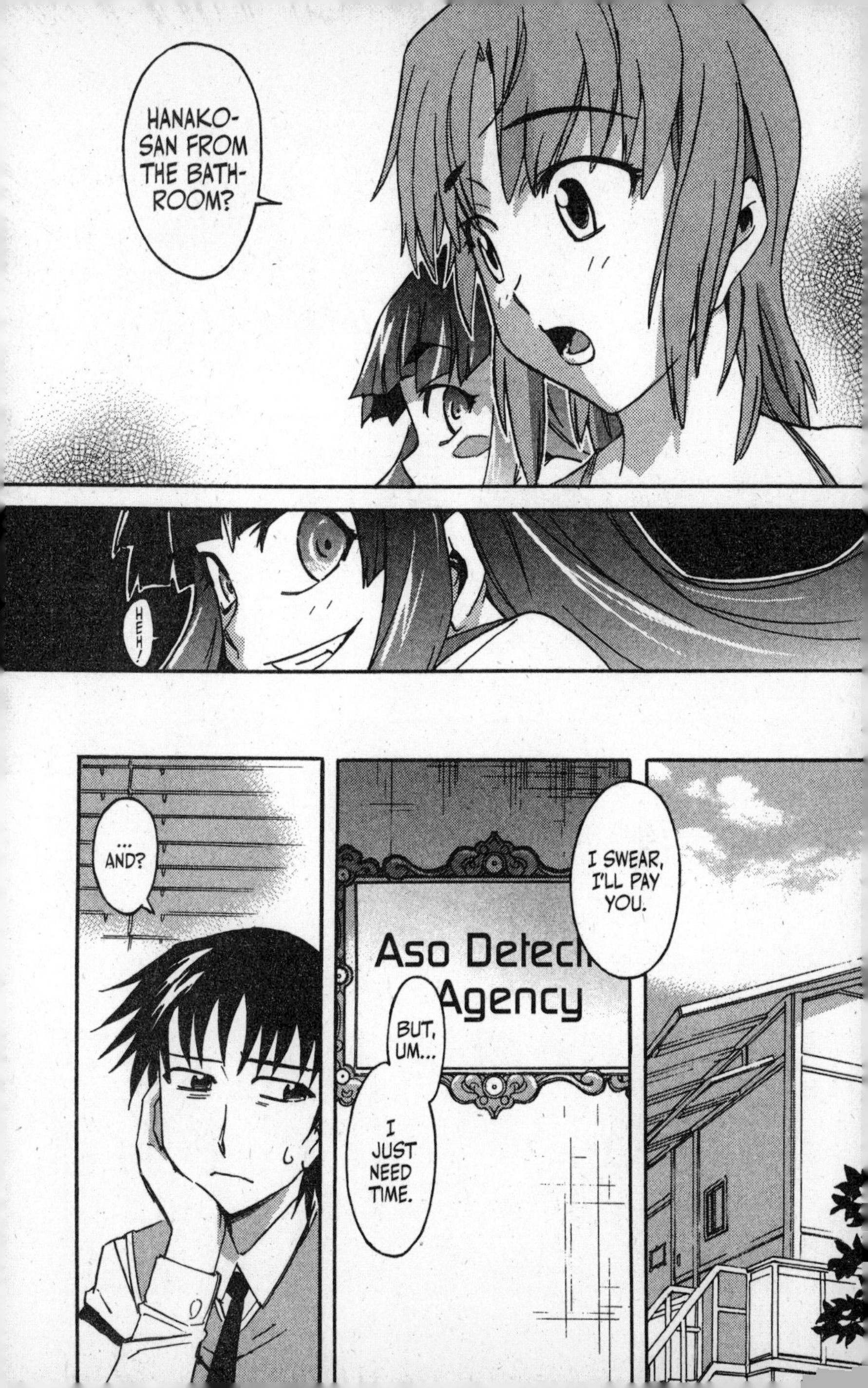
HANAKO-SAN FROM THE BATH-ROOM?
HEH!
I SWEAR, I'LL PAY YOU.
Aso Detec
Agency
BUT, UM...
I JUST NEED TIME.
... AND?

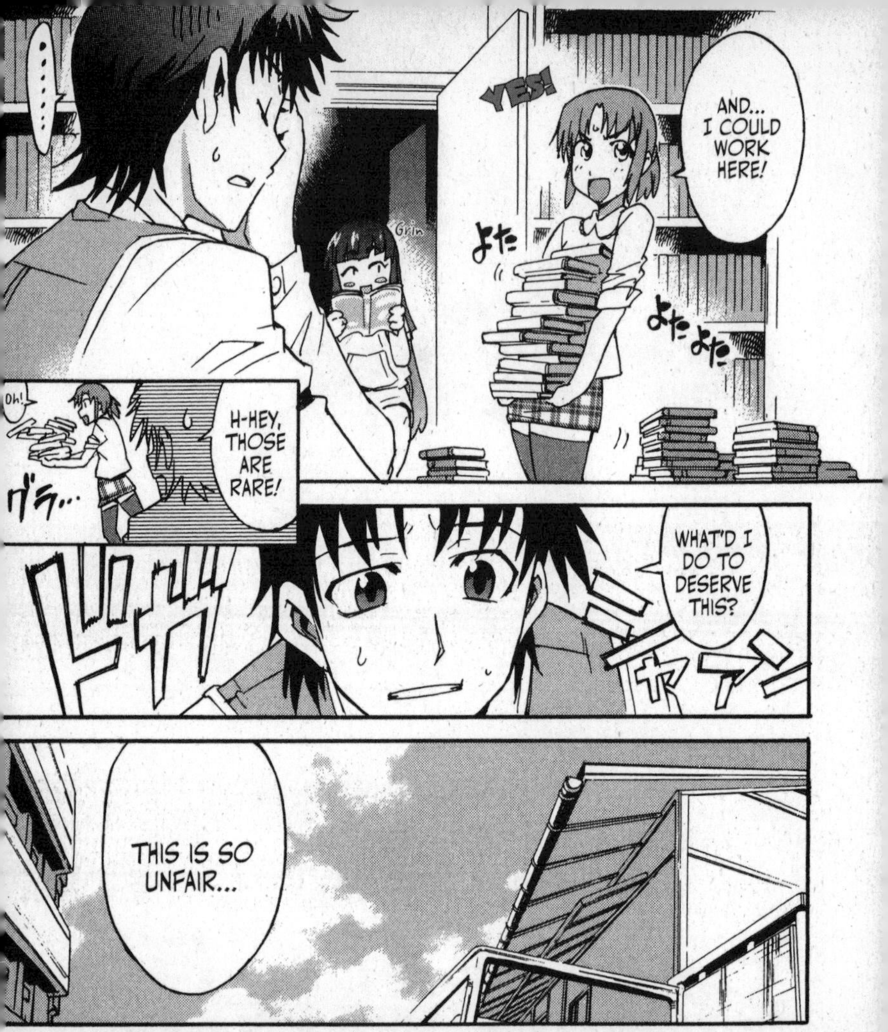
AND... I COULD WORK HERE!
YES!
よた
よたよた
Grin
......
H-HEY, THOSE ARE RARE!
Oh!
グラ...
WHAT'D I DO TO DESERVE THIS?
THIS IS SO UNFAIR...

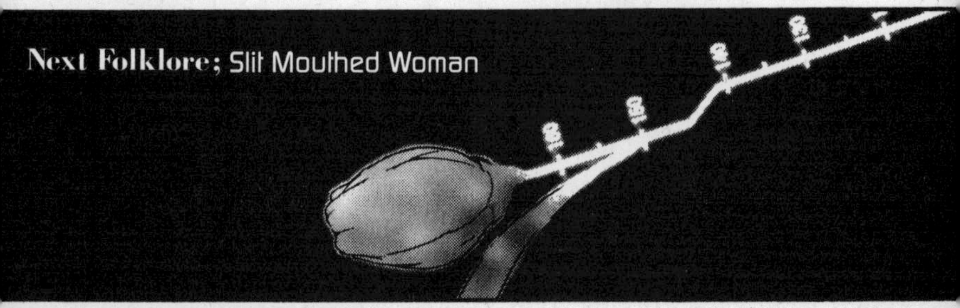
Next Folklore; Slit Mouthed Woman

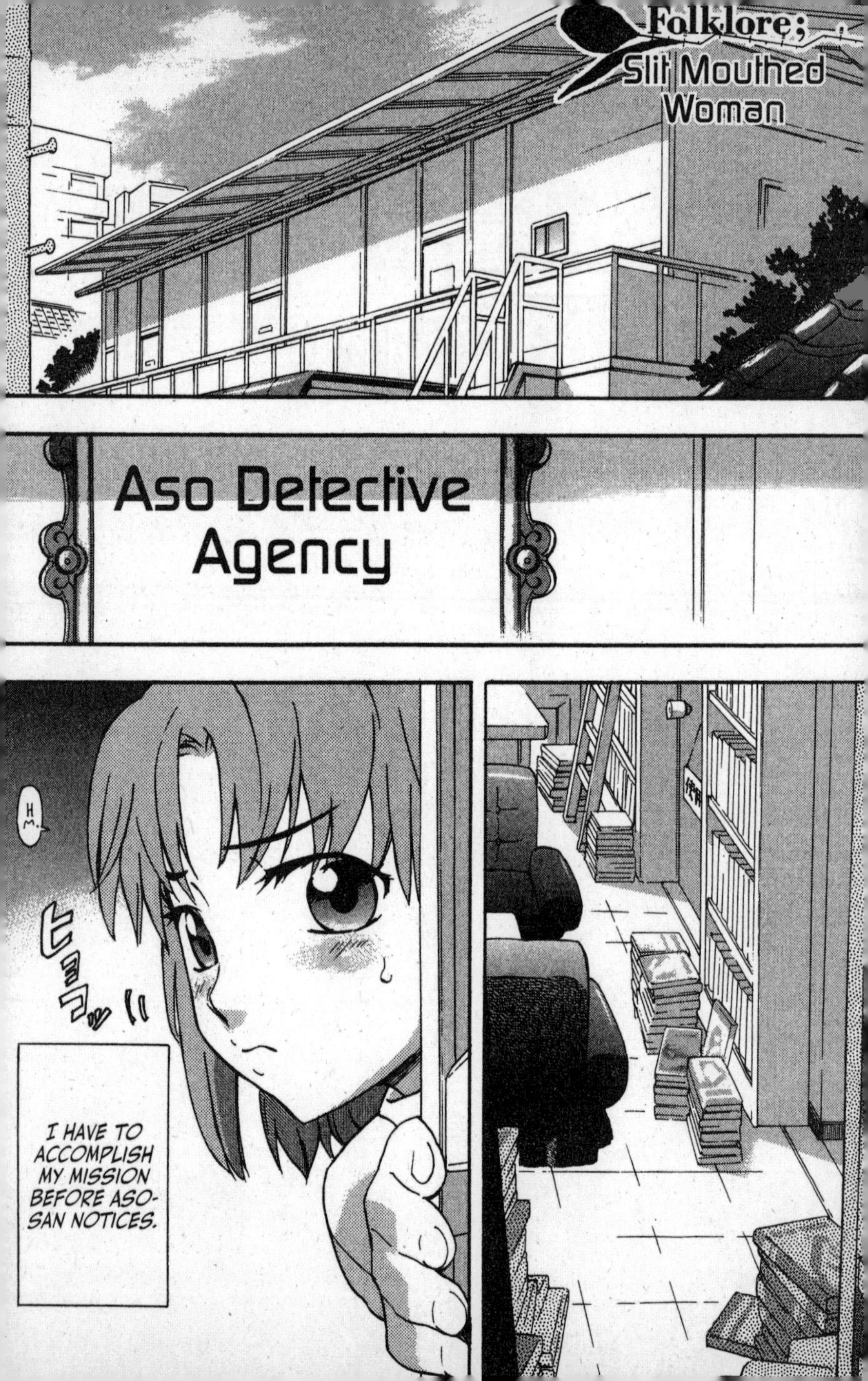
Folklore;
Slit Mouthed Woman
Aso Detective Agency
HM.
ヒョコッ
I HAVE TO ACCOMPLISH MY MISSION BEFORE ASO-SAN NOTICES.

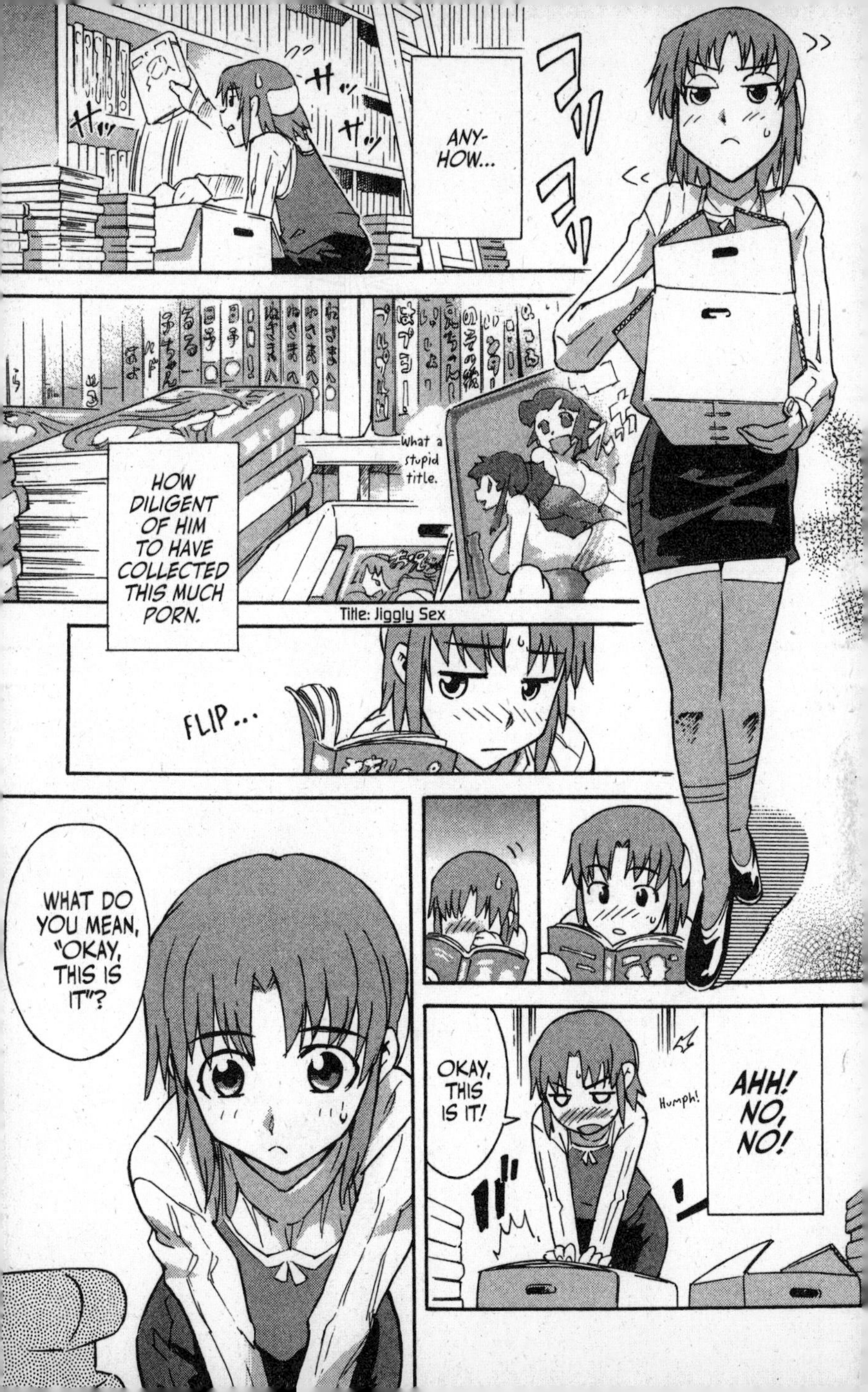
ANY-HOW...
HOW DILIGENT OF HIM TO HAVE COLLECTED THIS MUCH PORN.
What a stupid title.
Title: Jiggly Sex
FLIP...
AHH! NO, NO!
Humph!
OKAY, THIS IS IT!
WHAT DO YOU MEAN, "OKAY, THIS IS IT"?

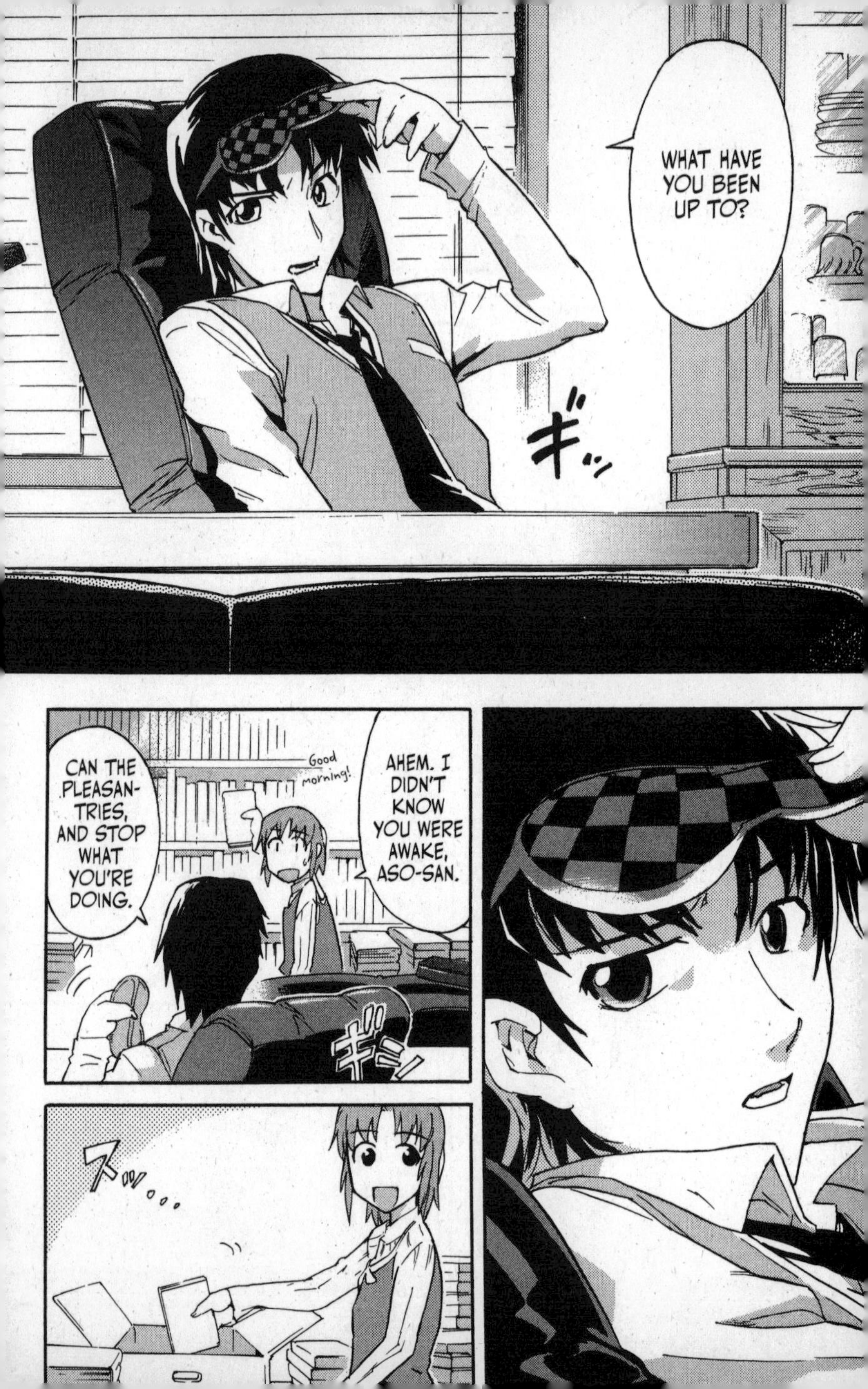
WHAT HAVE YOU BEEN UP TO?
ギッ
AHEM. I DIDN'T KNOW YOU WERE AWAKE, ASO-SAN.
Good morning!
CAN THE PLEASANTRIES, AND STOP WHAT YOU'RE DOING.
ギシ

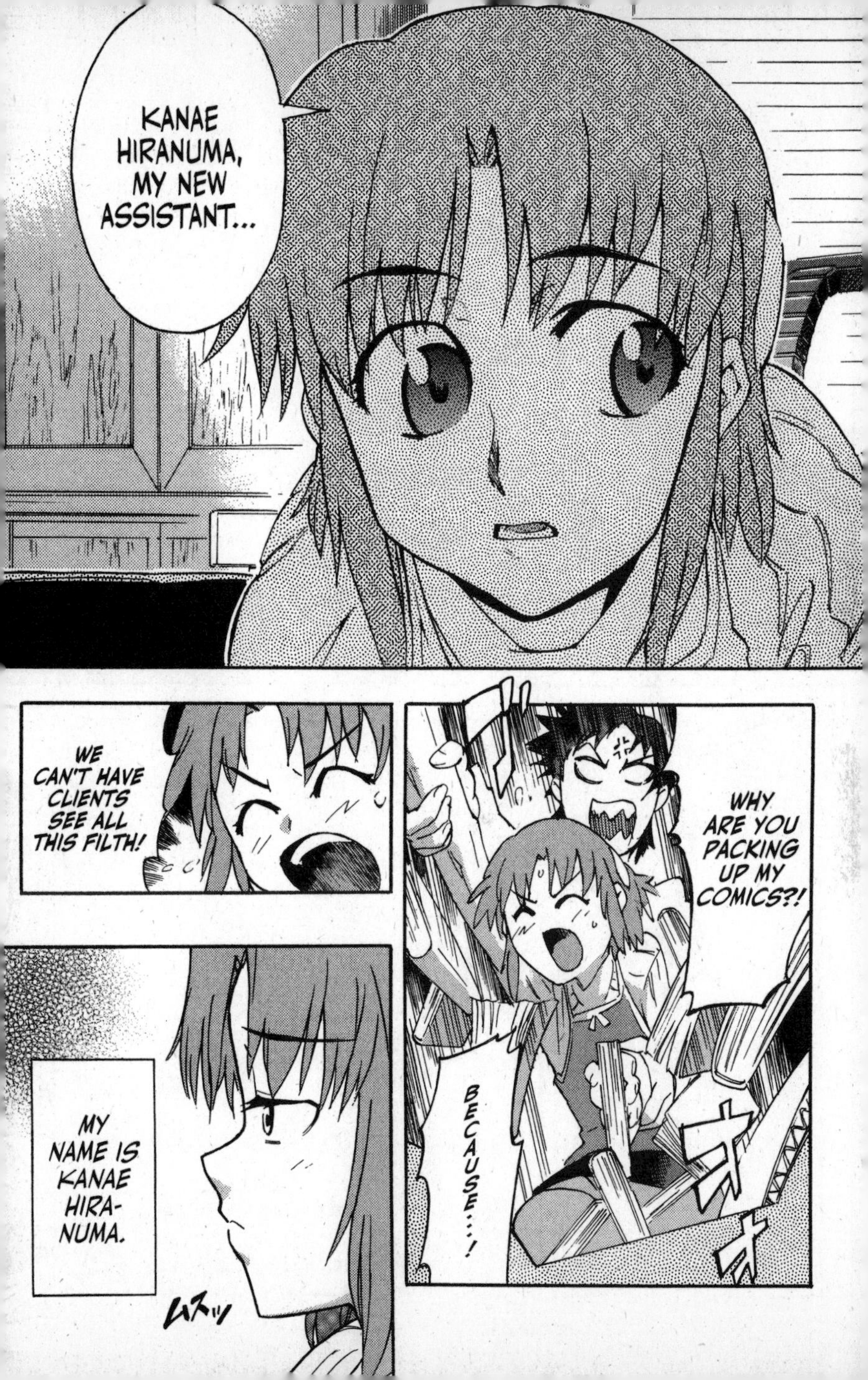
KANAE HIRANUMA, MY NEW ASSISTANT...
WHY ARE YOU PACKING UP MY COMICS?!
BECAUSE...!
WE CAN'T HAVE CLIENTS SEE ALL THIS FILTH!
MY NAME IS KANAE HIRA-NUMA.
ムスッ

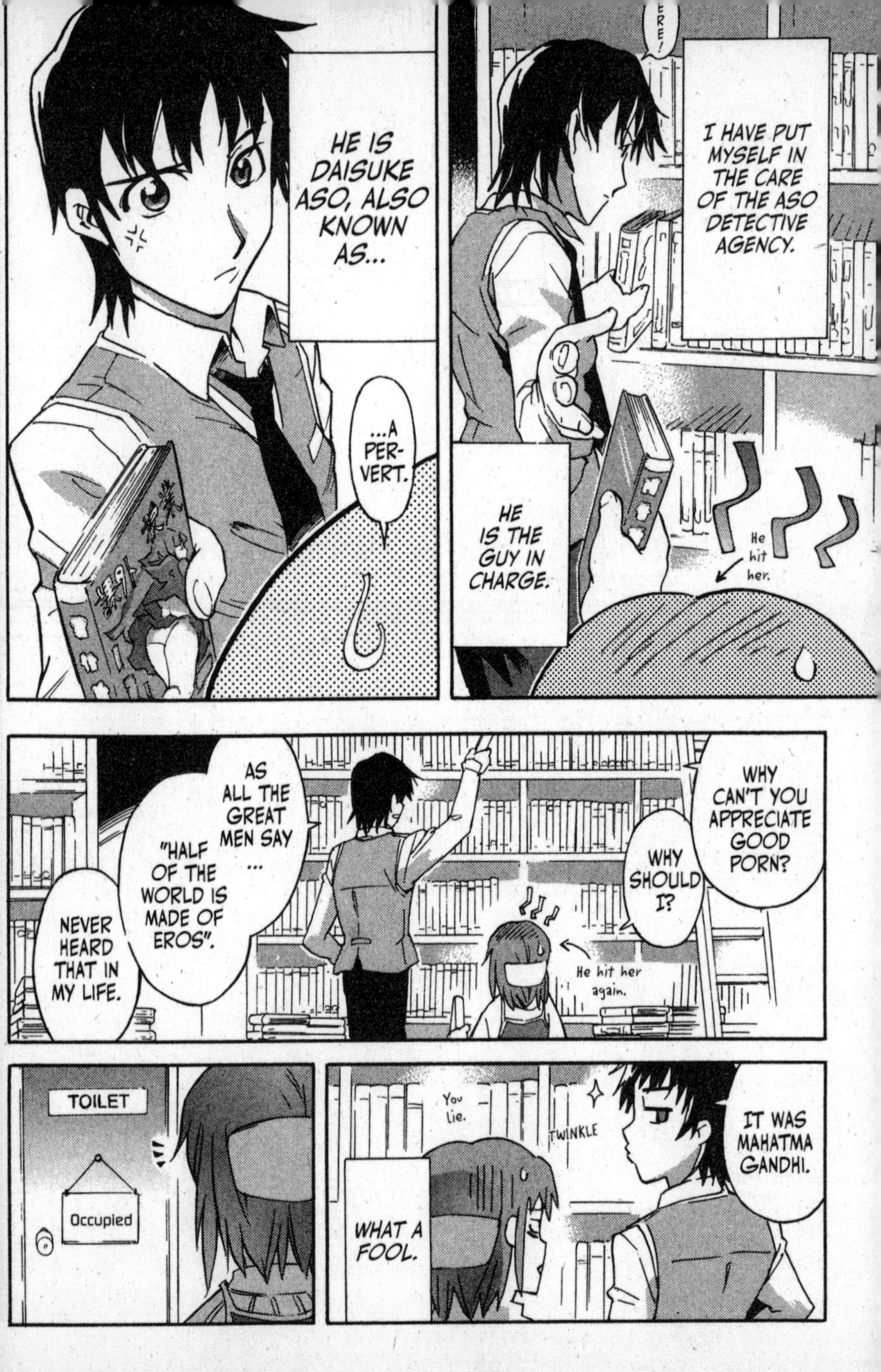
ERE!
I HAVE PUT MYSELF IN THE CARE OF THE ASO DETECTIVE AGENCY.
HE IS THE GUY IN CHARGE.
He hit her.
HE IS DAISUKE ASO, ALSO KNOWN AS...
...A PER-VERT.
WHY CAN'T YOU APPRECIATE GOOD PORN?
WHY SHOULD I?
He hit her again.
AS ALL THE GREAT MEN SAY ...
"HALF OF THE WORLD IS MADE OF EROS".
NEVER HEARD THAT IN MY LIFE.
IT WAS MAHATMA GANDHI.
TWINKLE
You lie.
WHAT A FOOL.
TOILET
Occupied

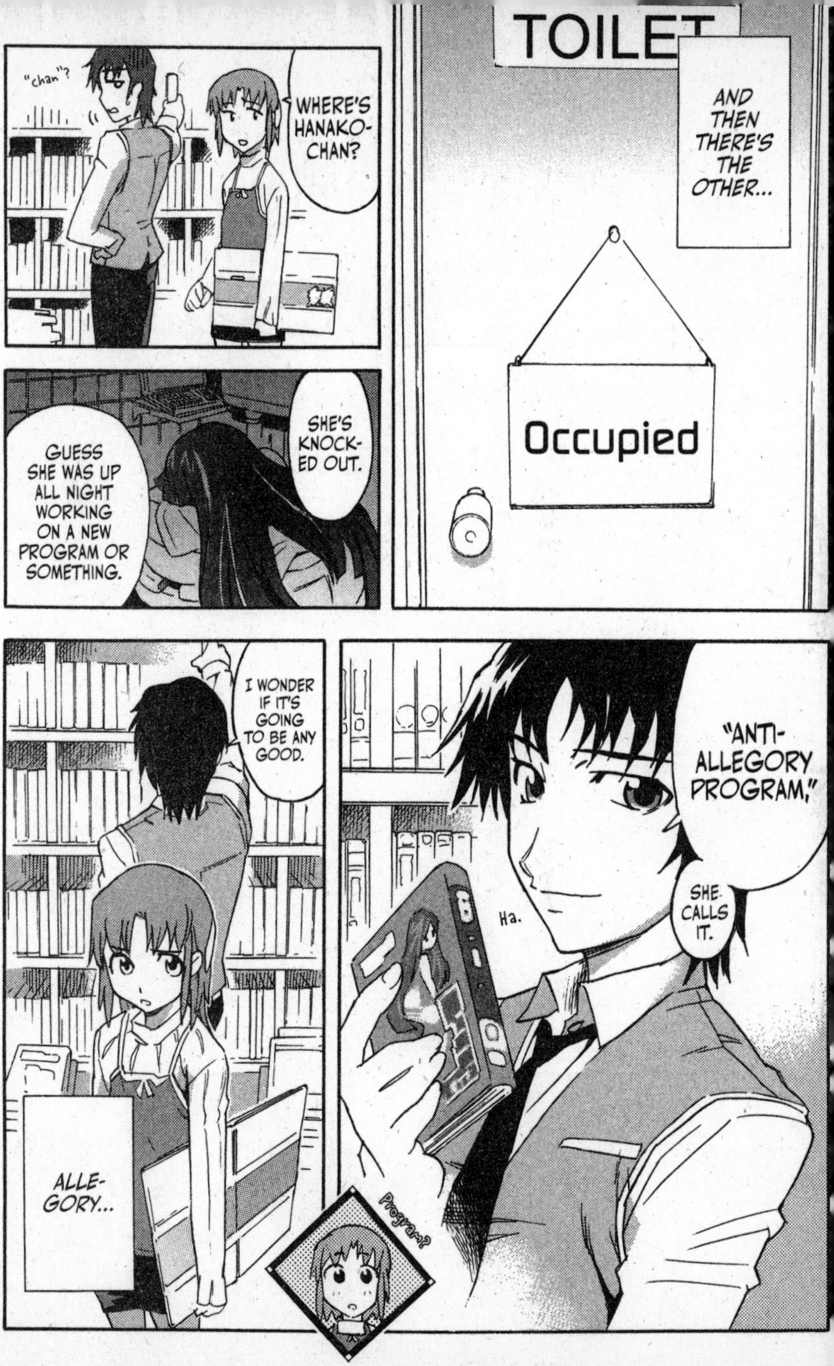
TOILET
AND THEN THERE'S THE OTHER...
Occupied
WHERE'S HANAKO-CHAN?
"chan"?
SHE'S KNOCKED OUT.
GUESS SHE WAS UP ALL NIGHT WORKING ON A NEW PROGRAM OR SOMETHING.
"ANTI-ALLEGORY PROGRAM,"
SHE CALLS IT.
Ha.
I WONDER IF IT'S GOING TO BE ANY GOOD.
ALLE-GORY...
Program?

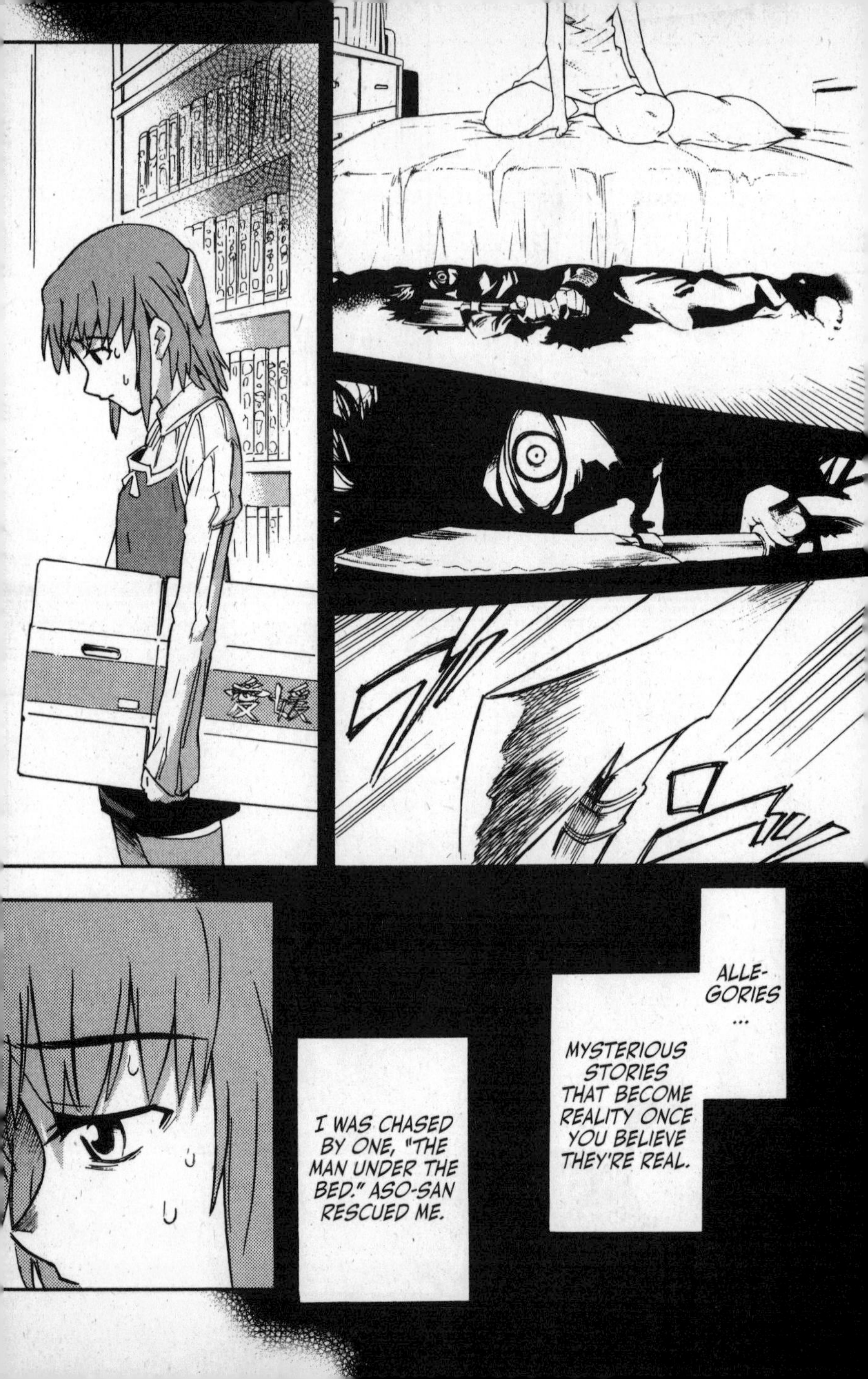
愛媛
ALLE-GORIES ...
MYSTERIOUS STORIES THAT BECOME REALITY ONCE YOU BELIEVE THEY'RE REAL.
I WAS CHASED BY ONE, "THE MAN UNDER THE BED." ASO-SAN RESCUED ME.

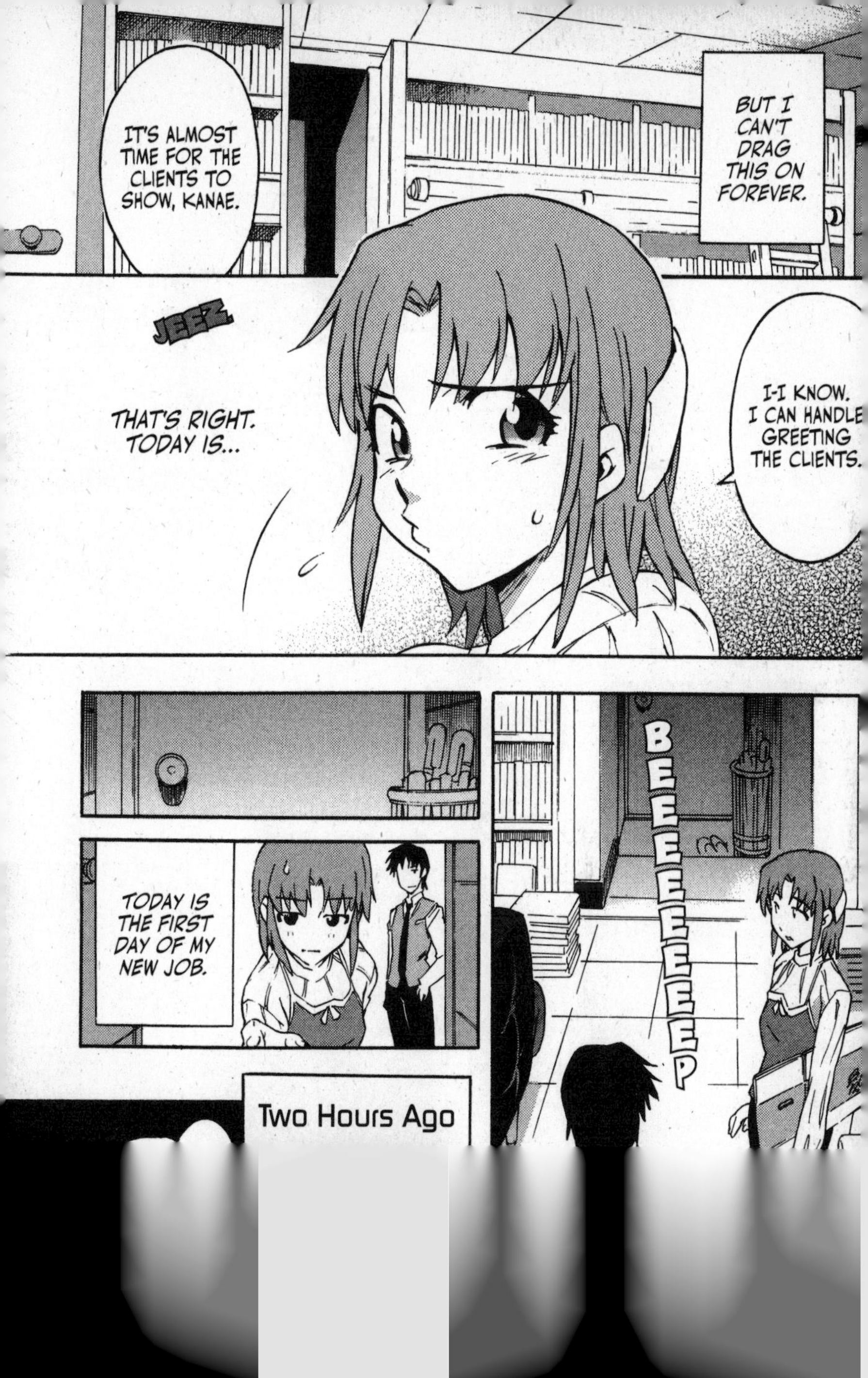
BUT I CAN'T DRAG THIS ON FOREVER.
IT'S ALMOST TIME FOR THE CLIENTS TO SHOW, KANAE.
I-I KNOW. I CAN HANDLE GREETING THE CLIENTS.
JEEZ
THAT'S RIGHT. TODAY IS...
BEEEEEEEEEP
TODAY IS THE FIRST DAY OF MY NEW JOB.
Two Hours Ago

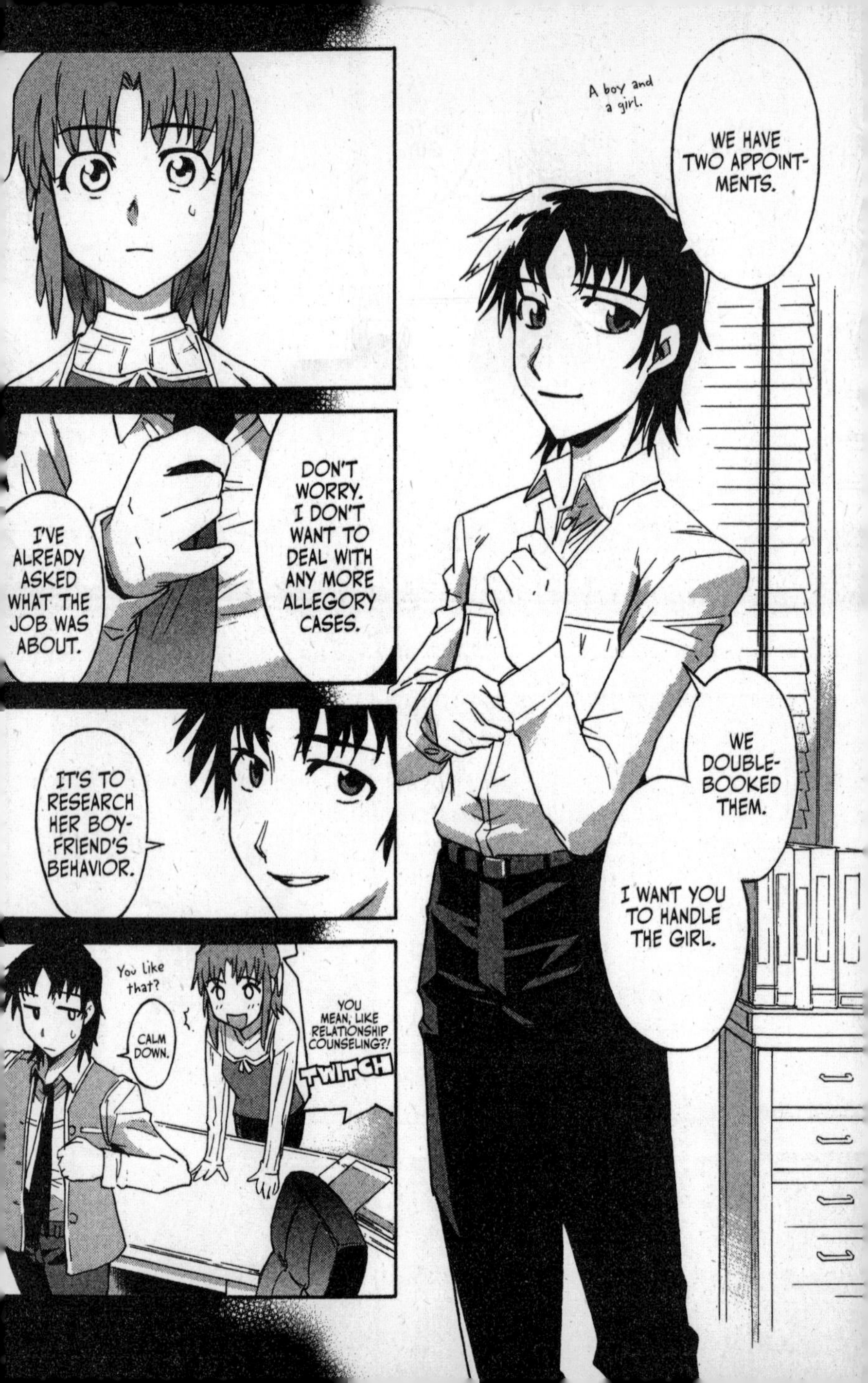
WE HAVE TWO APPOINT-MENTS.
A boy and a girl.
WE DOUBLE-BOOKED THEM.
I WANT YOU TO HANDLE THE GIRL.
DON'T WORRY. I DON'T WANT TO DEAL WITH ANY MORE ALLEGORY CASES.
I'VE ALREADY ASKED WHAT THE JOB WAS ABOUT.
IT'S TO RESEARCH HER BOY-FRIEND'S BEHAVIOR.
YOU MEAN, LIKE RELATIONSHIP COUNSELING?!
TWITCH
You like that?
CALM DOWN.

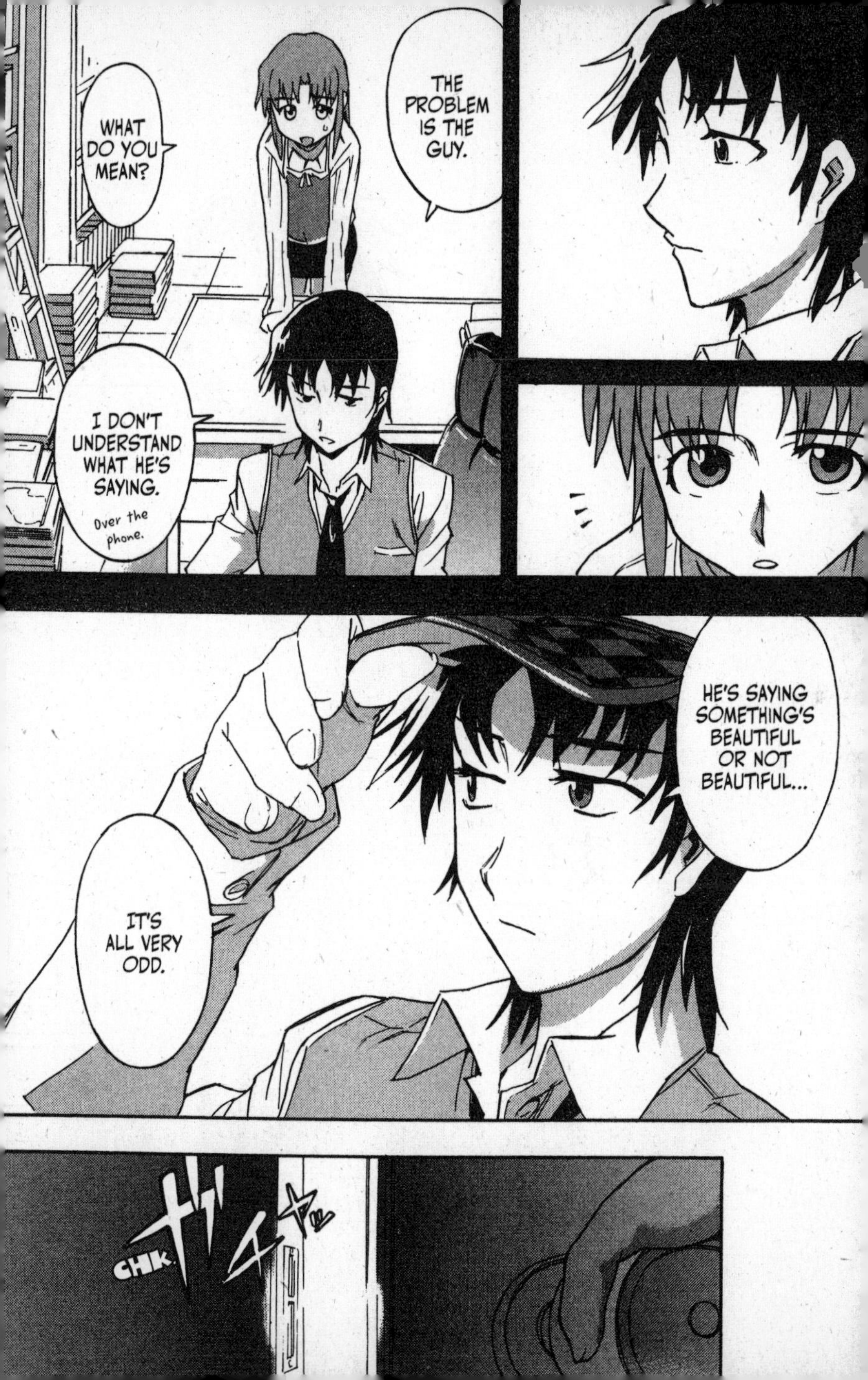
THE PROBLEM IS THE GUY.
WHAT DO YOU MEAN?
I DON'T UNDERSTAND WHAT HE'S SAYING.
Over the phone.
HE'S SAYING SOMETHING'S BEAUTIFUL OR NOT BEAUTIFUL...
IT'S ALL VERY ODD.
CHK.

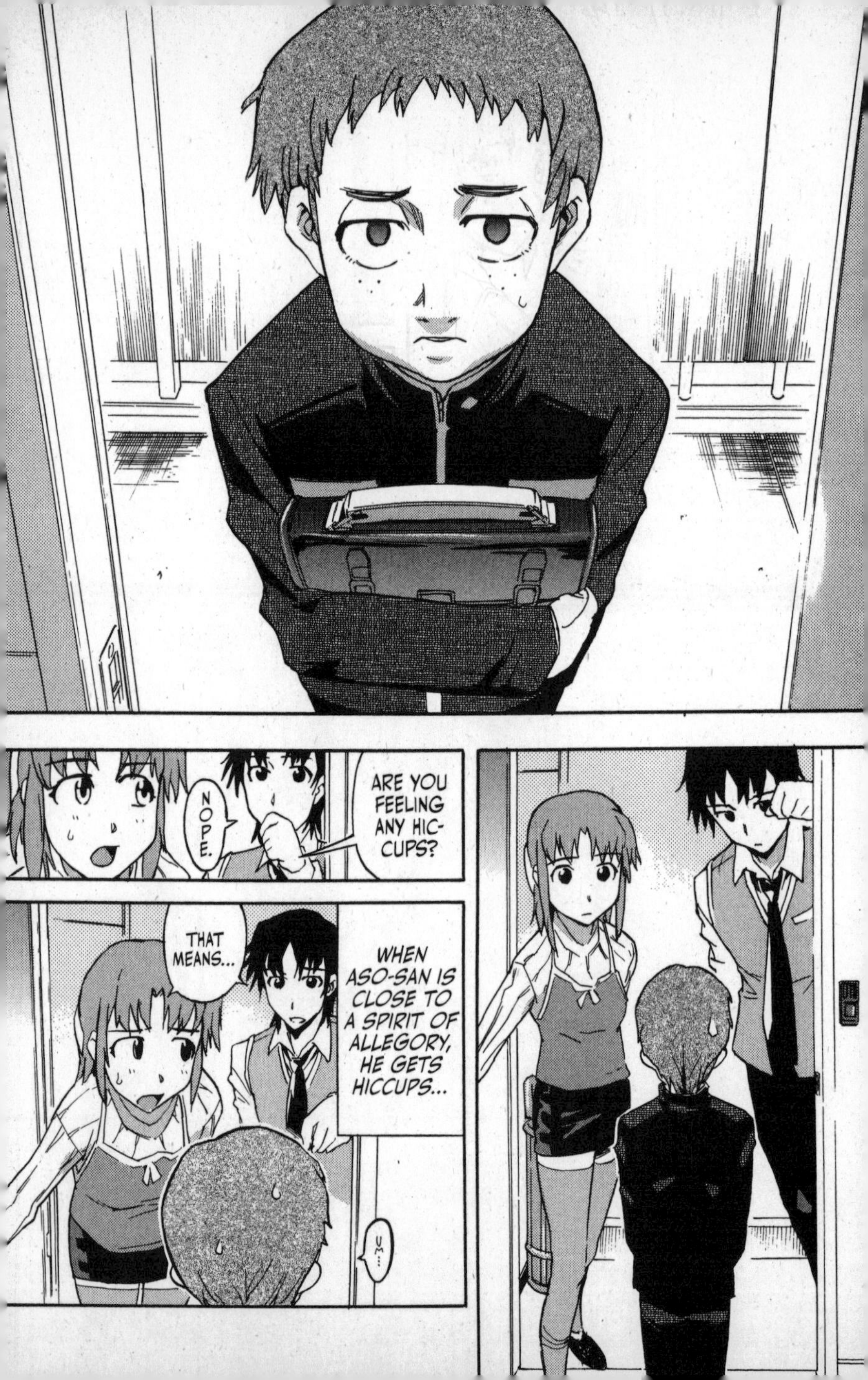
ARE YOU FEELING ANY HIC-CUPS?
NOPE.
WHEN ASO-SAN IS CLOSE TO A SPIRIT OF ALLEGORY, HE GETS HICCUPS...
THAT MEANS...
UM...

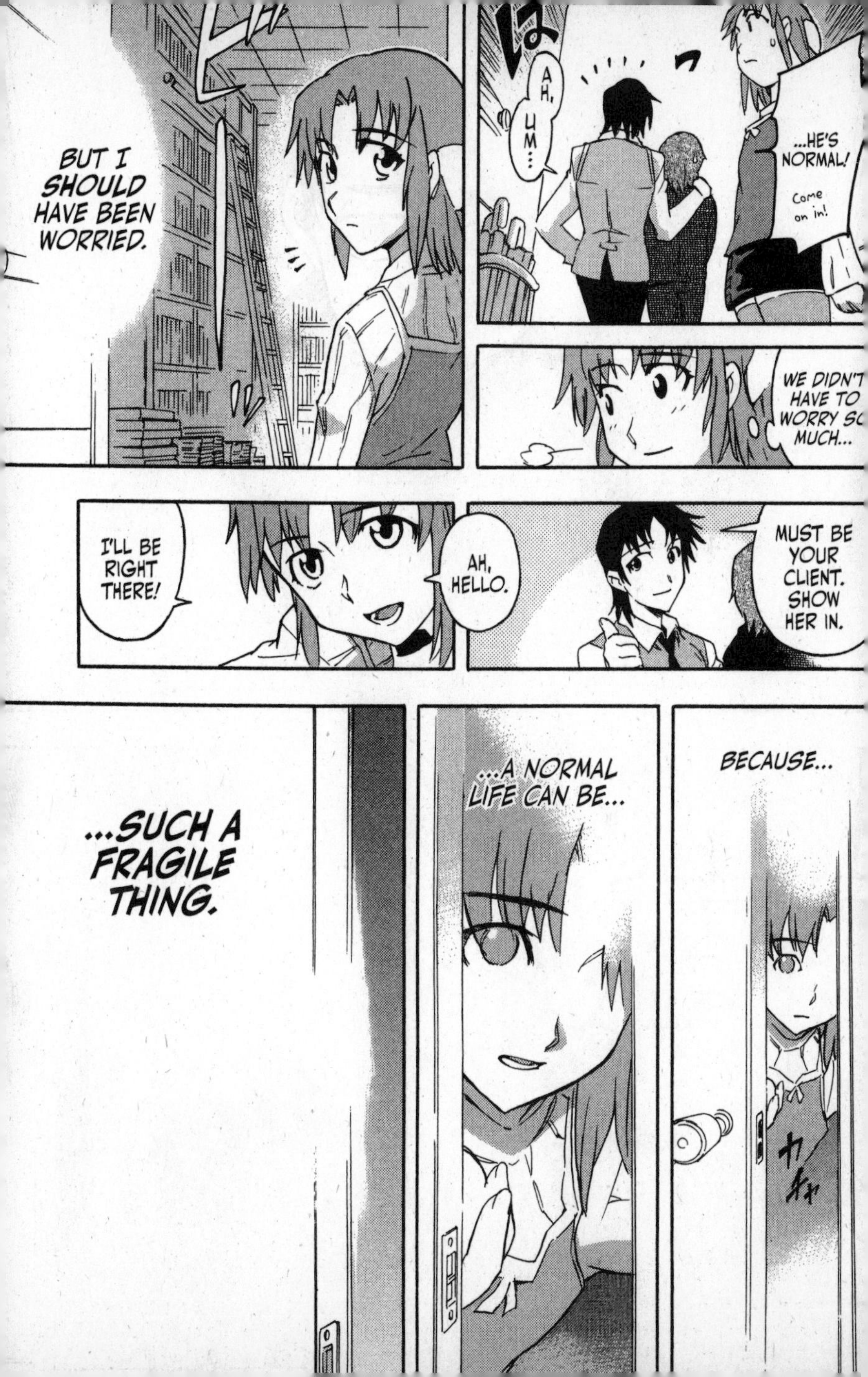
は
...HE'S NORMAL!
Come on in!
AH, UM...
WE DIDN'T HAVE TO WORRY SO MUCH...
BUT I SHOULD HAVE BEEN WORRIED.
MUST BE YOUR CLIENT. SHOW HER IN.
AH, HELLO.
I'LL BE RIGHT THERE!
BECAUSE...
...A NORMAL LIFE CAN BE...
...SUCH A FRAGILE THING.

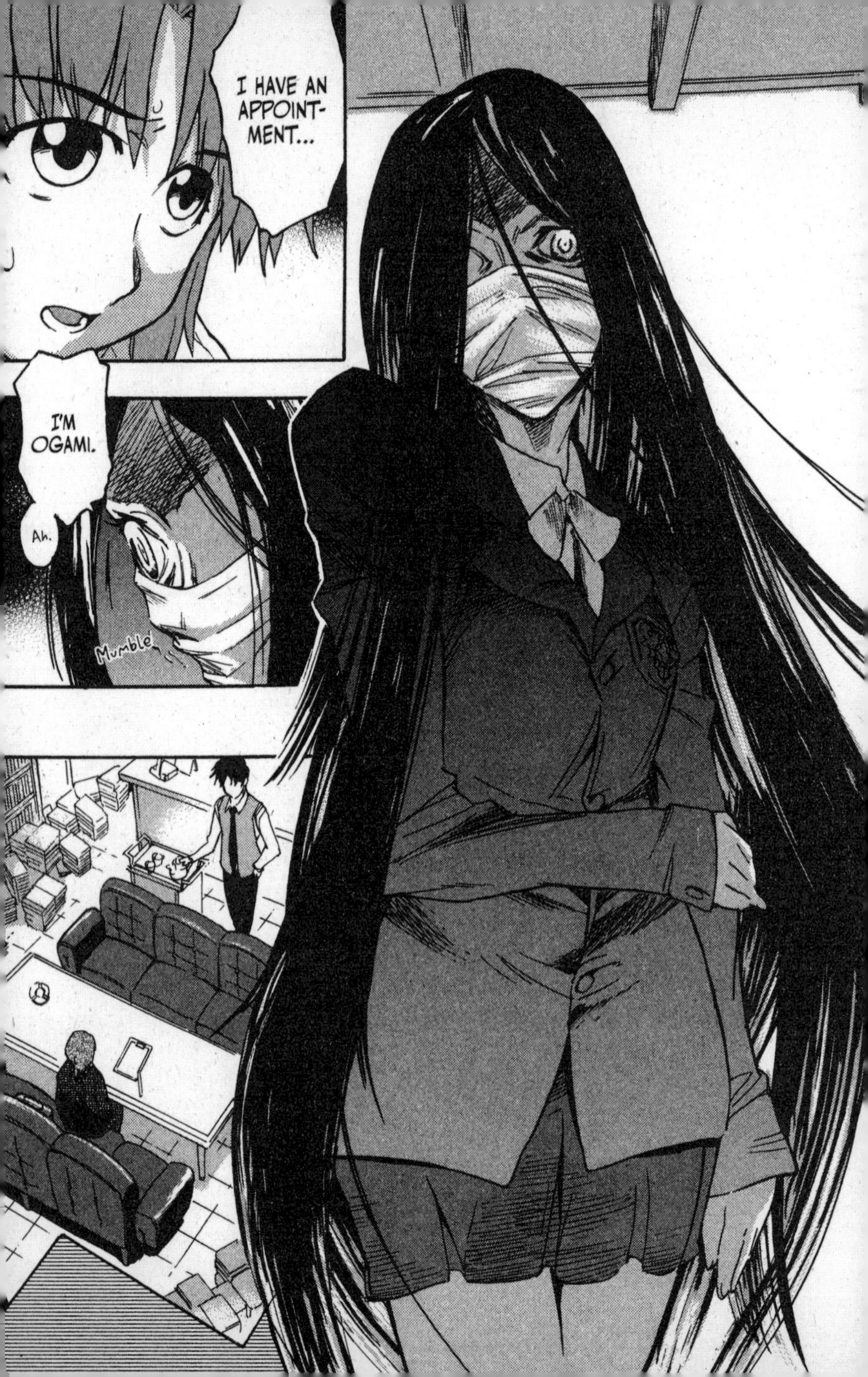

I HAVE AN APPOINT-MENT...
I'M OGAMI.
Ah.
Mumble

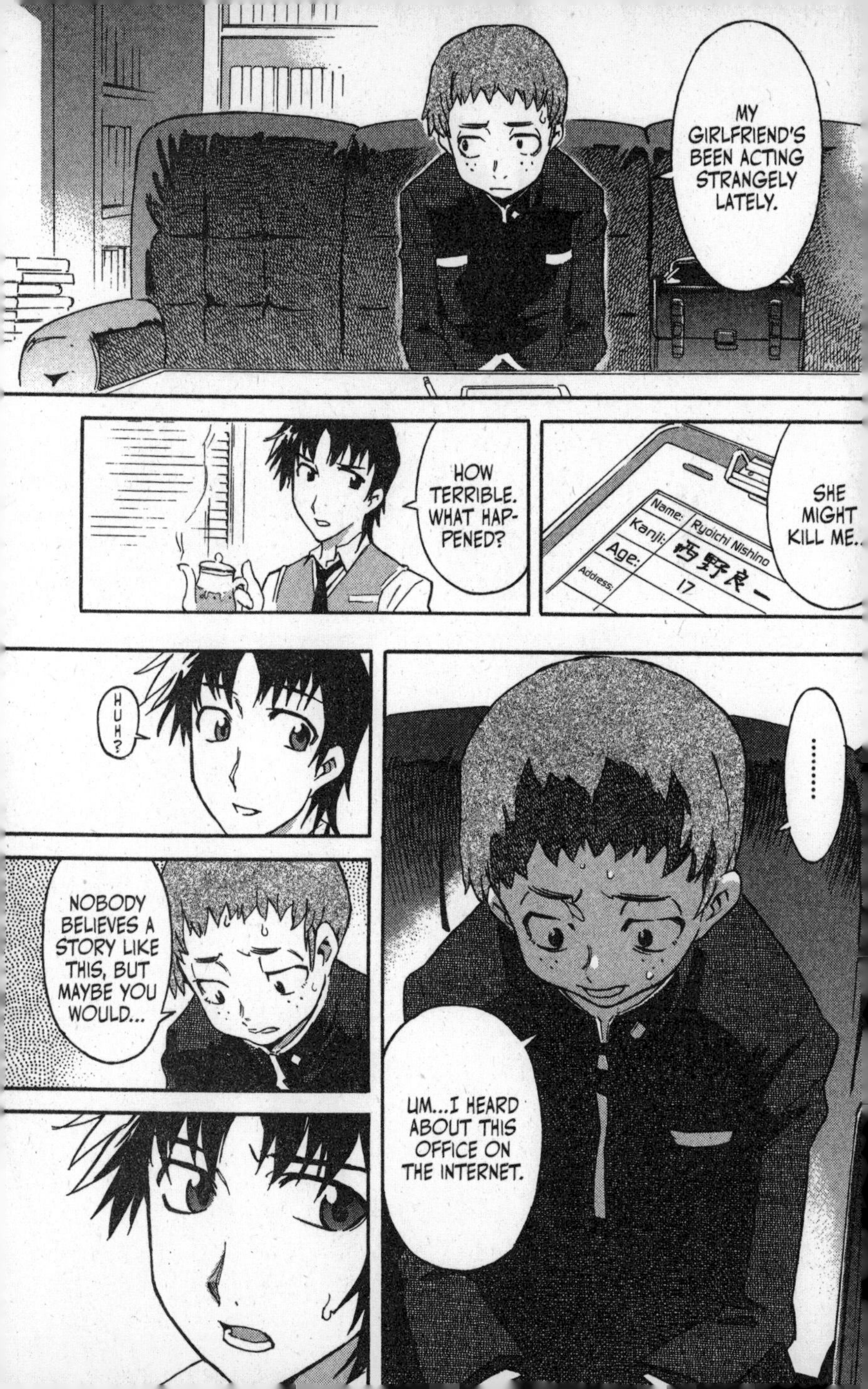
MY GIRLFRIEND'S BEEN ACTING STRANGELY LATELY.
SHE MIGHT KILL ME..
Name: Ryoichi Nishino
Kanji: 西野良一
Age: 17
Address:
HOW TERRIBLE. WHAT HAPPENED?
....
UM...I HEARD ABOUT THIS OFFICE ON THE INTERNET.
HUH?
NOBODY BELIEVES A STORY LIKE THIS, BUT MAYBE YOU WOULD...

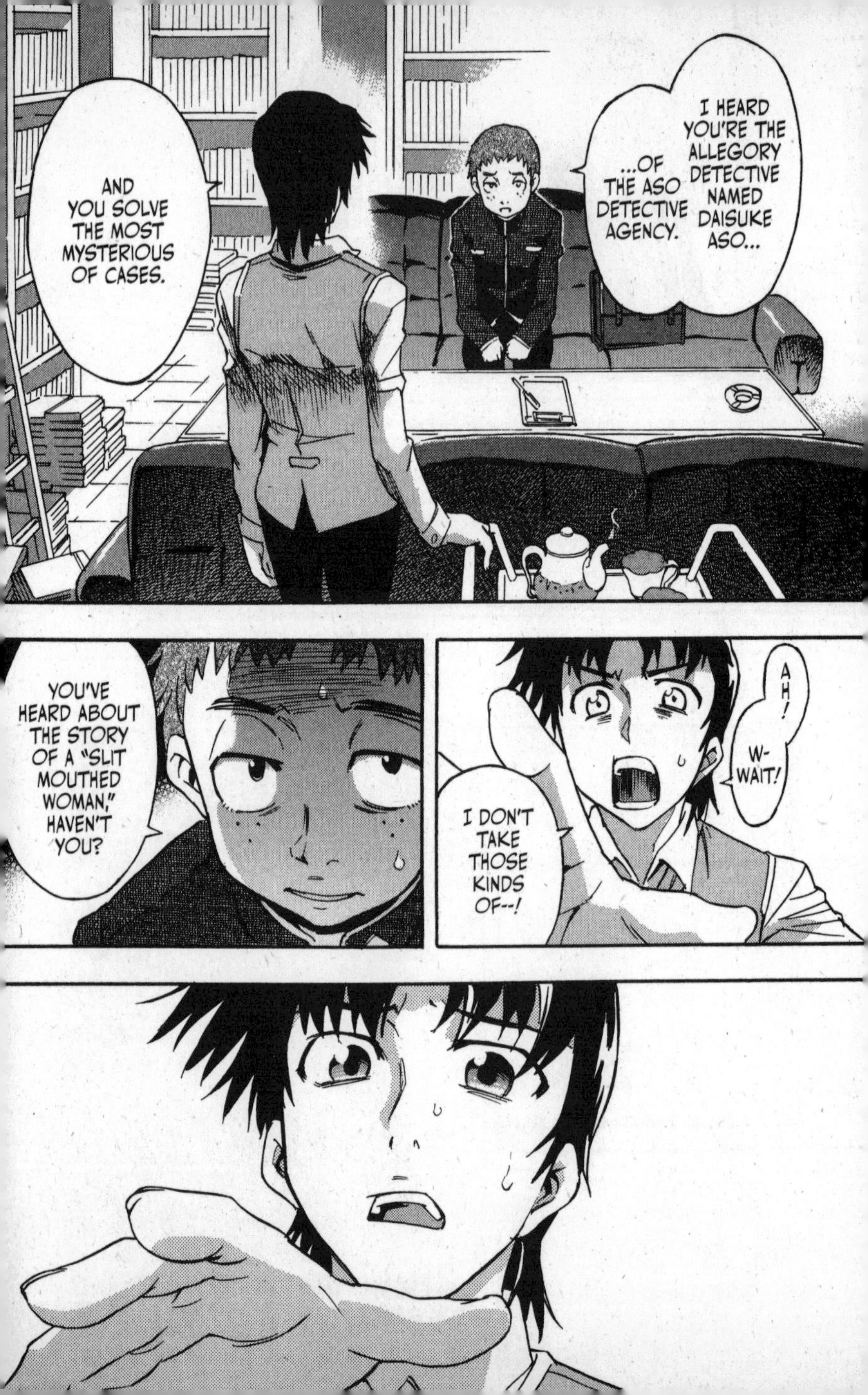
I HEARD YOU'RE THE ALLEGORY DETECTIVE NAMED DAISUKE ASO...
...OF THE ASO DETECTIVE AGENCY.
AND YOU SOLVE THE MOST MYSTERIOUS OF CASES.
AH! W-WAIT!
I DON'T TAKE THOSE KINDS OF--!
YOU'VE HEARD ABOUT THE STORY OF A "SLIT MOUTHED WOMAN," HAVEN'T YOU?

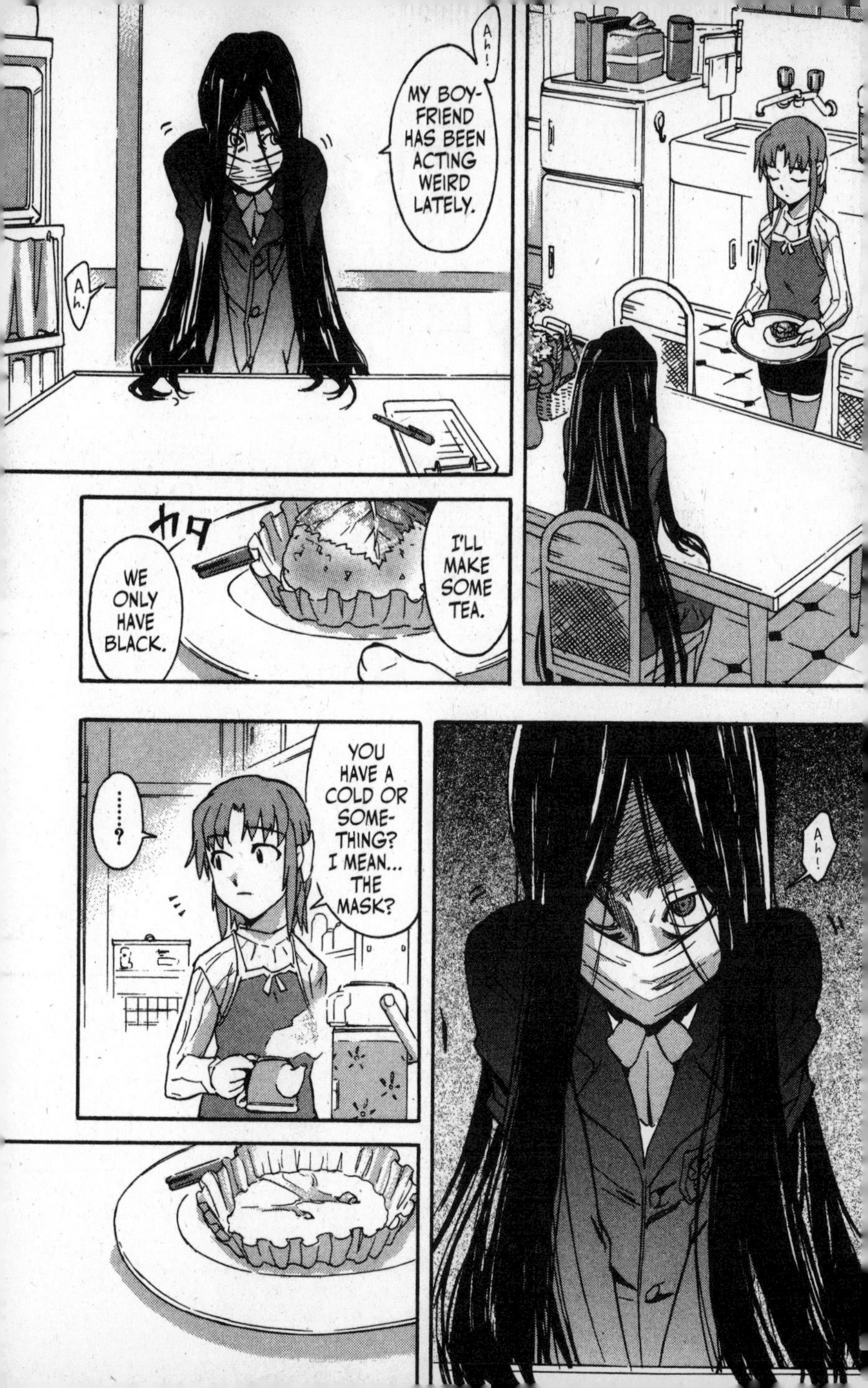
Ah!
MY BOYFRIEND HAS BEEN ACTING WEIRD LATELY.
Ah.
I'LL MAKE SOME TEA.
カタ
WE ONLY HAVE BLACK.
Ah!
YOU HAVE A COLD OR SOMETHING? I MEAN... THE MASK?
......?

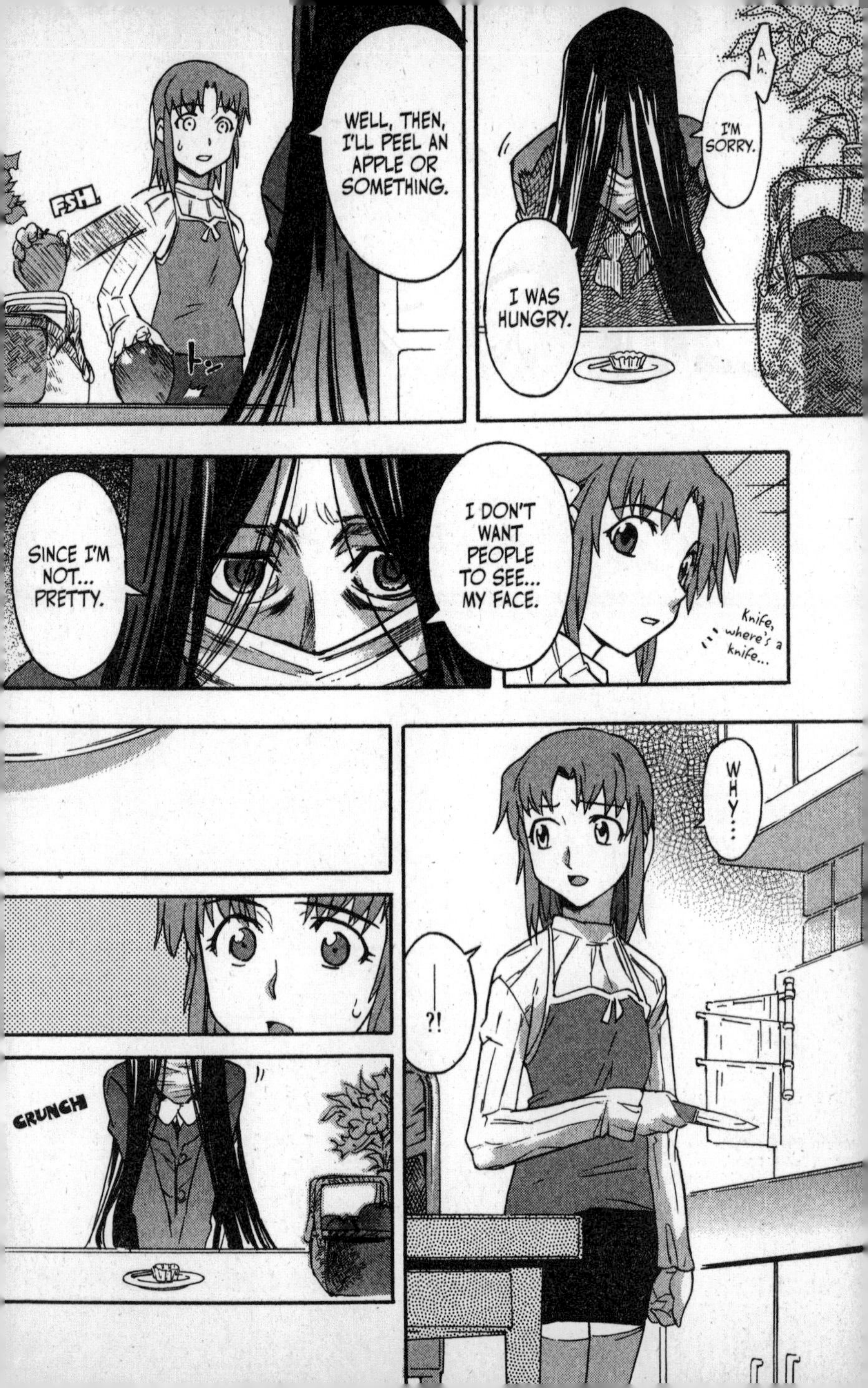
Ah.
I'M SORRY.
I WAS HUNGRY.
WELL, THEN, I'LL PEEL AN APPLE OR SOMETHING.
FSH.
I DON'T WANT PEOPLE TO SEE... MY FACE.
Knife, where's a knife...
SINCE I'M NOT... PRETTY.
WHY...
—?!
CRUNCH

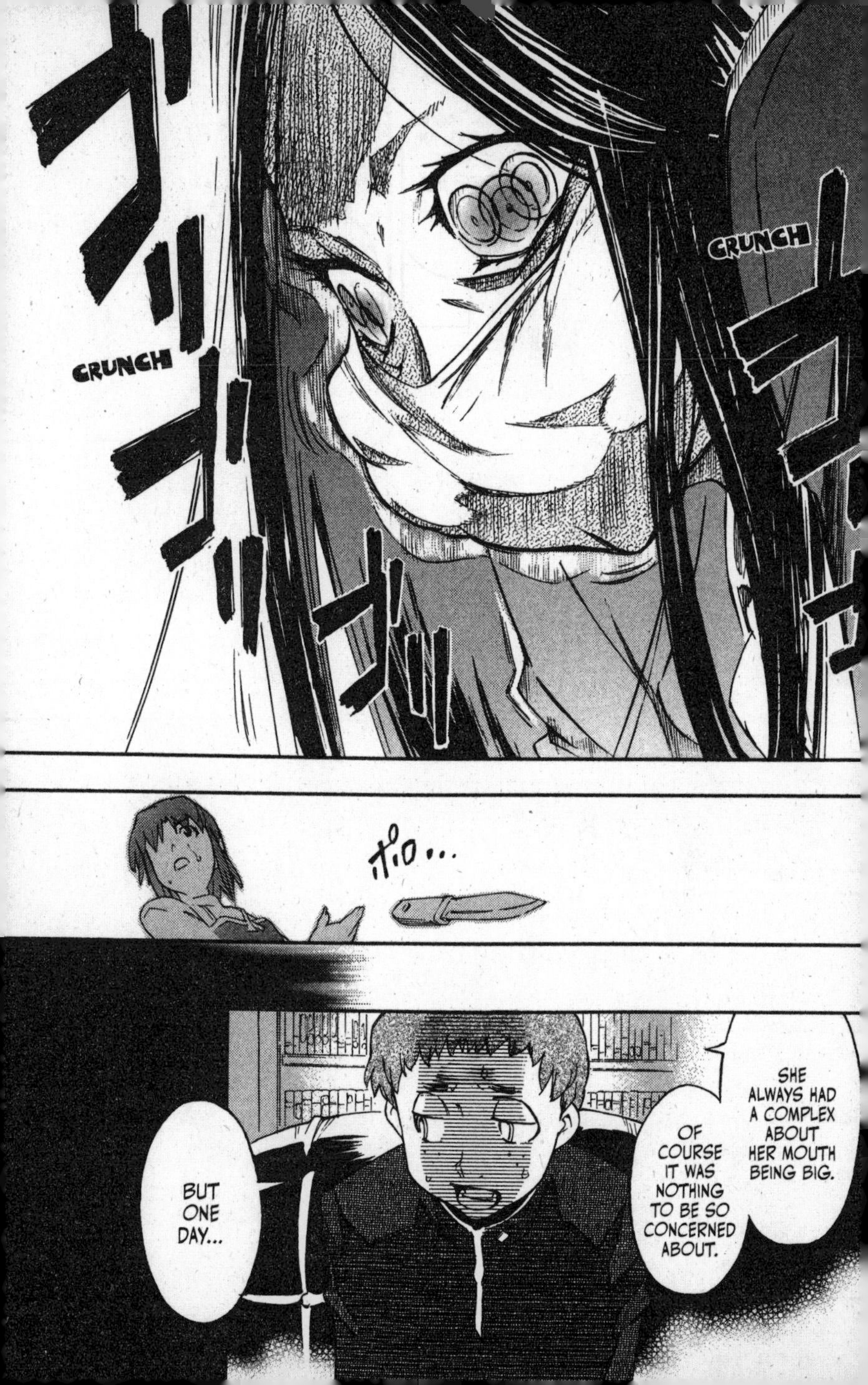
CRUNCH
CRUNCH
ポロ...
SHE ALWAYS HAD A COMPLEX ABOUT HER MOUTH BEING BIG.
OF COURSE IT WAS NOTHING TO BE SO CONCERNED ABOUT.
BUT ONE DAY...

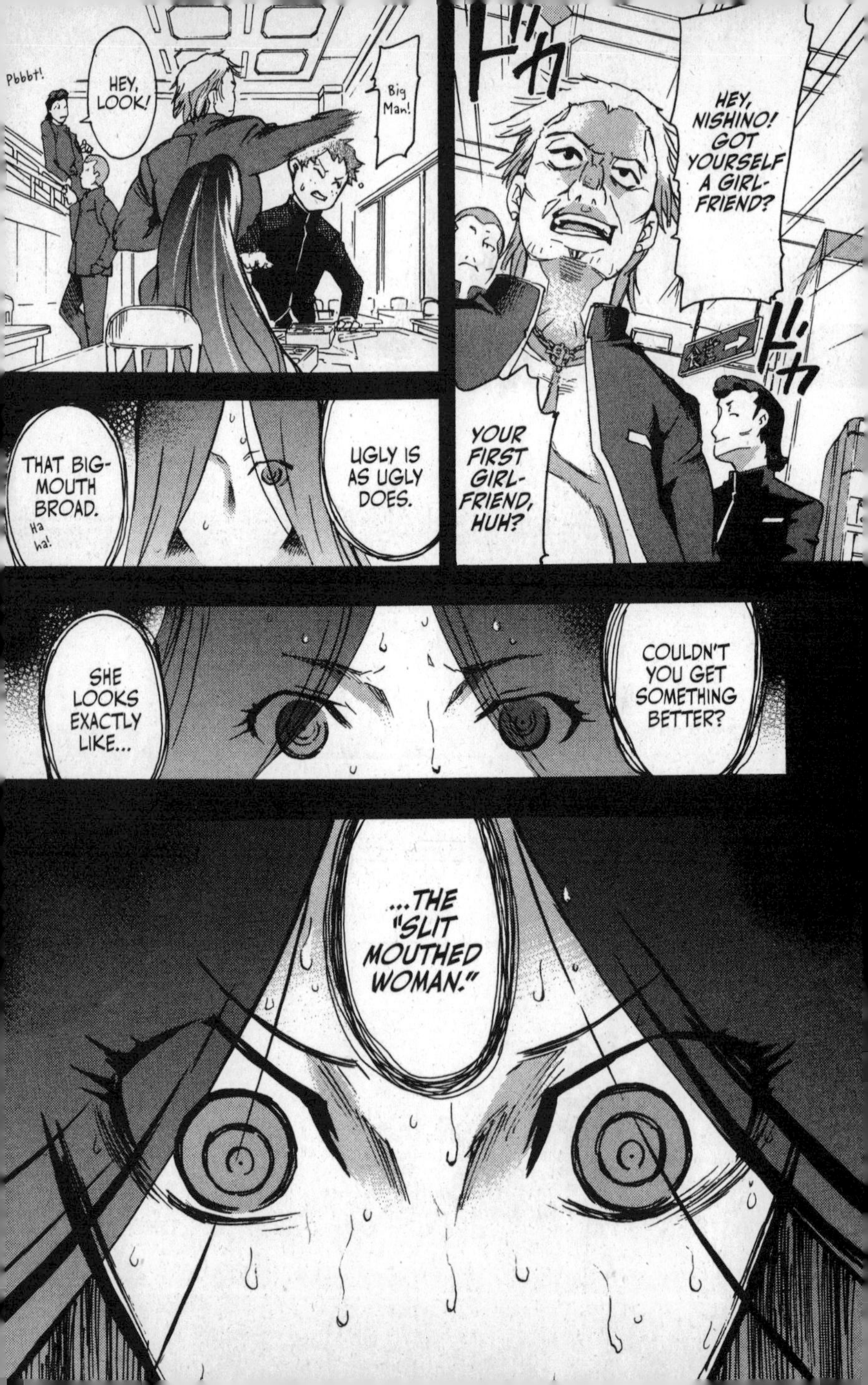
ドカ
HEY, NISHINO! GOT YOURSELF A GIRL-FRIEND?
ドカ
YOUR FIRST GIRL-FRIEND, HUH?
Big Man!
HEY, LOOK!
Pbbbt!
UGLY IS AS UGLY DOES.
THAT BIG-MOUTH BROAD.
Ha ha!
COULDN'T YOU GET SOMETHING BETTER?
SHE LOOKS EXACTLY LIKE...
...THE "SLIT MOUTHED WOMAN."

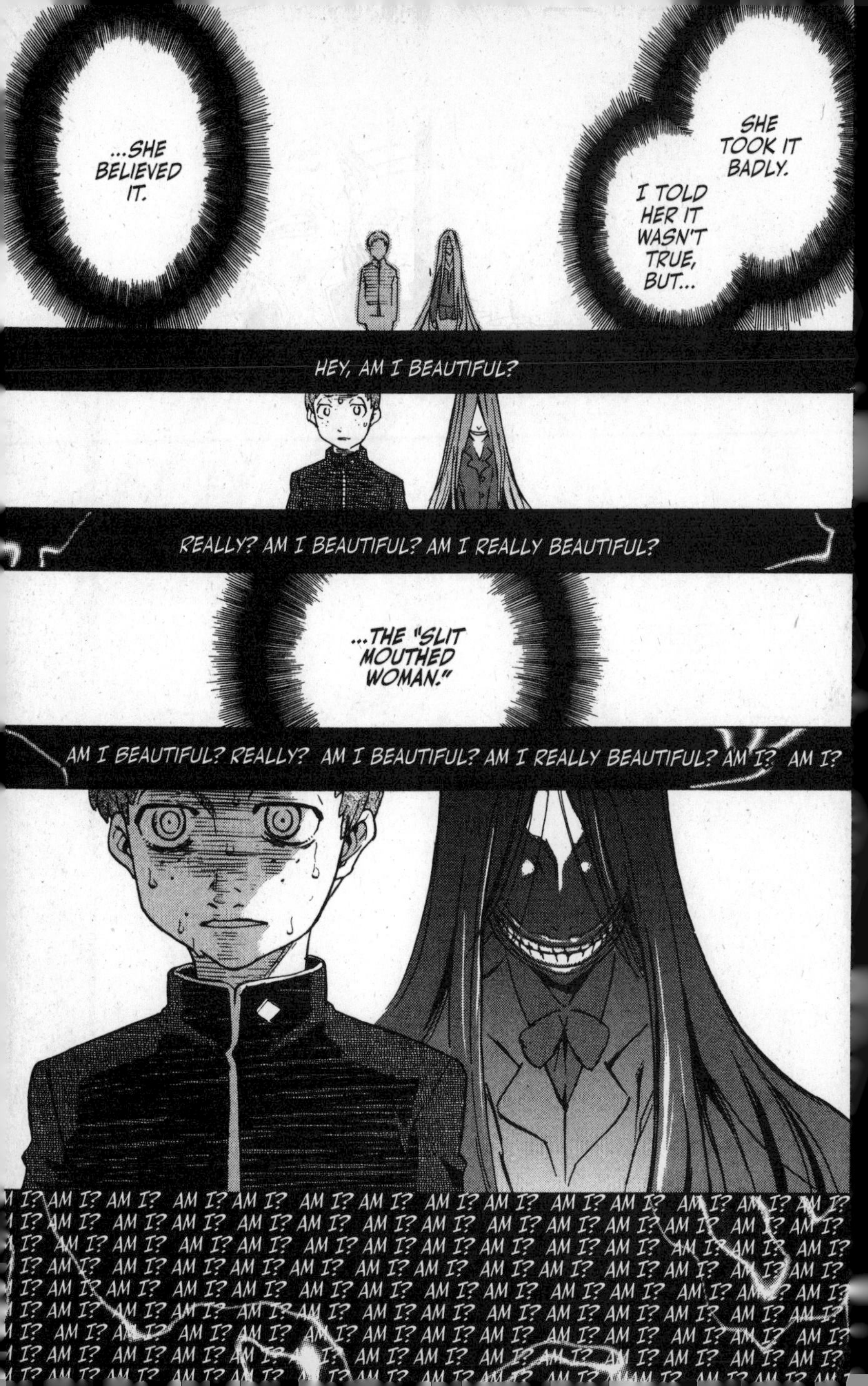
SHE TOOK IT BADLY.
I TOLD HER IT WASN'T TRUE, BUT...
...SHE BELIEVED IT.
HEY, AM I BEAUTIFUL?
REALLY? AM I BEAUTIFUL? AM I REALLY BEAUTIFUL?
...THE "SLIT MOUTHED WOMAN."
AM I BEAUTIFUL? REALLY? AM I BEAUTIFUL? AM I REALLY BEAUTIFUL? AM I? AM I?
AM I? AM I? AM I? AM I? AM I? AM I? AM I? AM I? AM I? AM I? AM I? AM I? AM I?

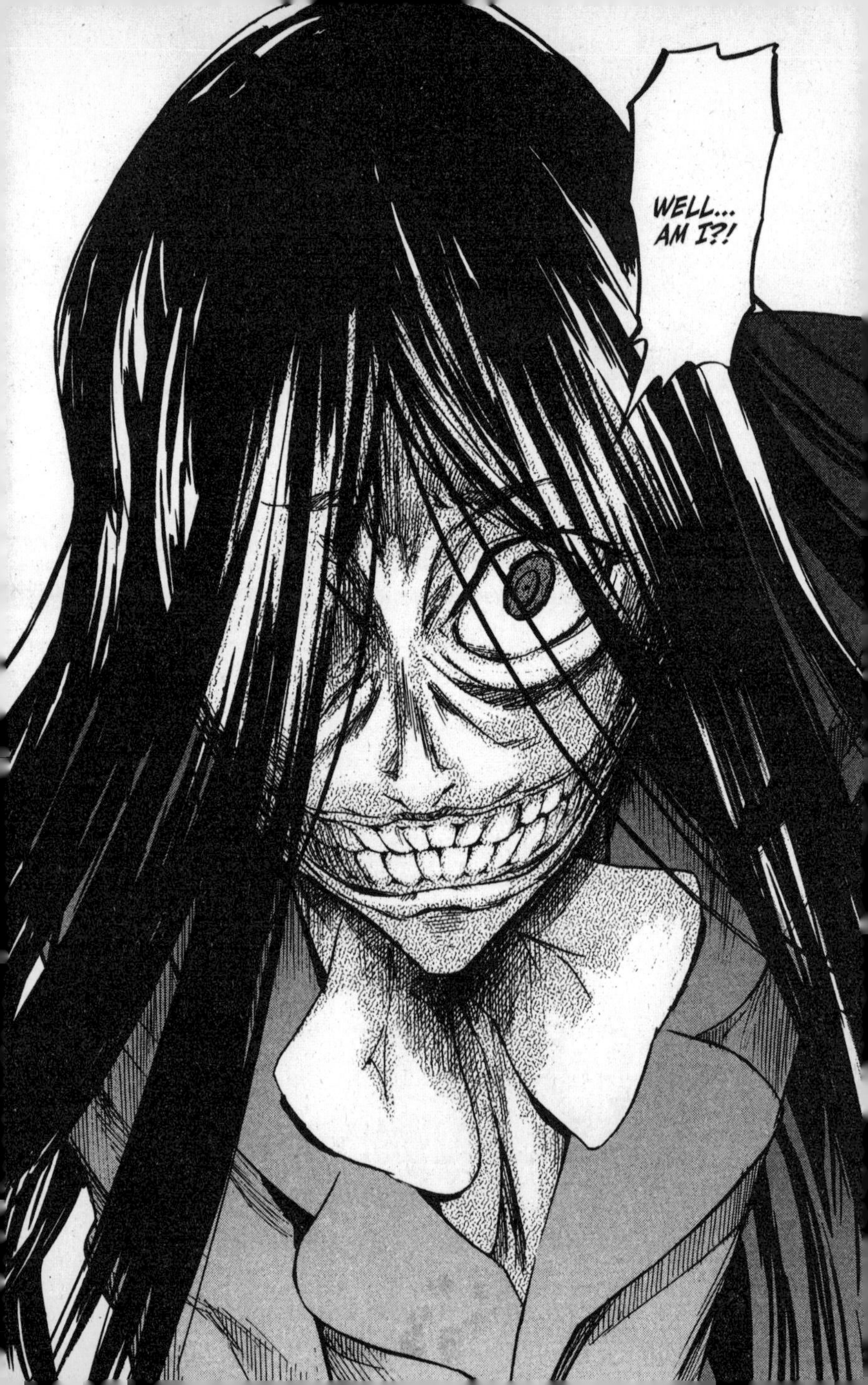
WELL... AM I?!

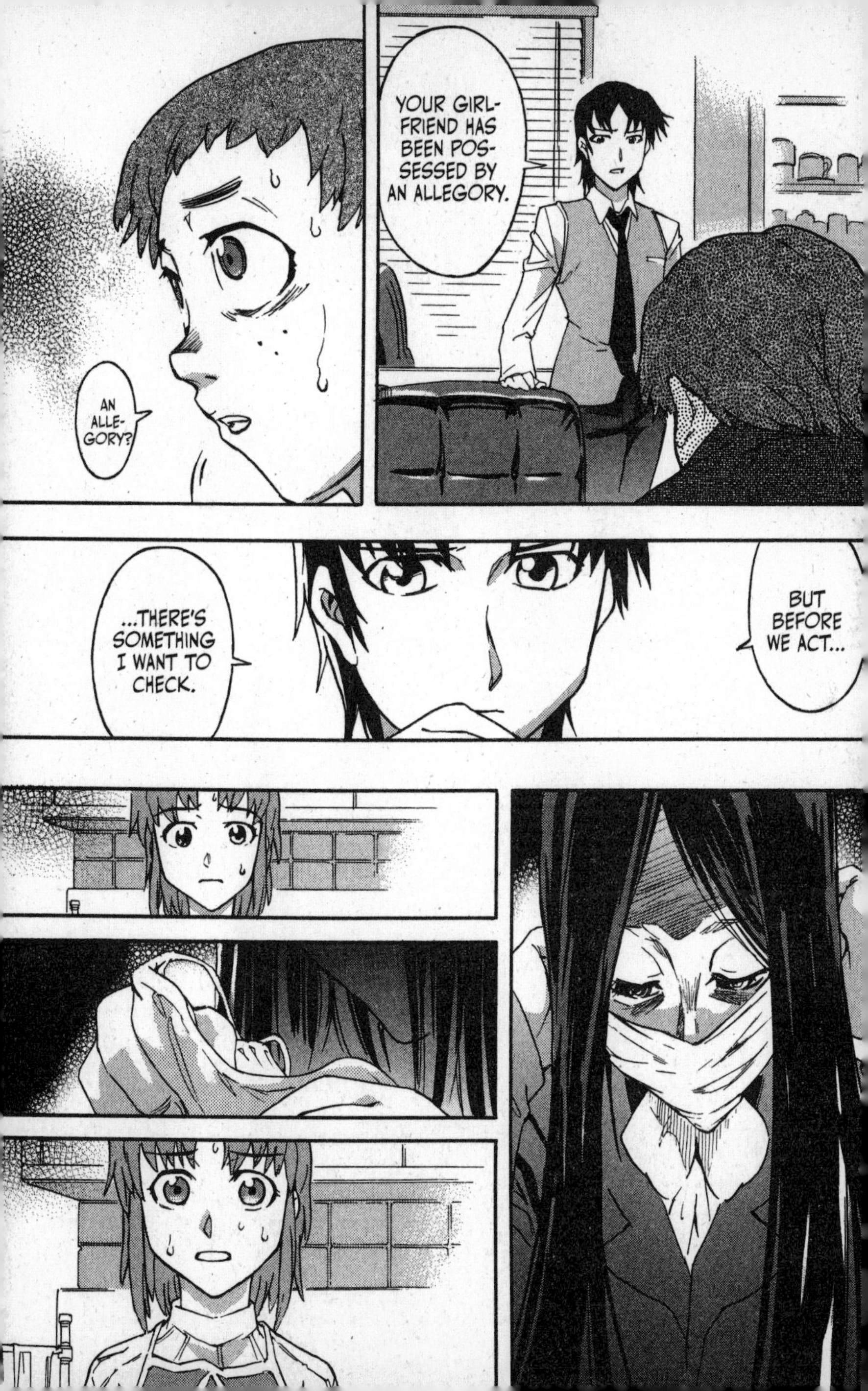
YOUR GIRL-FRIEND HAS BEEN POS-SESSED BY AN ALLEGORY.
AN ALLE-GORY?
BUT BEFORE WE ACT...
...THERE'S SOMETHING I WANT TO CHECK.

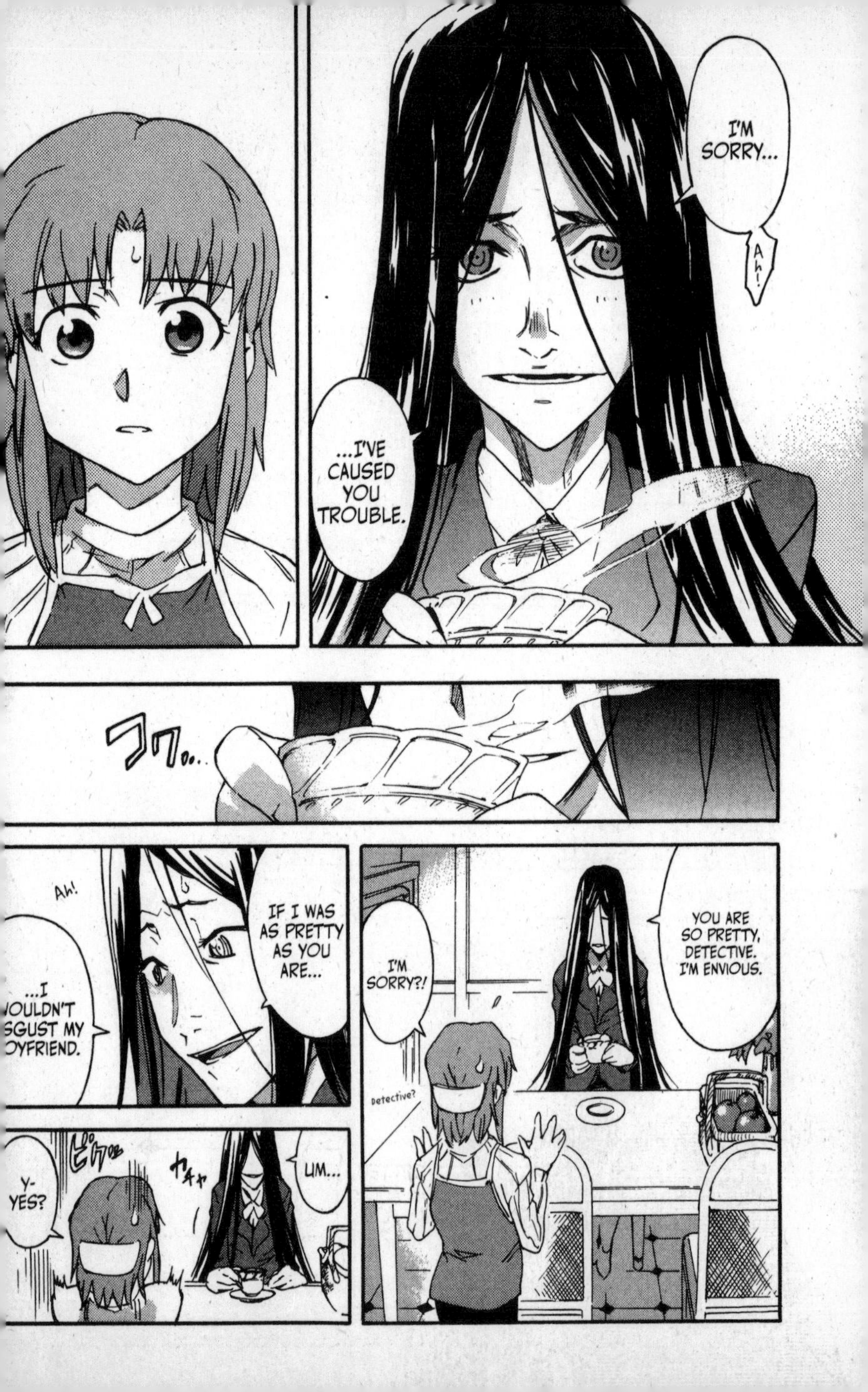
I'M SORRY...
Ah!
...I'VE CAUSED YOU TROUBLE.
フワ...
YOU ARE SO PRETTY, DETECTIVE. I'M ENVIOUS.
I'M SORRY?!
Detective?
IF I WAS AS PRETTY AS YOU ARE...
Ah!
...I OULDN'T SGUST MY OYFRIEND.
UM...
カチャ
ピクッ
Y-YES?

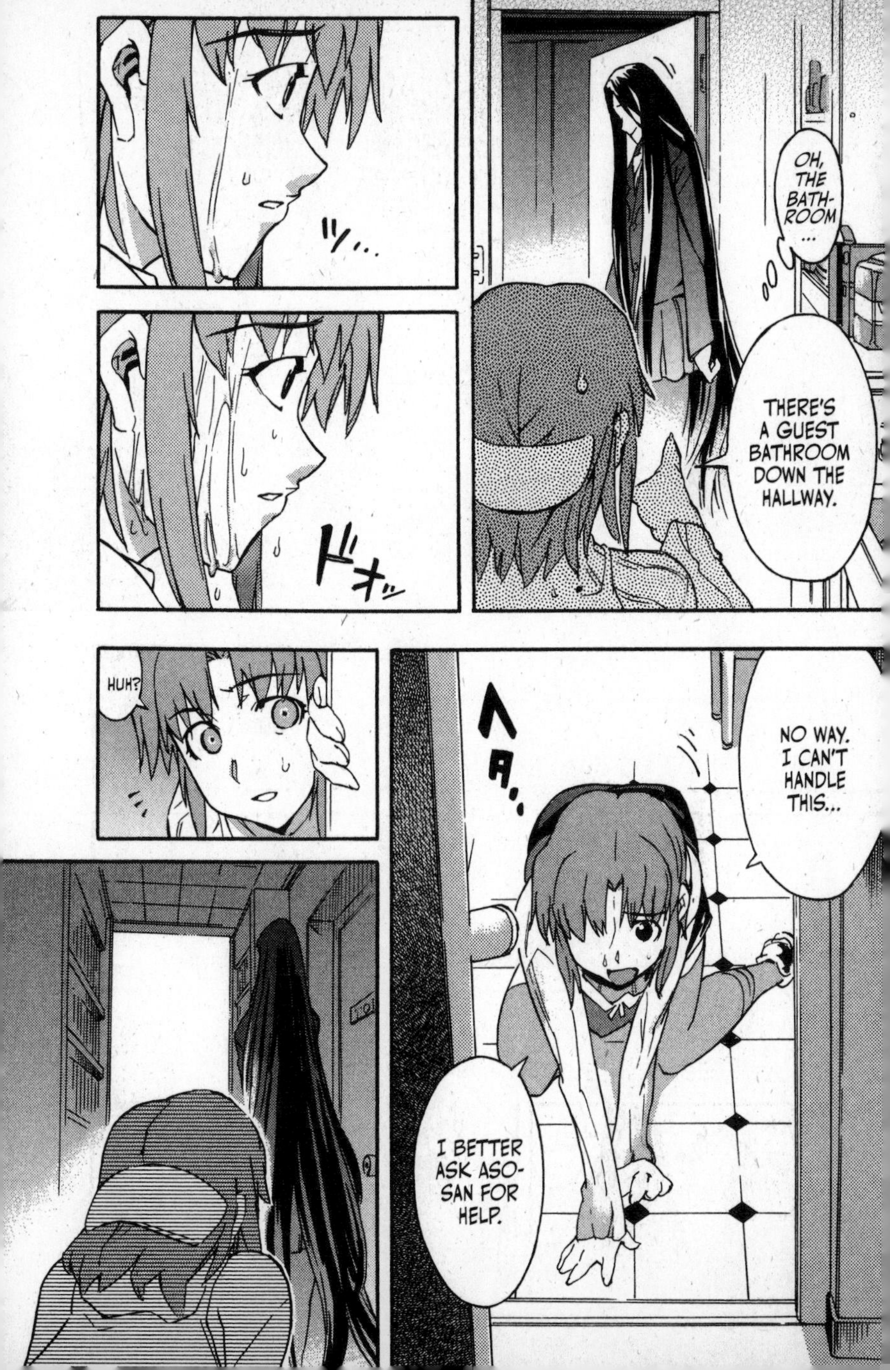
OH, THE BATHROOM...
THERE'S A GUEST BATHROOM DOWN THE HALLWAY.
ツ...
ドオッ
NO WAY. I CAN'T HANDLE THIS...
I BETTER ASK ASO-SAN FOR HELP.
HUH?

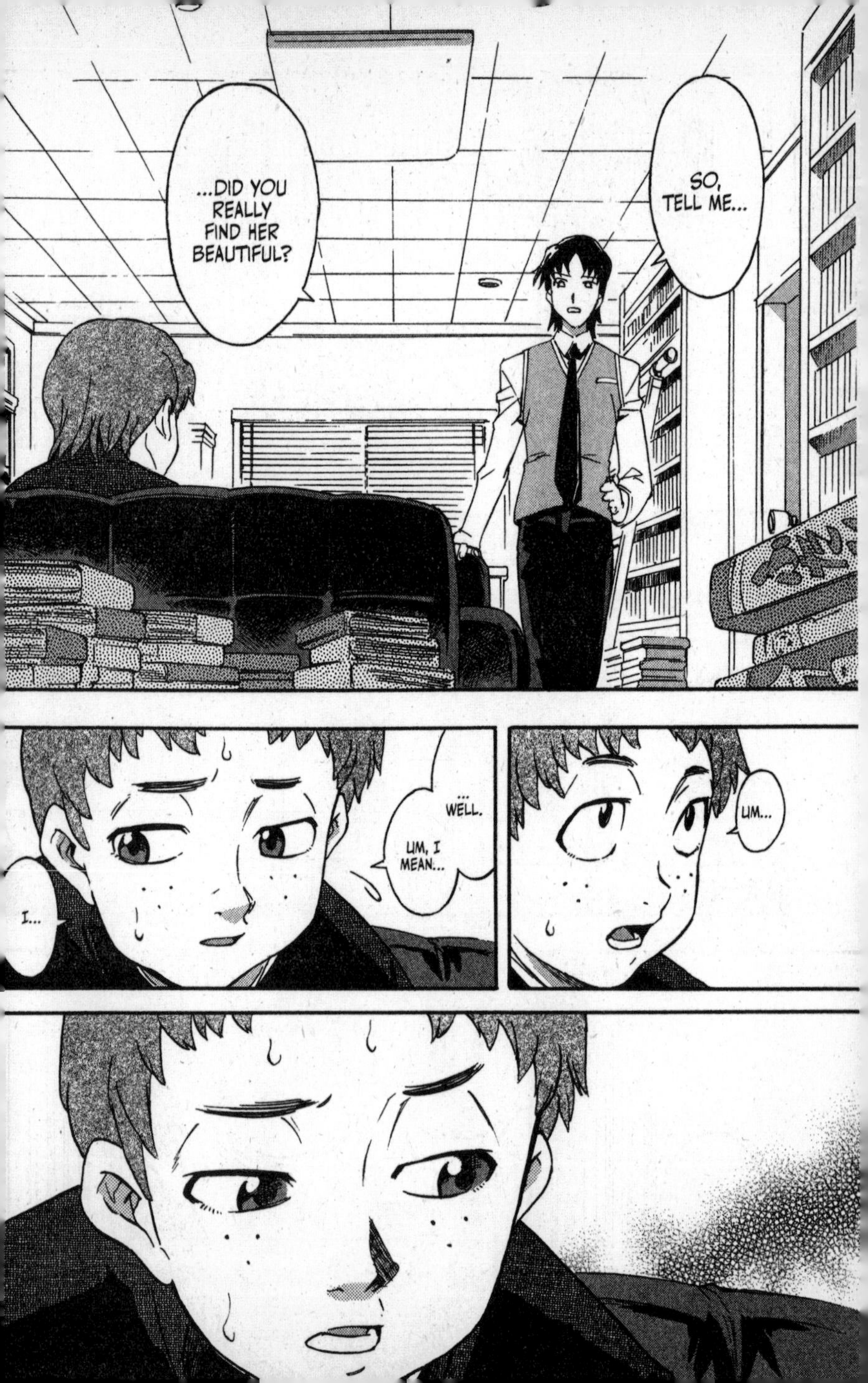
SO, TELL ME...
...DID YOU REALLY FIND HER BEAUTIFUL?
UM...
... WELL.
UM, I MEAN...
I...

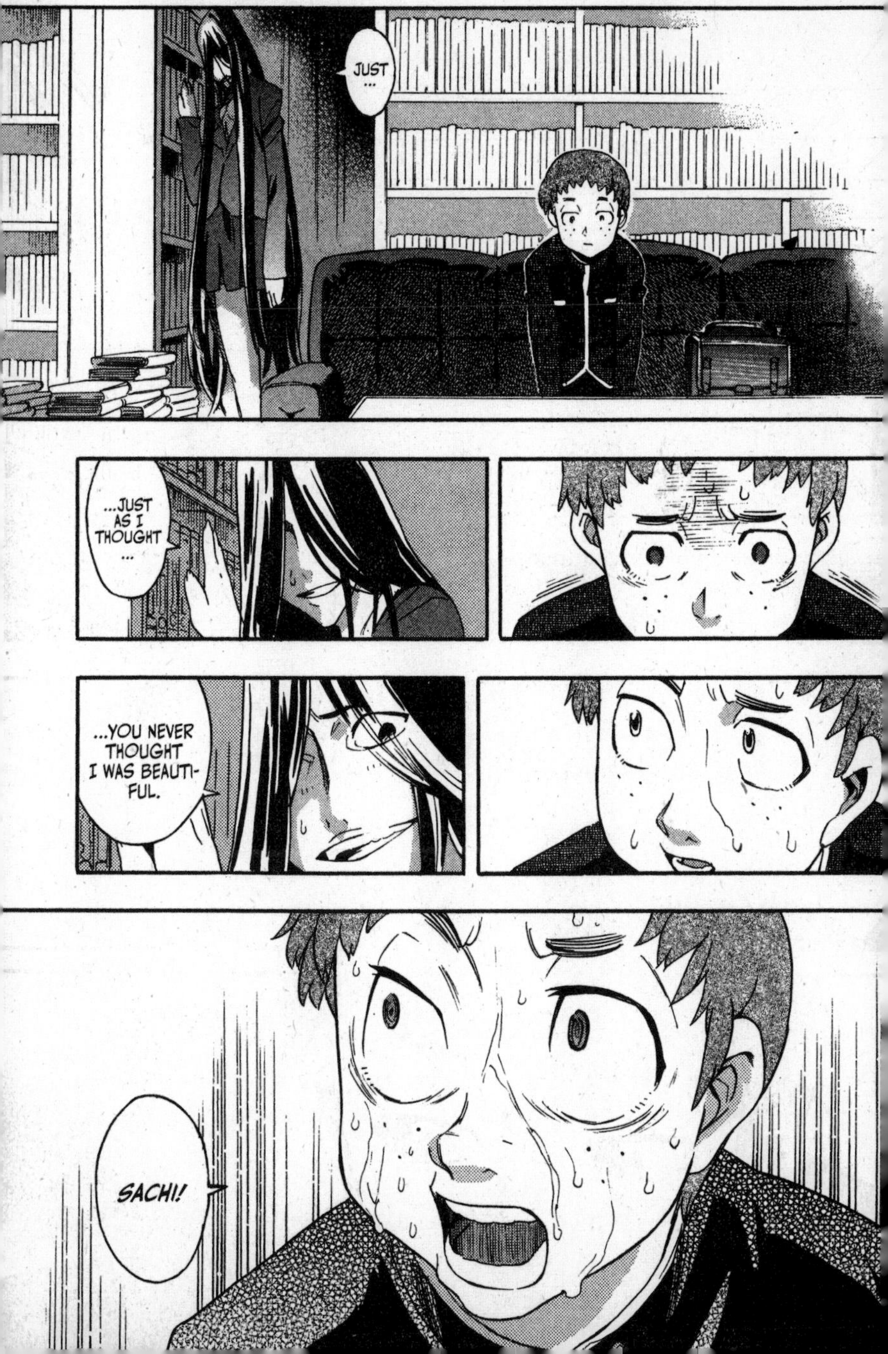
JUST ...
...JUST AS I THOUGHT ...
...YOU NEVER THOUGHT I WAS BEAUTI-FUL.
SACHI!

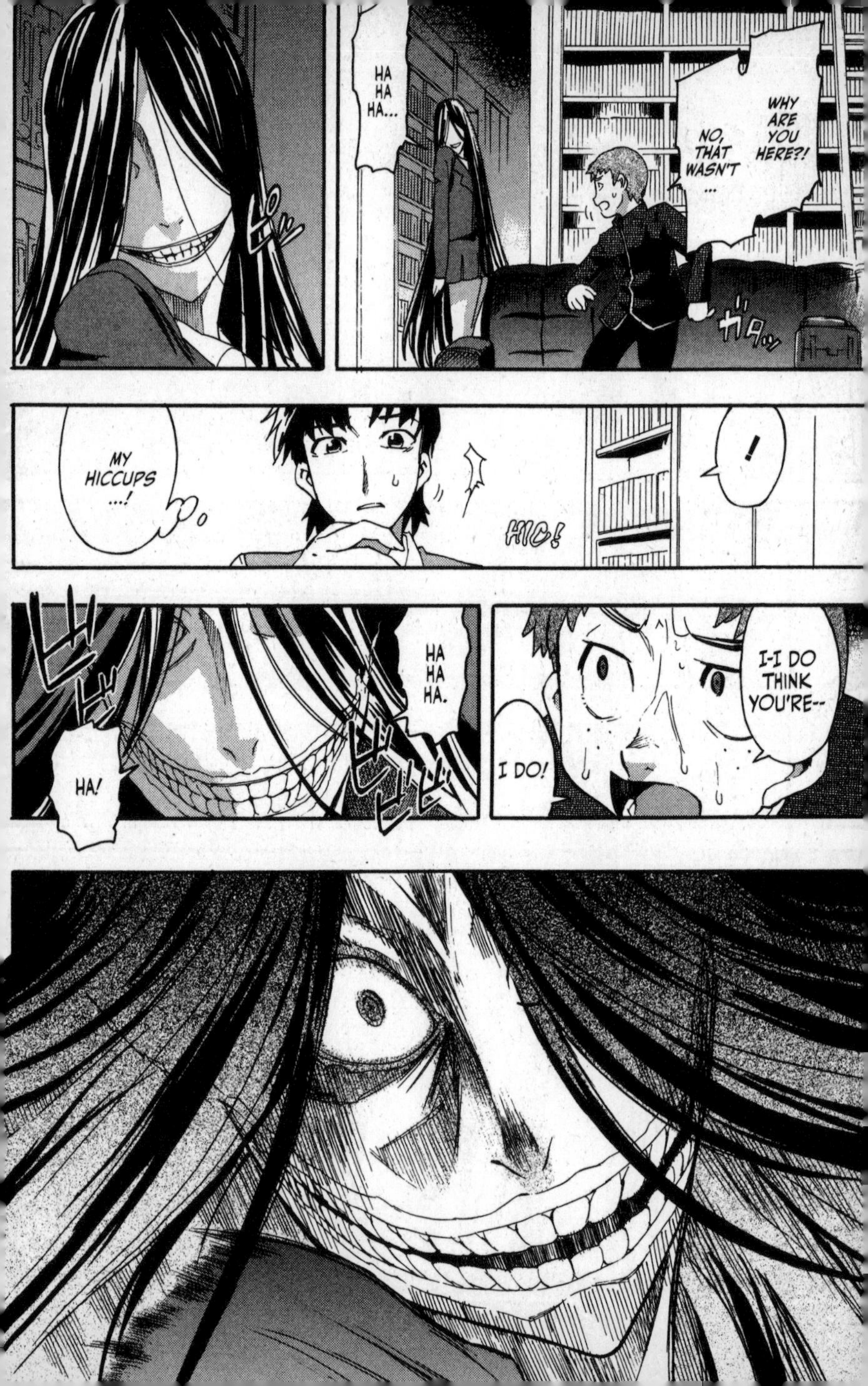
WHY ARE YOU HERE?!
NO, THAT WASN'T ...
HA HA HA...
!
HIC!
MY HICCUPS ...!
I-I DO THINK YOU'RE--
I DO!
HA HA HA.
HA!

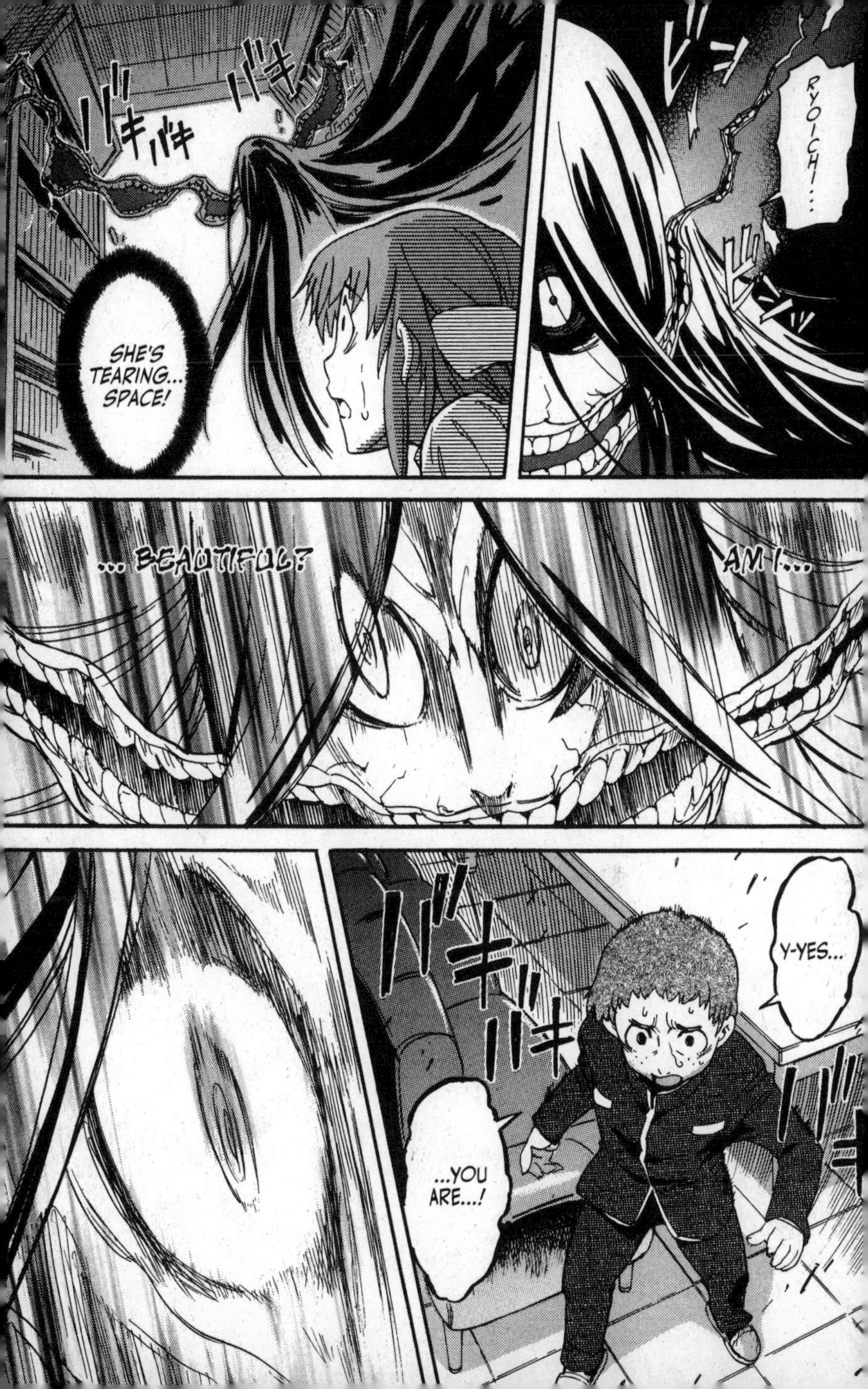
RYOICHI...
SHE'S TEARING... SPACE!
AM I...
... BEAUTIFUL?
Y-YES...
...YOU ARE...!

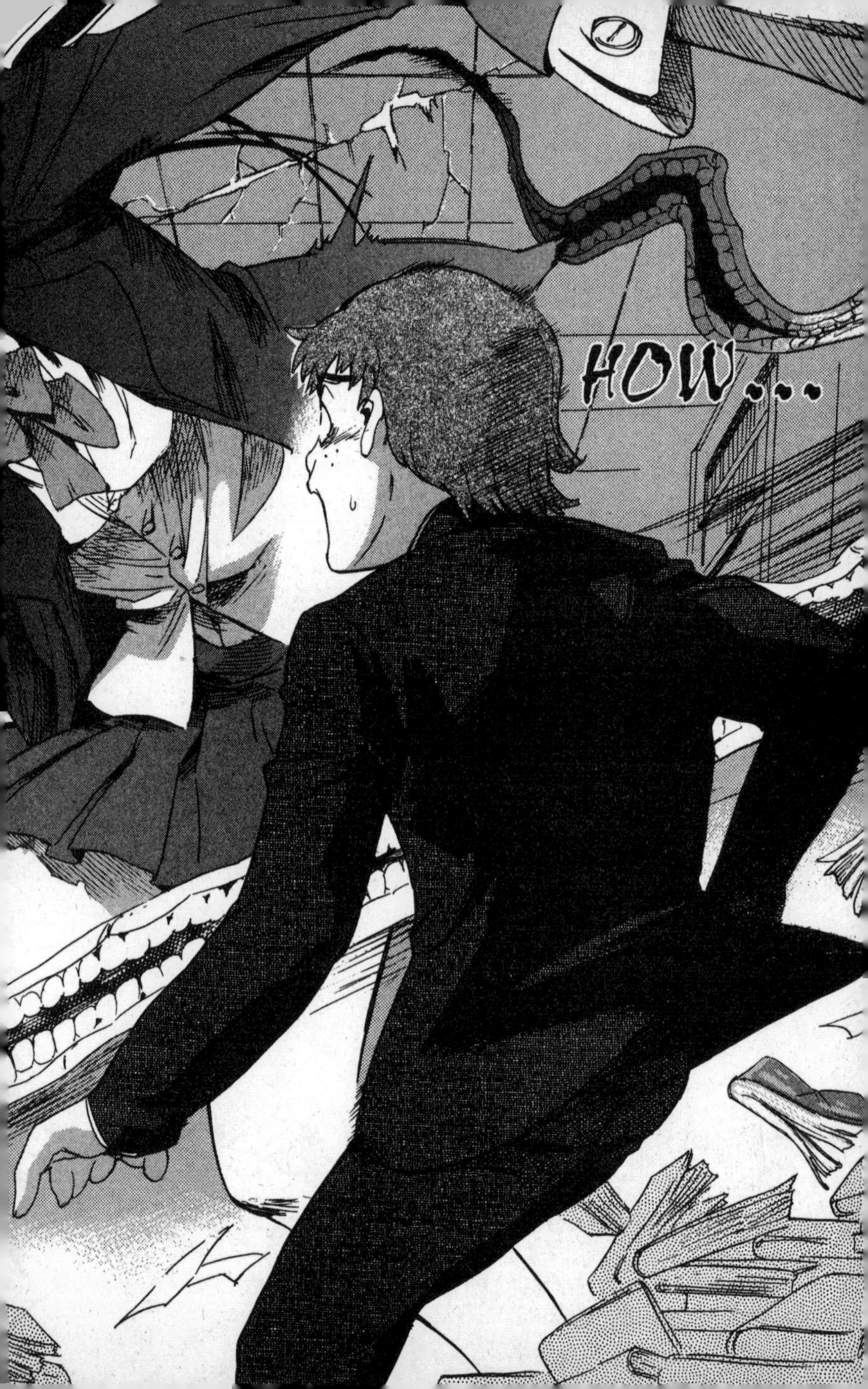
HOW...

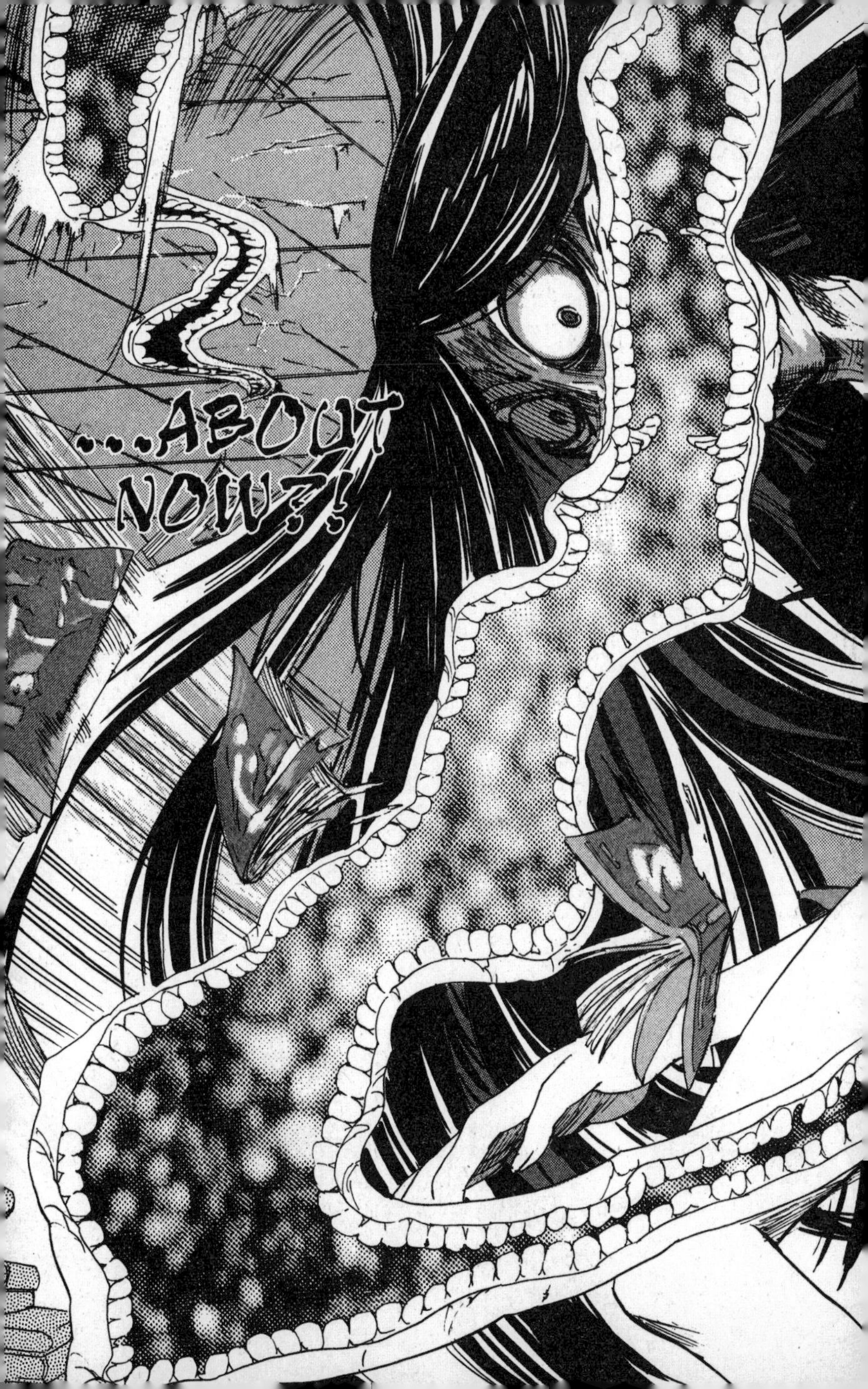
...ABOUT NOW?!

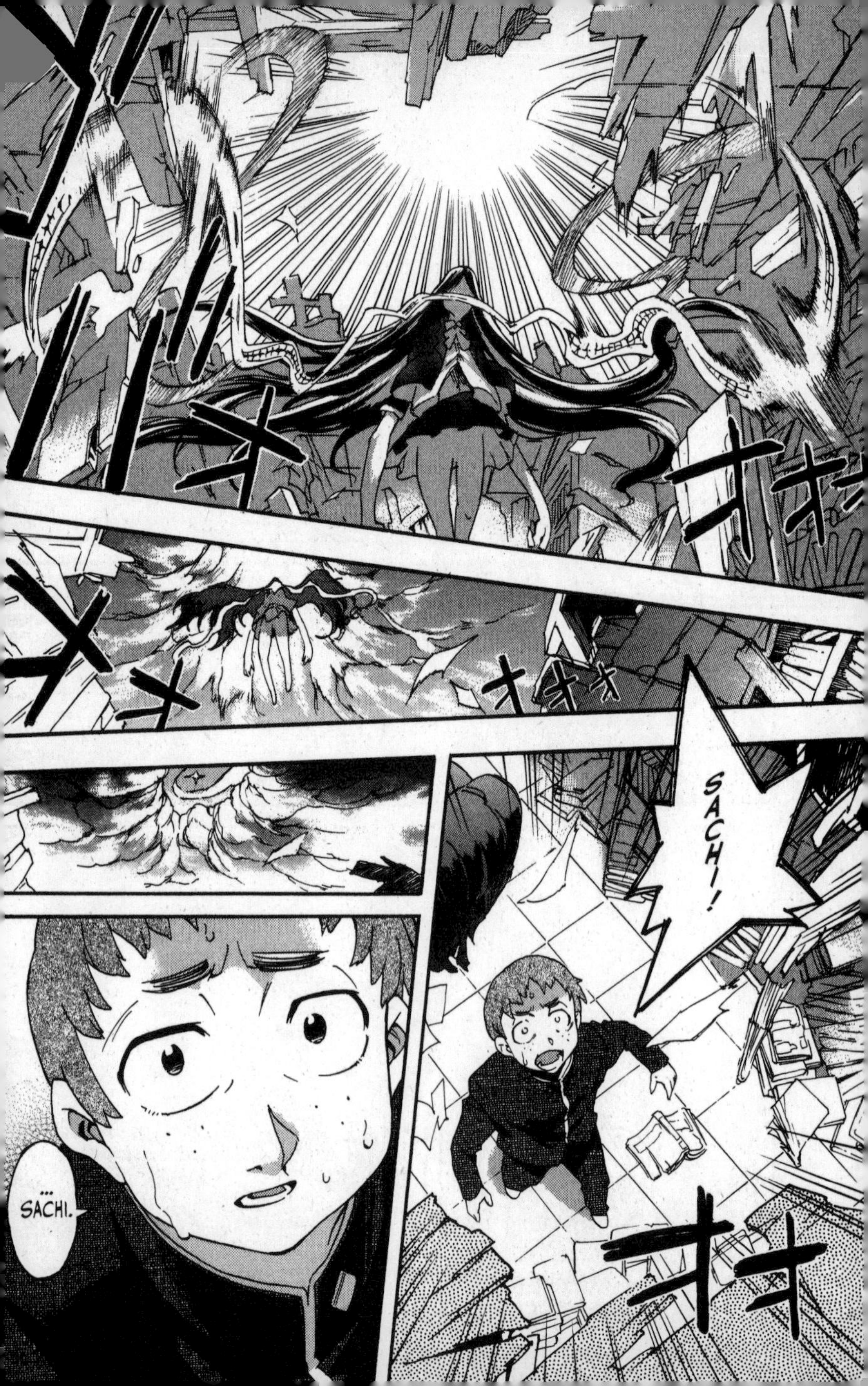
SACHI!
... SACHI.

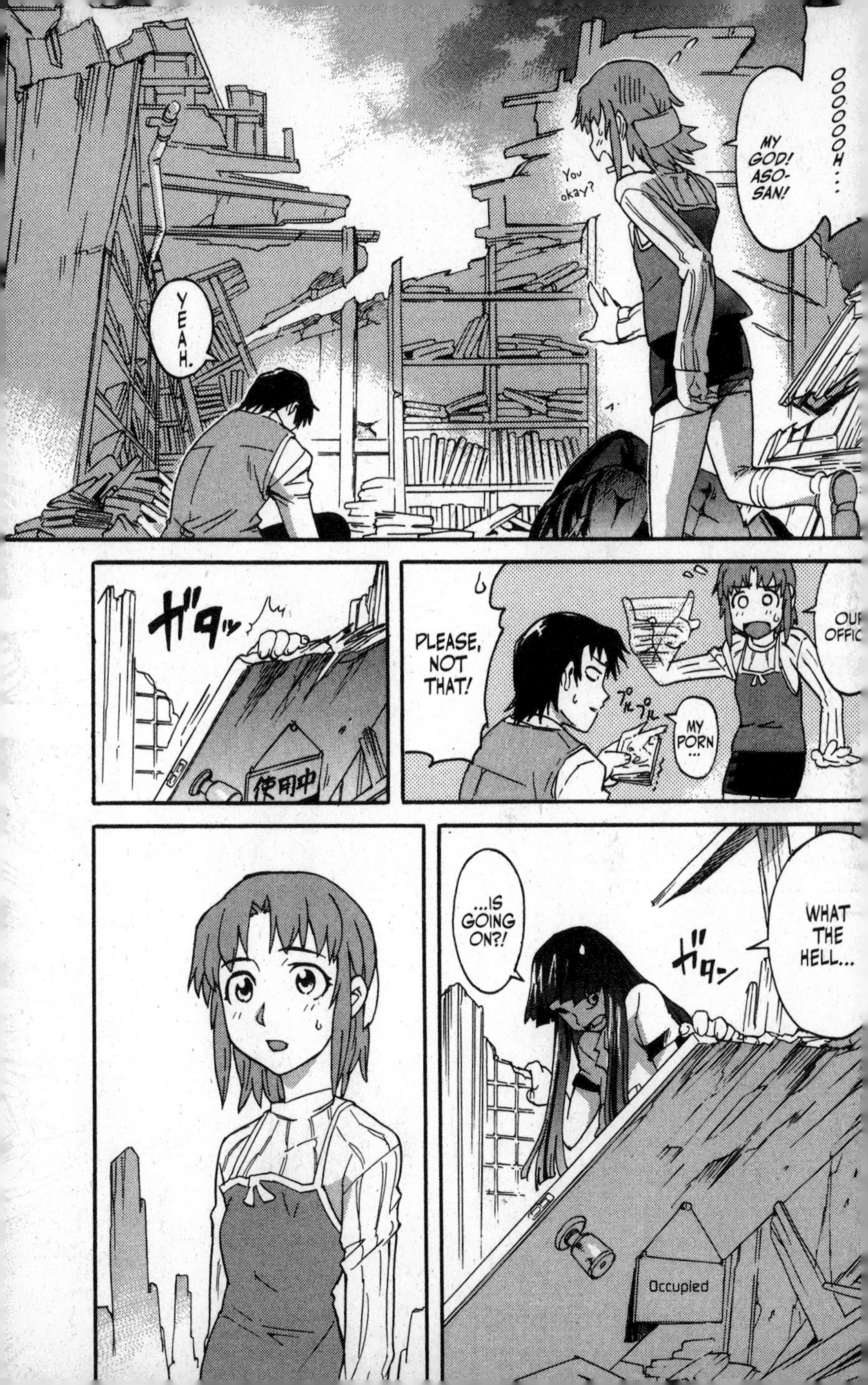
OOOOOOOH...
MY GOD! ASO-SAN!
You okay?
YEAH.
OUR OFFIC
PLEASE, NOT THAT!
MY PORN...
ガタッ
使用中
WHAT THE HELL...
ガタン
...IS GOING ON?!
Occupied

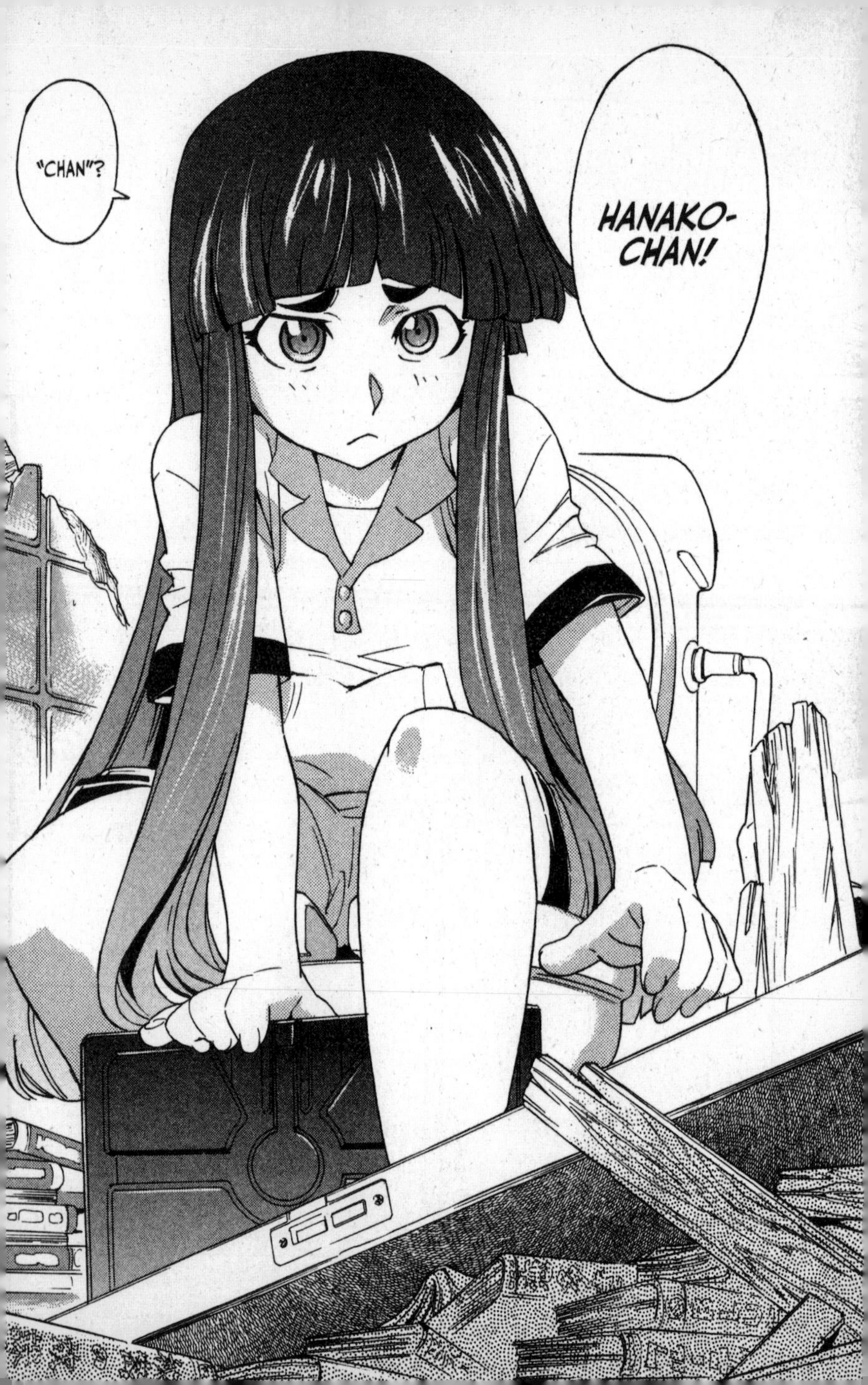
HANAKO-CHAN!
"CHAN"?

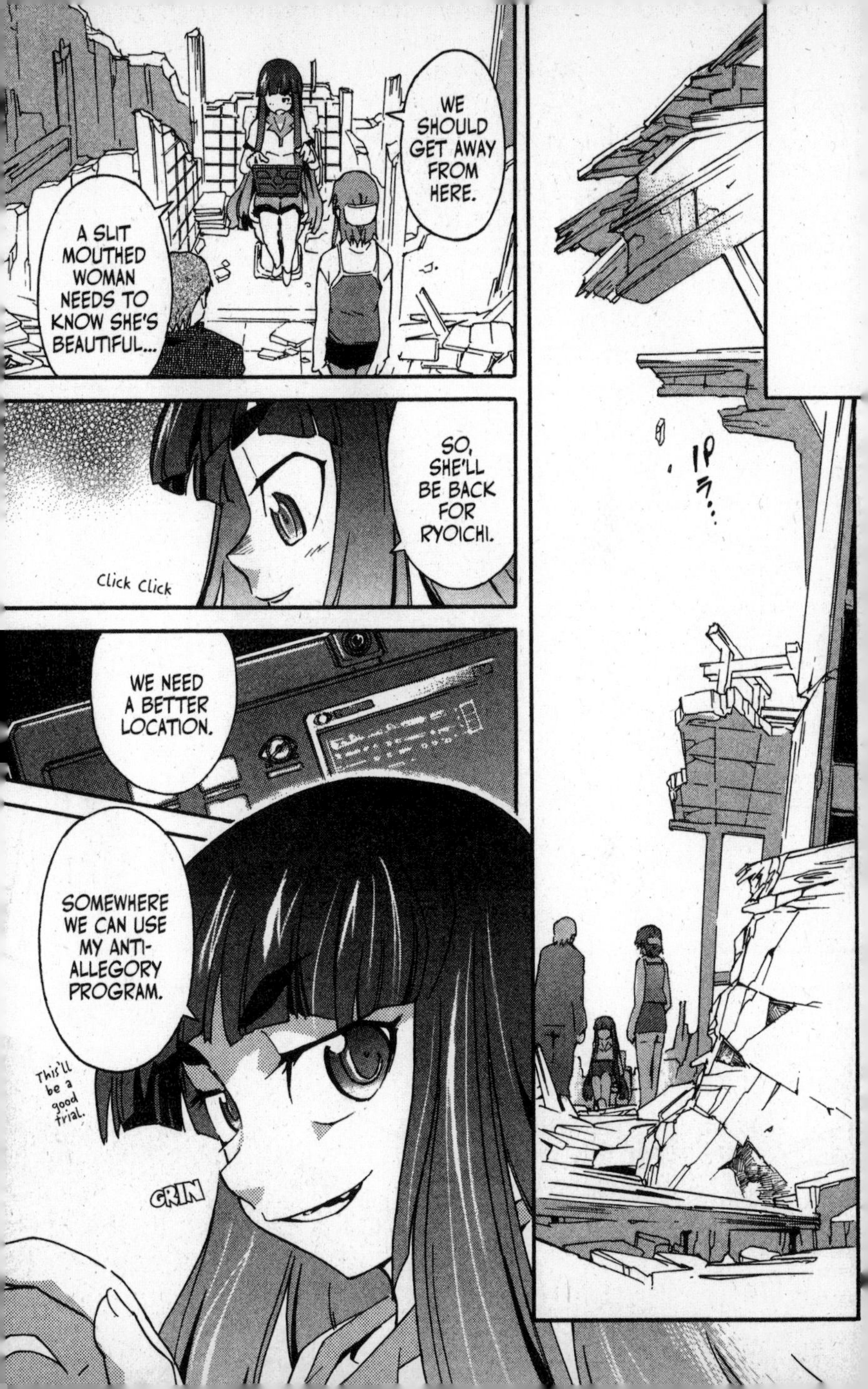
WE SHOULD GET AWAY FROM HERE.
A SLIT MOUTHED WOMAN NEEDS TO KNOW SHE'S BEAUTIFUL...
SO, SHE'LL BE BACK FOR RYOICHI.
Click Click
WE NEED A BETTER LOCATION.
SOMEWHERE WE CAN USE MY ANTI-ALLEGORY PROGRAM.
This'll be a good trial.
GRIN

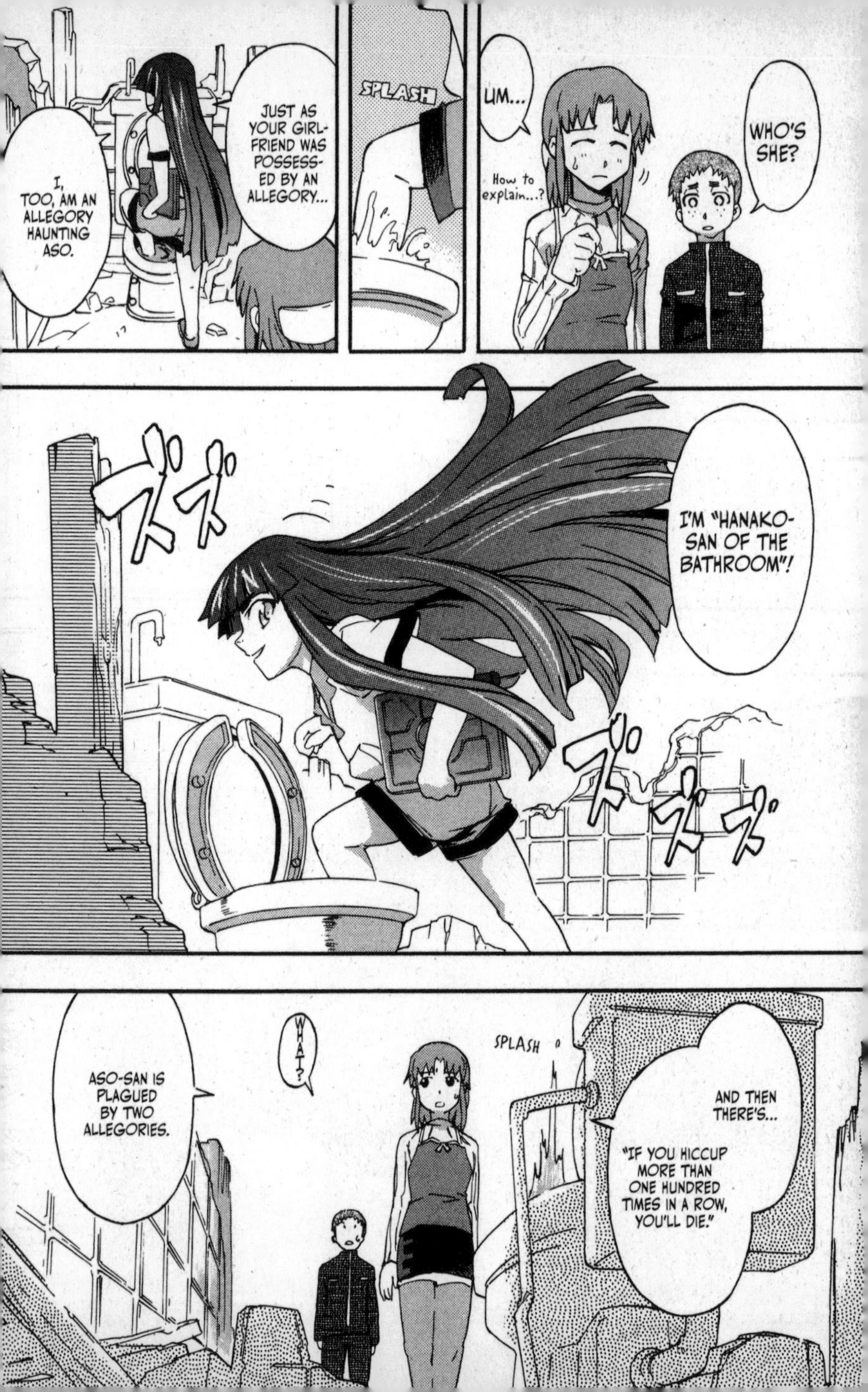
WHO'S SHE?
UM...
How to explain...?
SPLASH
JUST AS YOUR GIRLFRIEND WAS POSSESSED BY AN ALLEGORY...
I, TOO, AM AN ALLEGORY HAUNTING ASO.
I'M "HANAKO-SAN OF THE BATHROOM"!
ズズズズ
ズズ
AND THEN THERE'S...
"IF YOU HICCUP MORE THAN ONE HUNDRED TIMES IN A ROW, YOU'LL DIE."
SPLASH
WHAT?
ASO-SAN IS PLAGUED BY TWO ALLEGORIES.

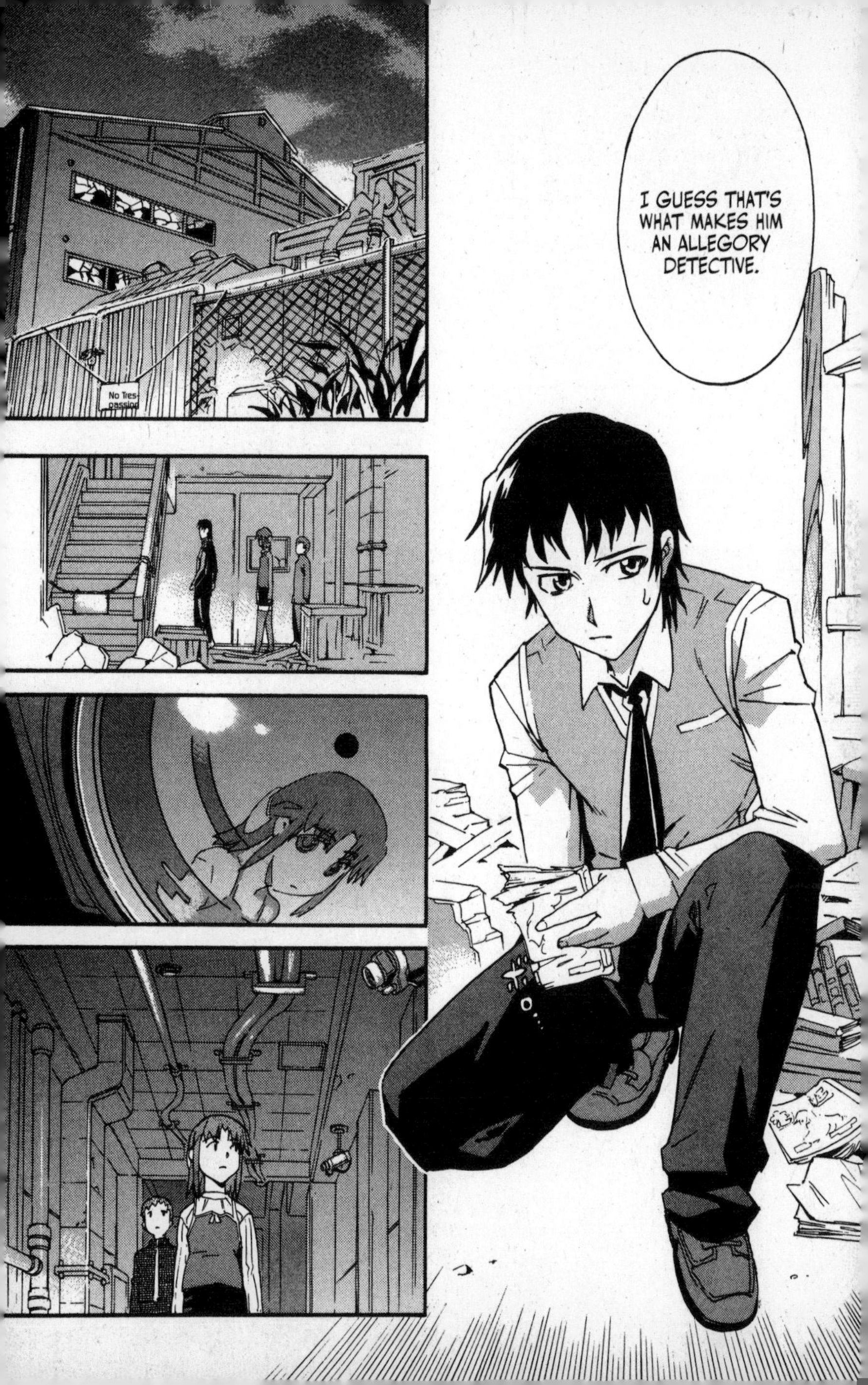
I GUESS THAT'S WHAT MAKES HIM AN ALLEGORY DETECTIVE.
No Tres-passing

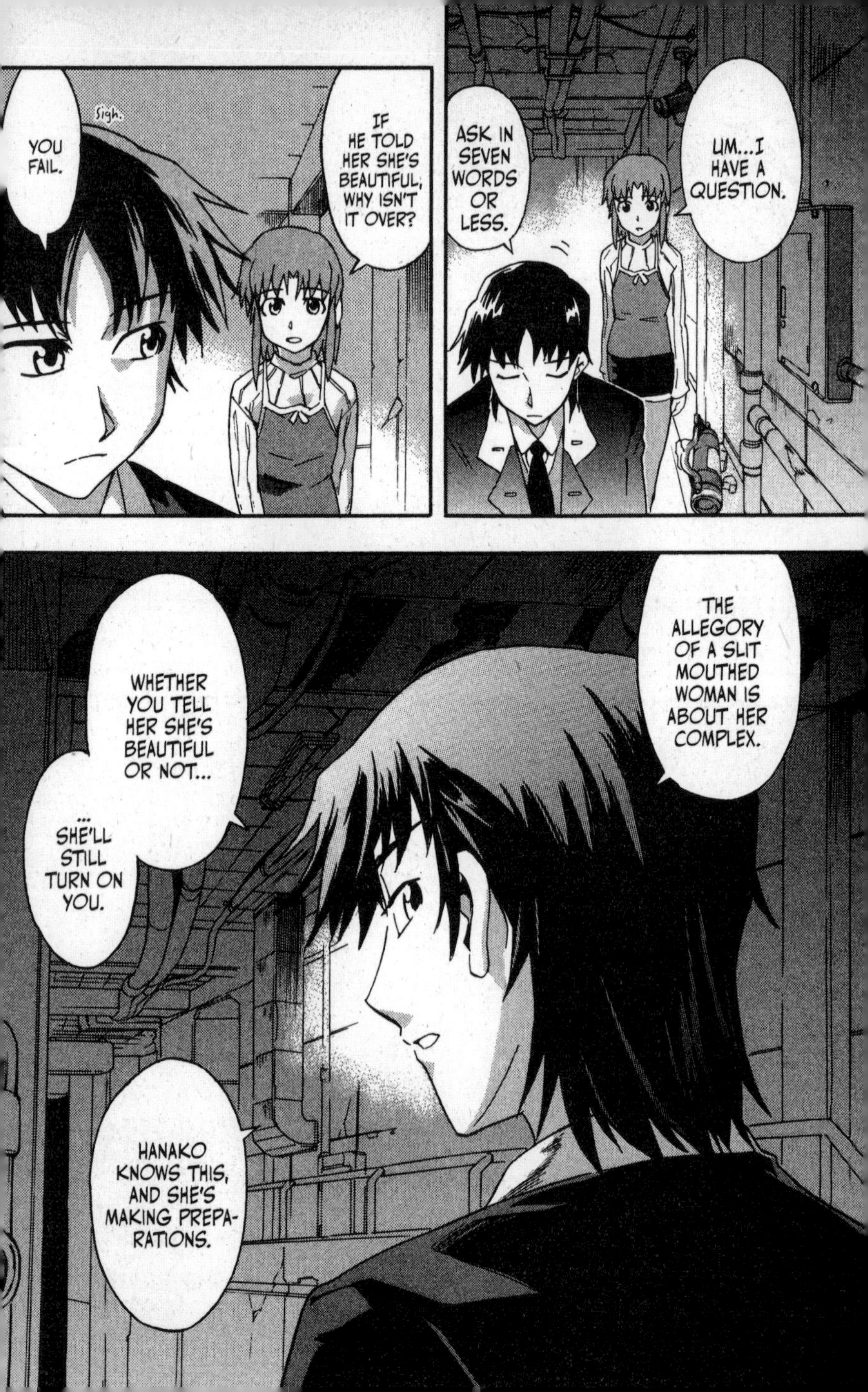
UM...I HAVE A QUESTION.
ASK IN SEVEN WORDS OR LESS.
IF HE TOLD HER SHE'S BEAUTIFUL, WHY ISN'T IT OVER?
Sigh.
YOU FAIL.
THE ALLEGORY OF A SLIT MOUTHED WOMAN IS ABOUT HER COMPLEX.
WHETHER YOU TELL HER SHE'S BEAUTIFUL OR NOT...
...SHE'LL STILL TURN ON YOU.
HANAKO KNOWS THIS, AND SHE'S MAKING PREPARATIONS.

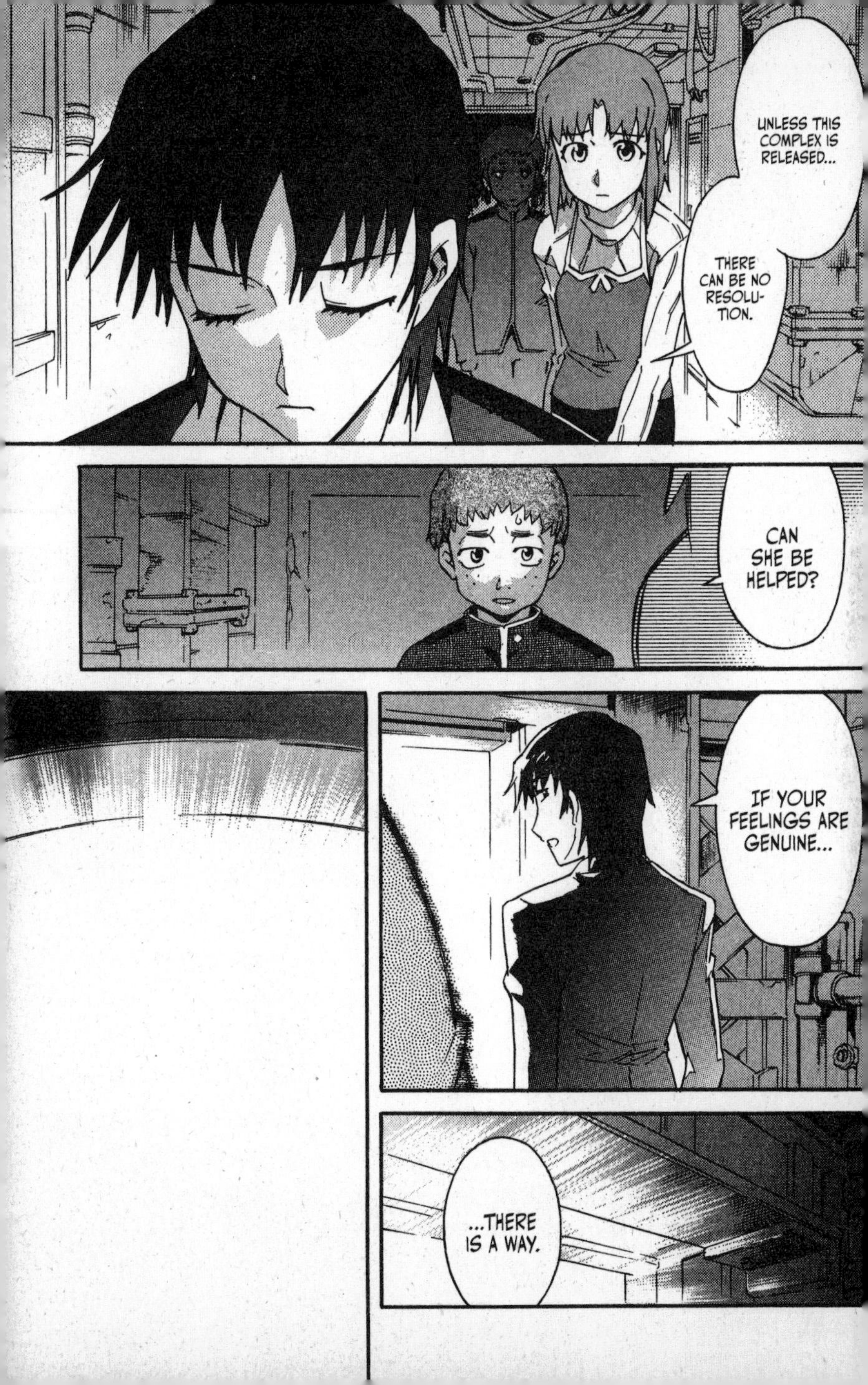
UNLESS THIS COMPLEX IS RELEASED...
THERE CAN BE NO RESOLU-TION.
CAN SHE BE HELPED?
IF YOUR FEELINGS ARE GENUINE...
...THERE IS A WAY.

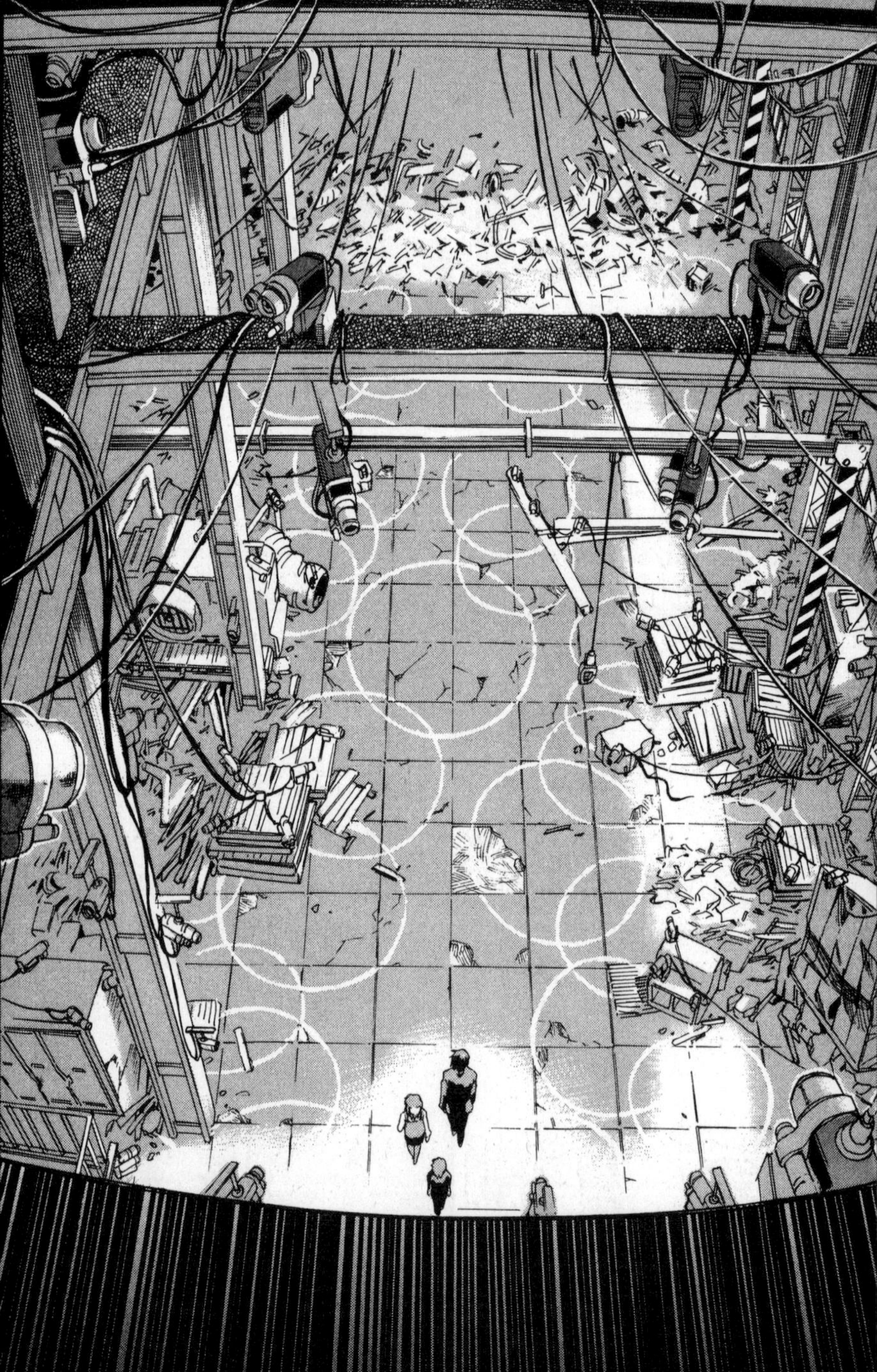

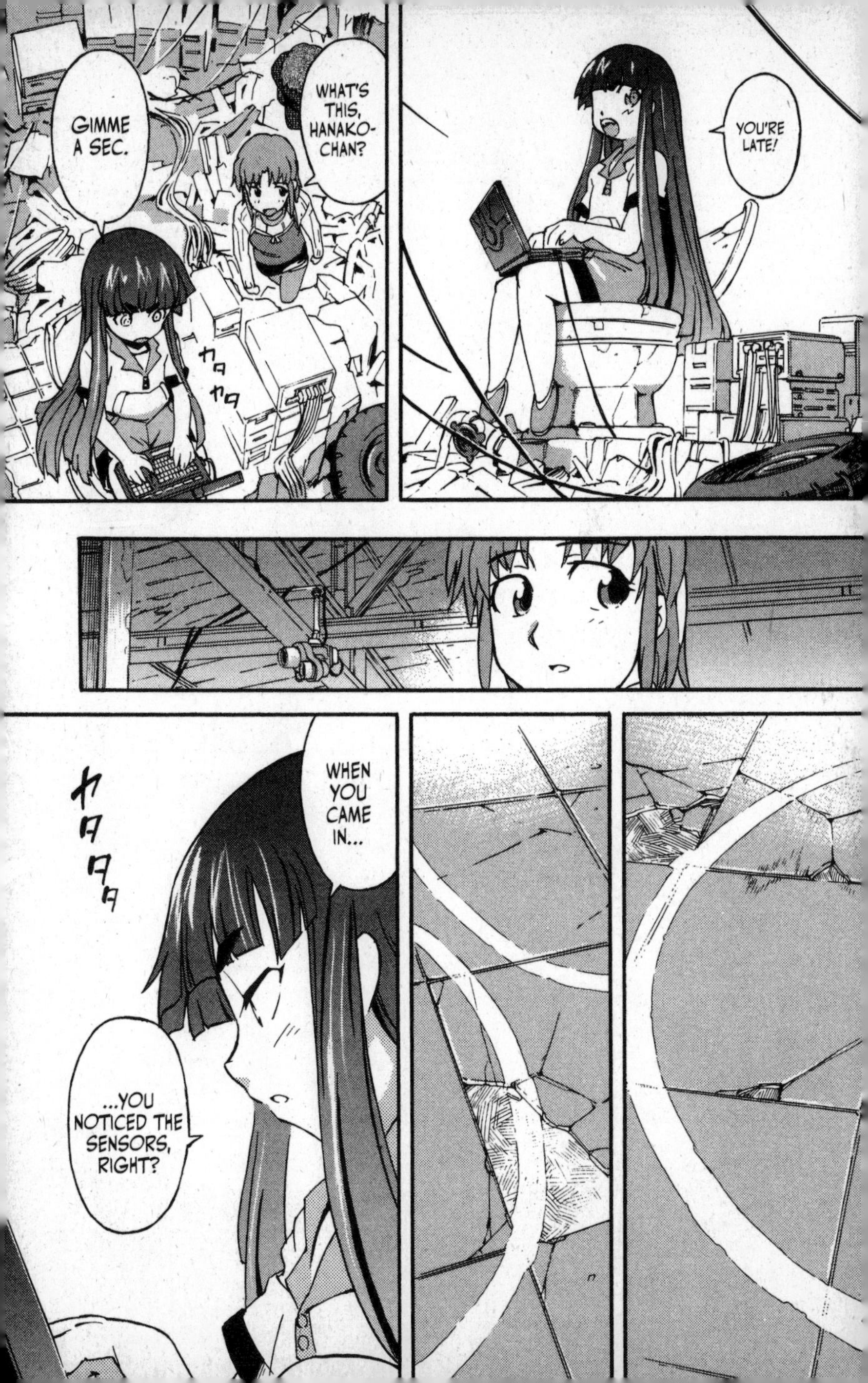
YOU'RE LATE!
WHAT'S THIS, HANAKO-CHAN?
GIMME A SEC.
カタカタ
WHEN YOU CAME IN...
カタタタ
...YOU NOTICED THE SENSORS, RIGHT?

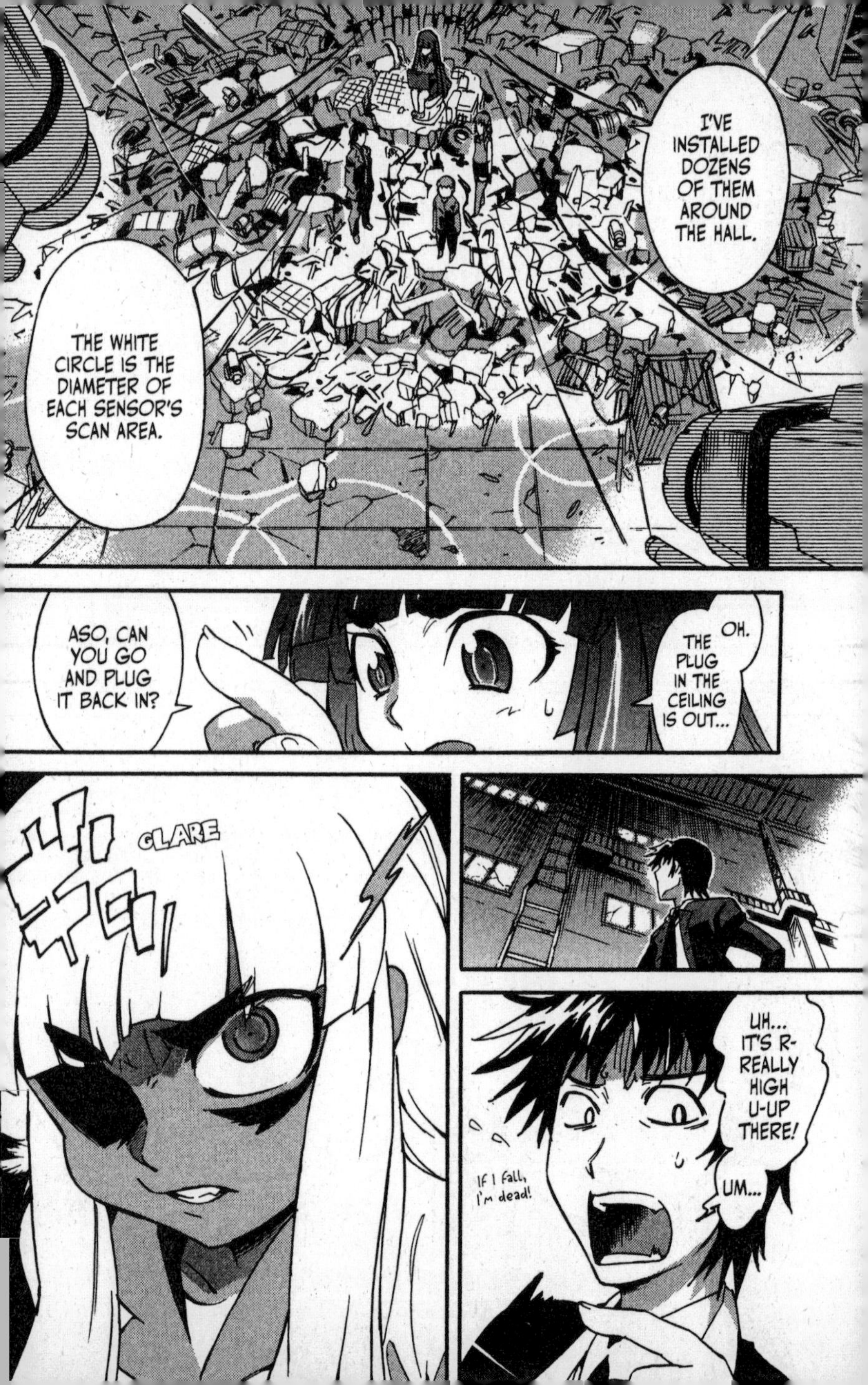
I'VE INSTALLED DOZENS OF THEM AROUND THE HALL.
THE WHITE CIRCLE IS THE DIAMETER OF EACH SENSOR'S SCAN AREA.
OH. THE PLUG IN THE CEILING IS OUT...
ASO, CAN YOU GO AND PLUG IT BACK IN?
UH... IT'S R-REALLY HIGH U-UP THERE!
UM...
If I fall, I'm dead!
GLARE

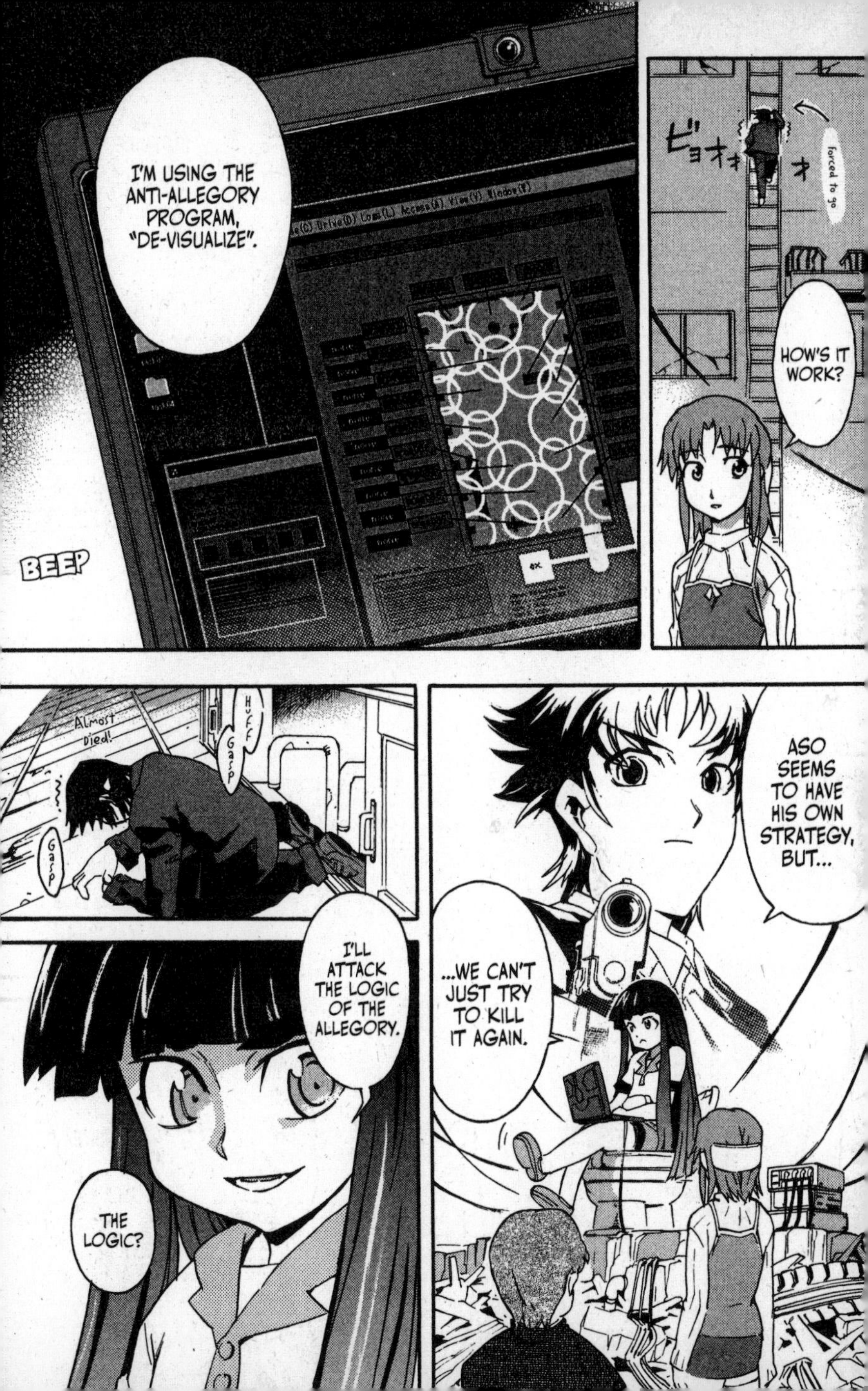
forced to go
ビョオオオ
HOW'S IT WORK?
I'M USING THE ANTI-ALLEGORY PROGRAM, "DE-VISUALIZE".
BEEP
ASO SEEMS TO HAVE HIS OWN STRATEGY, BUT...
...WE CAN'T JUST TRY TO KILL IT AGAIN.
Almost Died!
HUFF
Gasp
Gasp
I'LL ATTACK THE LOGIC OF THE ALLEGORY.
THE LOGIC?

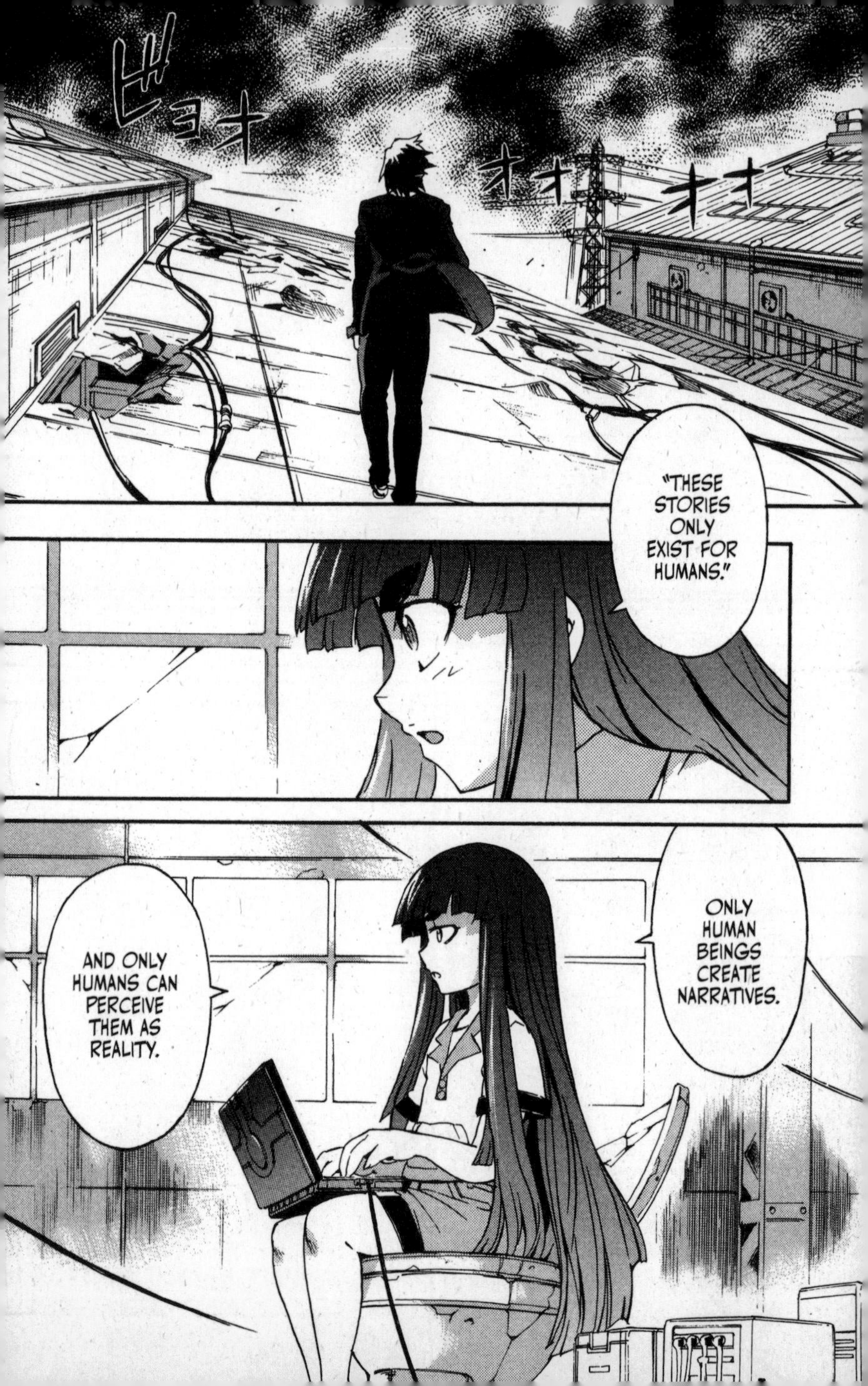
ビュオオオオ
"THESE STORIES ONLY EXIST FOR HUMANS."
ONLY HUMAN BEINGS CREATE NARRATIVES.
AND ONLY HUMANS CAN PERCEIVE THEM AS REALITY.

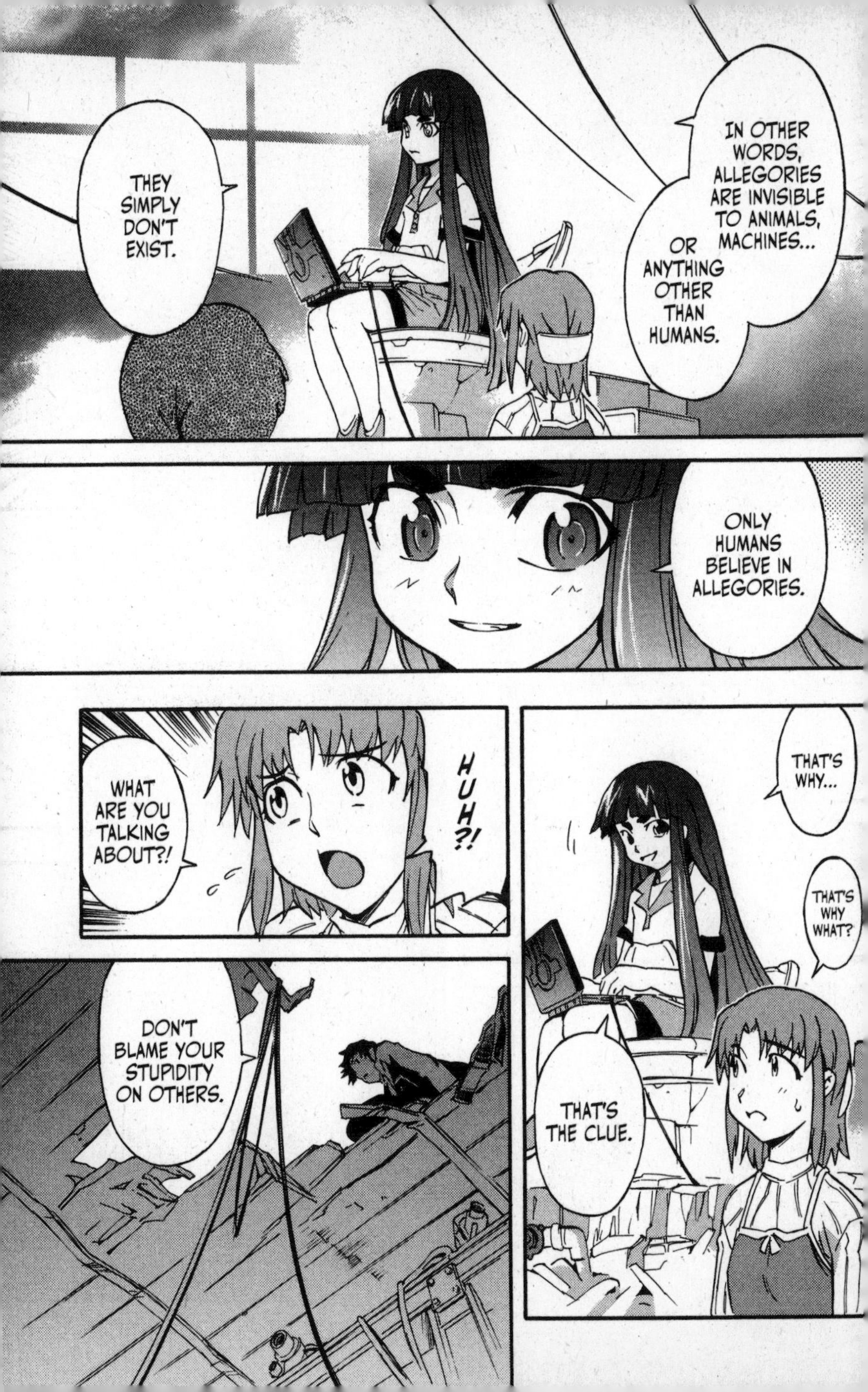
IN OTHER WORDS, ALLEGORIES ARE INVISIBLE TO ANIMALS, MACHINES...
OR ANYTHING OTHER THAN HUMANS.
THEY SIMPLY DON'T EXIST.
ONLY HUMANS BELIEVE IN ALLEGORIES.
THAT'S WHY...
THAT'S WHY WHAT?
THAT'S THE CLUE.
HUH?!
WHAT ARE YOU TALKING ABOUT?!
DON'T BLAME YOUR STUPIDITY ON OTHERS.

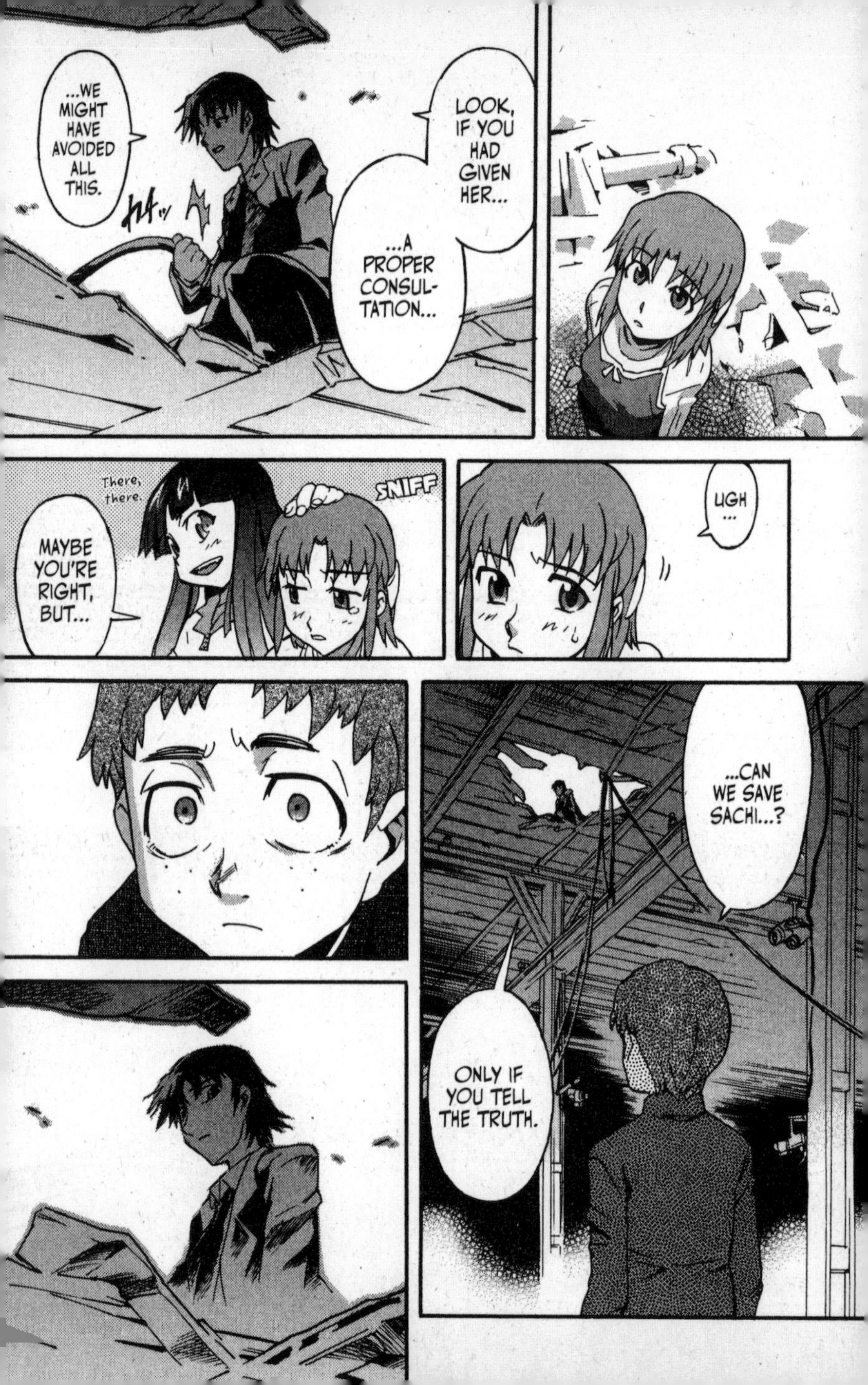
LOOK, IF YOU HAD GIVEN HER...
...A PROPER CONSULTATION...
...WE MIGHT HAVE AVOIDED ALL THIS.
UGH ...
SNIFF
There, there.
MAYBE YOU'RE RIGHT, BUT...
...CAN WE SAVE SACHI...?
ONLY IF YOU TELL THE TRUTH.

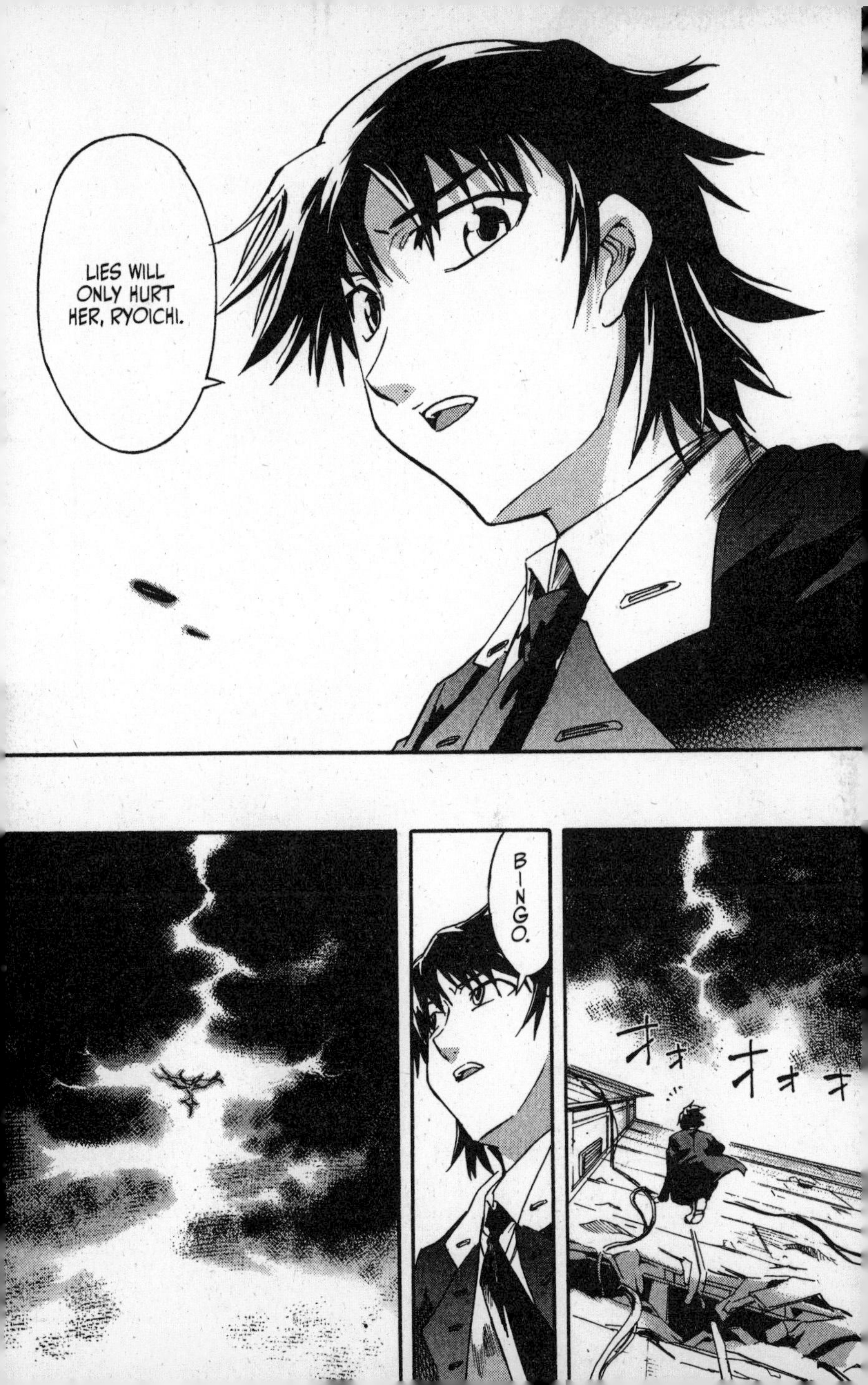
LIES WILL ONLY HURT HER, RYOICHI.
オォ オォォ
BINGO.

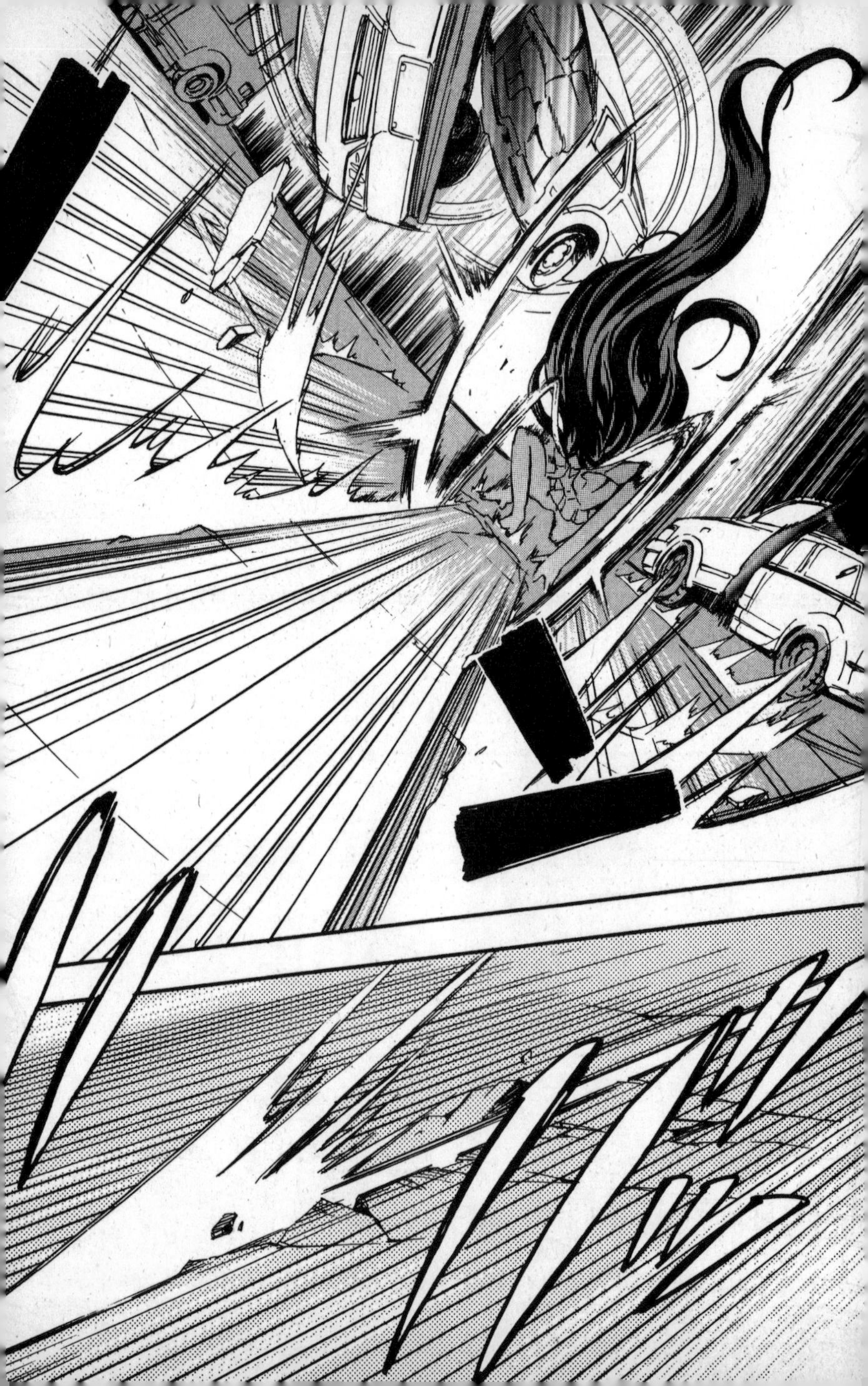

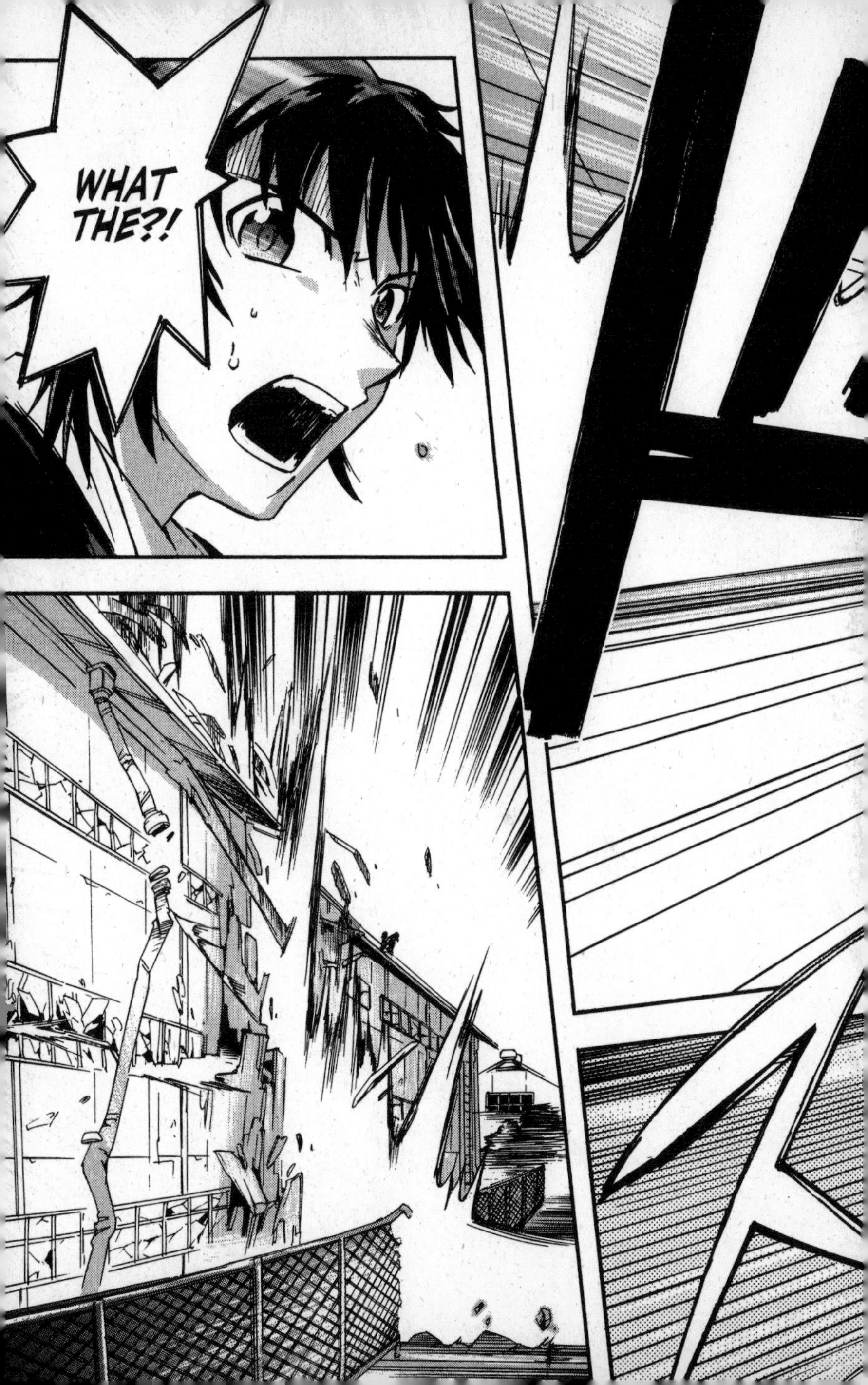
WHAT THE?!

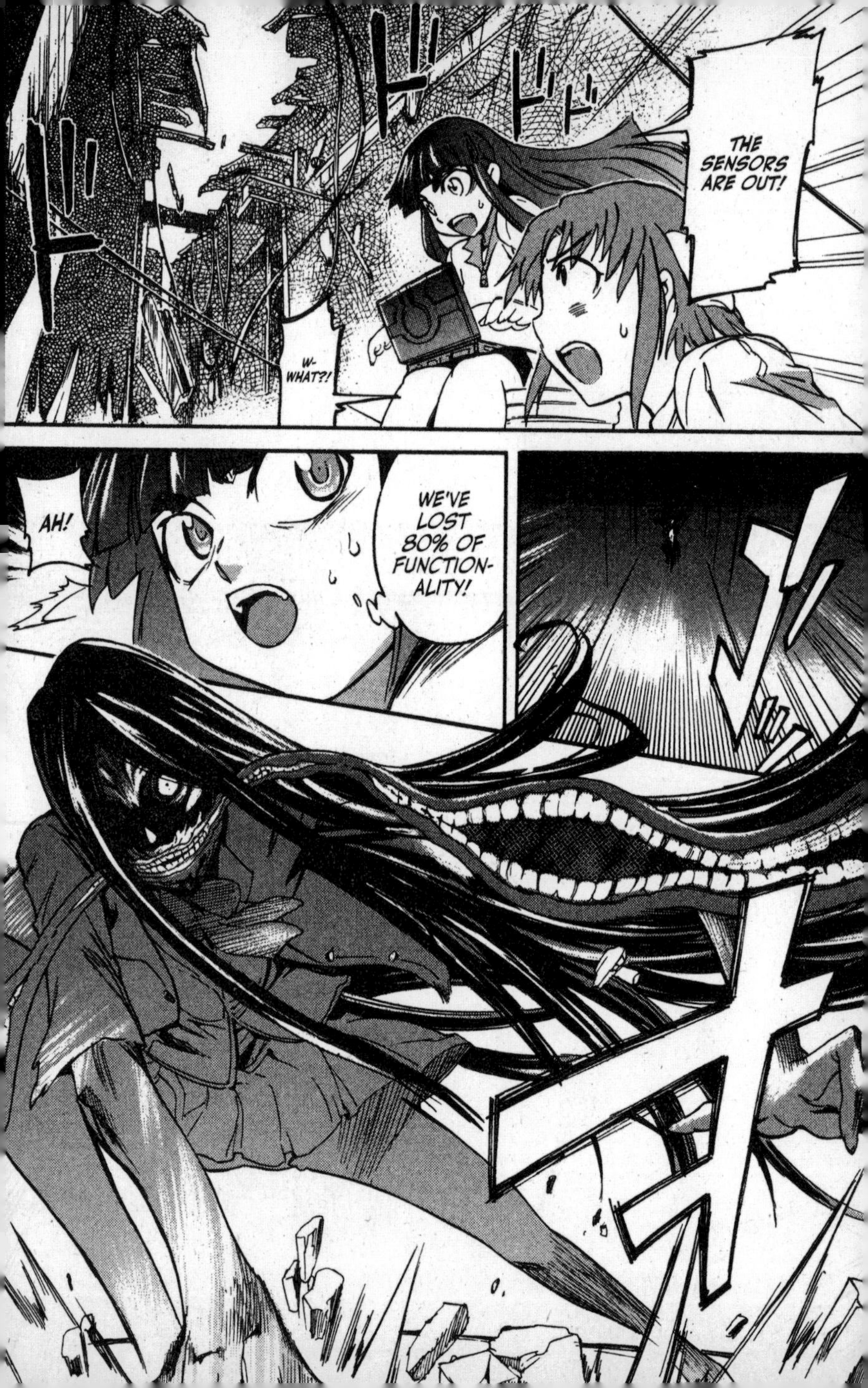
THE SENSORS ARE OUT!
W-WHAT?!
WE'VE LOST 80% OF FUNCTION-ALITY!
AH!

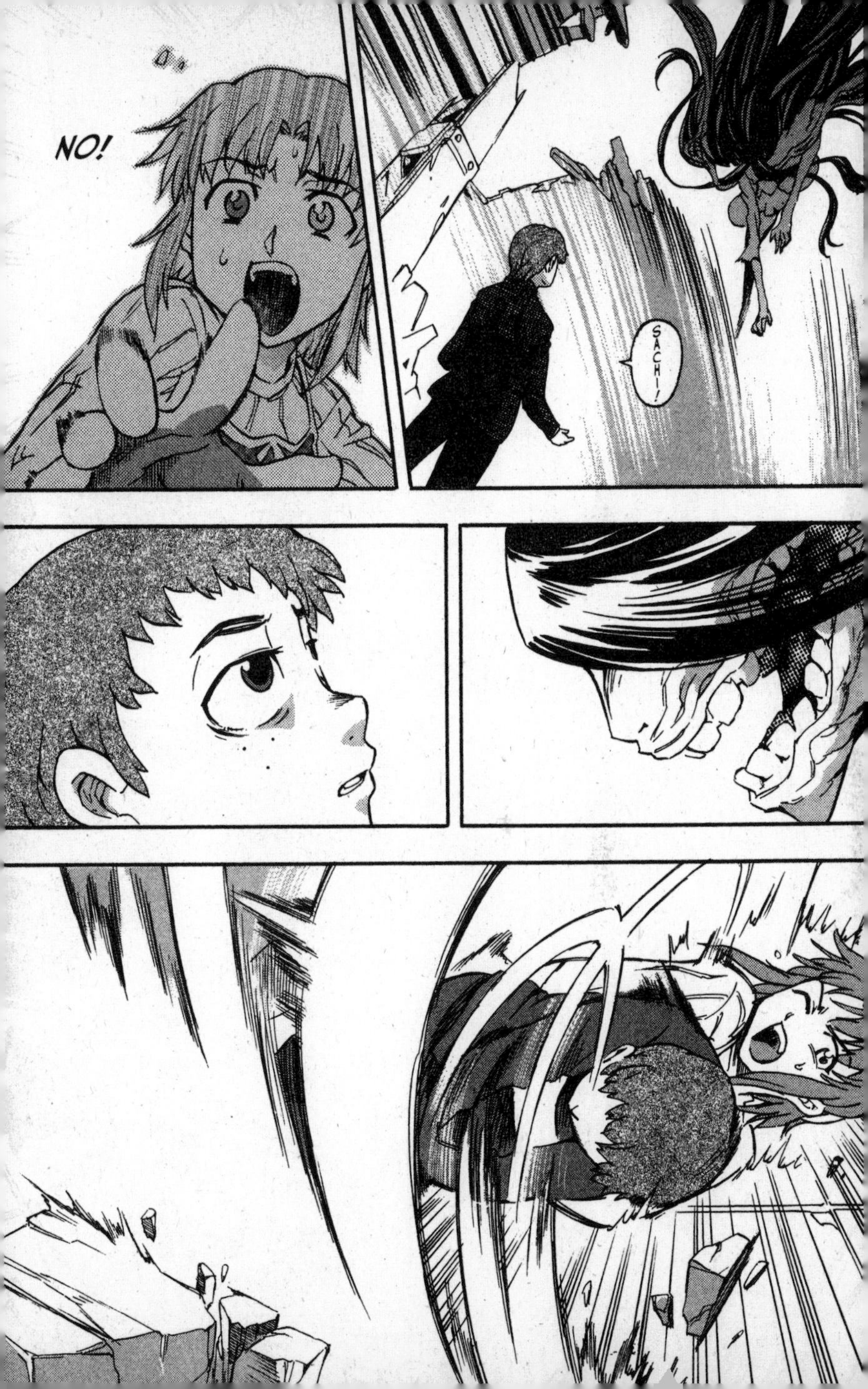
SACHI!
NO!

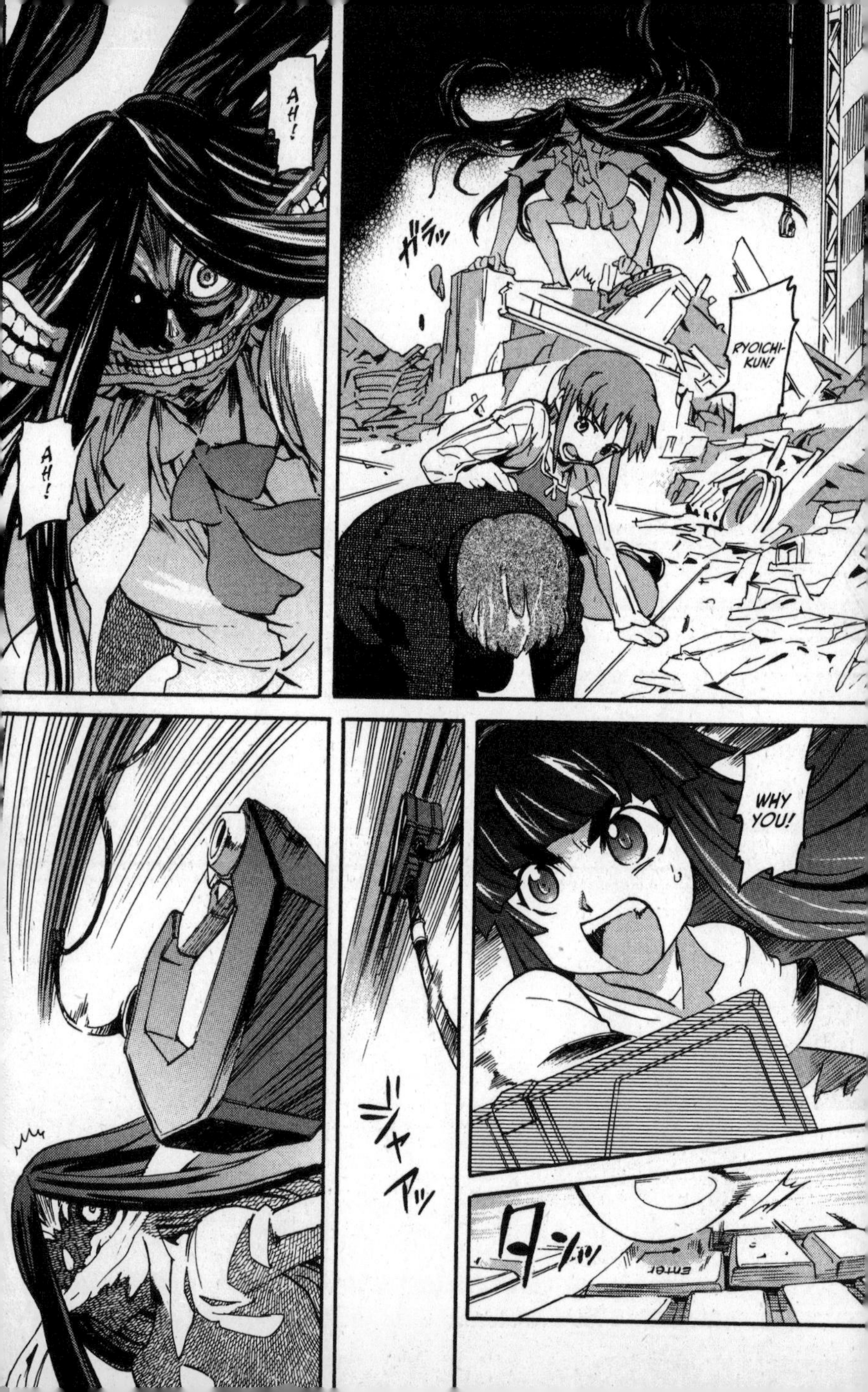
ガラッ
RYOICHI-KUN!
AH!
AH!
WHY YOU!
ジャアッ

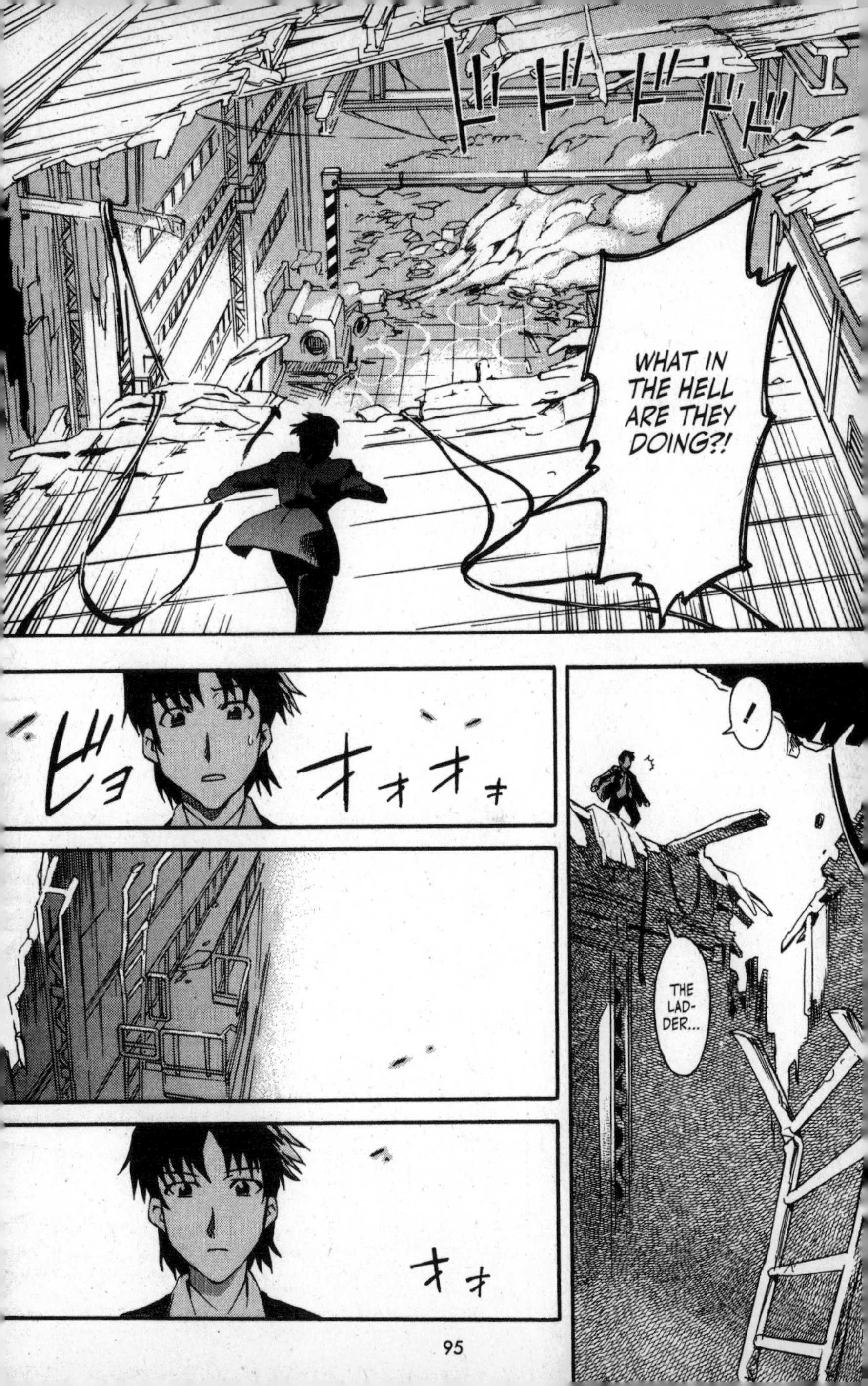
WHAT IN THE HELL ARE THEY DOING?!
!
THE LAD-DER...

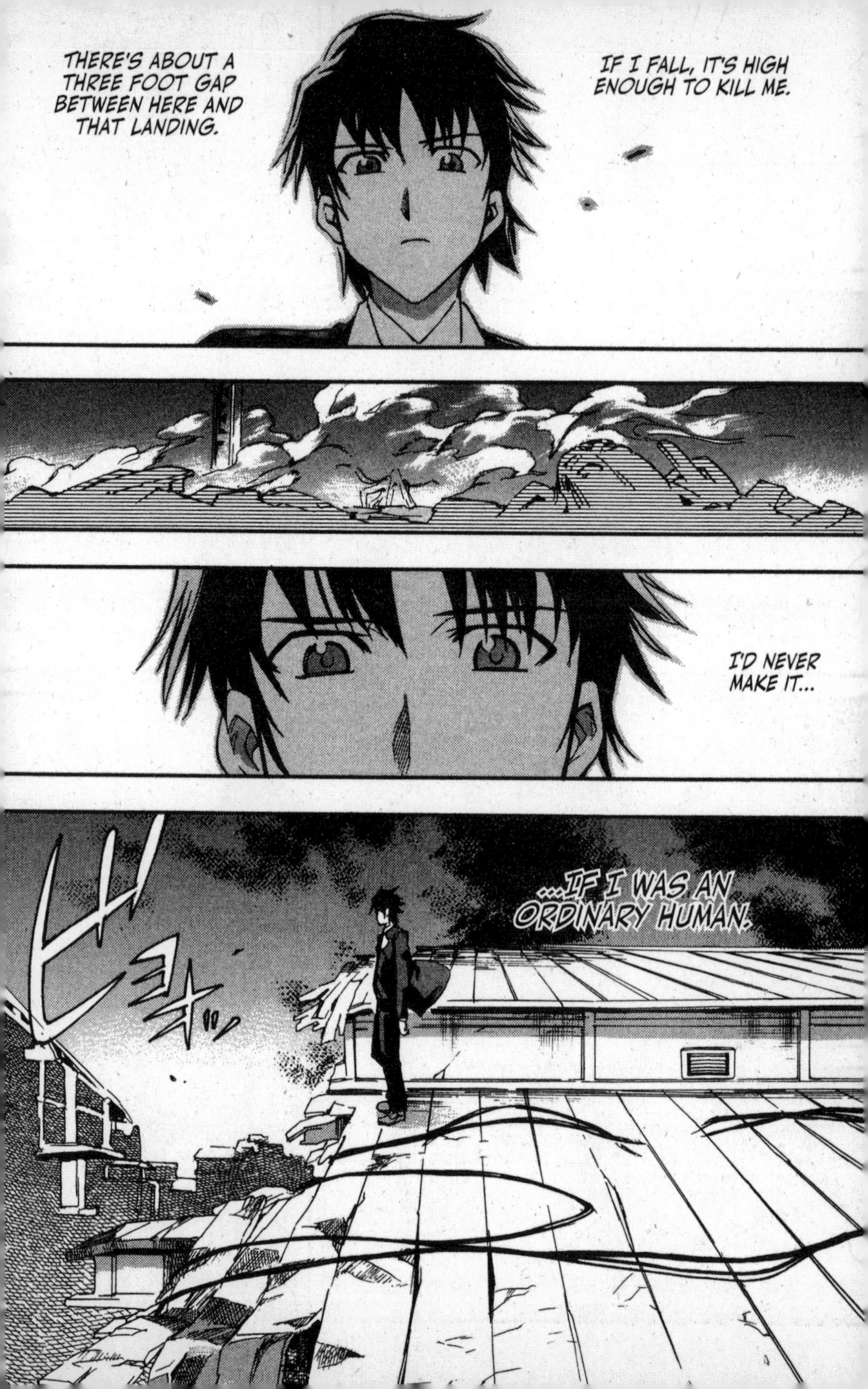
IF I FALL, IT'S HIGH ENOUGH TO KILL ME.
THERE'S ABOUT A THREE FOOT GAP BETWEEN HERE AND THAT LANDING.
I'D NEVER MAKE IT...
...IF I WAS AN ORDINARY HUMAN.

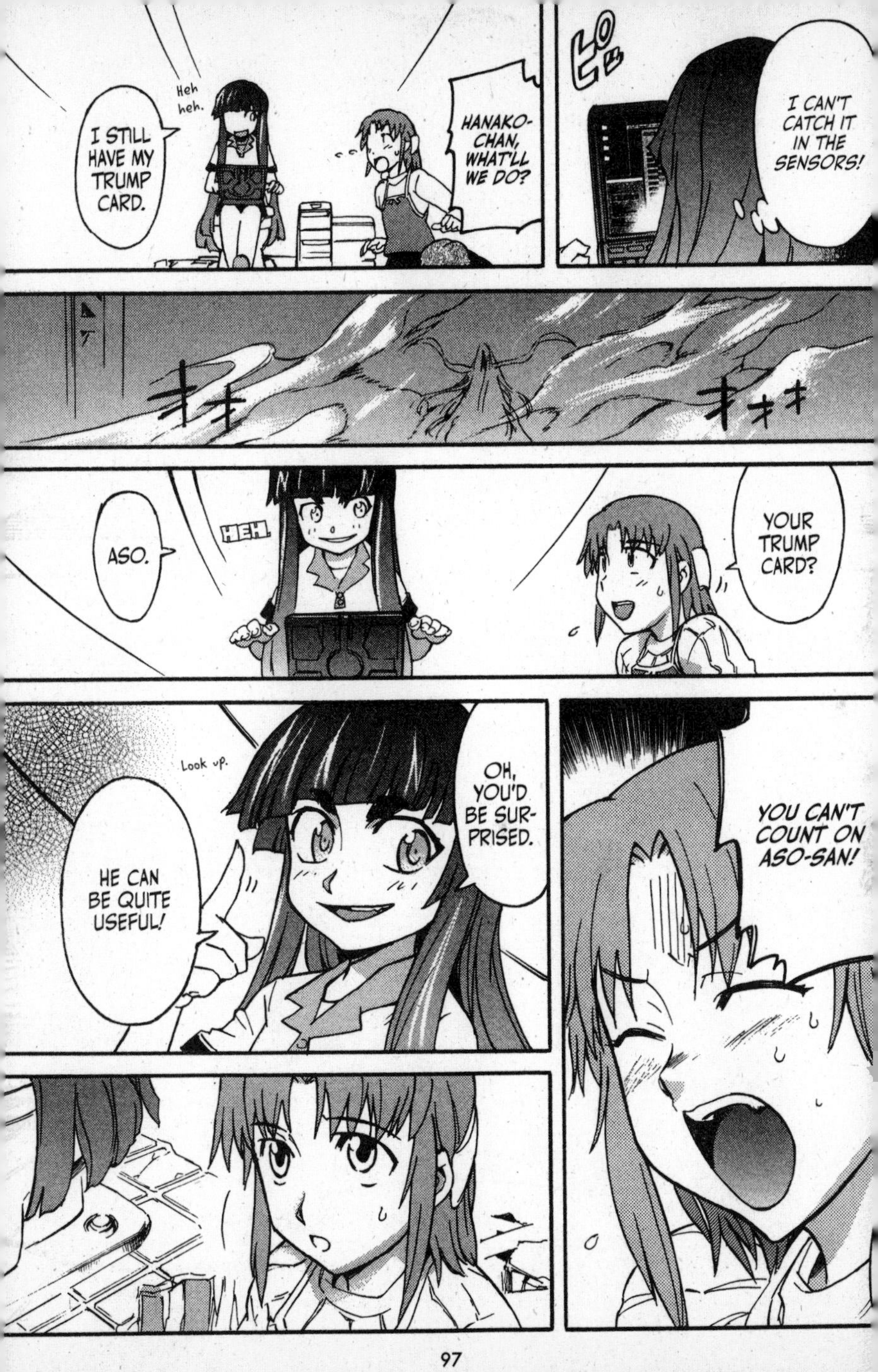
I CAN'T CATCH IT IN THE SENSORS!
HANAKO-CHAN, WHAT'LL WE DO?
Heh heh.
I STILL HAVE MY TRUMP CARD.
YOUR TRUMP CARD?
HEH.
ASO.
YOU CAN'T COUNT ON ASO-SAN!
OH, YOU'D BE SURPRISED.
Look up.
HE CAN BE QUITE USEFUL!

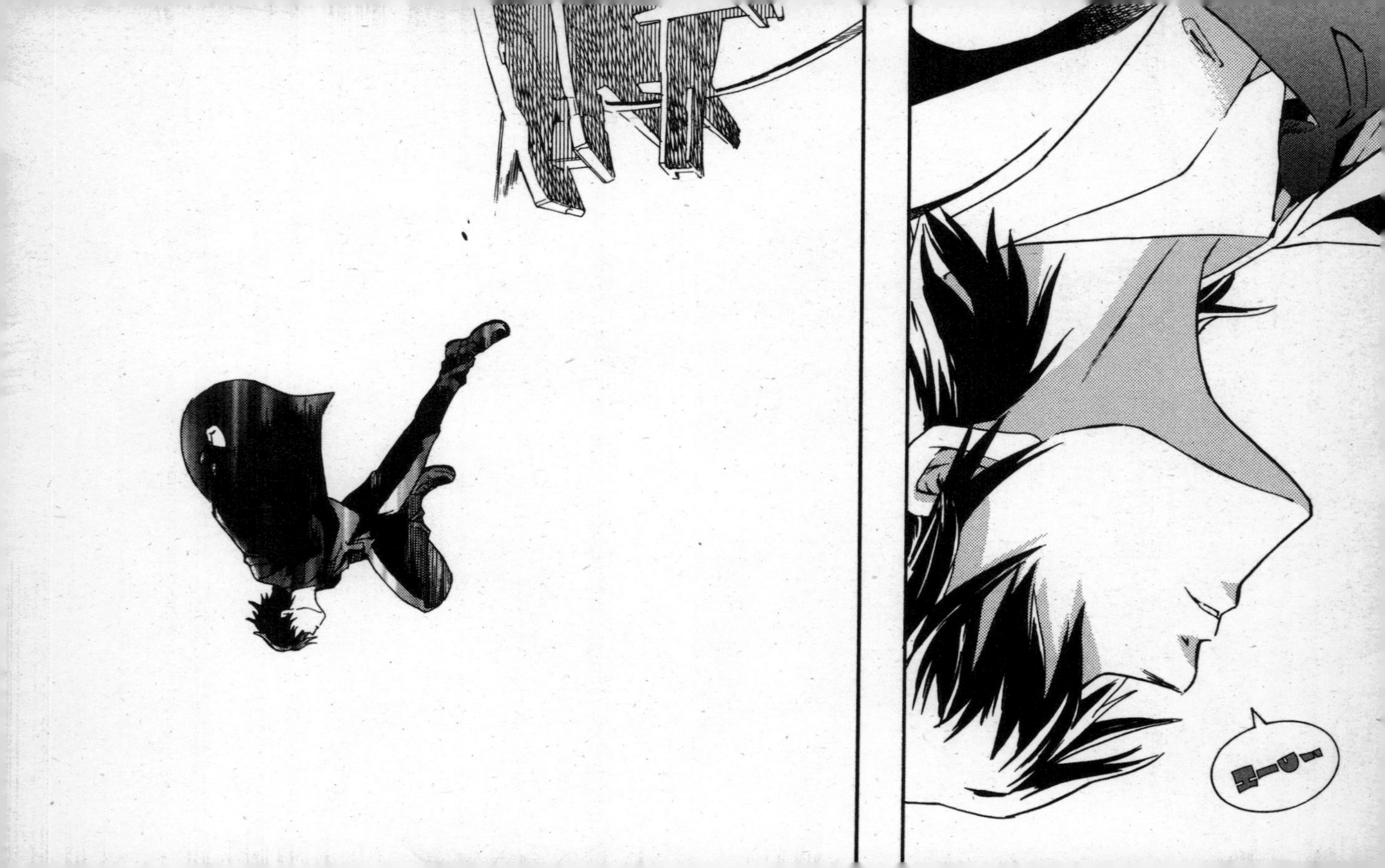
HIC!

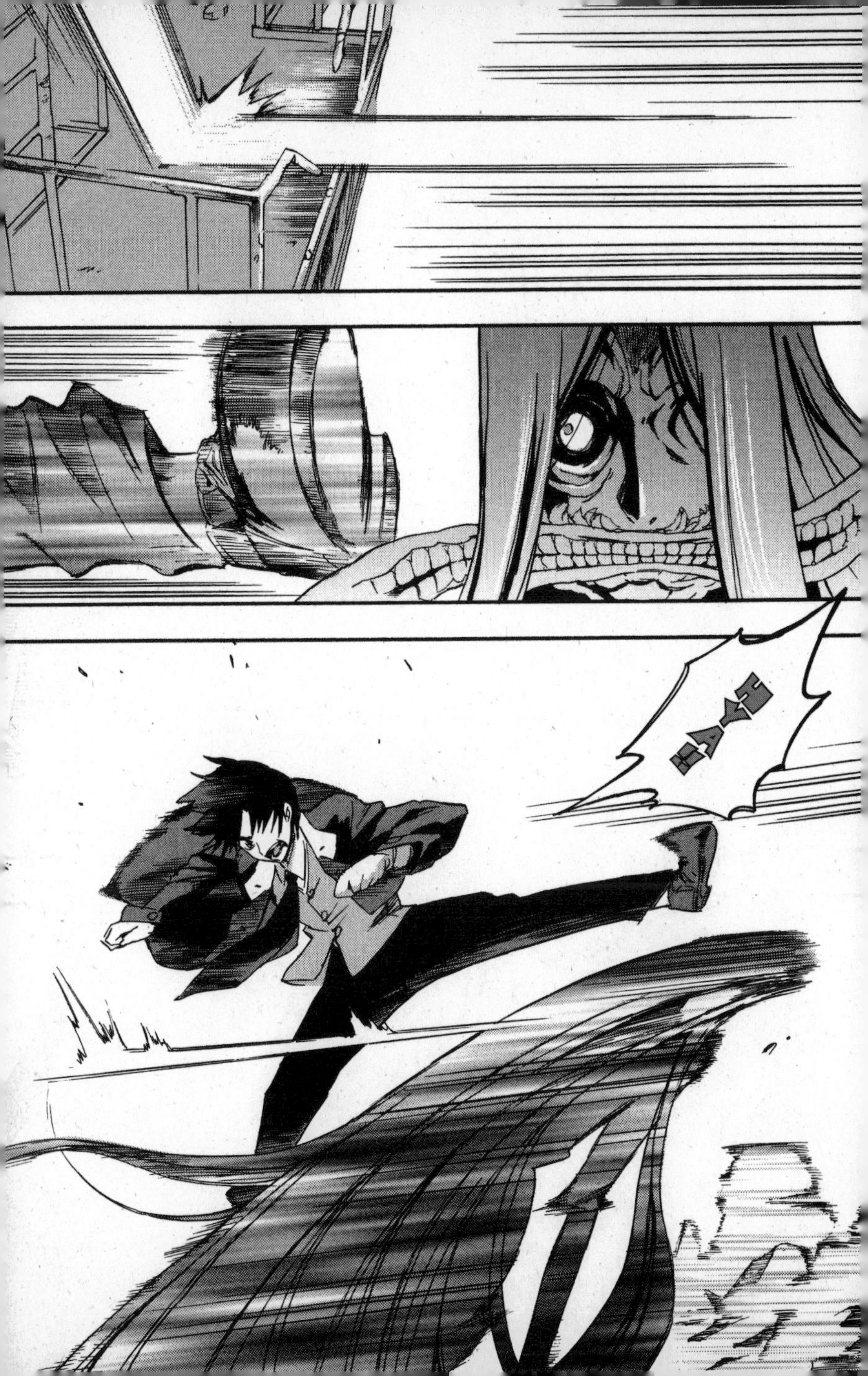

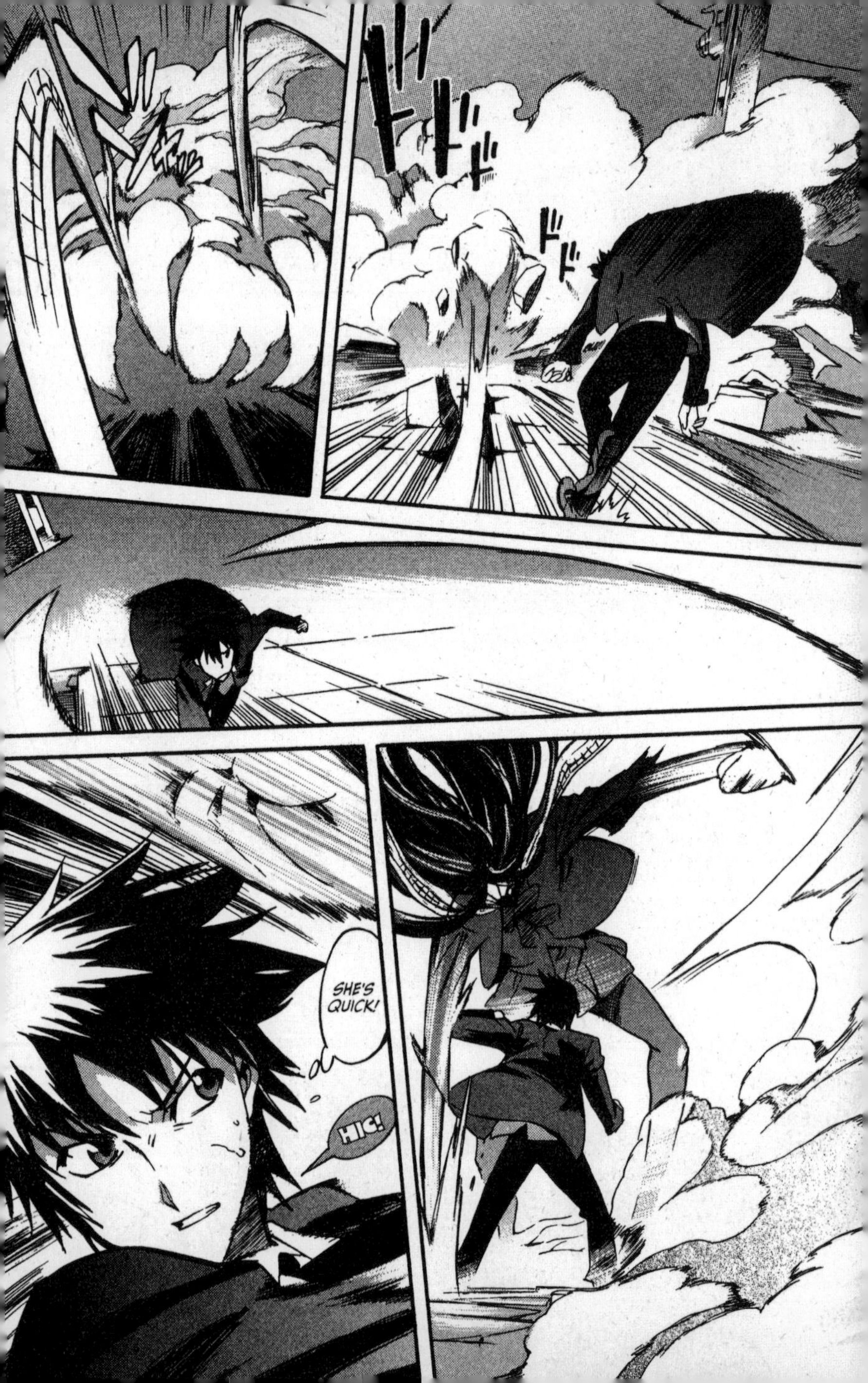
SHE'S QUICK!
HIC!

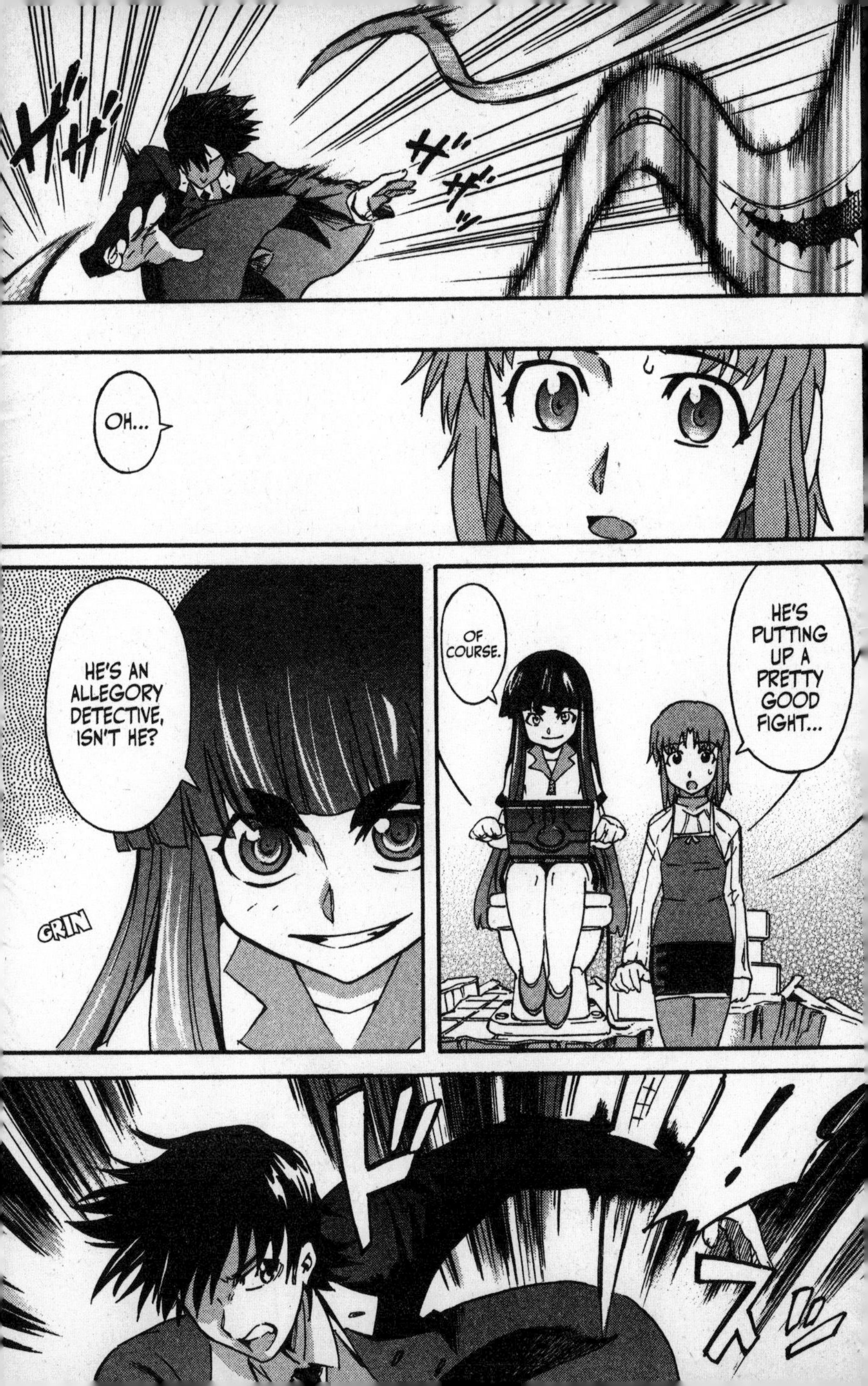
OH...
HE'S PUTTING UP A PRETTY GOOD FIGHT...
OF COURSE.
HE'S AN ALLEGORY DETECTIVE, ISN'T HE?
GRIN

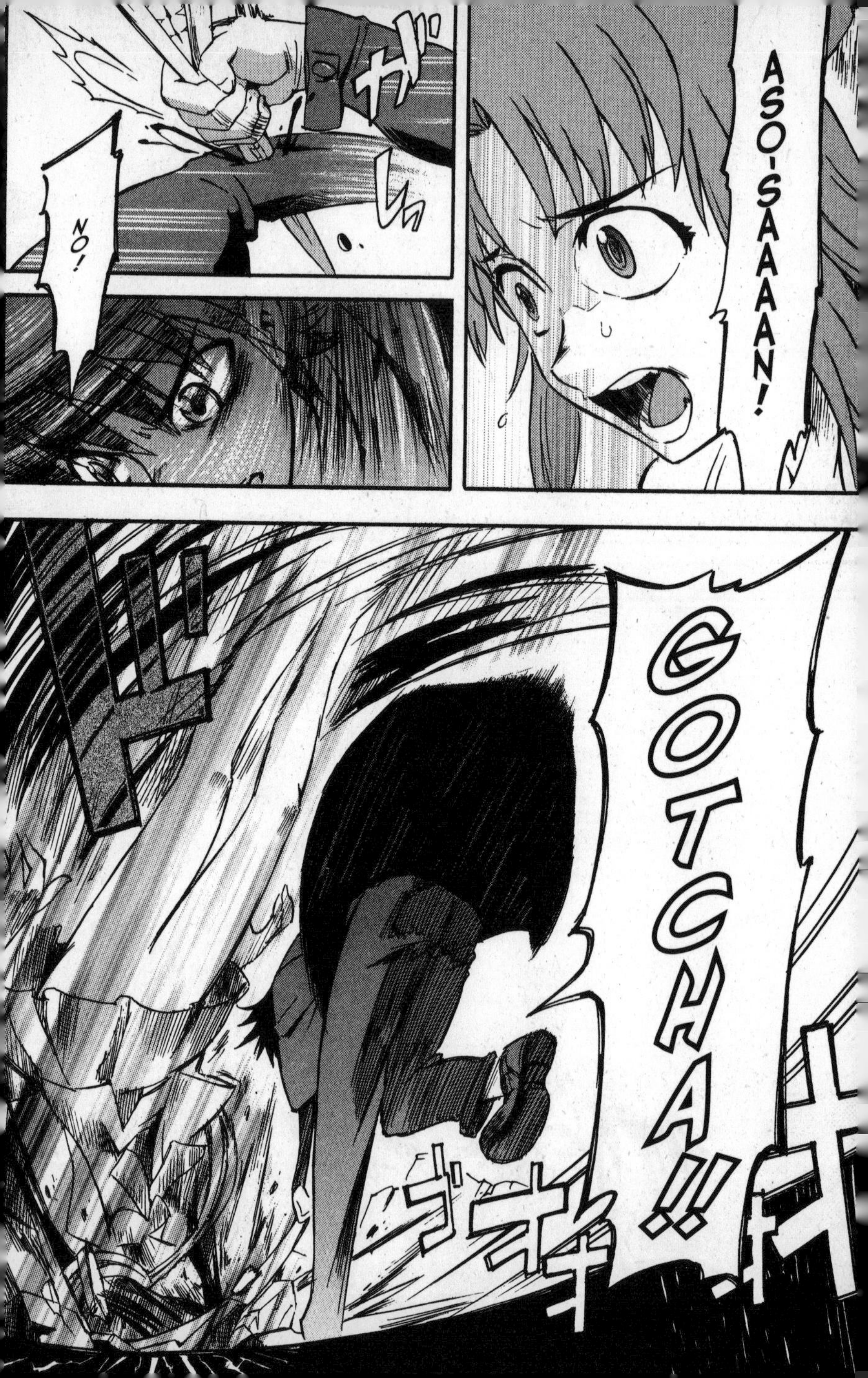
ASO-SAAAN!
NO!
GOTCHA!!

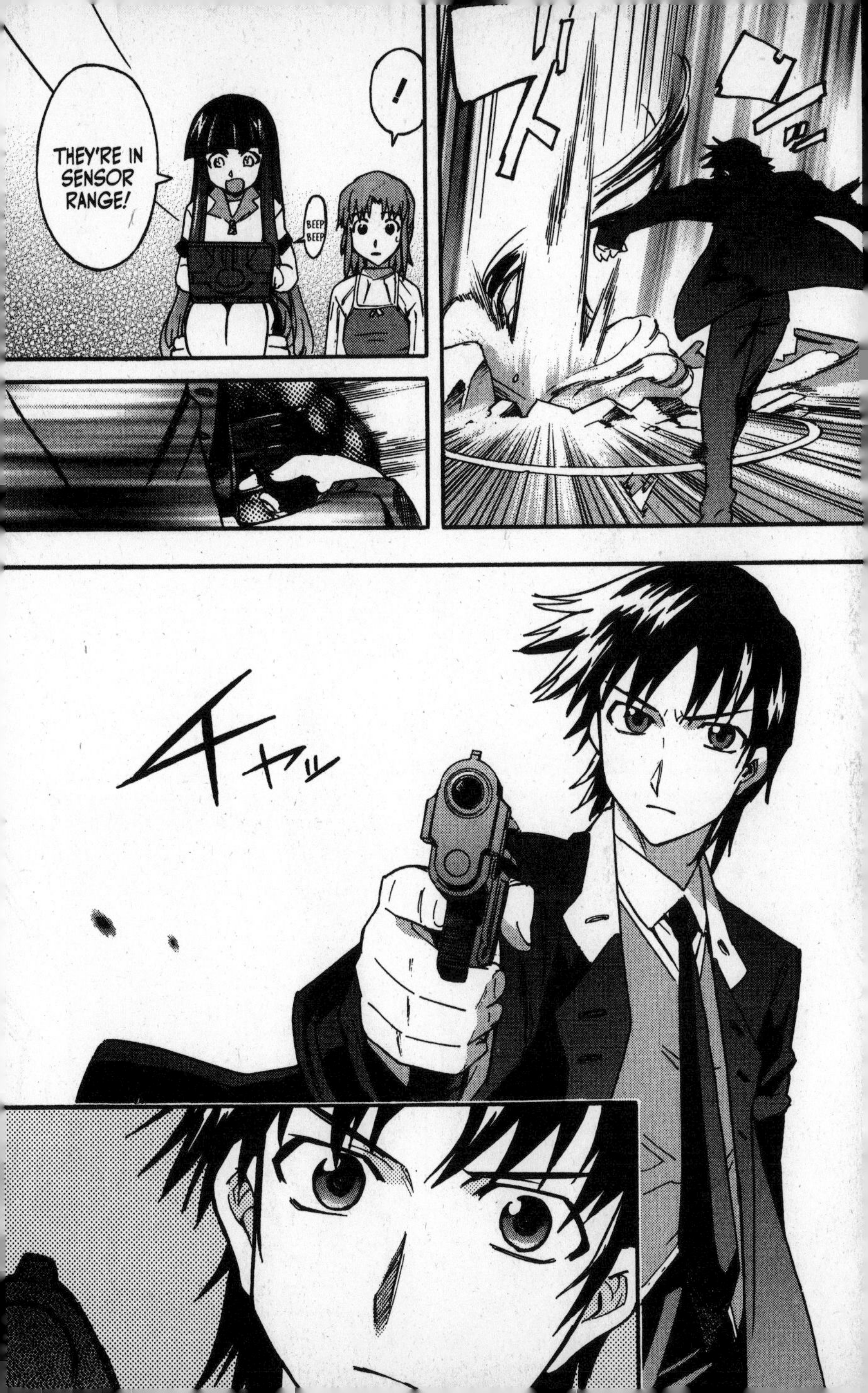

!
THEY'RE IN SENSOR RANGE!
BEEP BEEP

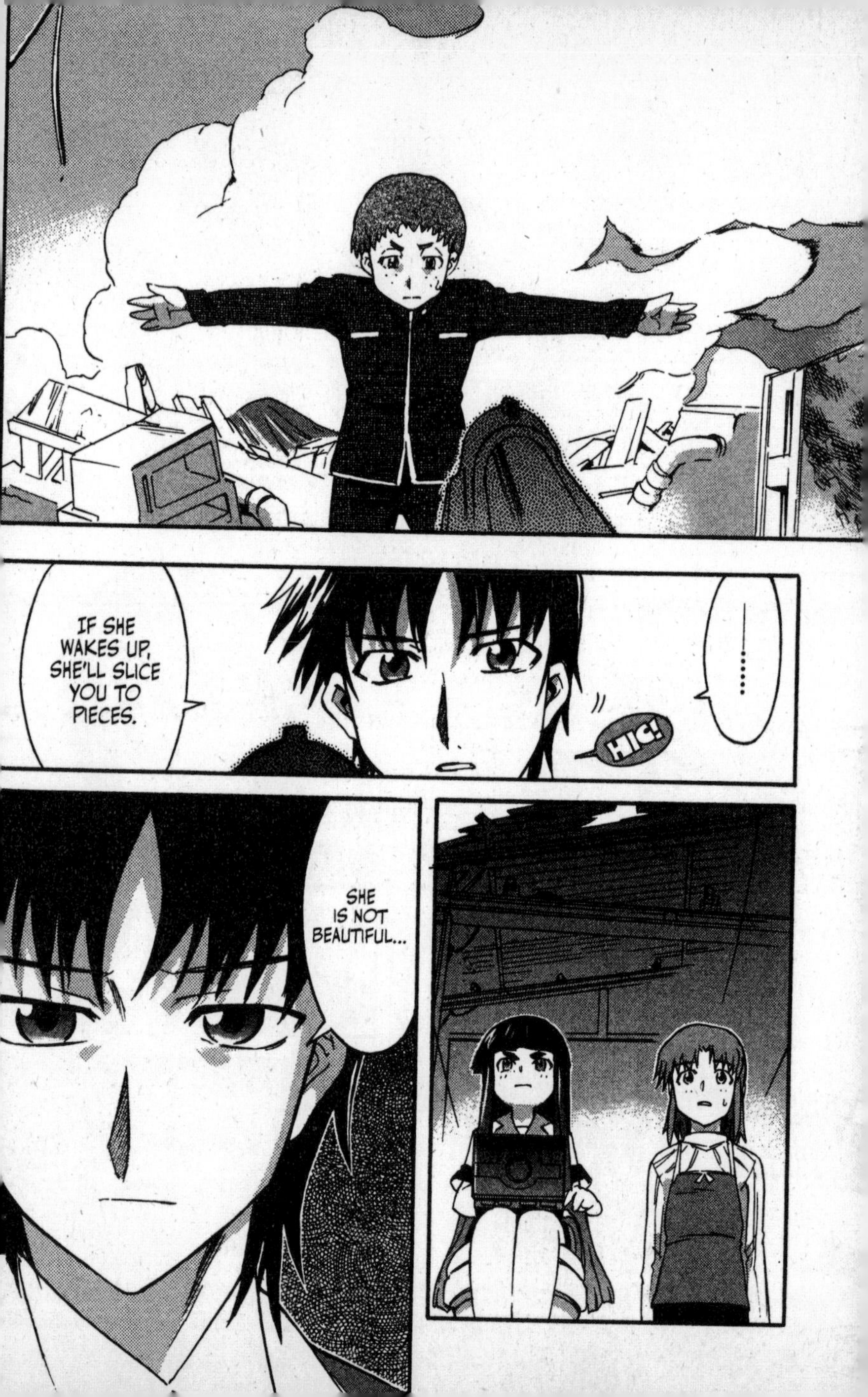
......
HIC!
IF SHE WAKES UP, SHE'LL SLICE YOU TO PIECES.
SHE IS NOT BEAUTIFUL...

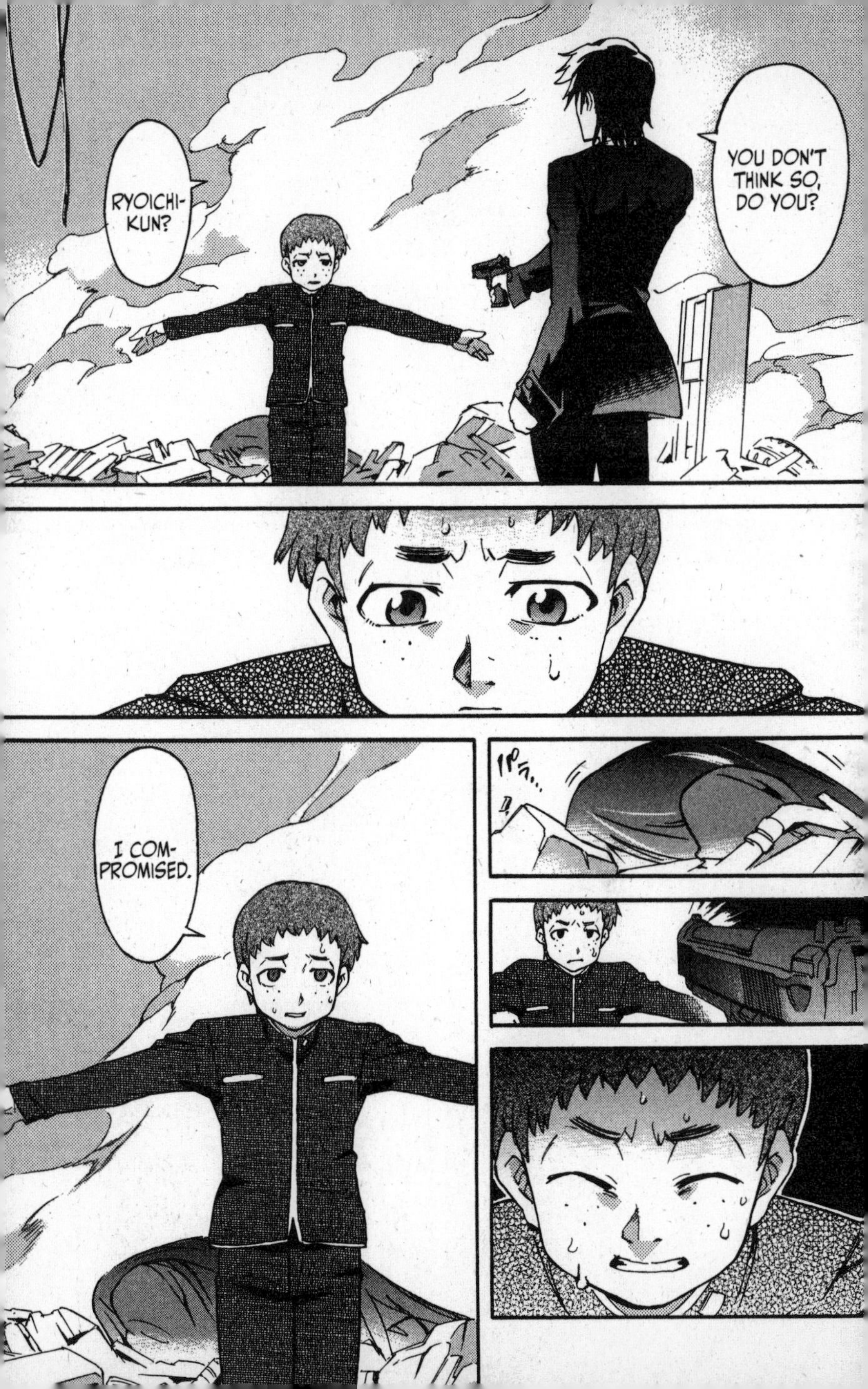
YOU DON'T THINK SO, DO YOU?
RYOICHI-KUN?
I COM-PROMISED.

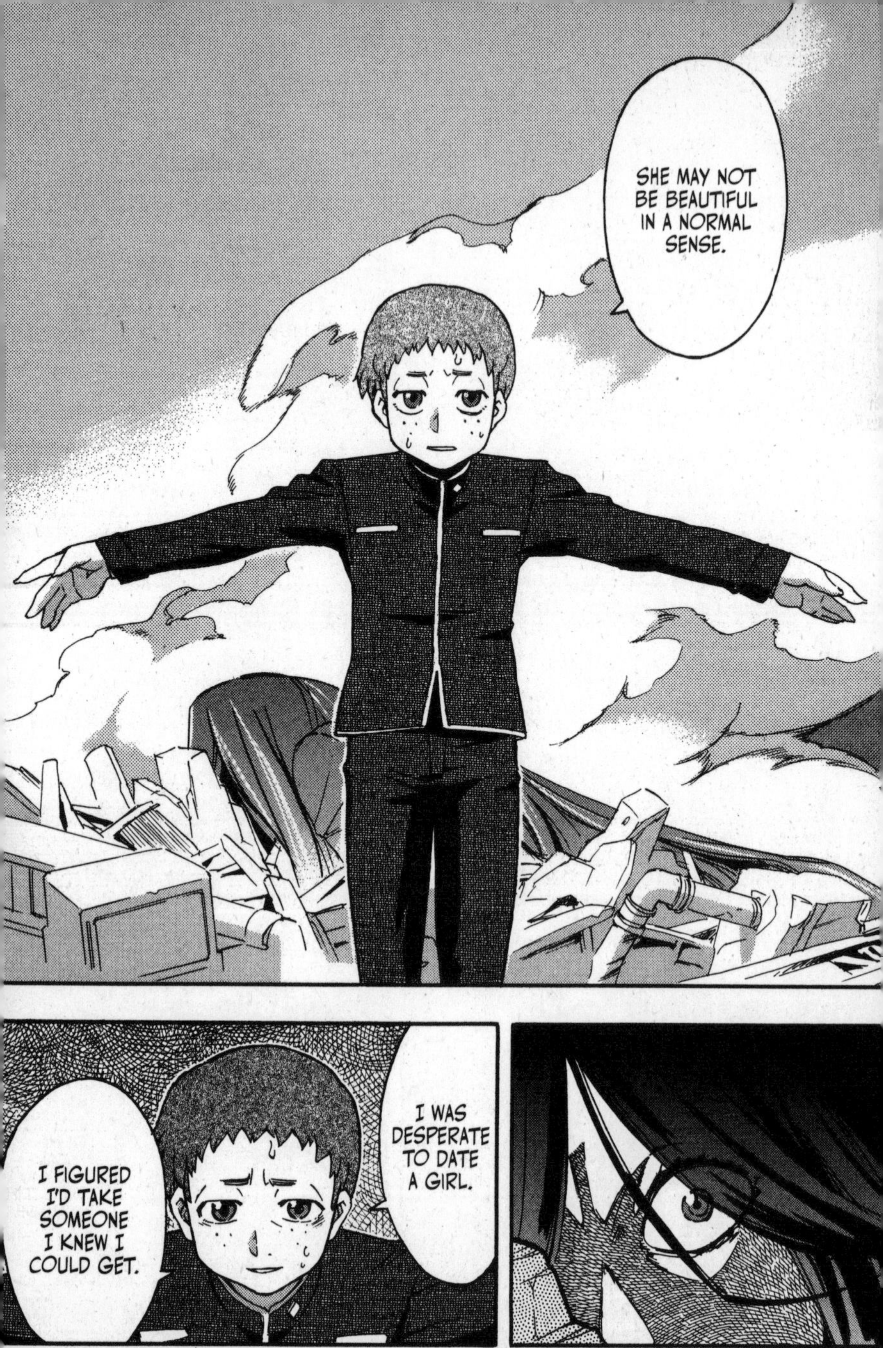
SHE MAY NOT BE BEAUTIFUL IN A NORMAL SENSE.
I WAS DESPERATE TO DATE A GIRL.
I FIGURED I'D TAKE SOMEONE I KNEW I COULD GET.

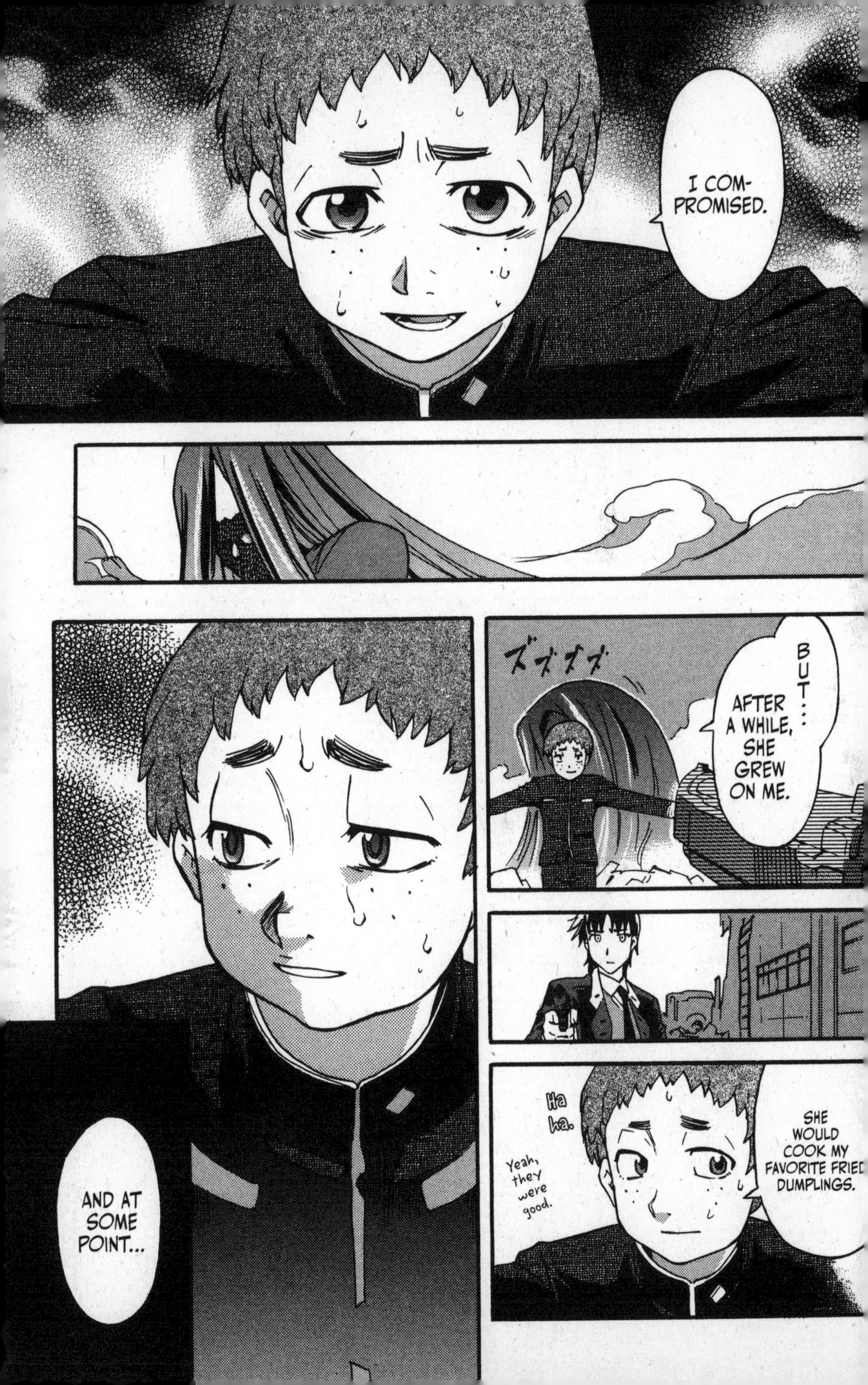
I COMPROMISED.
ズズズズ
BUT... AFTER A WHILE, SHE GREW ON ME.
SHE WOULD COOK MY FAVORITE FRIED DUMPLINGS.
Ha ha.
Yeah, they were good.
AND AT SOME POINT...

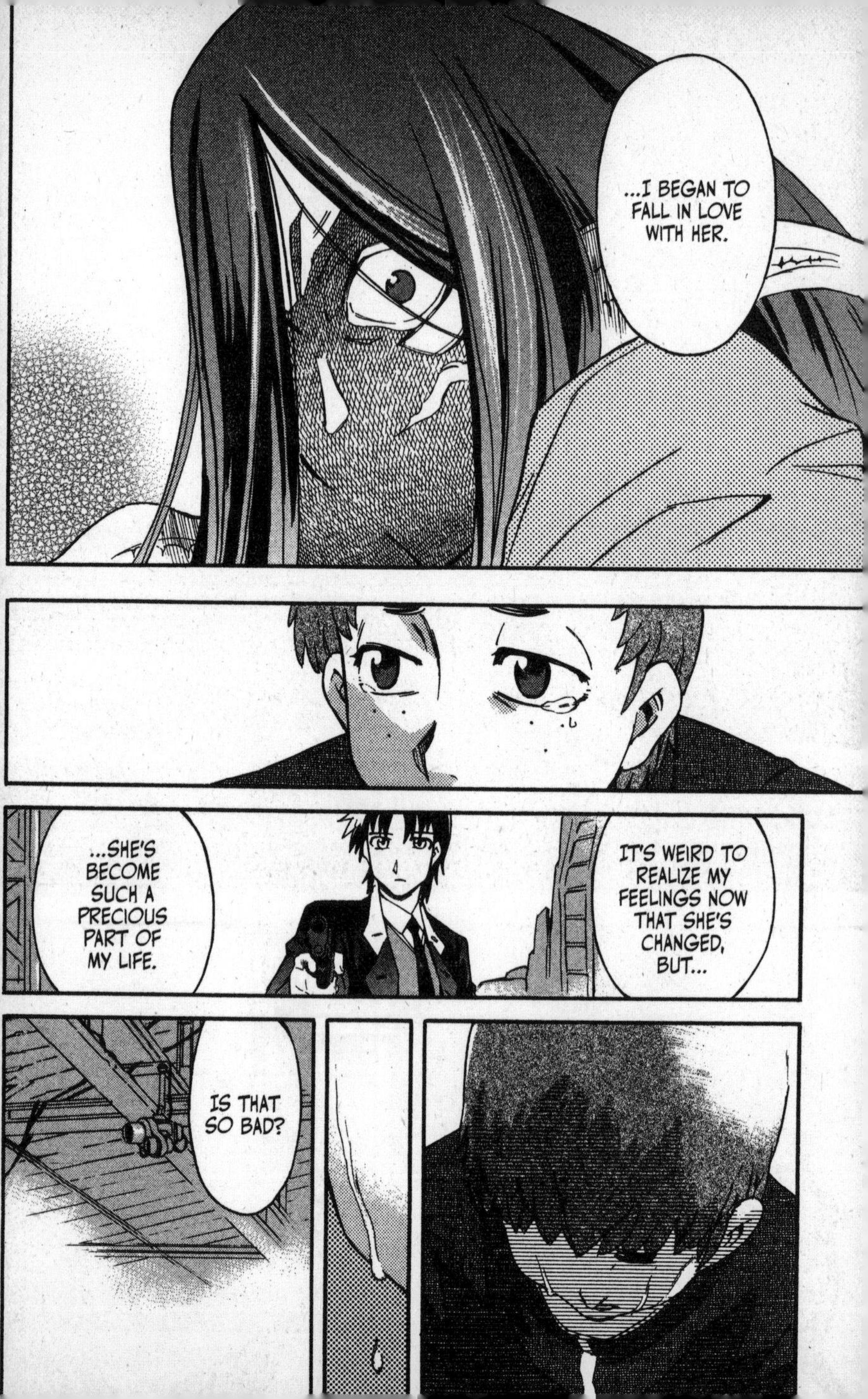
...I BEGAN TO FALL IN LOVE WITH HER.
IT'S WEIRD TO REALIZE MY FEELINGS NOW THAT SHE'S CHANGED, BUT...
...SHE'S BECOME SUCH A PRECIOUS PART OF MY LIFE.
IS THAT SO BAD?

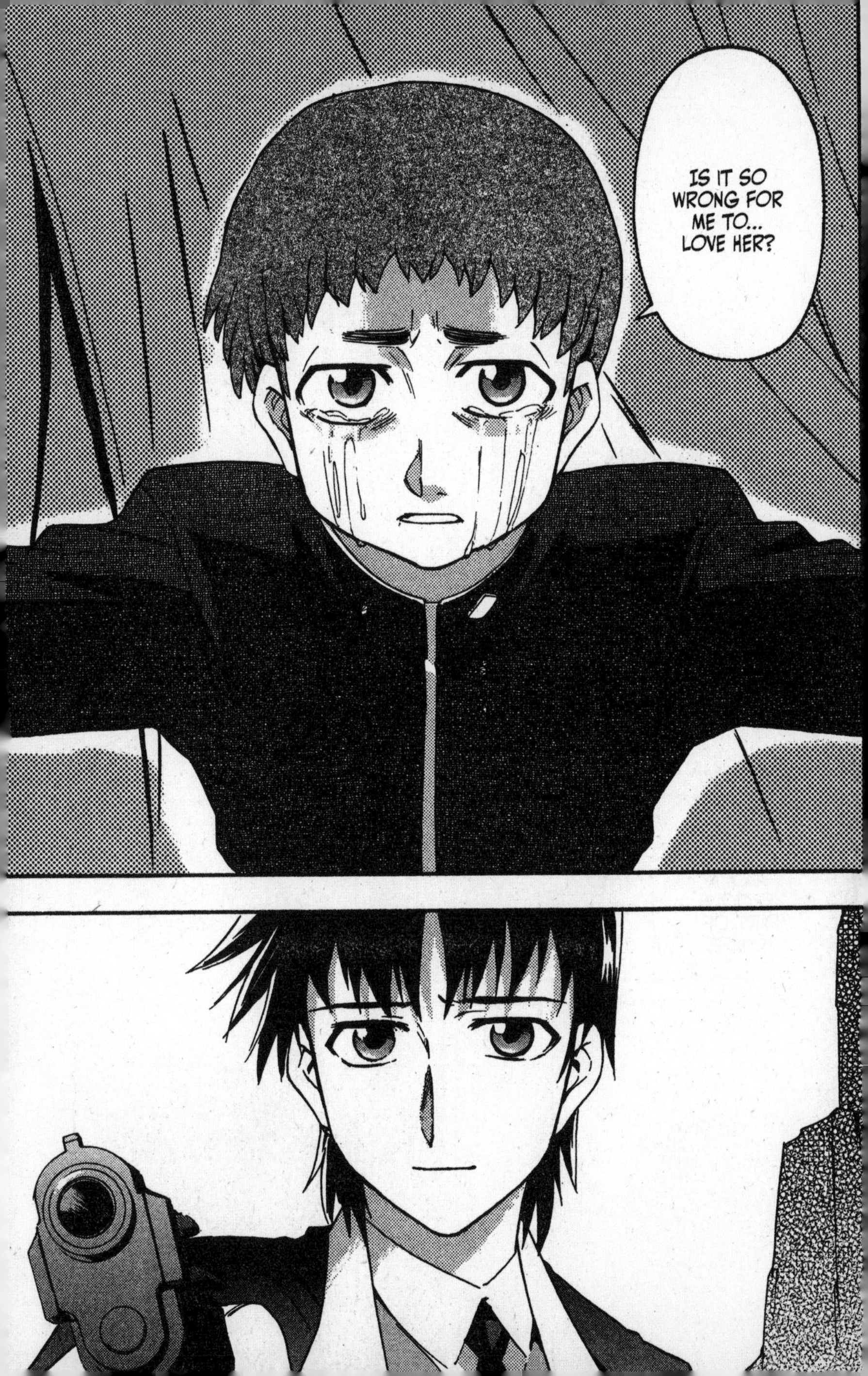
IS IT SO WRONG FOR ME TO... LOVE HER?

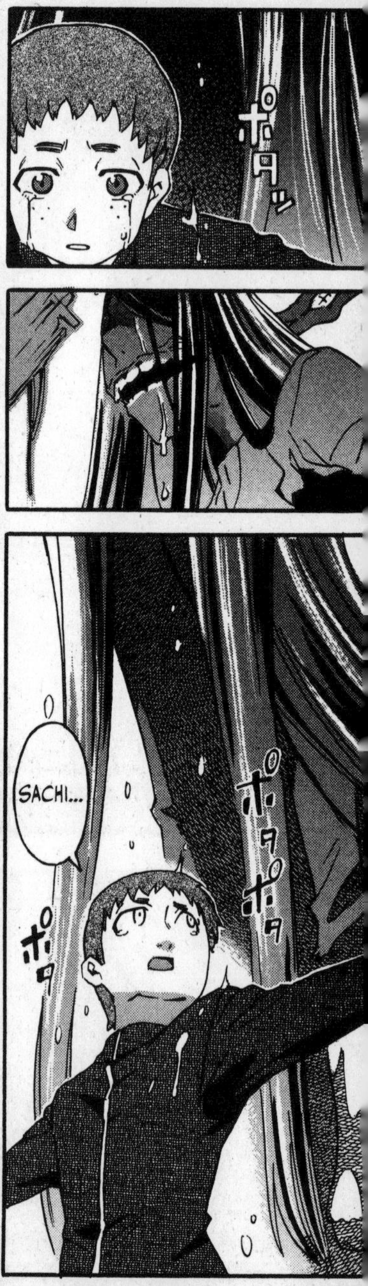
ポタッ
SACHI...
ポタポタ
ポタ
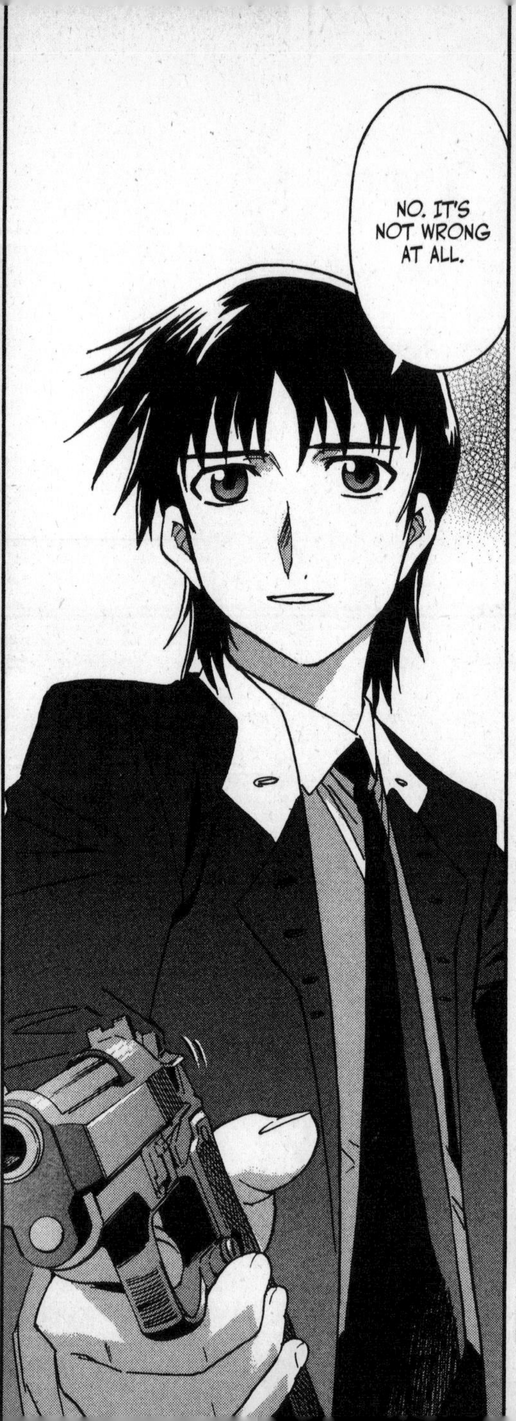
NO. IT'S NOT WRONG AT ALL.

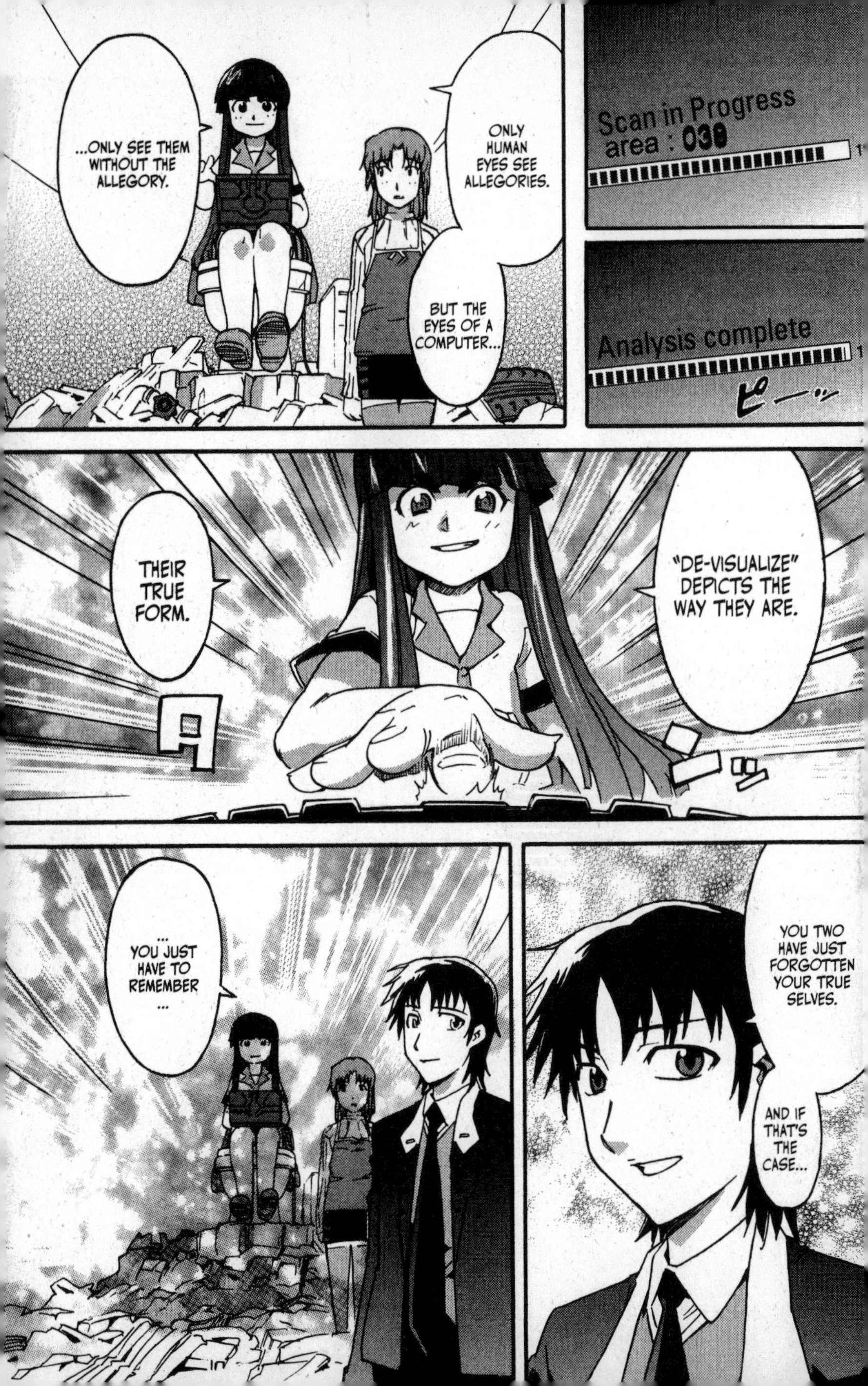

Scan in Progress
area : 038
Analysis complete
ピーッ
ONLY HUMAN EYES SEE ALLEGORIES.
BUT THE EYES OF A COMPUTER...
...ONLY SEE THEM WITHOUT THE ALLEGORY.
"DE-VISUALIZE" DEPICTS THE WAY THEY ARE.
THEIR TRUE FORM.
YOU TWO HAVE JUST FORGOTTEN YOUR TRUE SELVES.
AND IF THAT'S THE CASE...
... YOU JUST HAVE TO REMEMBER ...

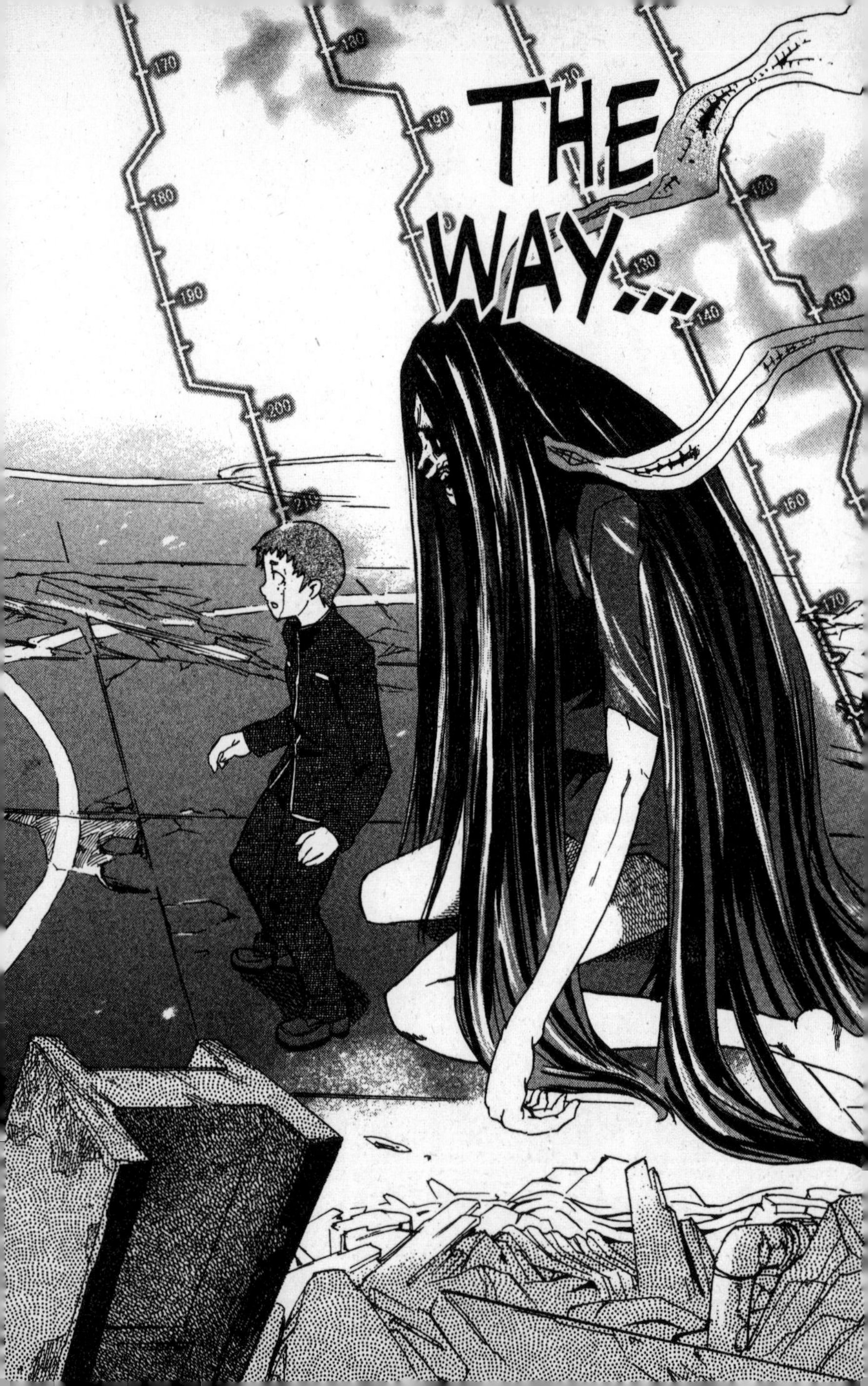
THE WAY...

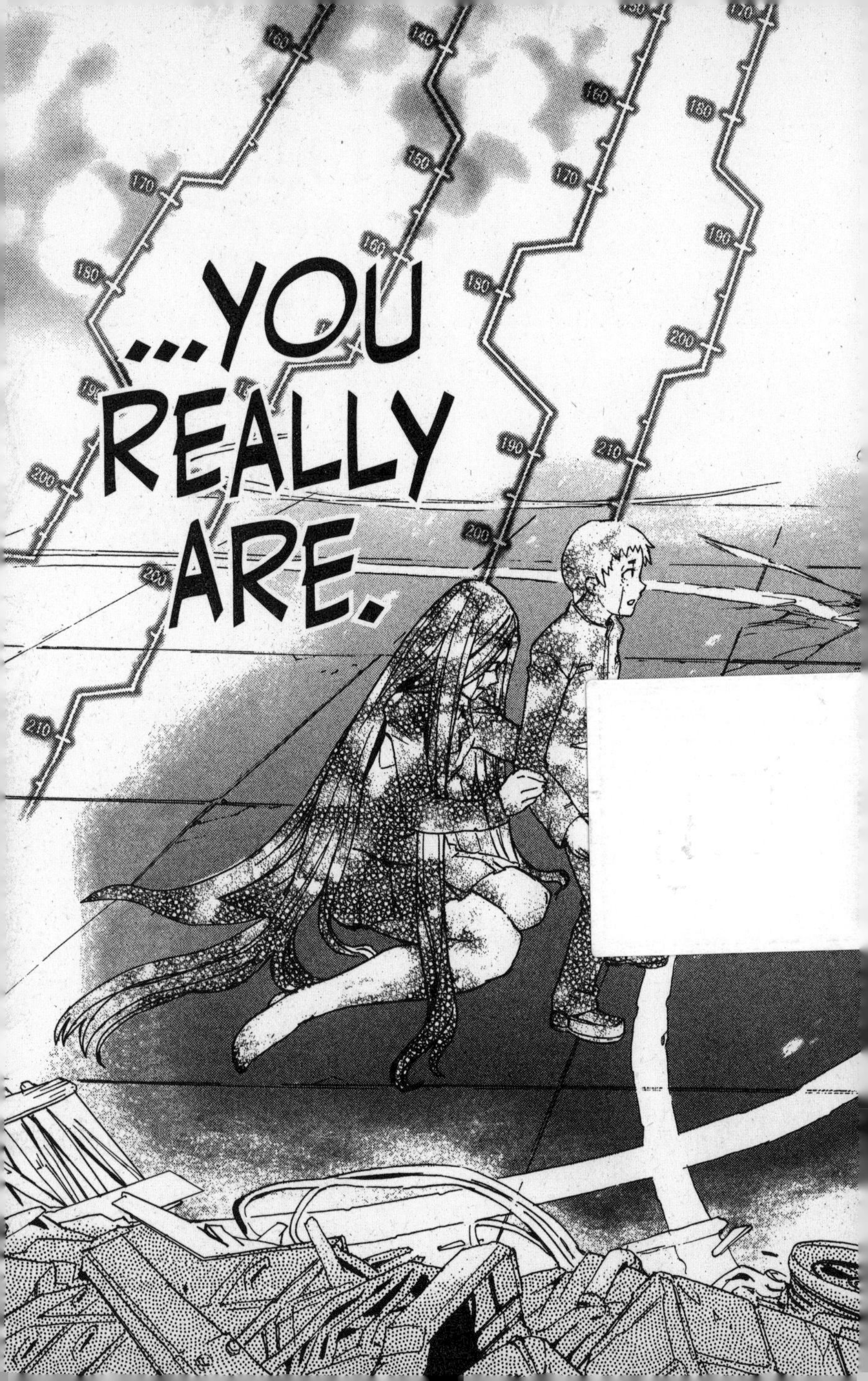
...YOU REALLY ARE.

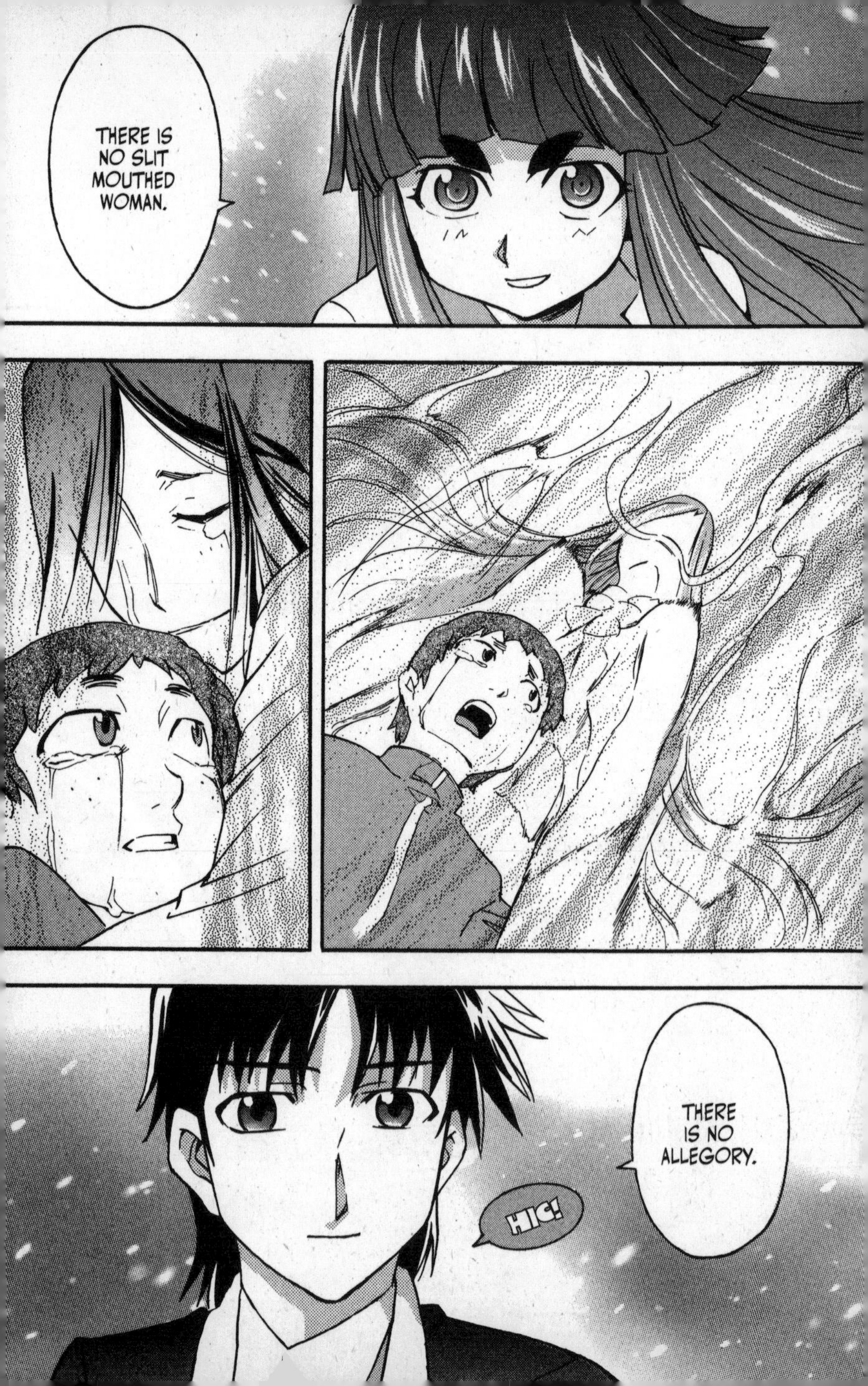
THERE IS NO SLIT MOUTHED WOMAN.
THERE IS NO ALLEGORY.
HIC!

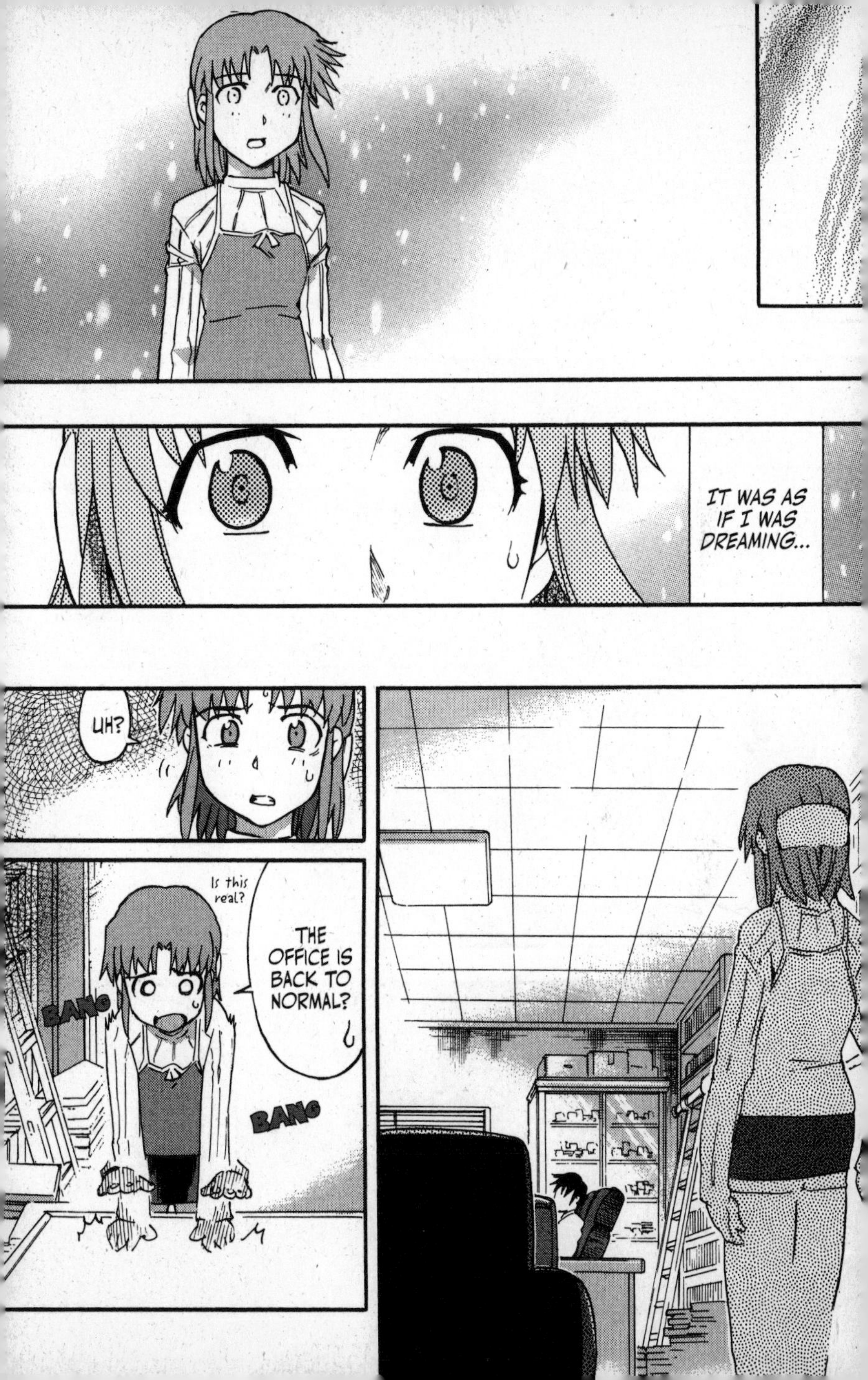
IT WAS AS IF I WAS DREAMING...
UH?
THE OFFICE IS BACK TO NORMAL?
Is this real?
BANG
BANG

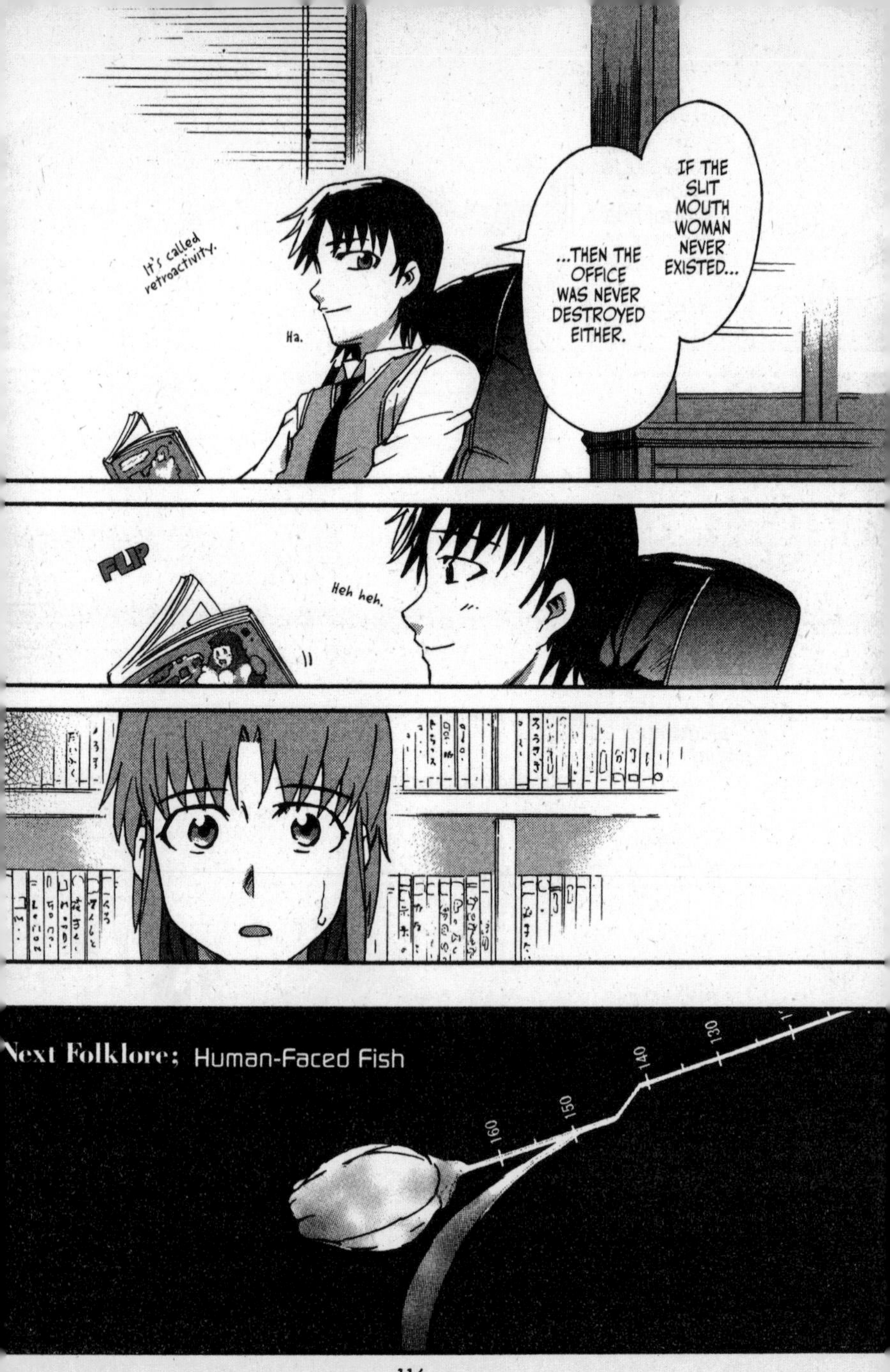
IF THE SLIT MOUTH WOMAN NEVER EXISTED...
...THEN THE OFFICE WAS NEVER DESTROYED EITHER.
It's called retroactivity.
Ha.
Heh heh.
FLIP
Next Folklore; Human-Faced Fish
130
140
150
160

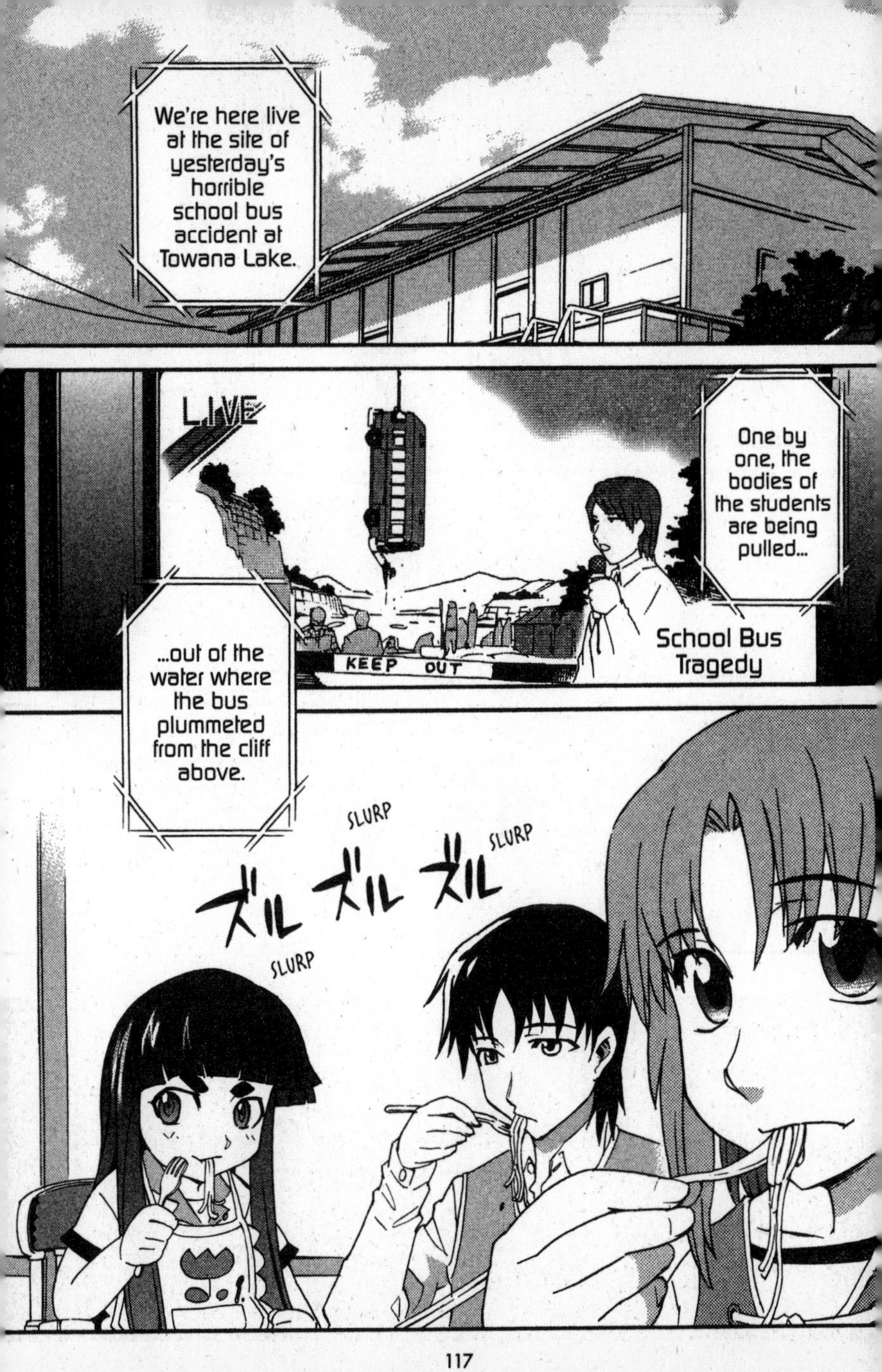
We're here live at the site of yesterday's horrible school bus accident at Towana Lake.
One by one, the bodies of the students are being pulled...
LIVE
School Bus Tragedy
...out of the water where the bus plummeted from the cliff above.
SLURP
SLURP
ズル ズル ズル
SLURP

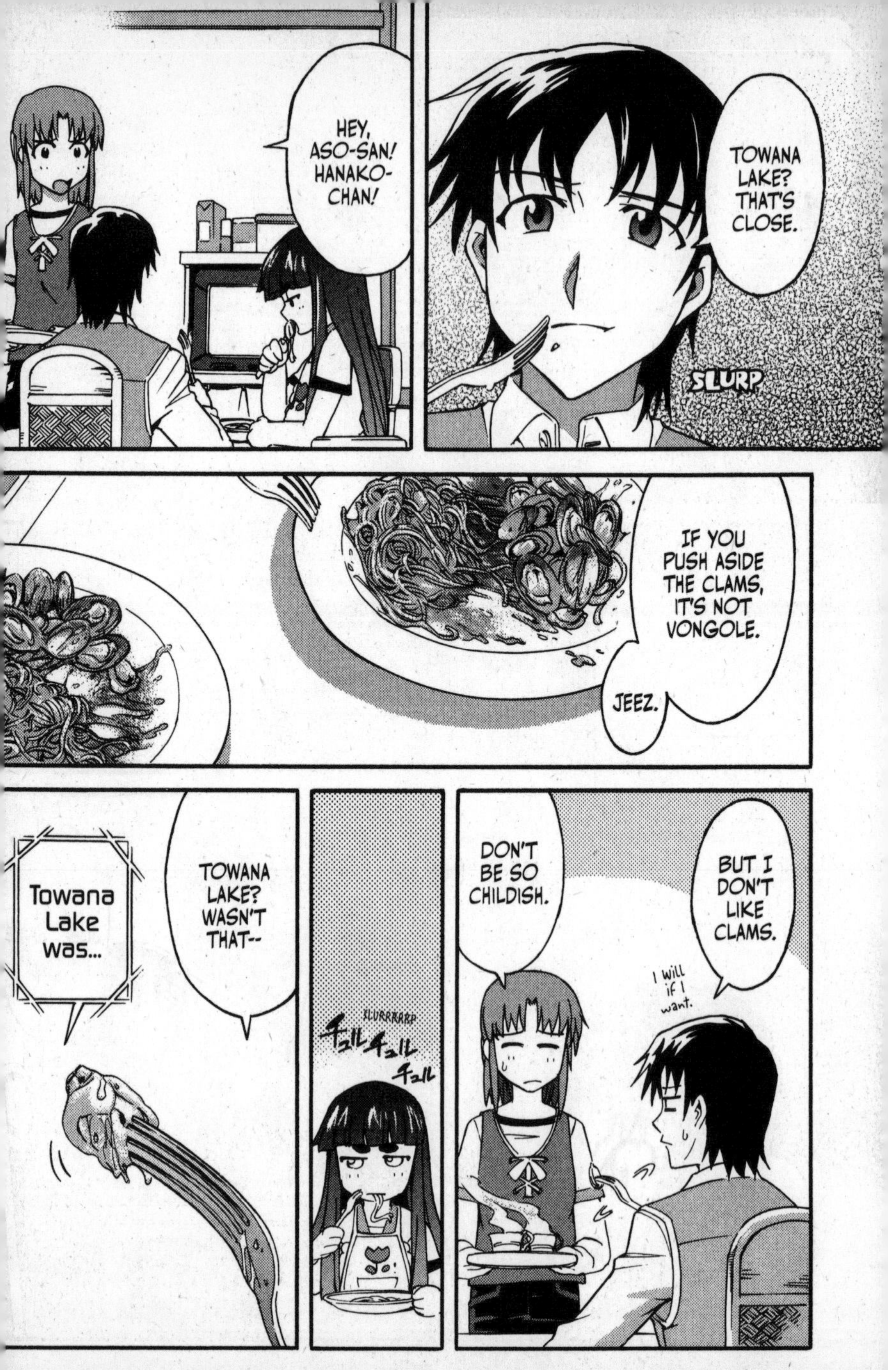
TOWANA LAKE? THAT'S CLOSE.
SLURP
HEY, ASO-SAN! HANAKO-CHAN!
IF YOU PUSH ASIDE THE CLAMS, IT'S NOT VONGOLE.
JEEZ.
BUT I DON'T LIKE CLAMS.
DON'T BE SO CHILDISH.
I will if I want.
SLURRRRRP
チュルチュルチュル
TOWANA LAKE? WASN'T THAT--
Towana Lake was...

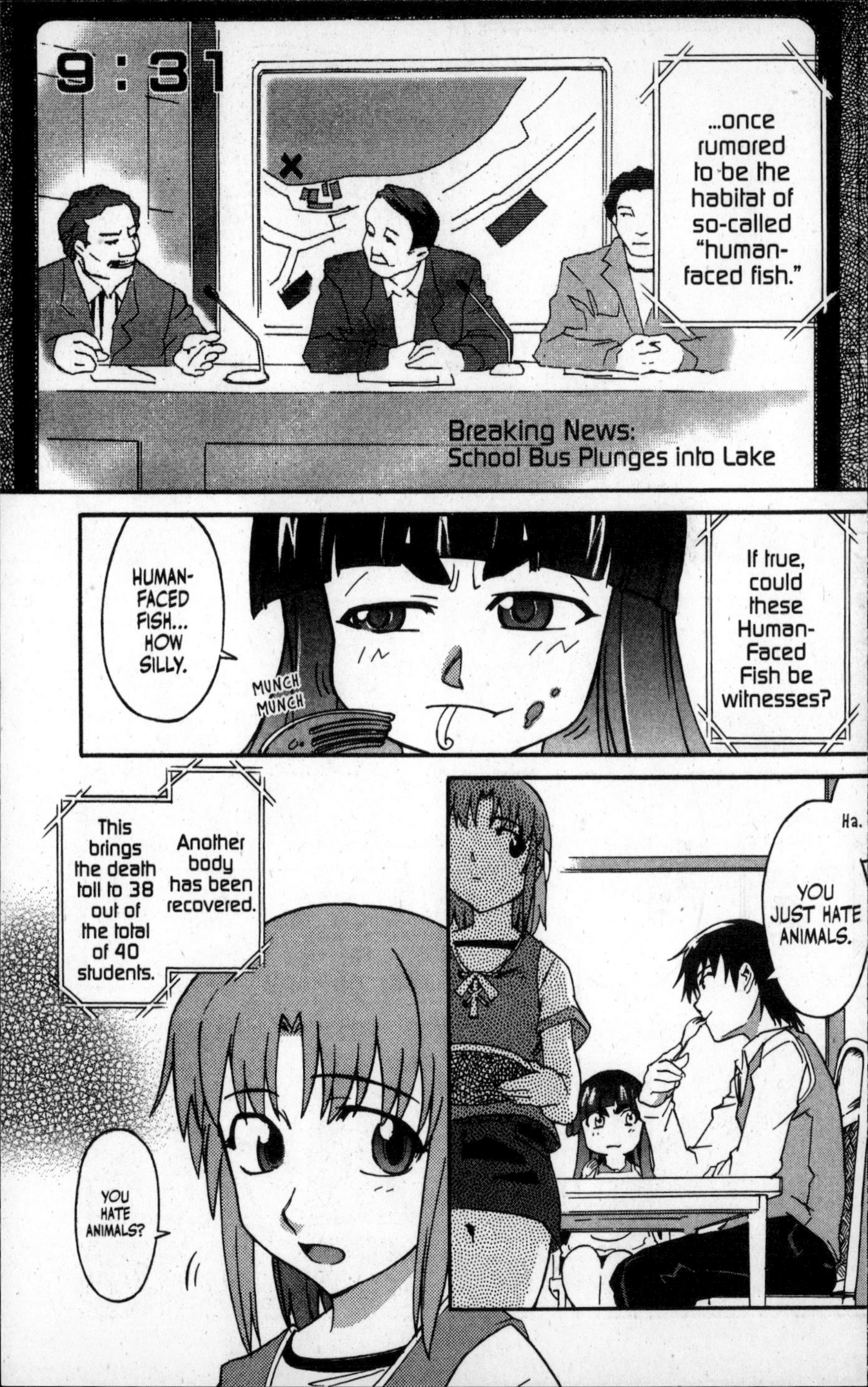
9:31
...once rumored to be the habitat of so-called "human-faced fish."
Breaking News: School Bus Plunges into Lake
If true, could these Human-Faced Fish be witnesses?
HUMAN-FACED FISH... HOW SILLY.
MUNCH MUNCH
Ha.
YOU JUST HATE ANIMALS.
Another body has been recovered.
This brings the death toll to 38 out of the total of 40 students.
YOU HATE ANIMALS?

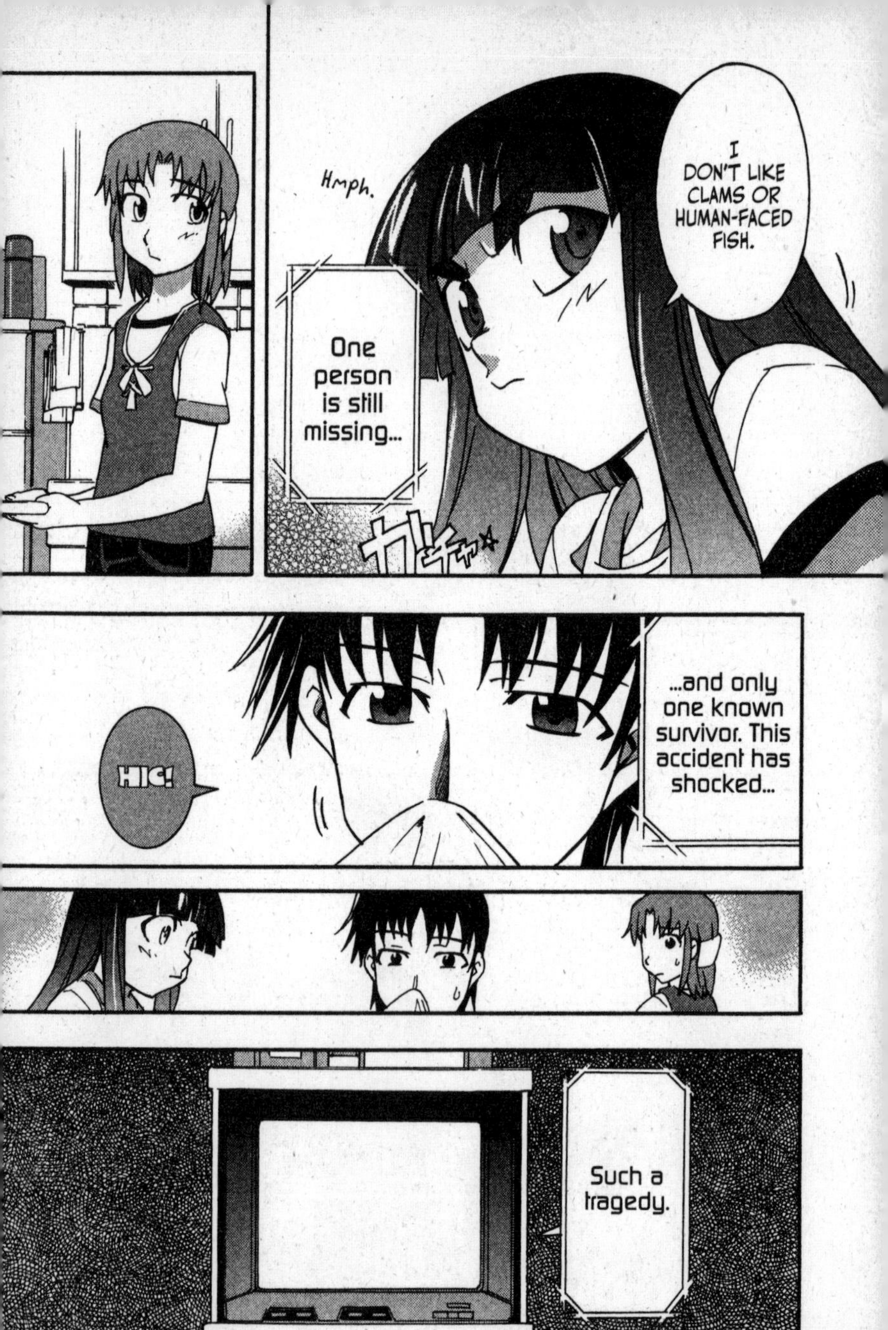
I DON'T LIKE CLAMS OR HUMAN-FACED FISH.
Hmph.
One person is still missing...
ガチャ☆
...and only one known survivor. This accident has shocked...
HIC!
Such a tragedy.

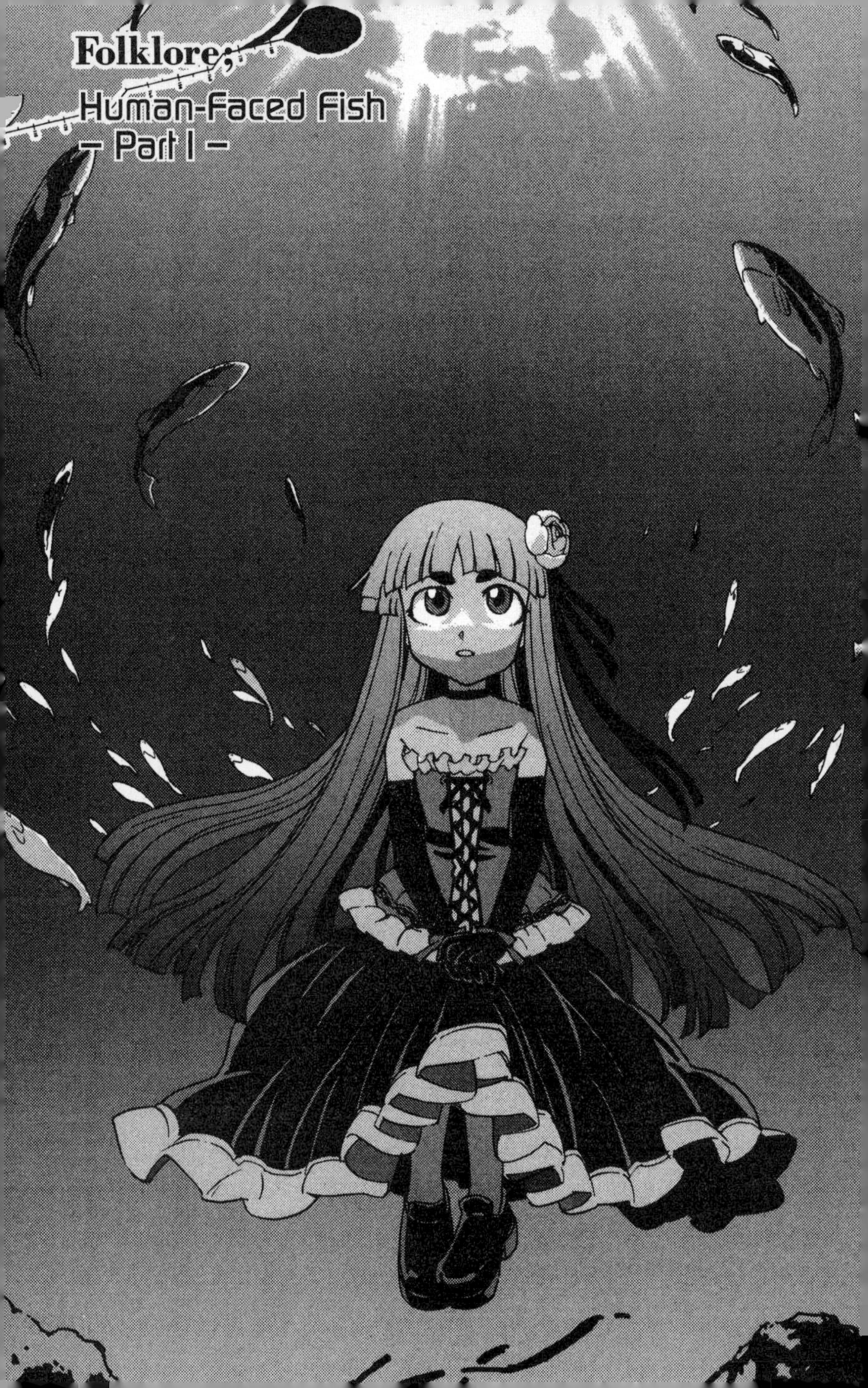
Folklore;
Human-Faced Fish
– Part I –

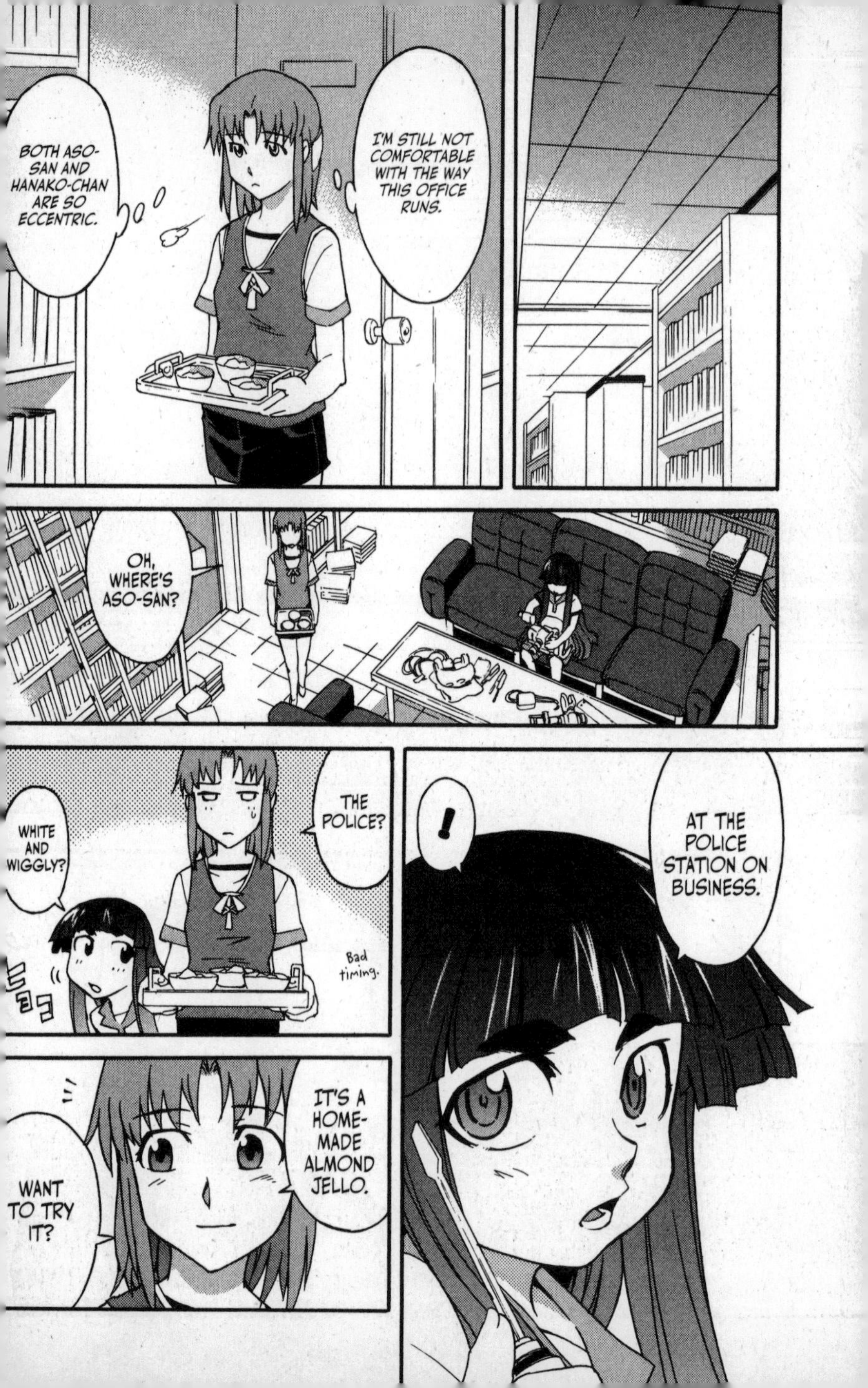
I'M STILL NOT COMFORTABLE WITH THE WAY THIS OFFICE RUNS.
BOTH ASO-SAN AND HANAKO-CHAN ARE SO ECCENTRIC.
OH, WHERE'S ASO-SAN?
AT THE POLICE STATION ON BUSINESS.
!
THE POLICE?
Bad timing.
WHITE AND WIGGLY?
IT'S A HOME-MADE ALMOND JELLO.
WANT TO TRY IT?

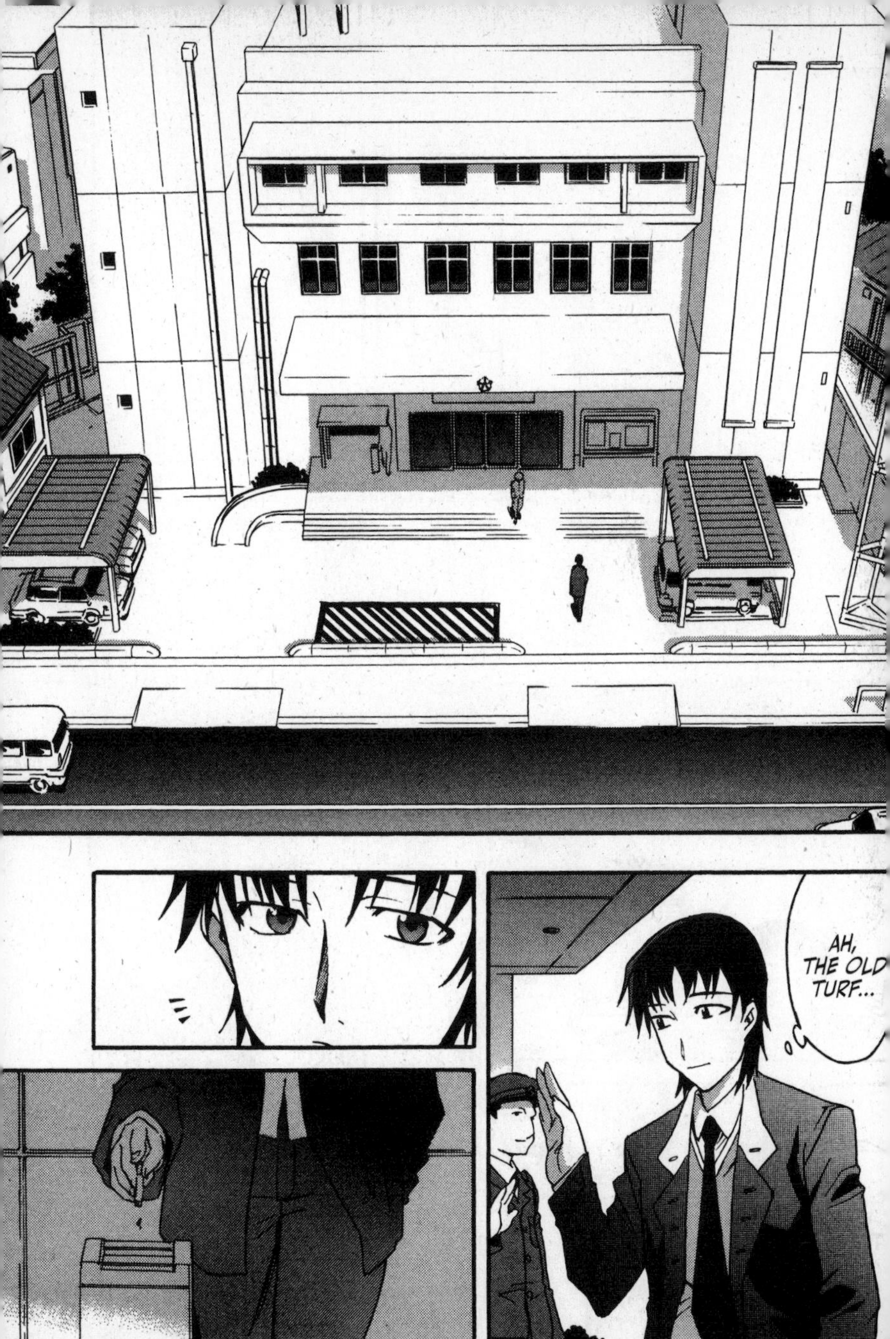
AH, THE OLD TURF...

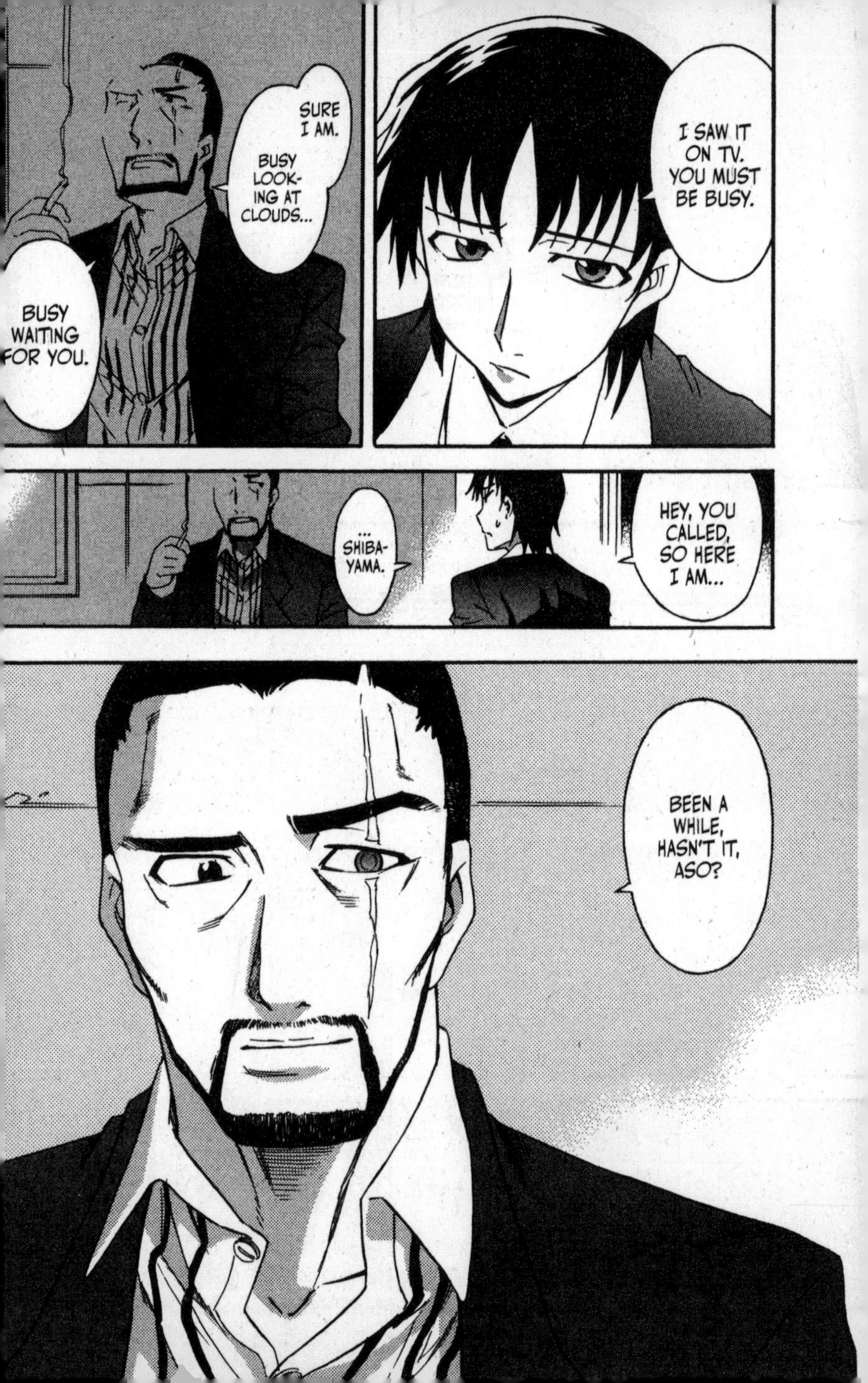
I SAW IT ON TV. YOU MUST BE BUSY.
SURE I AM.
BUSY LOOKING AT CLOUDS...
BUSY WAITING FOR YOU.
HEY, YOU CALLED, SO HERE I AM...
...SHIBAYAMA.
BEEN A WHILE, HASN'T IT, ASO?

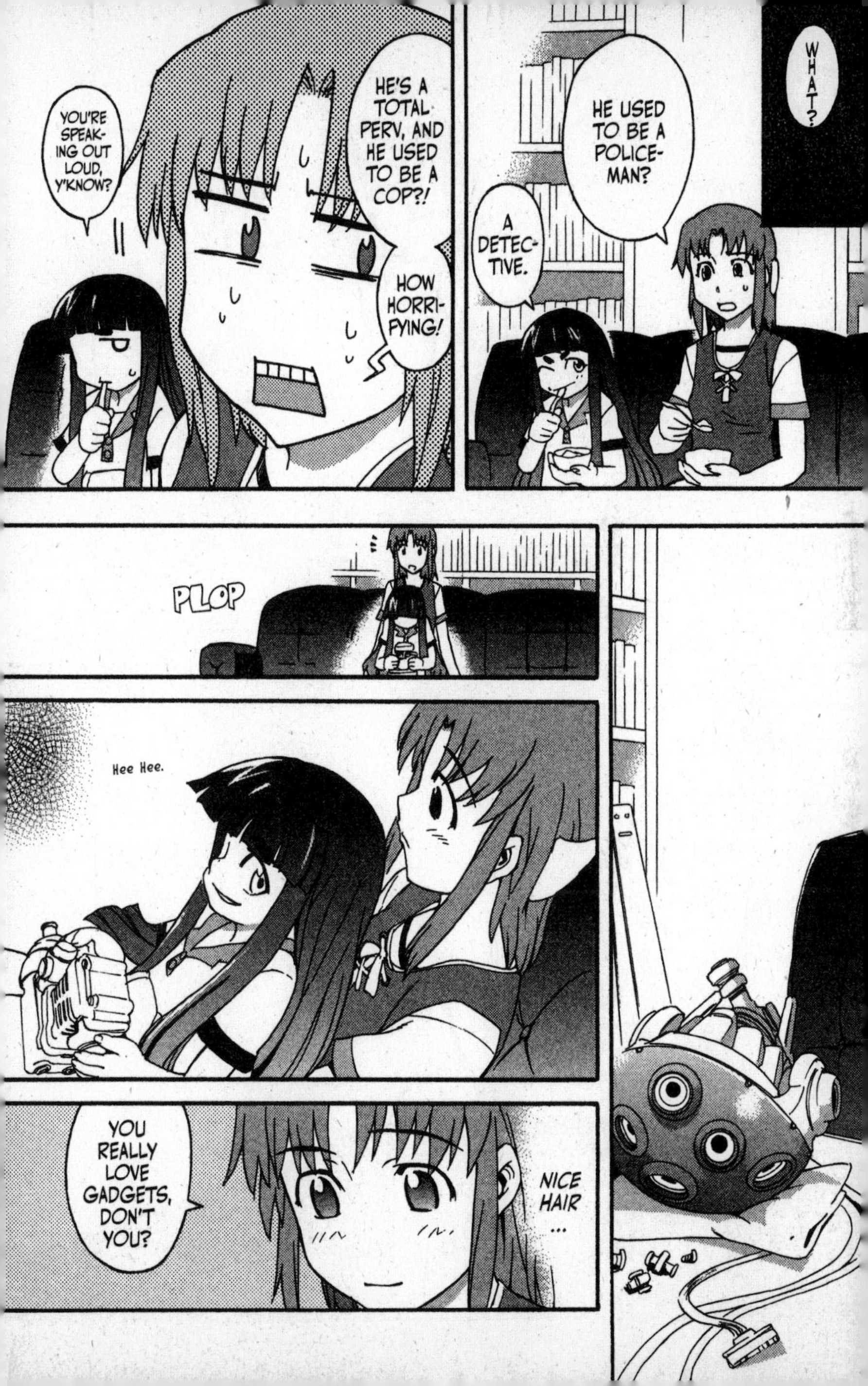
WHAT?!
HE USED TO BE A POLICEMAN?
A DETECTIVE.
HE'S A TOTAL PERV, AND HE USED TO BE A COP?!
HOW HORRIFYING!
YOU'RE SPEAKING OUT LOUD, Y'KNOW?
PLOP
Hee Hee.
NICE HAIR...
YOU REALLY LOVE GADGETS, DON'T YOU?

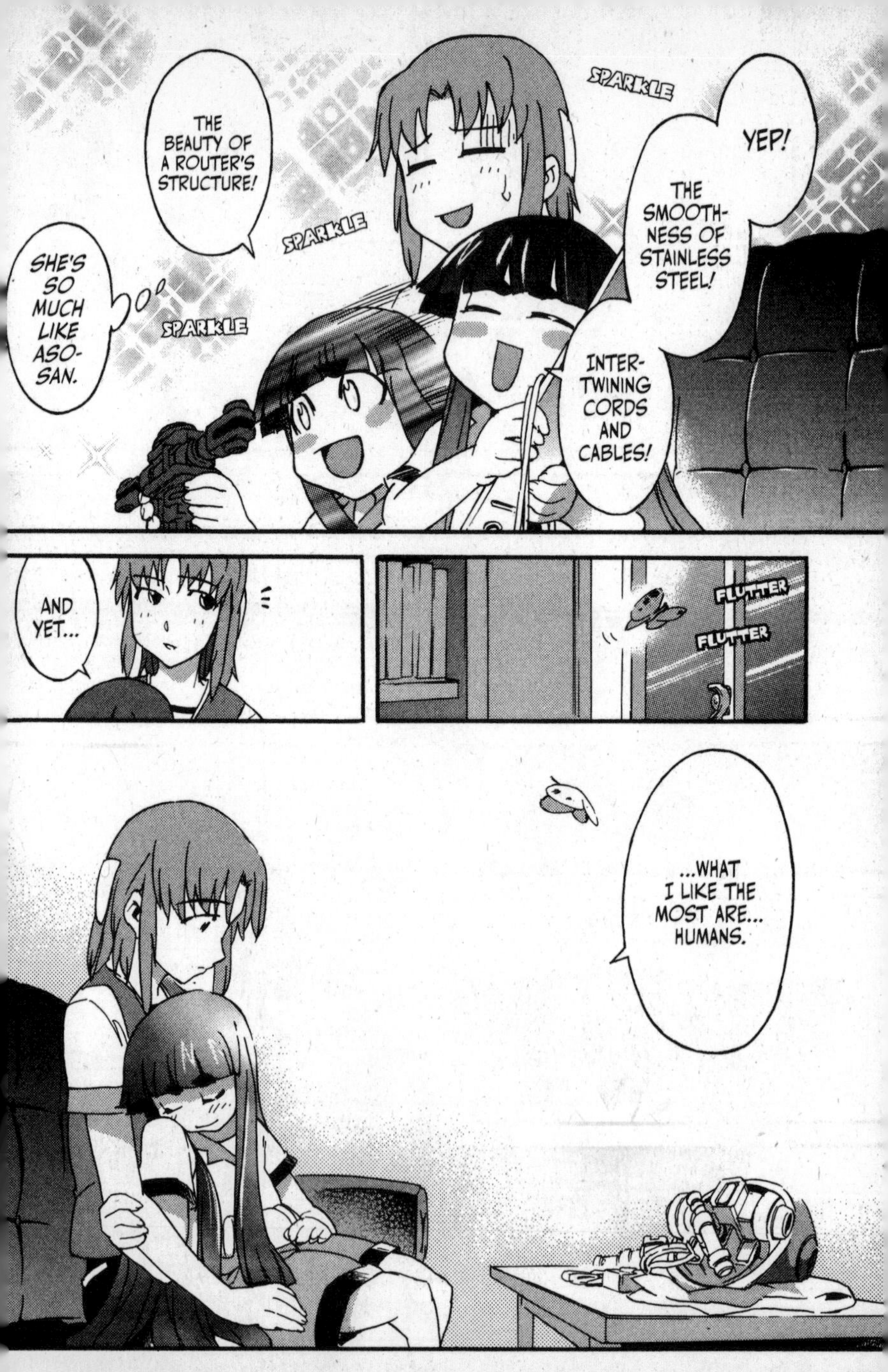
SPARKLE
YEP!
THE SMOOTHNESS OF STAINLESS STEEL!
INTER-TWINING CORDS AND CABLES!
THE BEAUTY OF A ROUTER'S STRUCTURE!
SPARKLE
SHE'S SO MUCH LIKE ASO-SAN.
SPARKLE
FLUTTER
FLUTTER
AND YET...
...WHAT I LIKE THE MOST ARE... HUMANS.

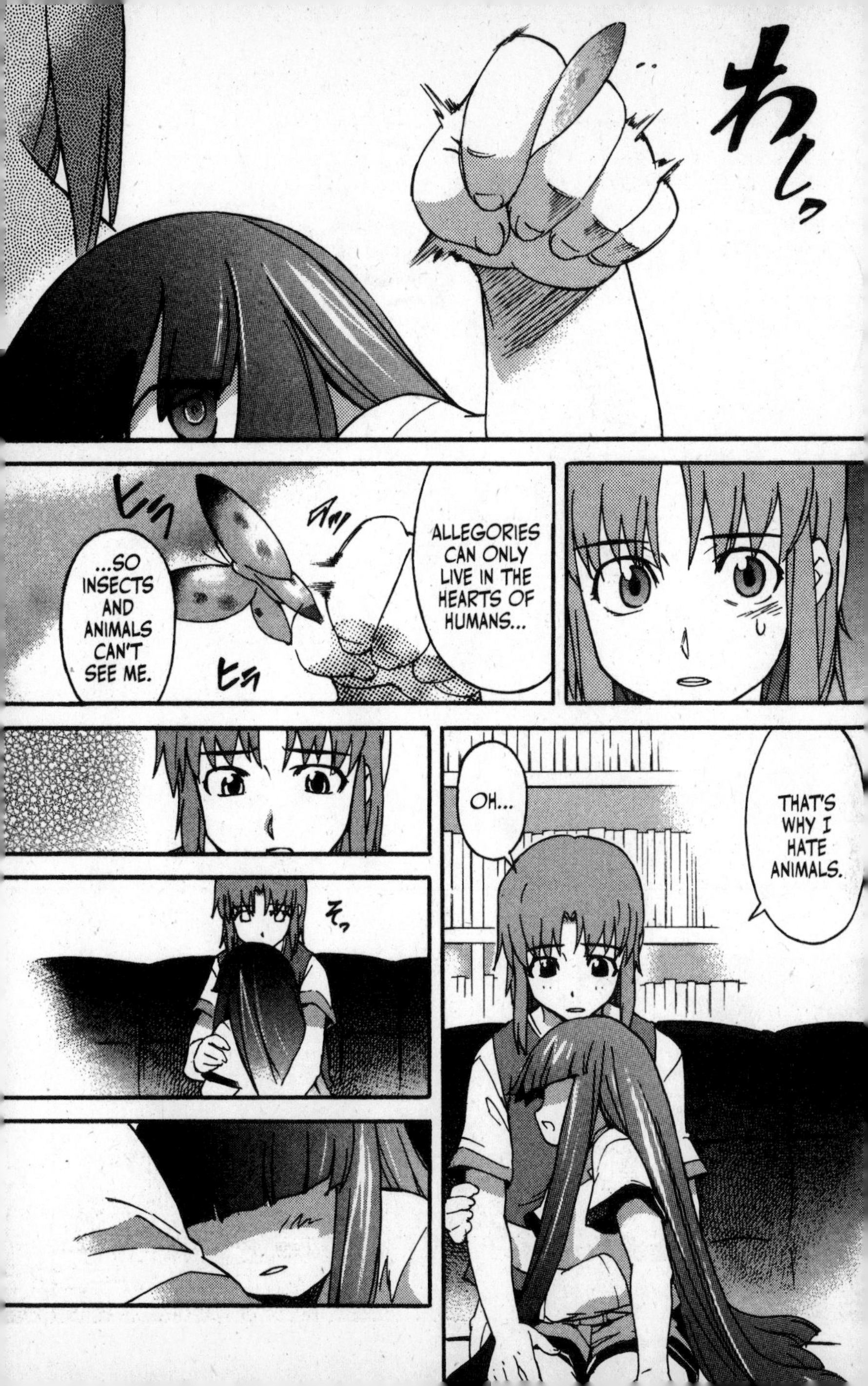
わしっ
ALLEGORIES CAN ONLY LIVE IN THE HEARTS OF HUMANS...
バッ
ヒラ
...SO INSECTS AND ANIMALS CAN'T SEE ME.
ヒラ
THAT'S WHY I HATE ANIMALS.
OH...
そっ

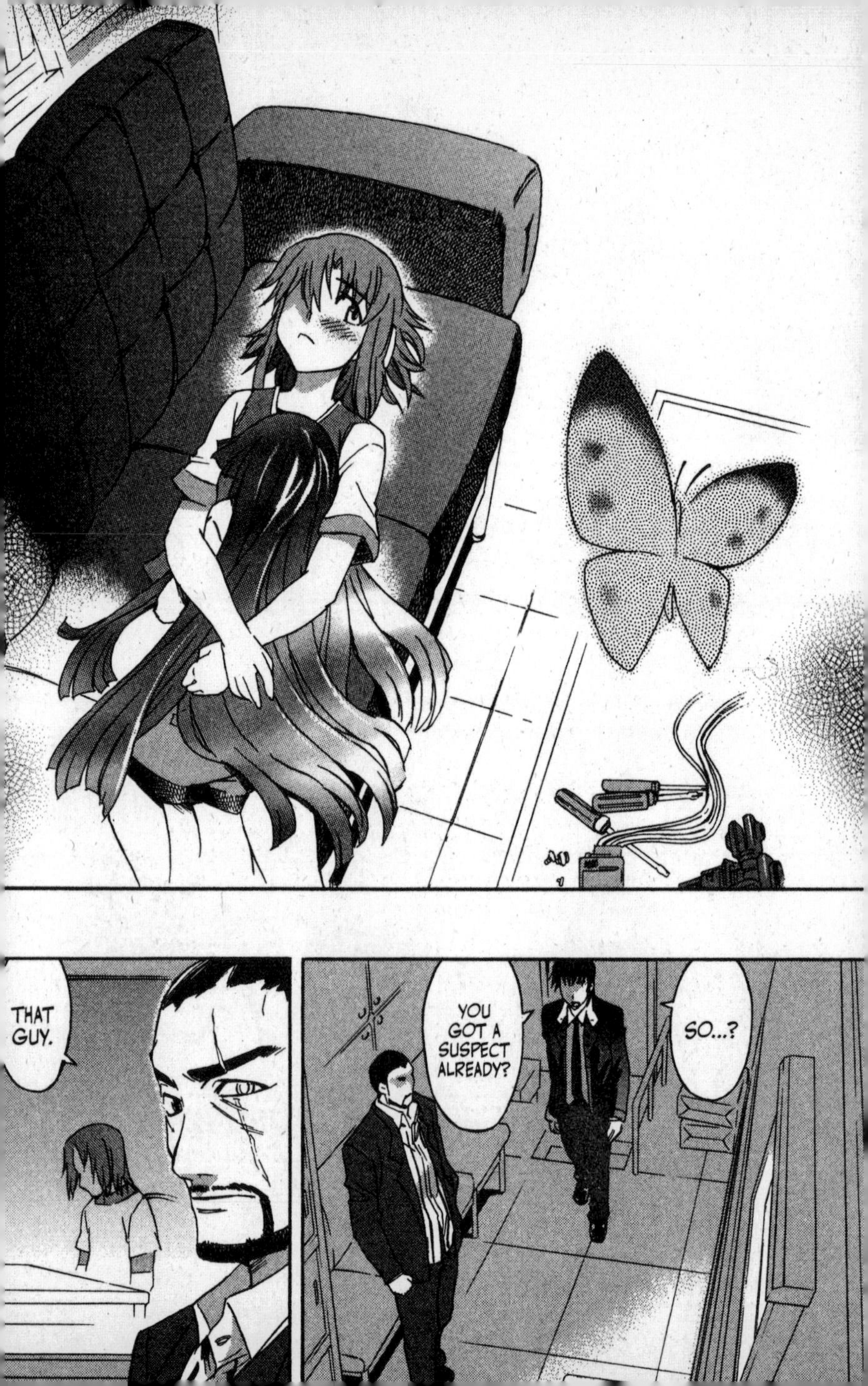
SO...?
YOU GOT A SUSPECT ALREADY?
THAT GUY.

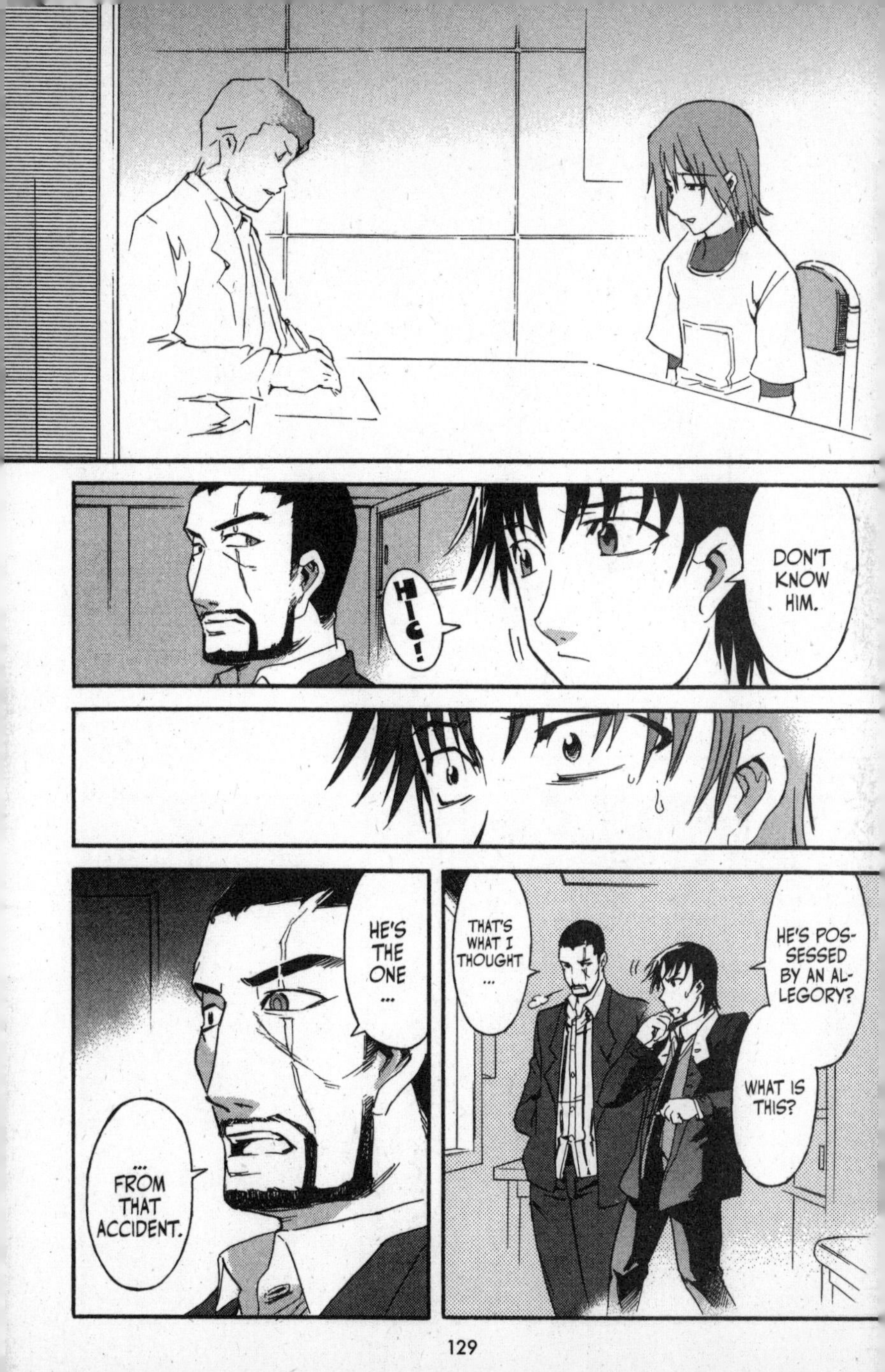
DON'T KNOW HIM.
HIC!
HE'S POSSESSED BY AN ALLEGORY?
WHAT IS THIS?
THAT'S WHAT I THOUGHT ...
HE'S THE ONE ...
... FROM THAT ACCIDENT.

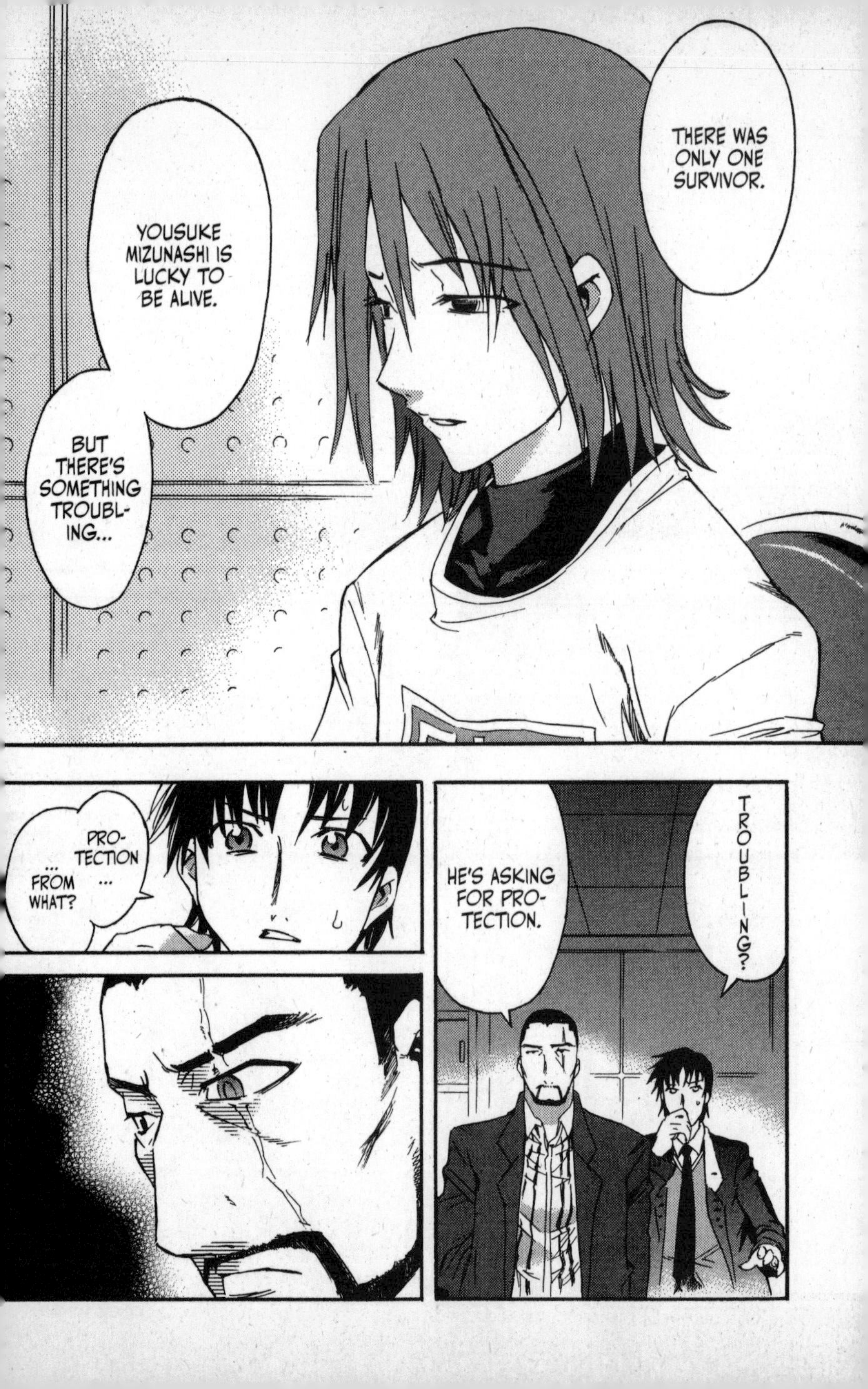
THERE WAS ONLY ONE SURVIVOR.
YOUSUKE MIZUNASHI IS LUCKY TO BE ALIVE.
BUT THERE'S SOMETHING TROUBLING...
TROUBLING?
HE'S ASKING FOR PROTECTION.
PROTECTION... ...FROM WHAT?

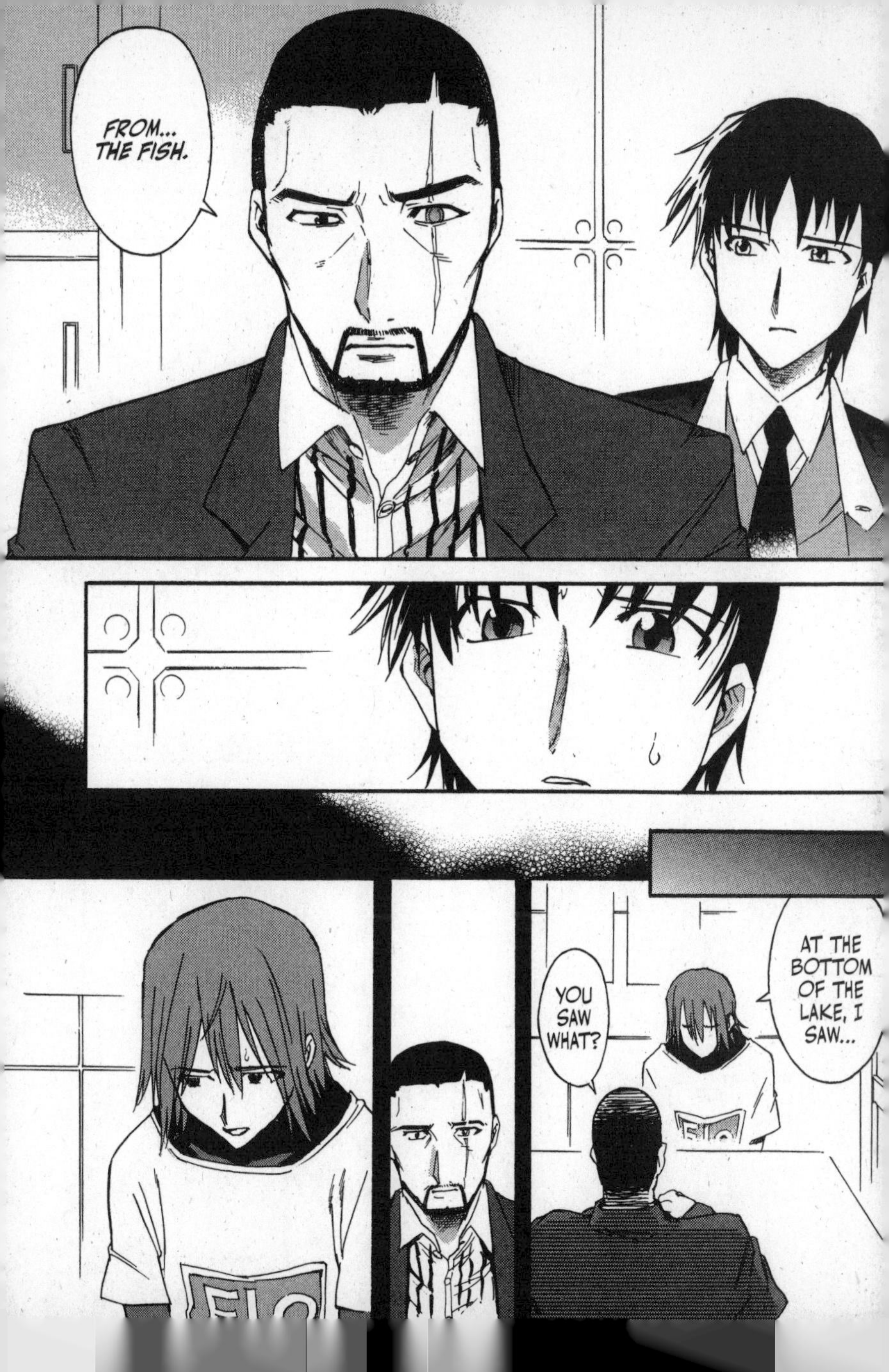
FROM... THE FISH.
AT THE BOTTOM OF THE LAKE, I SAW...
YOU SAW WHAT?

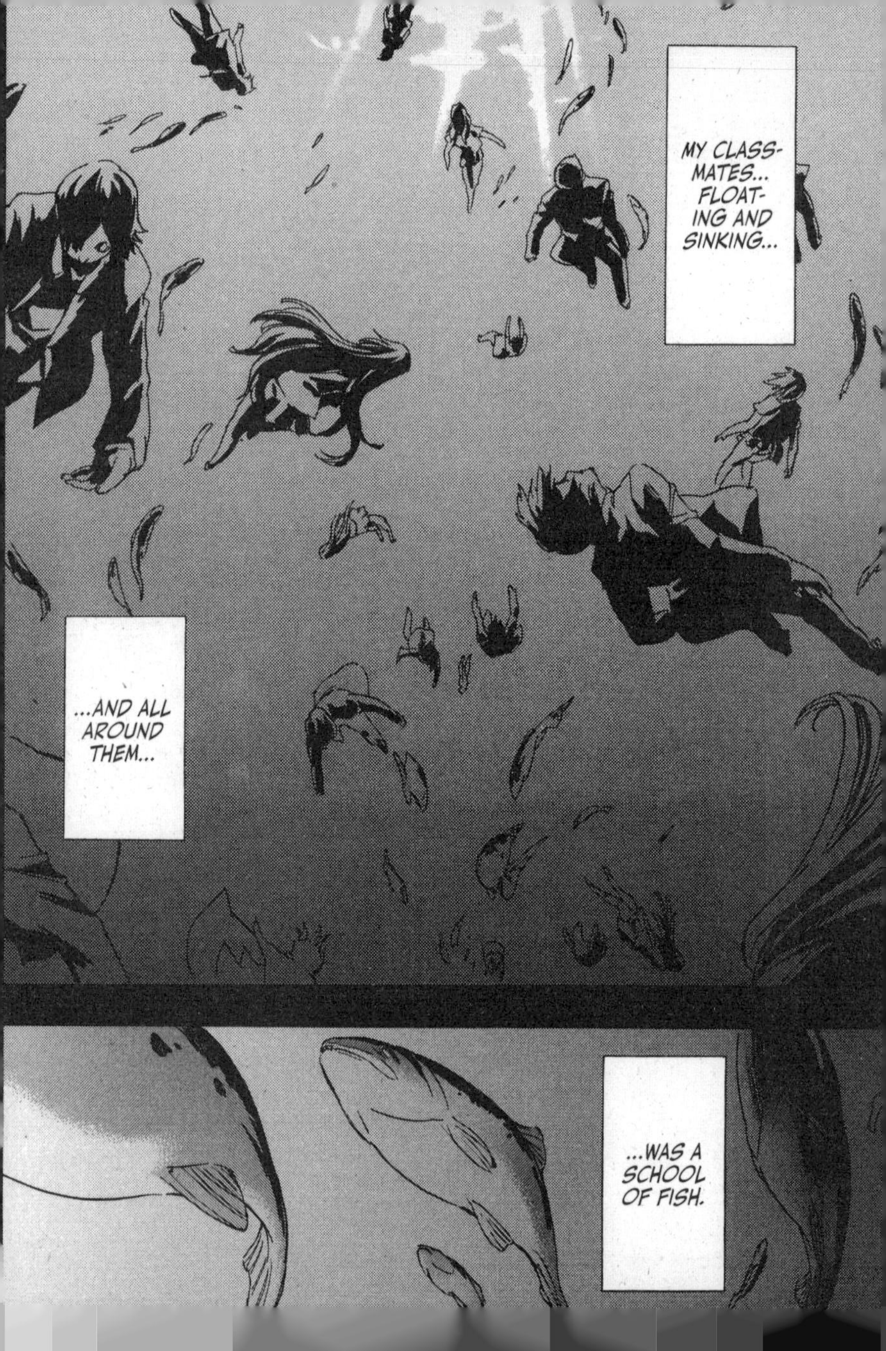
MY CLASS-MATES... FLOAT-ING AND SINKING...
...AND ALL AROUND THEM...
...WAS A SCHOOL OF FISH.

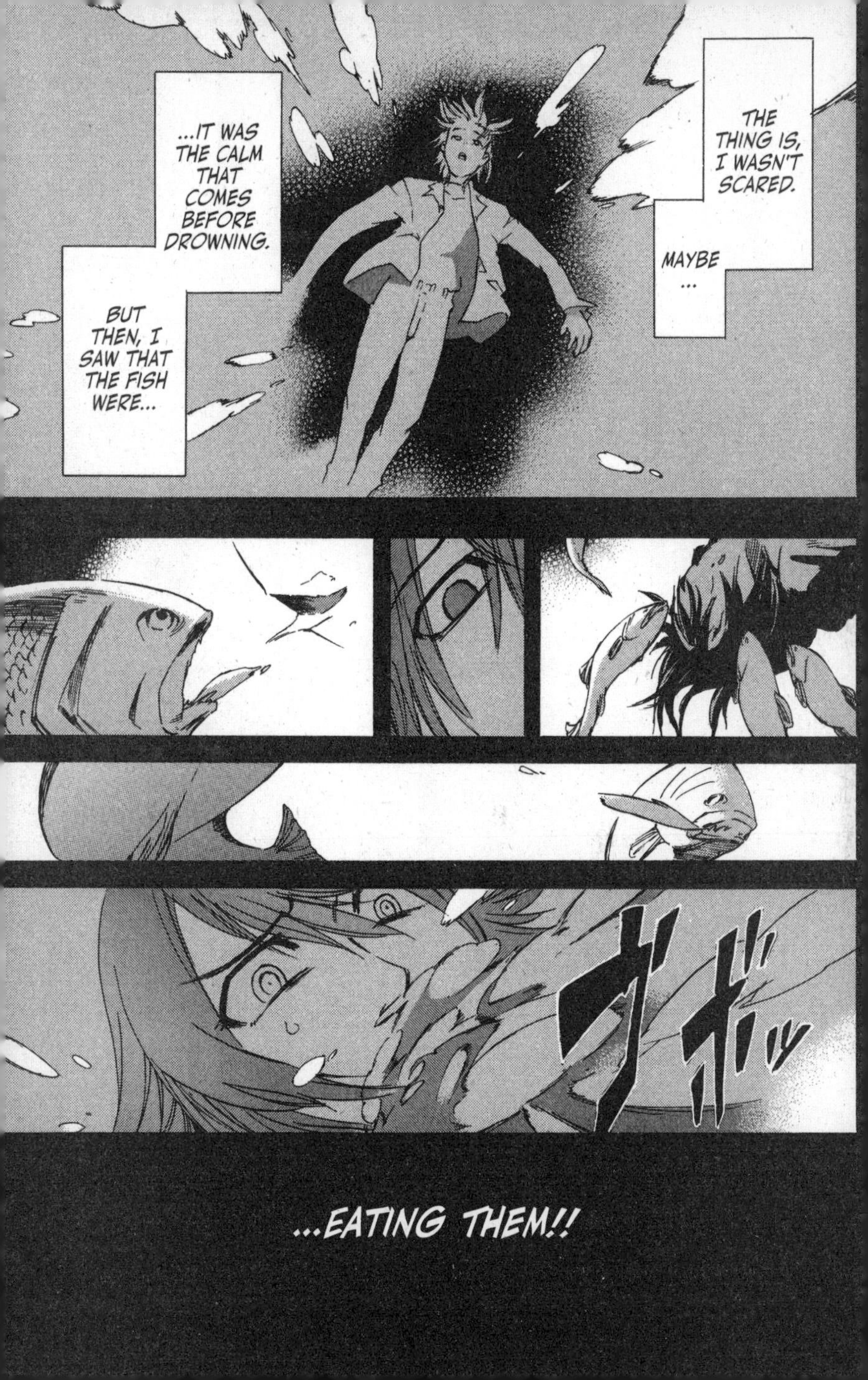
THE THING IS, I WASN'T SCARED.
MAYBE ...
...IT WAS THE CALM THAT COMES BEFORE DROWNING.
BUT THEN, I SAW THAT THE FISH WERE...
ヴボッ
...EATING THEM!!

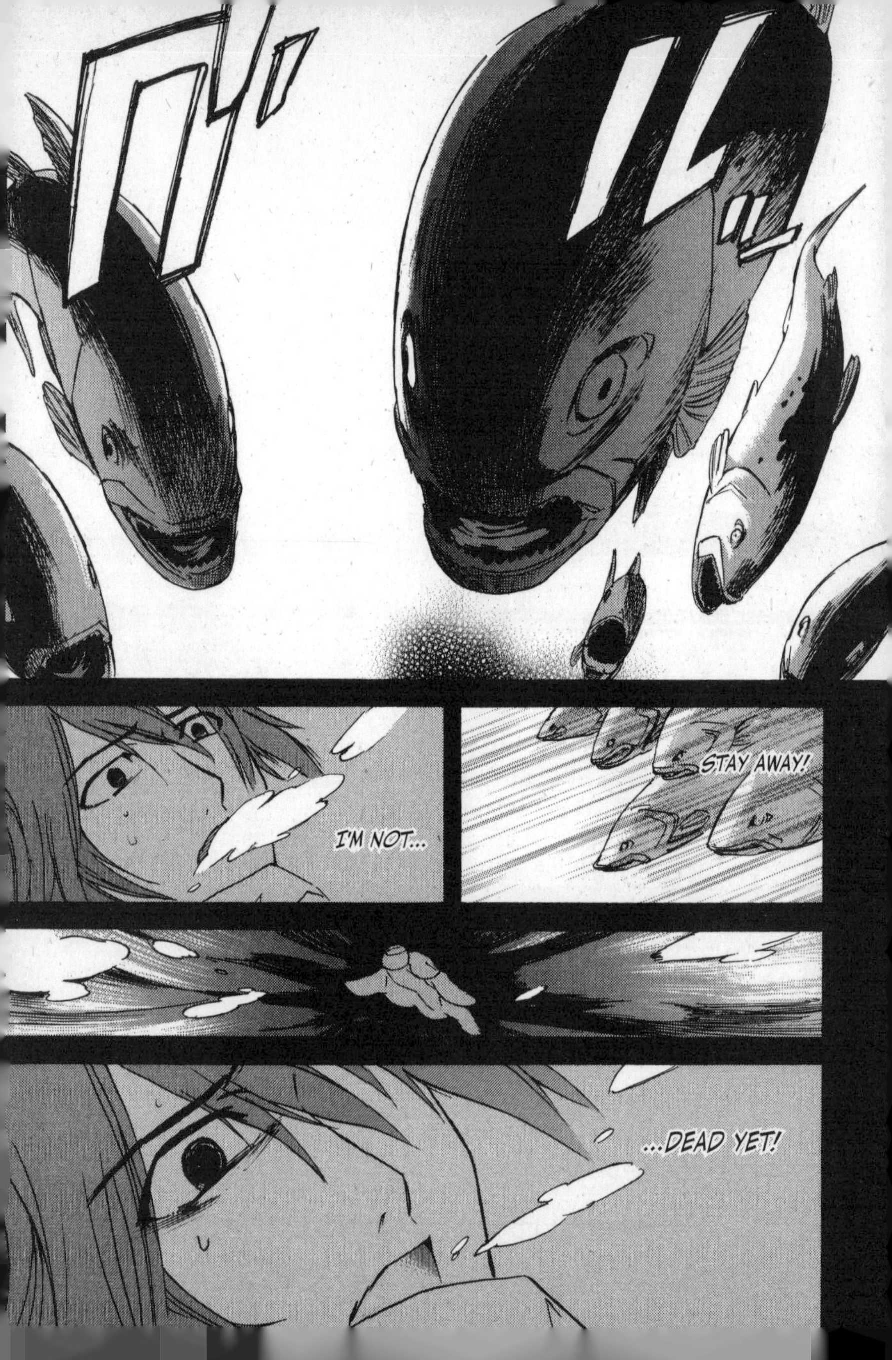
STAY AWAY!
I'M NOT...
...DEAD YET!

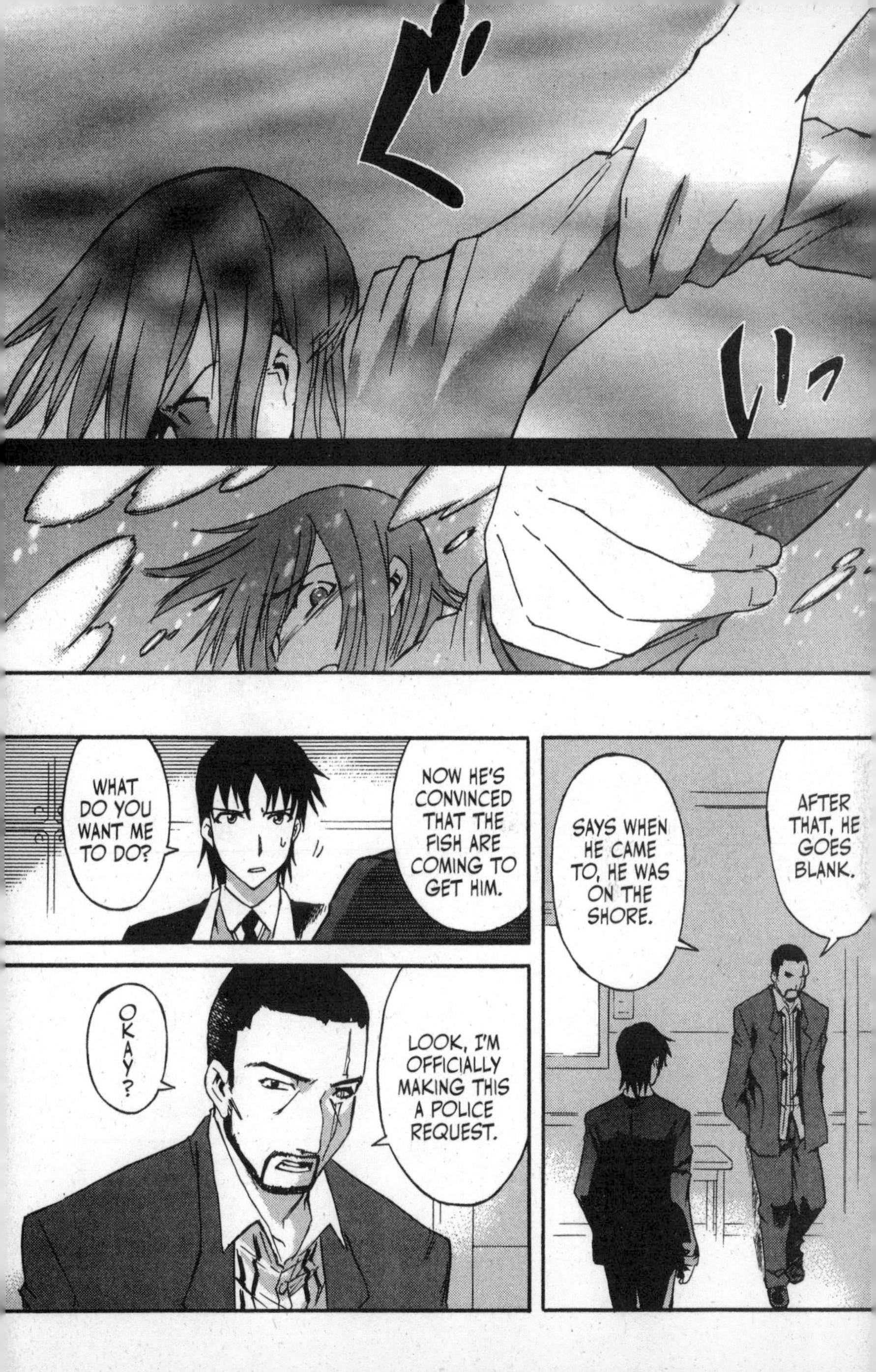
ぐ
いっ
AFTER THAT, HE GOES BLANK.
SAYS WHEN HE CAME TO, HE WAS ON THE SHORE.
NOW HE'S CONVINCED THAT THE FISH ARE COMING TO GET HIM.
WHAT DO YOU WANT ME TO DO?
LOOK, I'M OFFICIALLY MAKING THIS A POLICE REQUEST.
OKAY?

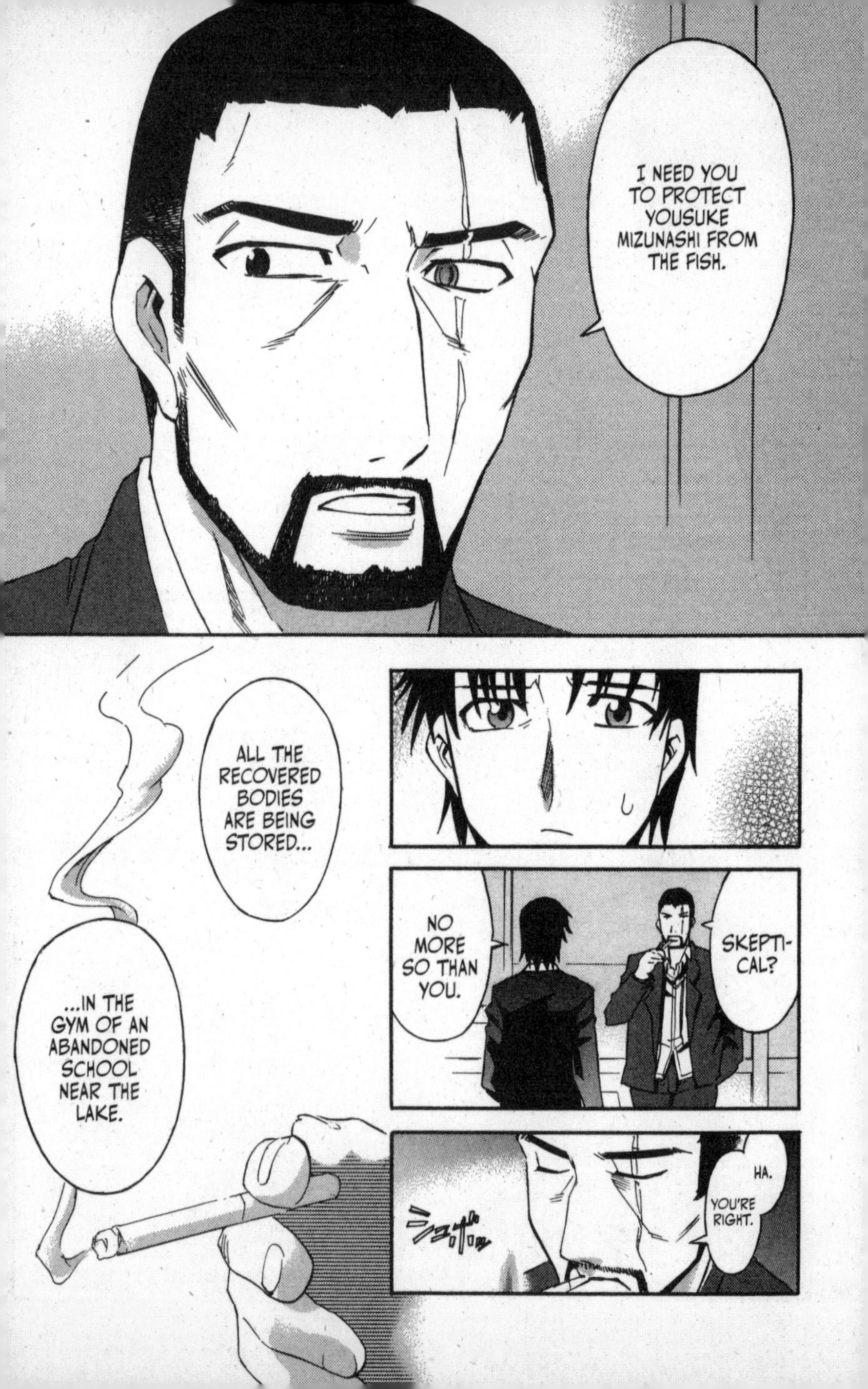
I NEED YOU TO PROTECT YOUSUKE MIZUNASHI FROM THE FISH.
SKEPTICAL?
NO MORE SO THAN YOU.
HA.
YOU'RE RIGHT.
ALL THE RECOVERED BODIES ARE BEING STORED...
...IN THE GYM OF AN ABANDONED SCHOOL NEAR THE LAKE.

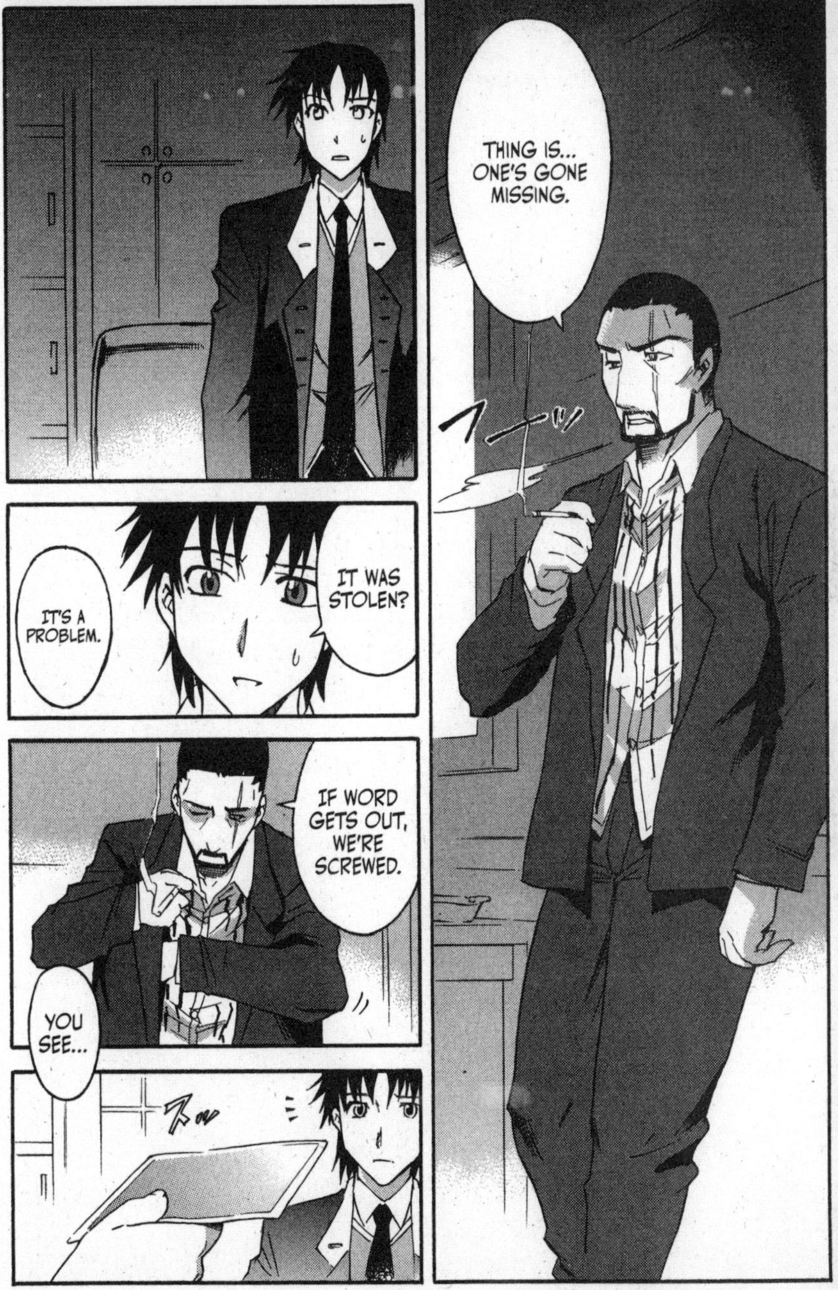
THING IS... ONE'S GONE MISSING.
IT WAS STOLEN?
IT'S A PROBLEM.
IF WORD GETS OUT, WE'RE SCREWED.
YOU SEE...

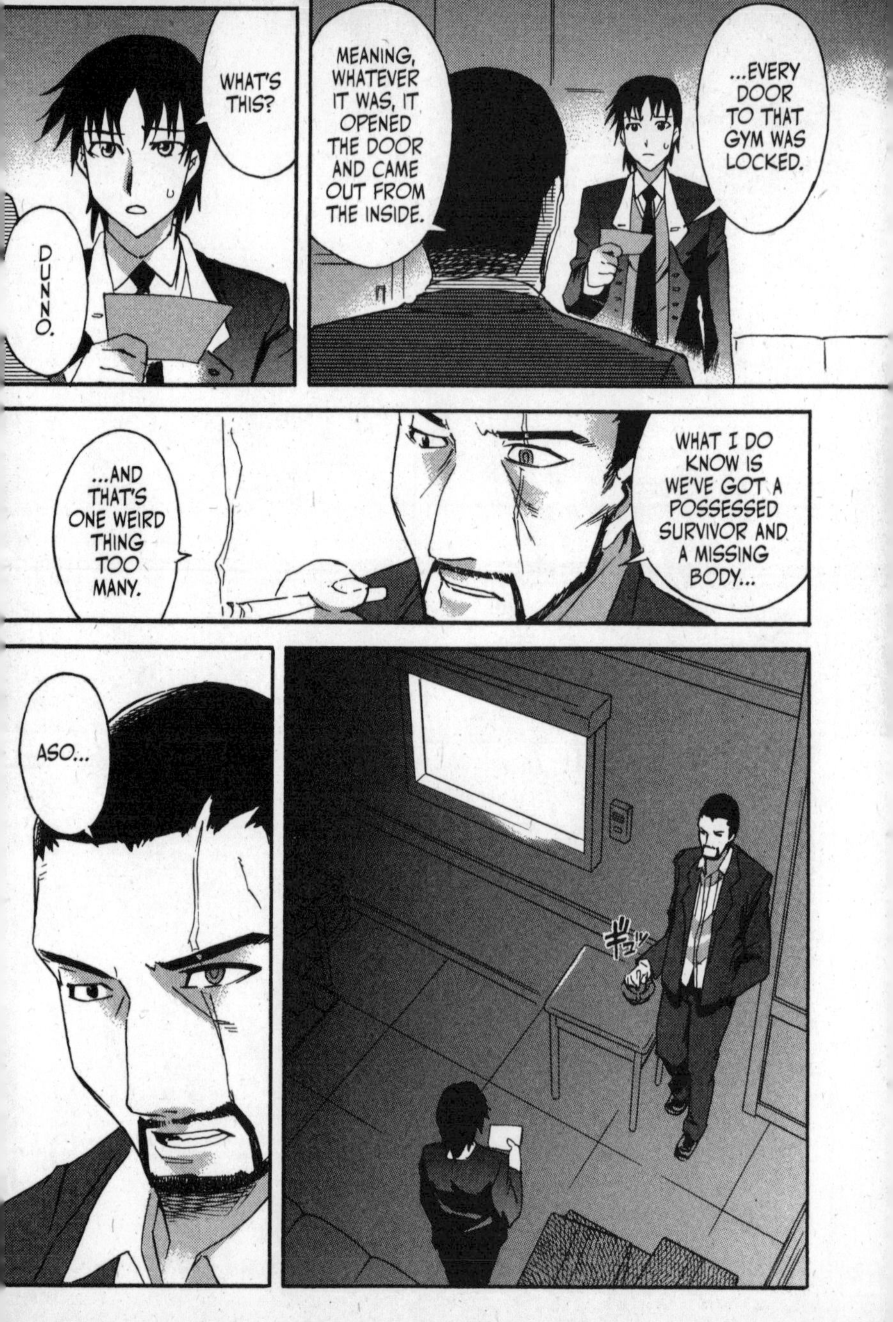
...EVERY DOOR TO THAT GYM WAS LOCKED.
MEANING, WHATEVER IT WAS, IT OPENED THE DOOR AND CAME OUT FROM THE INSIDE.
WHAT'S THIS?
DUNNO.
WHAT I DO KNOW IS WE'VE GOT A POSSESSED SURVIVOR AND A MISSING BODY...
...AND THAT'S ONE WEIRD THING TOO MANY.
ギュッ
ASO...

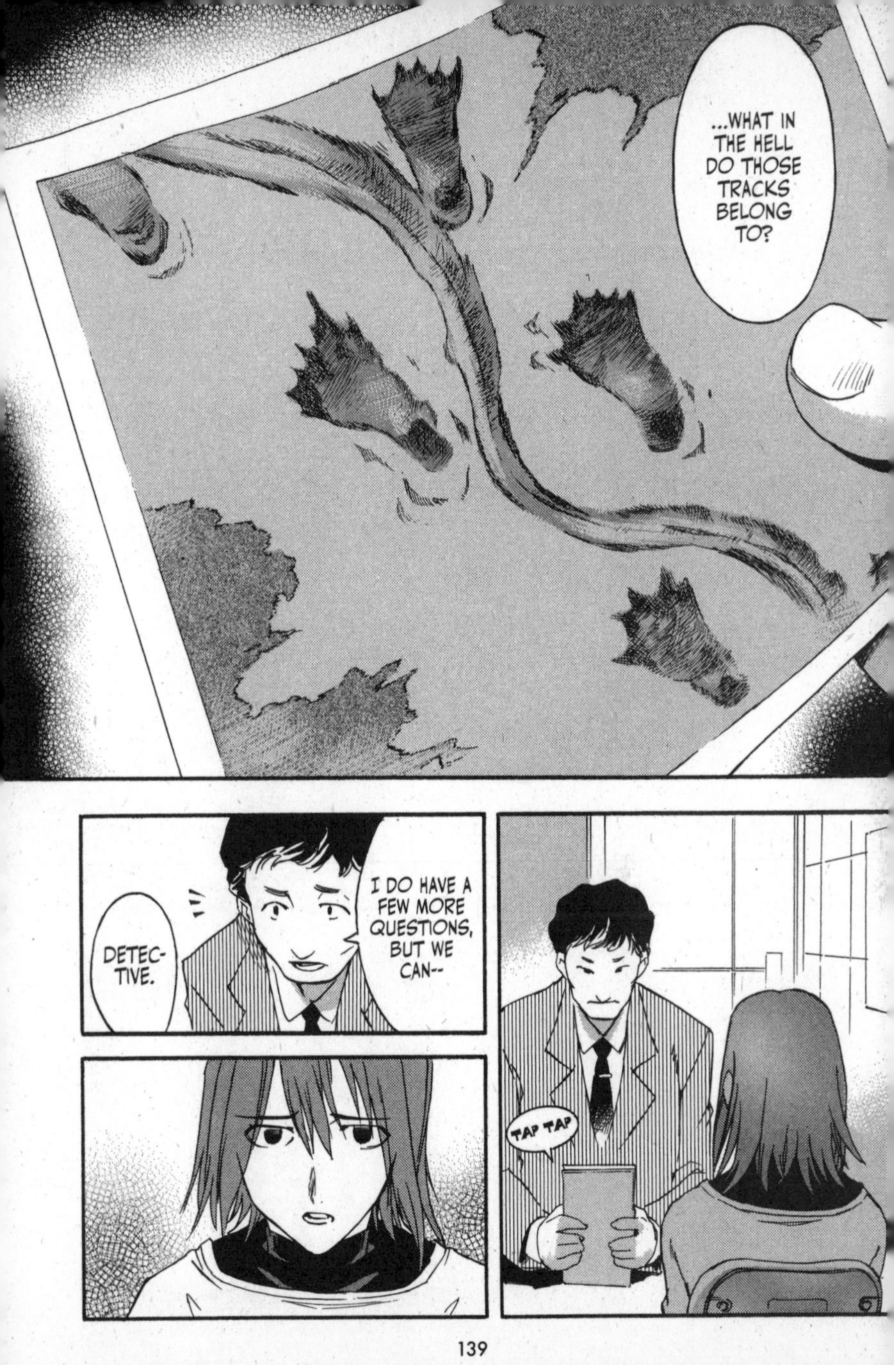

...WHAT IN THE HELL DO THOSE TRACKS BELONG TO?
TAP TAP
I DO HAVE A FEW MORE QUESTIONS, BUT WE CAN--
DETEC-TIVE.

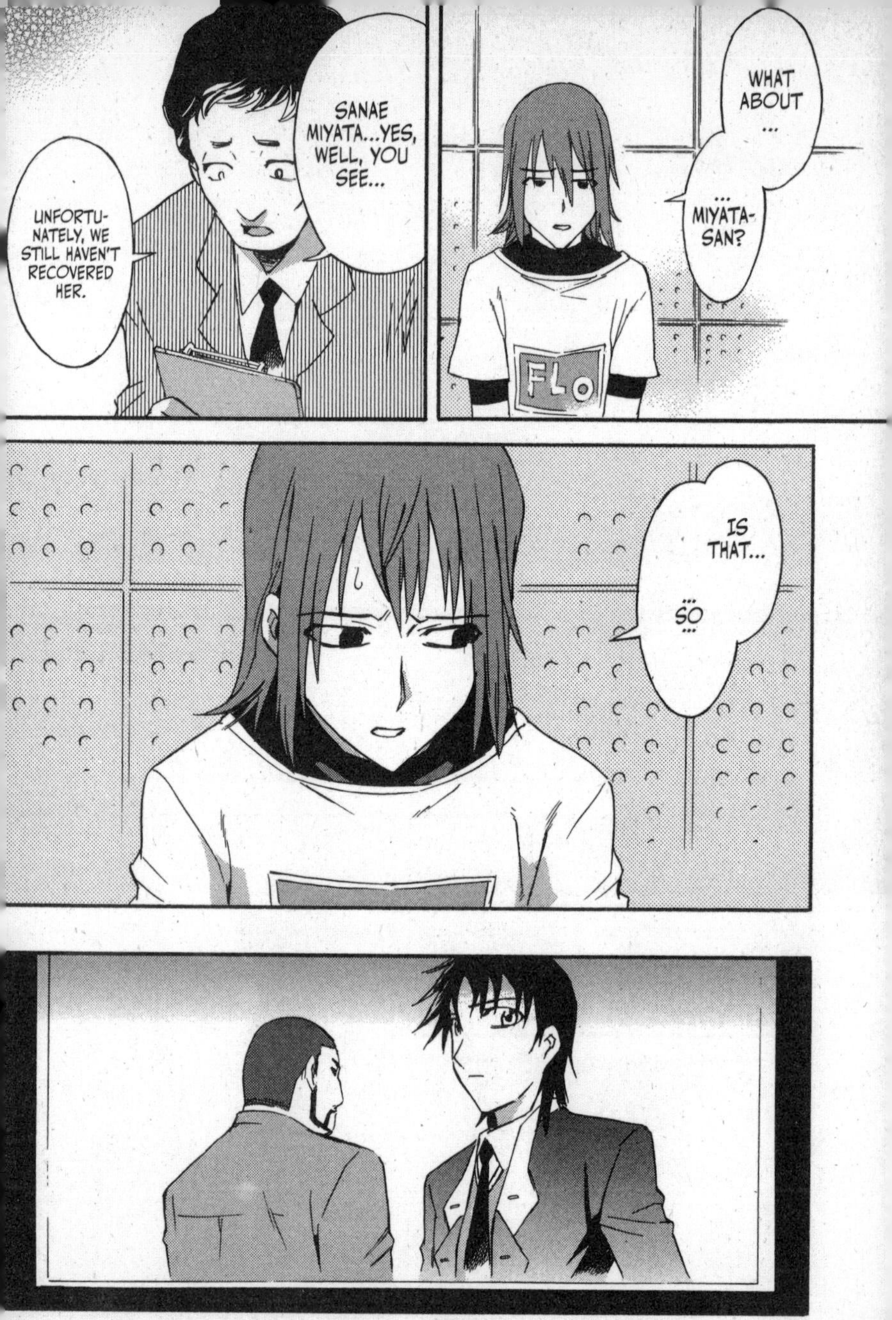
WHAT ABOUT ...
... MIYATA-SAN?
SANAE MIYATA...YES, WELL, YOU SEE...
UNFORTU-NATELY, WE STILL HAVEN'T RECOVERED HER.
IS THAT... ...SO...

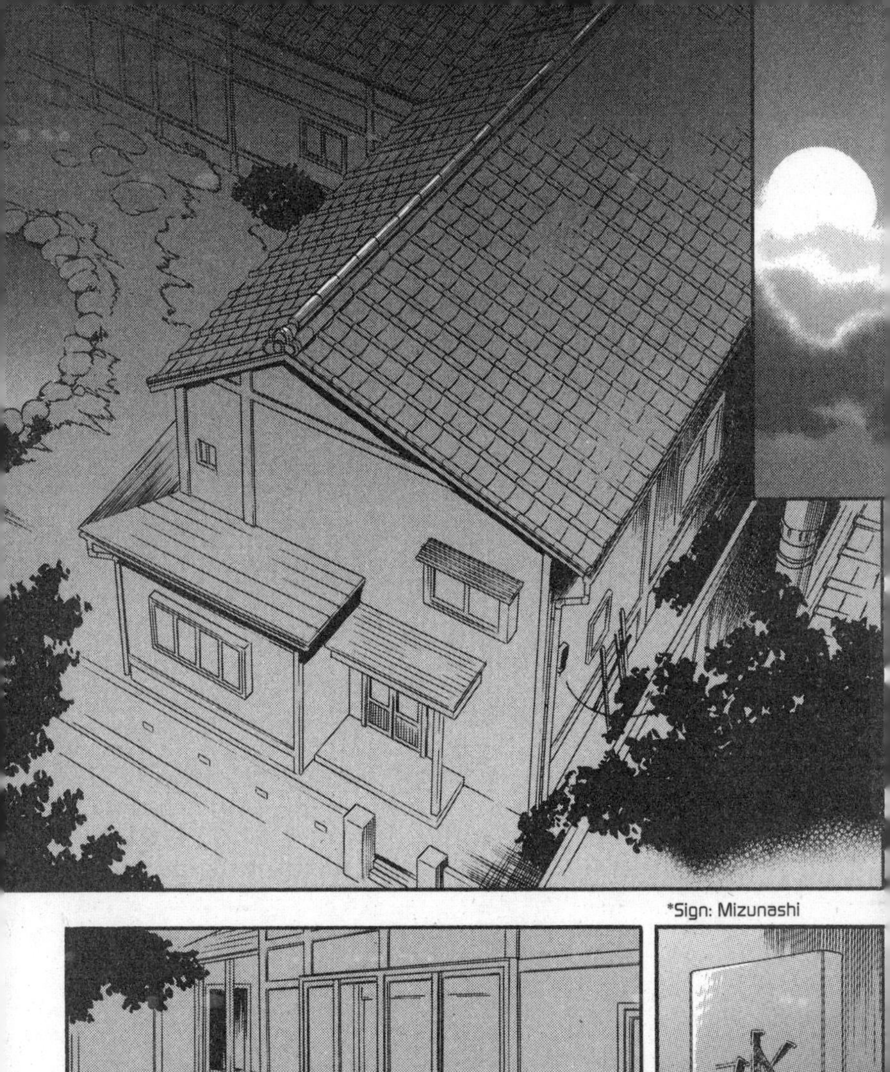

*Sign: Mizunashi

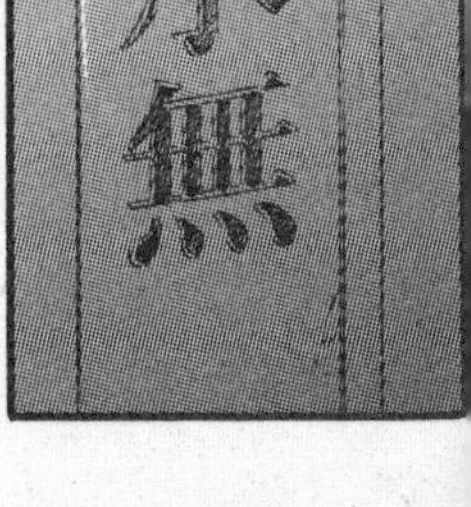
水無

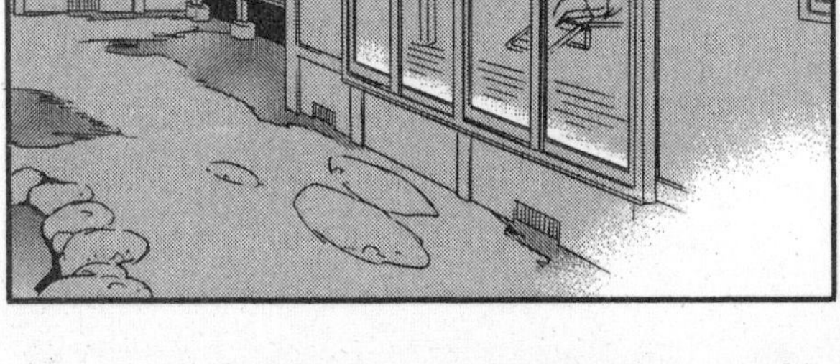

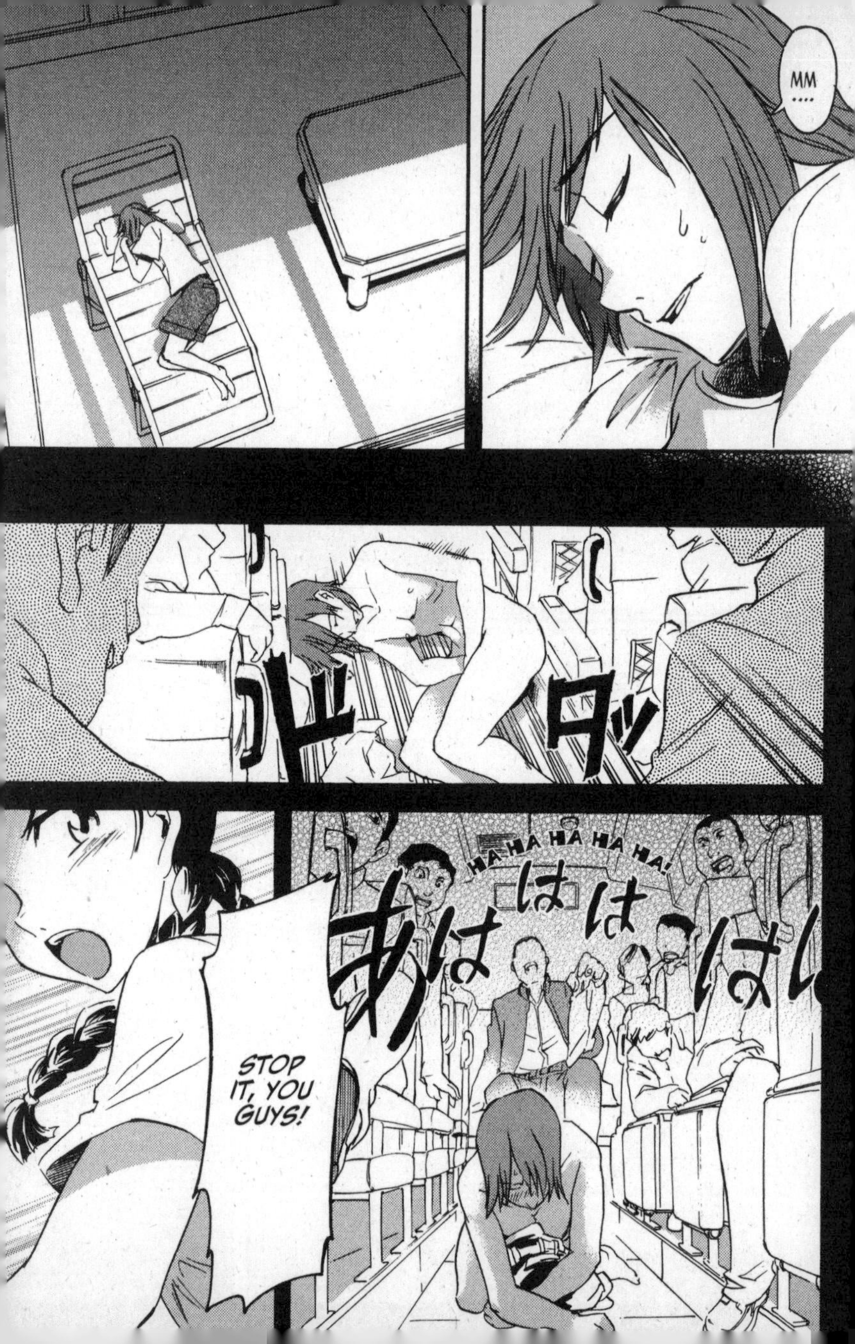
MM....
HA HA HA HA HA!
STOP IT, YOU GUYS!

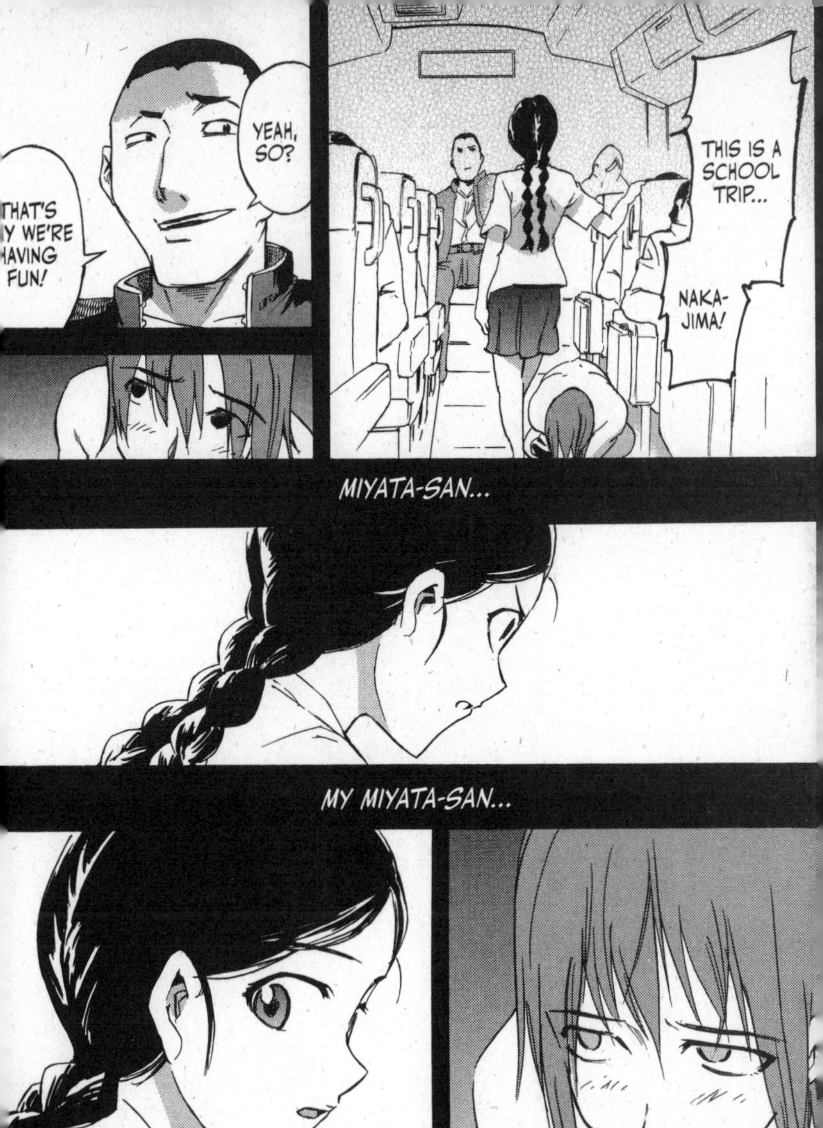
THIS IS A SCHOOL TRIP...
NAKA-JIMA!
YEAH, SO?
THAT'S Y WE'RE HAVING FUN!
MIYATA-SAN...
MY MIYATA-SAN...

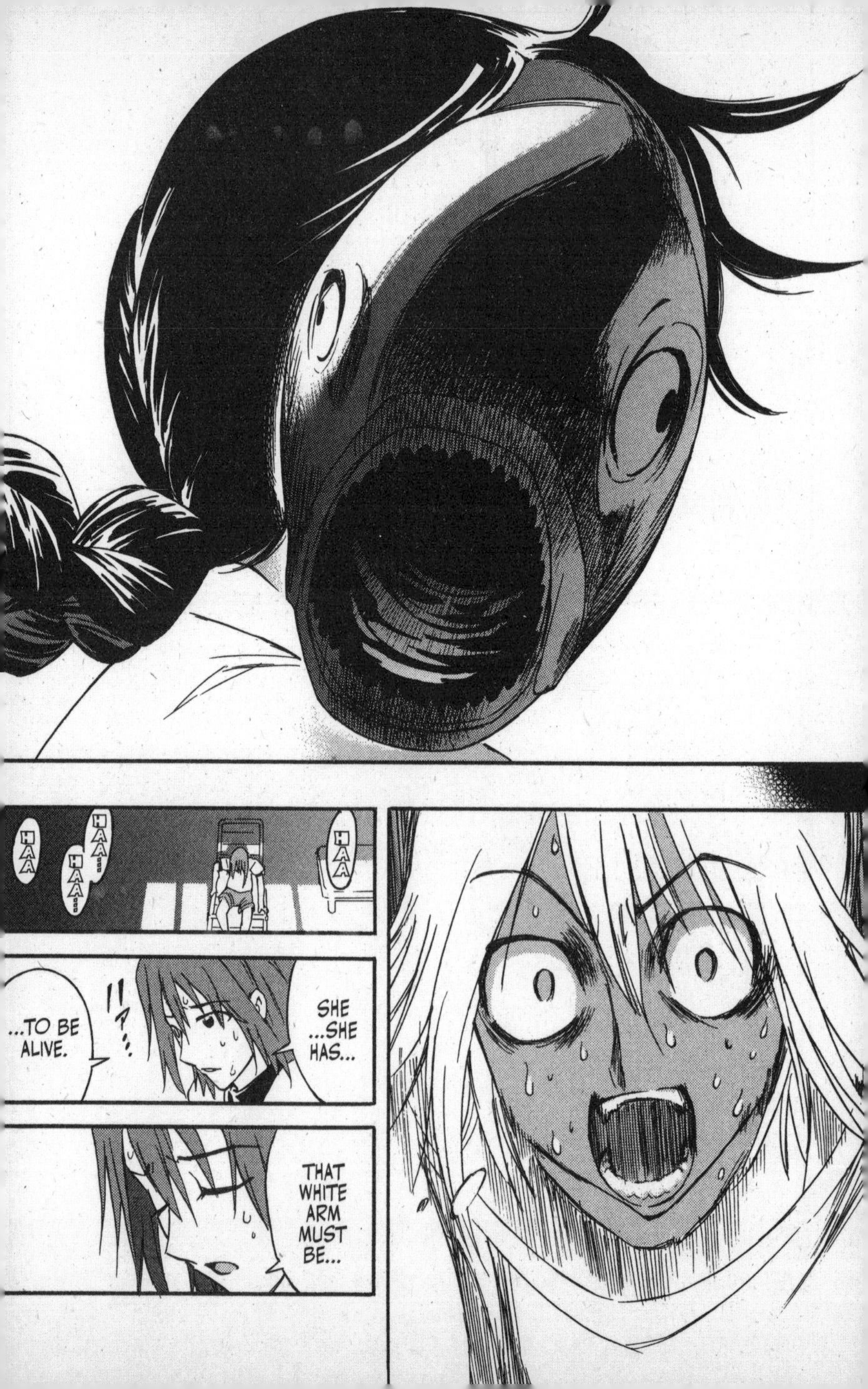
HAA
HAA...
HAA...
HAA
SHE ...SHE HAS...
...TO BE ALIVE.
THAT WHITE ARM MUST BE...

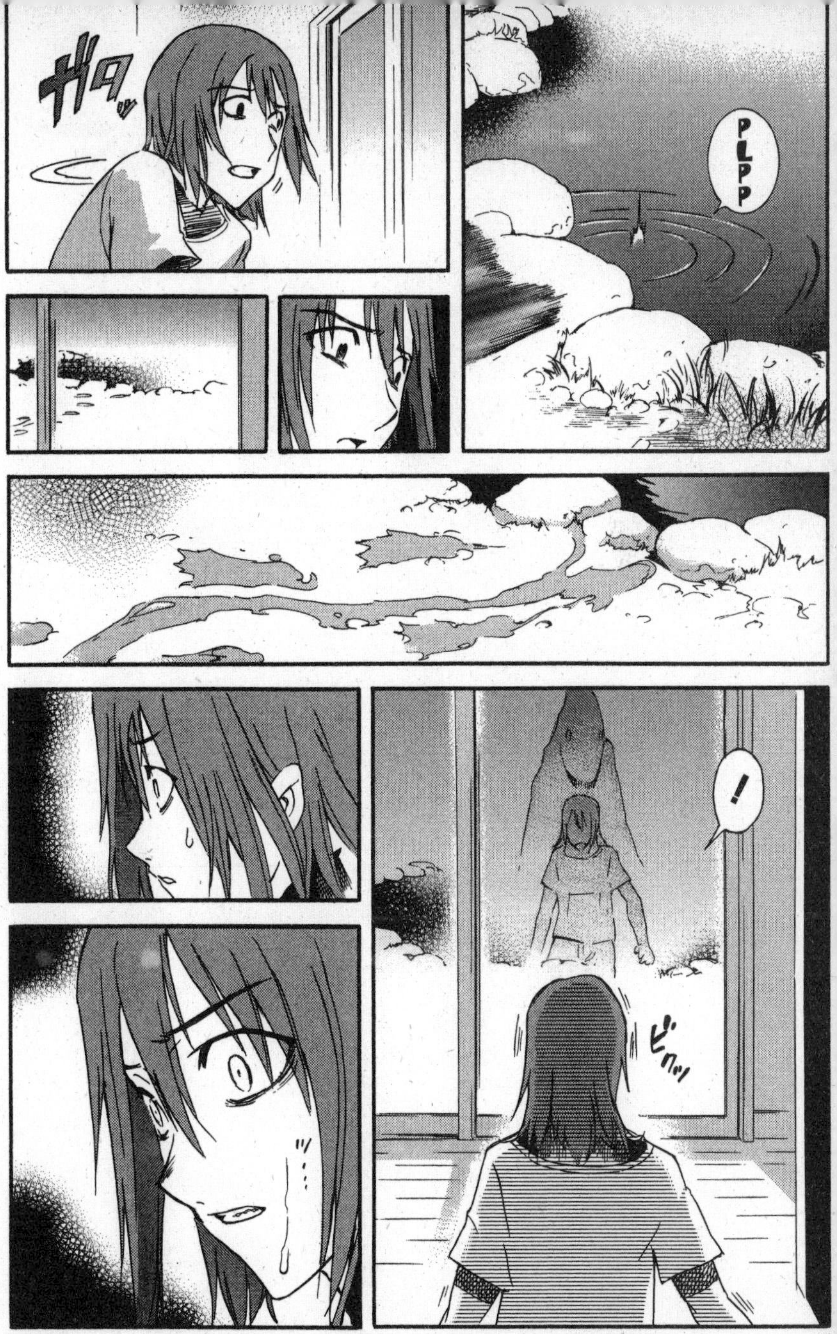
PLPP
ガタッ
!
ビクッ

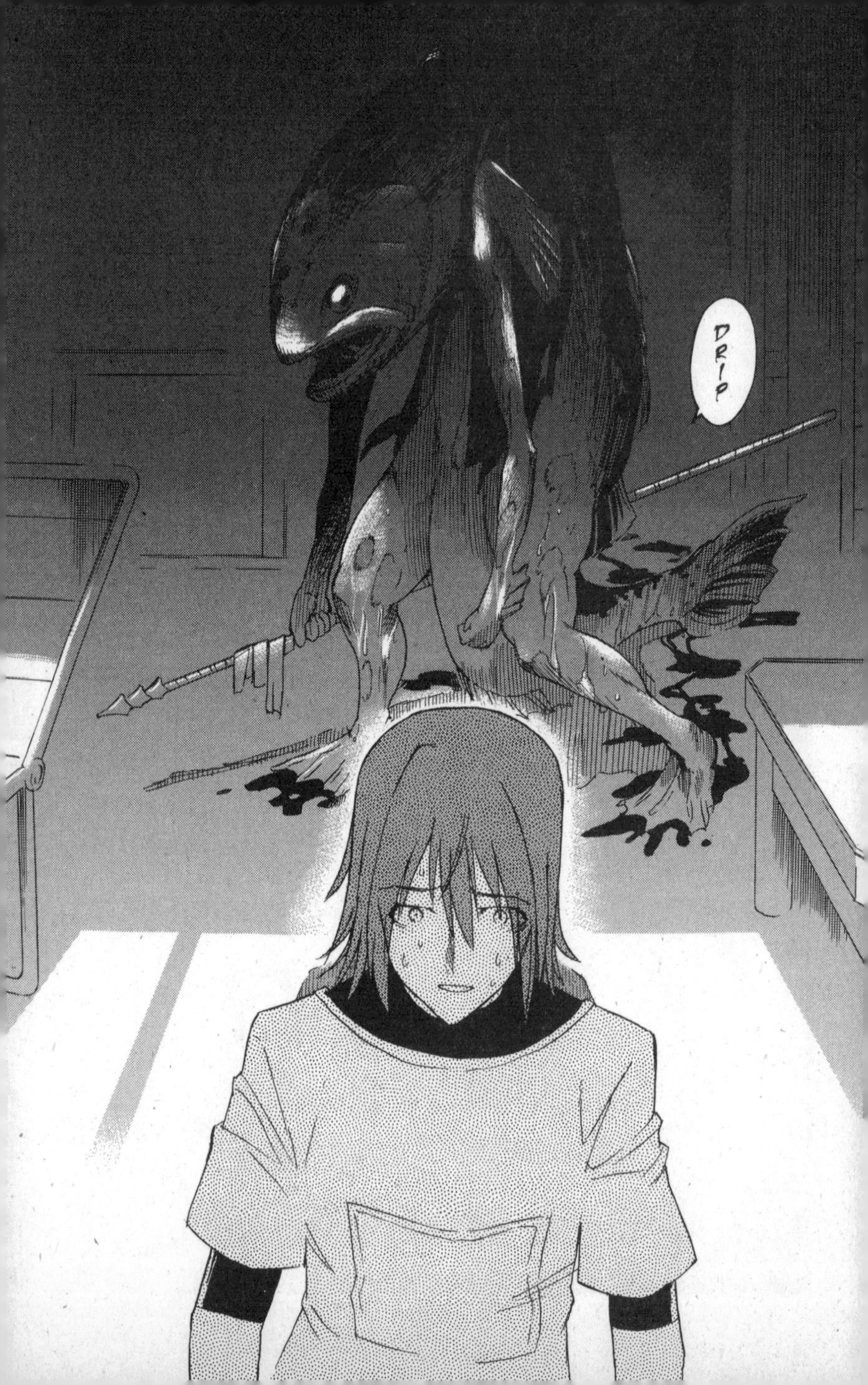
DRIP

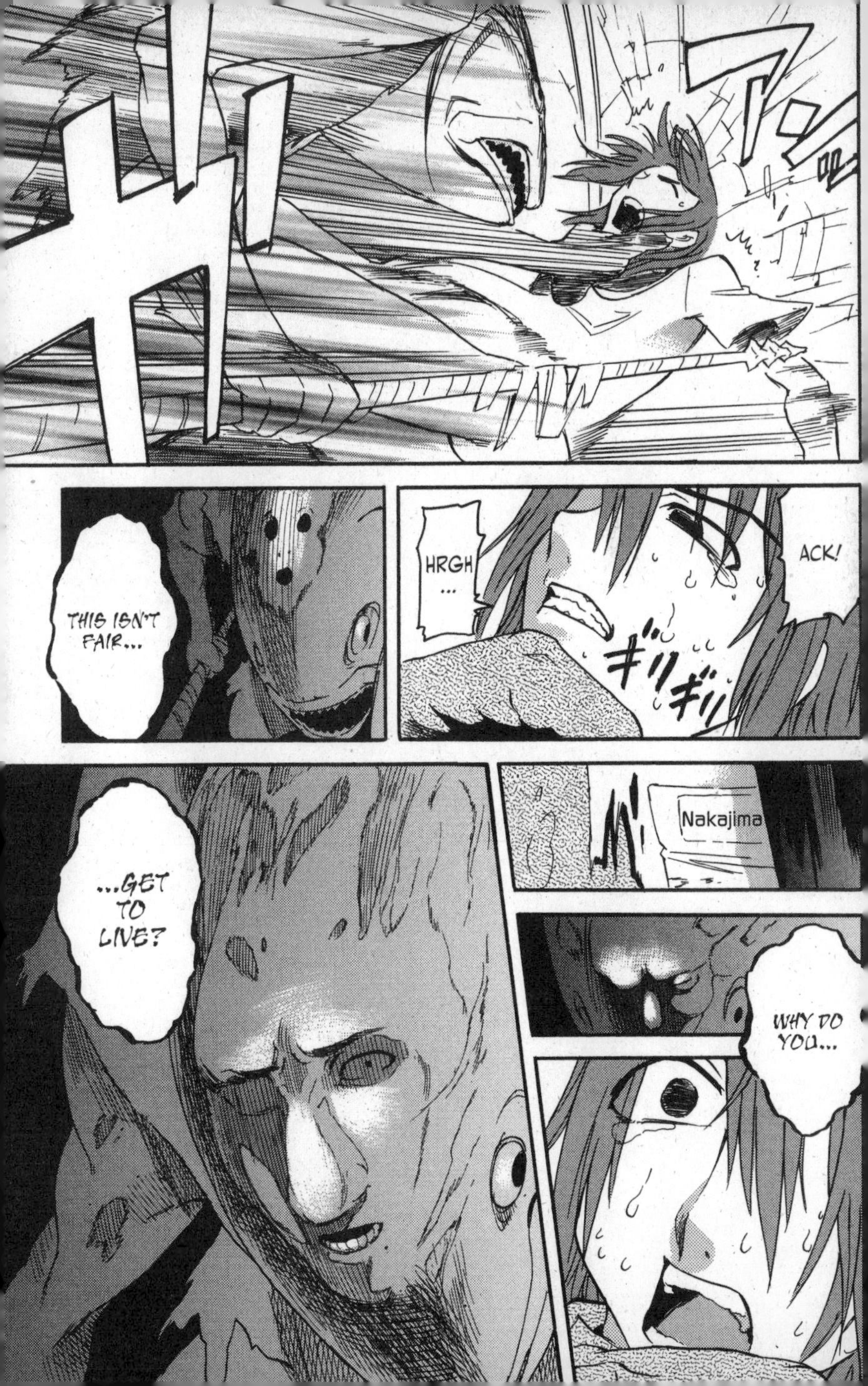
ACK!
HRGH ...
ギリギリ
THIS ISN'T FAIR...
Nakajima
WHY DO YOU...
...GET TO LIVE?

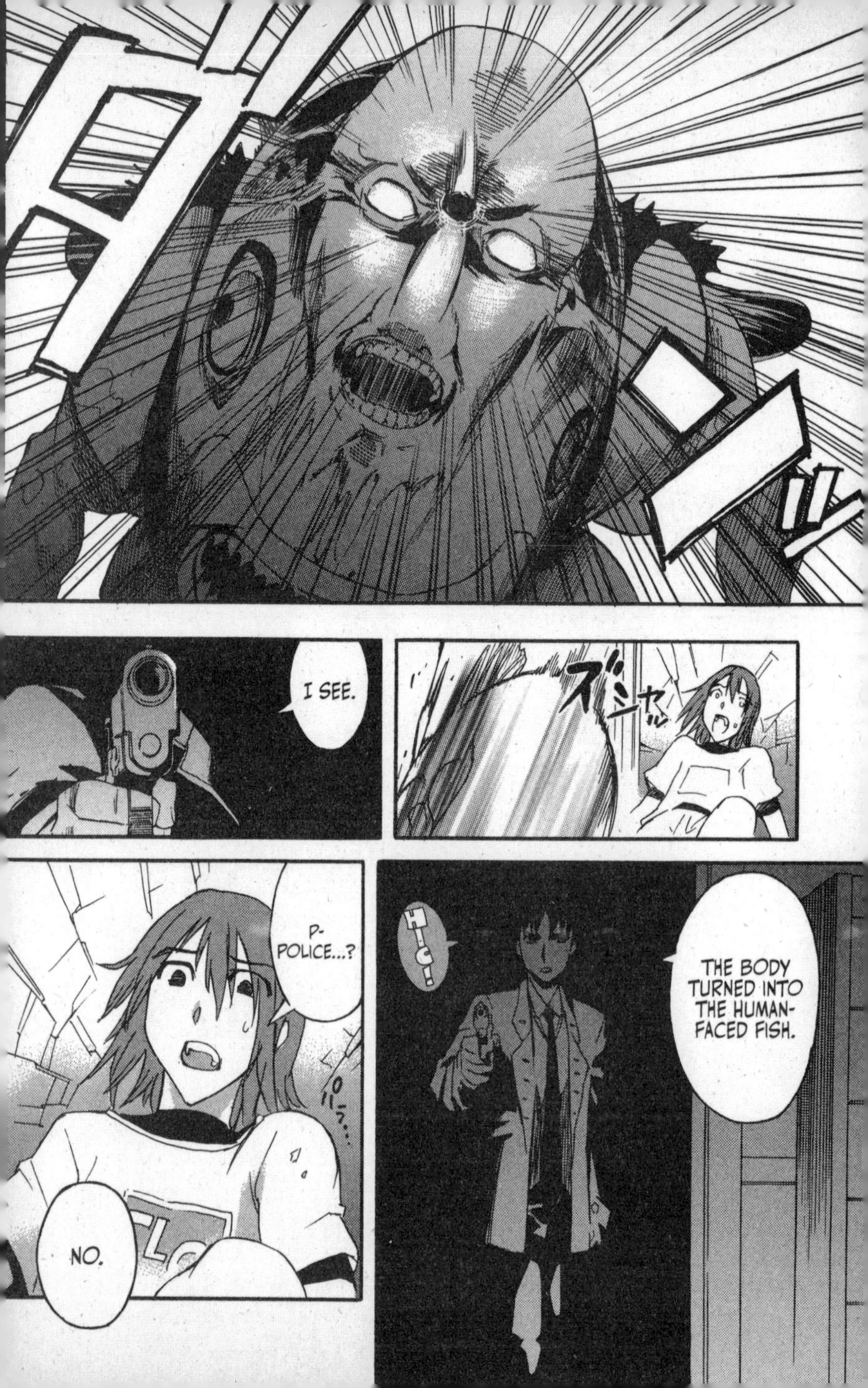
I SEE.
THE BODY TURNED INTO THE HUMAN-FACED FISH.
HIC!
P-POLICE...?
NO.

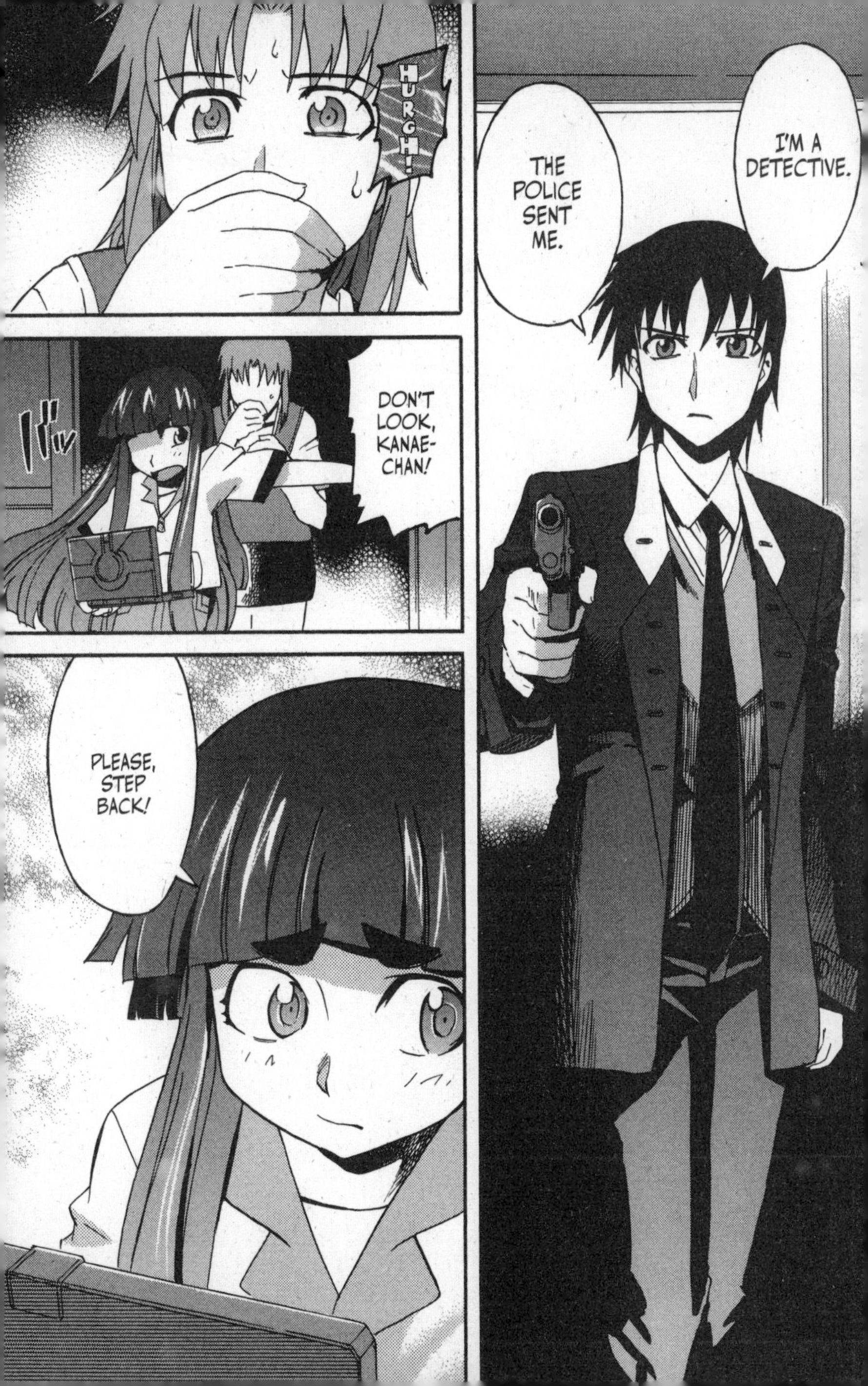
I'M A DETECTIVE.
THE POLICE SENT ME.
HURGH!
DON'T LOOK, KANAE-CHAN!
バッ
PLEASE, STEP BACK!

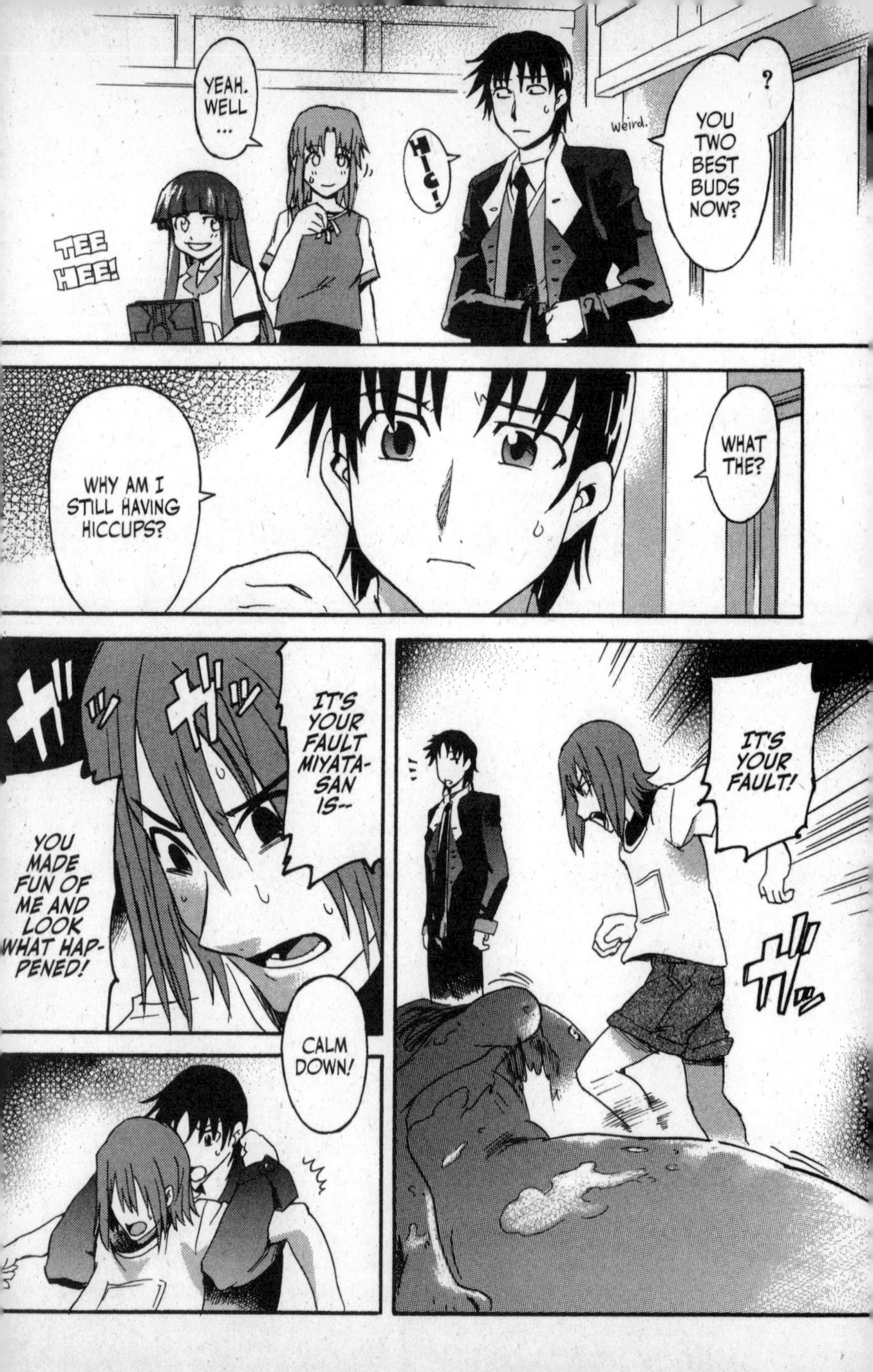
?
YOU TWO BEST BUDS NOW?
Weird.
HIC!
YEAH. WELL ...
TEE HEE!
WHAT THE?
WHY AM I STILL HAVING HICCUPS?
IT'S YOUR FAULT!
IT'S YOUR FAULT MIYATA-SAN IS--
YOU MADE FUN OF ME AND LOOK WHAT HAP-PENED!
CALM DOWN!

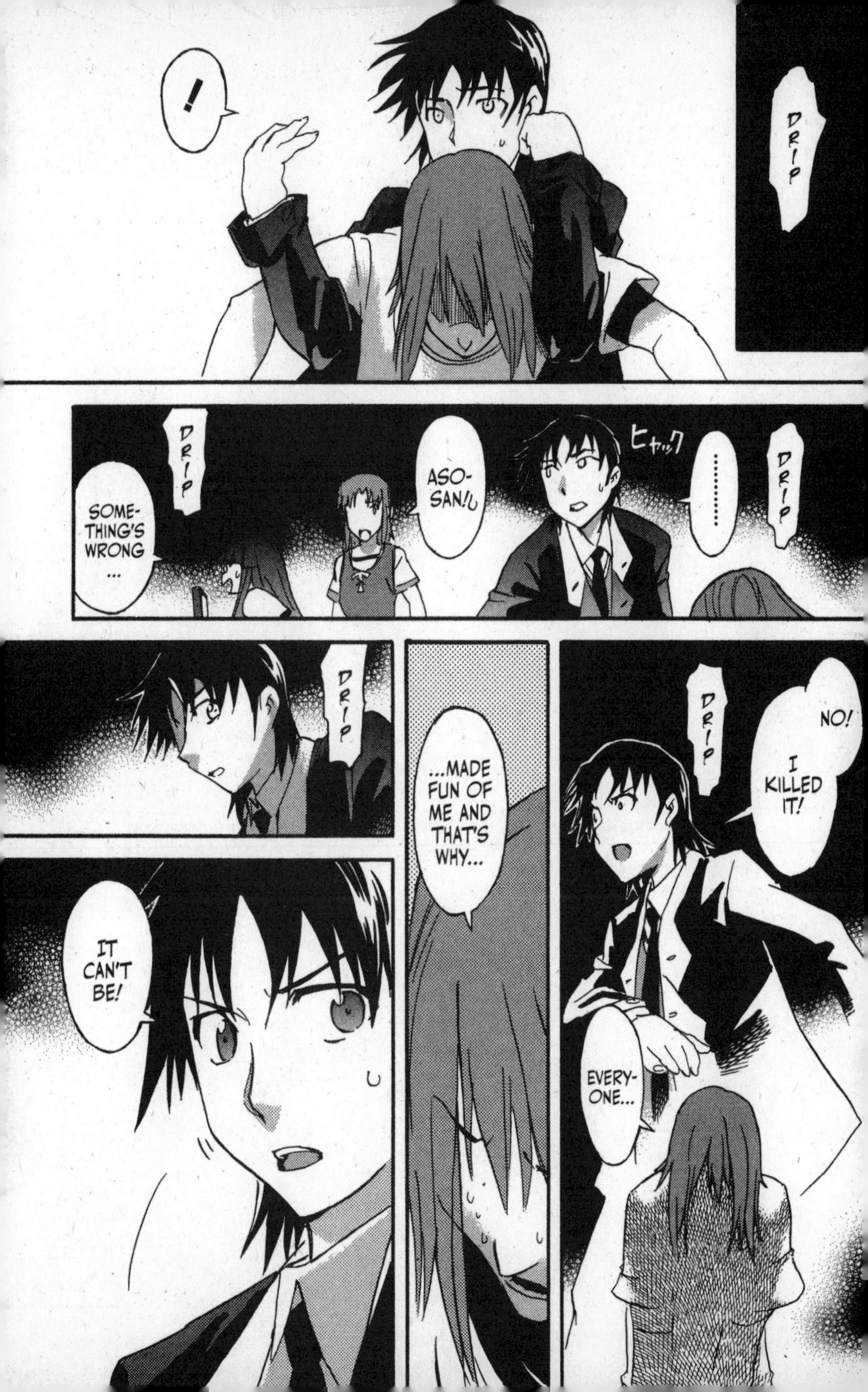
DRIP
!
DRIP
......
ASO-SAN!
DRIP
SOME-THING'S WRONG ...
NO!
I KILLED IT!
DRIP
EVERY-ONE...
...MADE FUN OF ME AND THAT'S WHY...
DRIP
IT CAN'T BE!

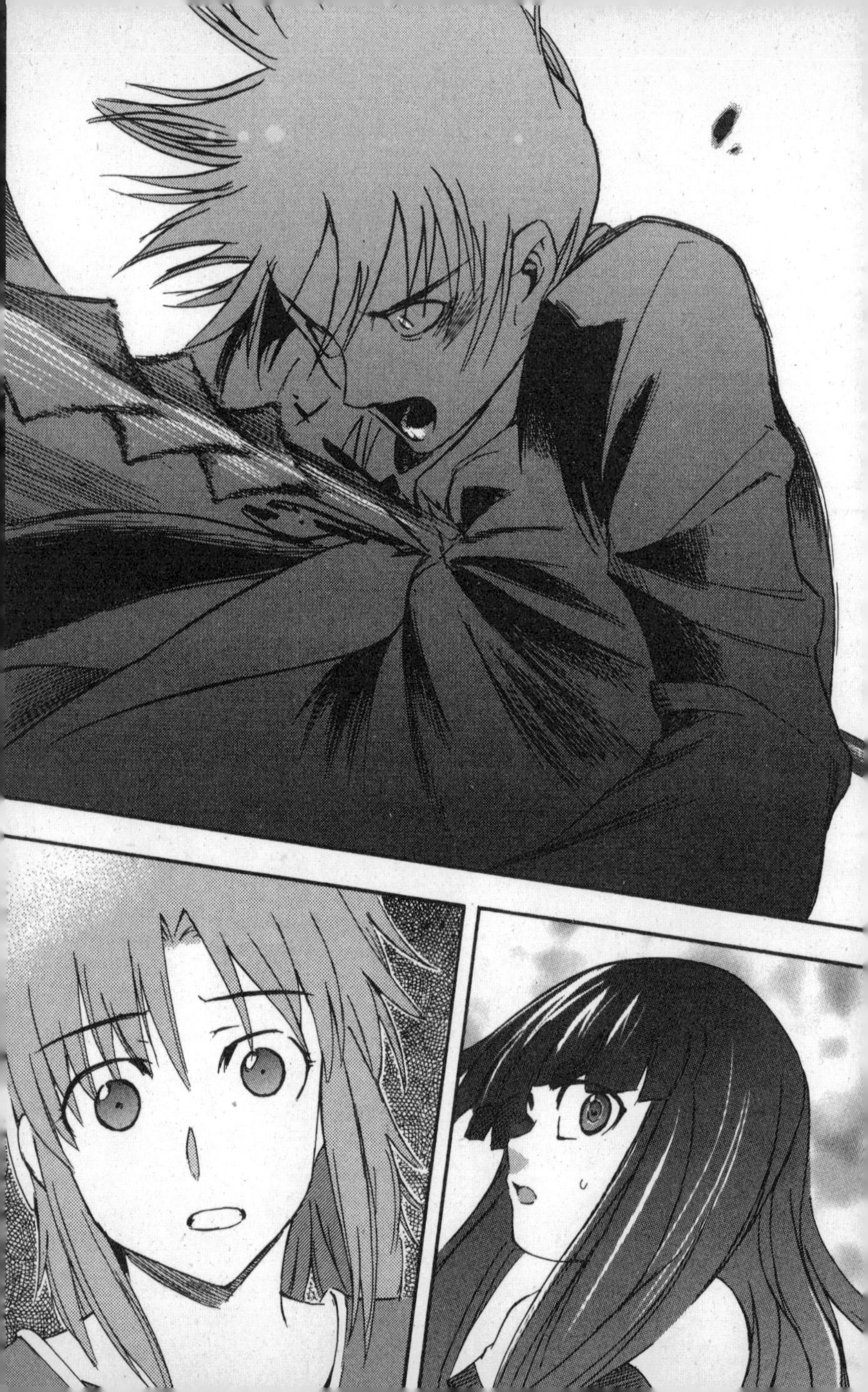

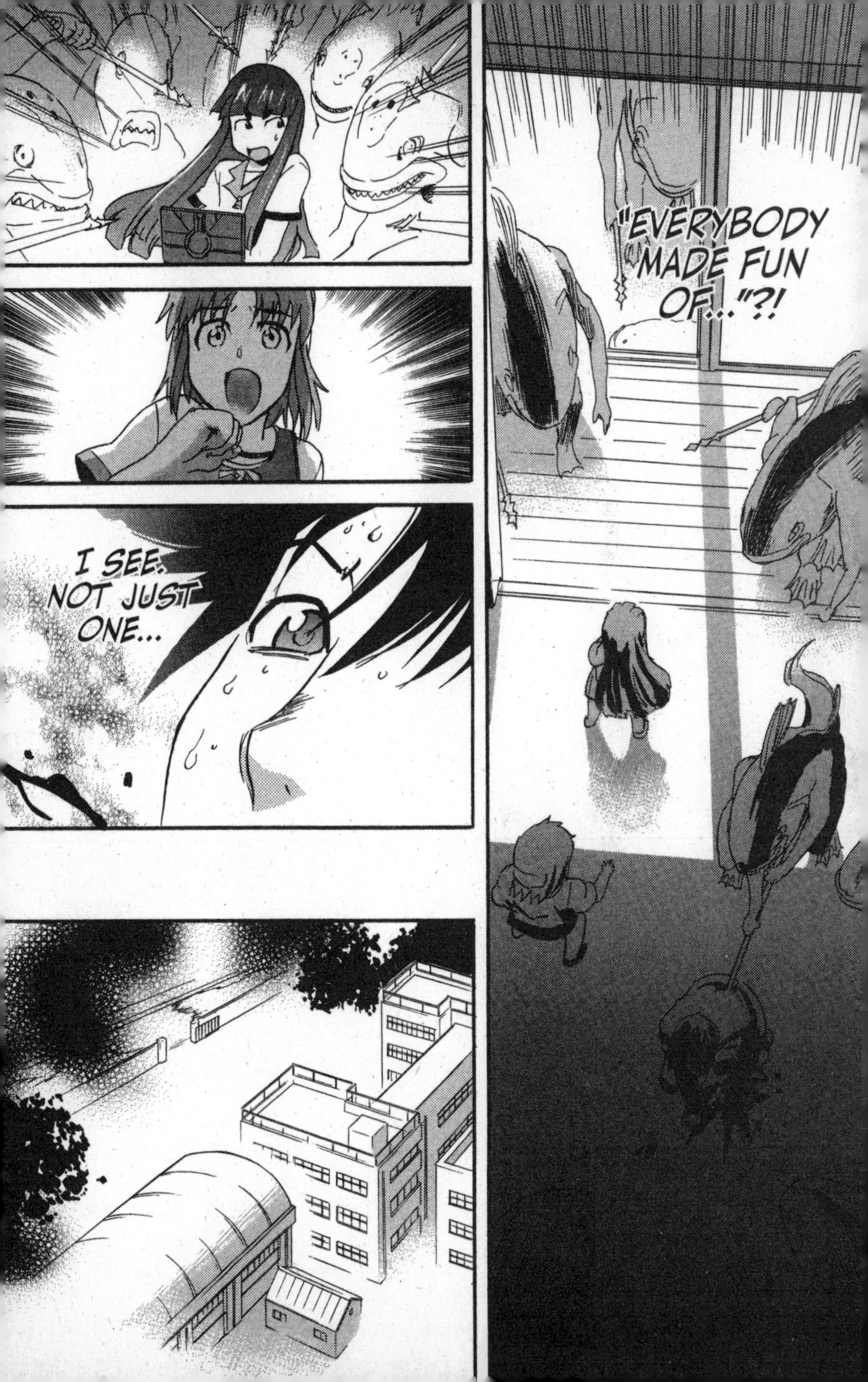
"EVERYBODY MADE FUN OF..."?!
I SEE. NOT JUST ONE...

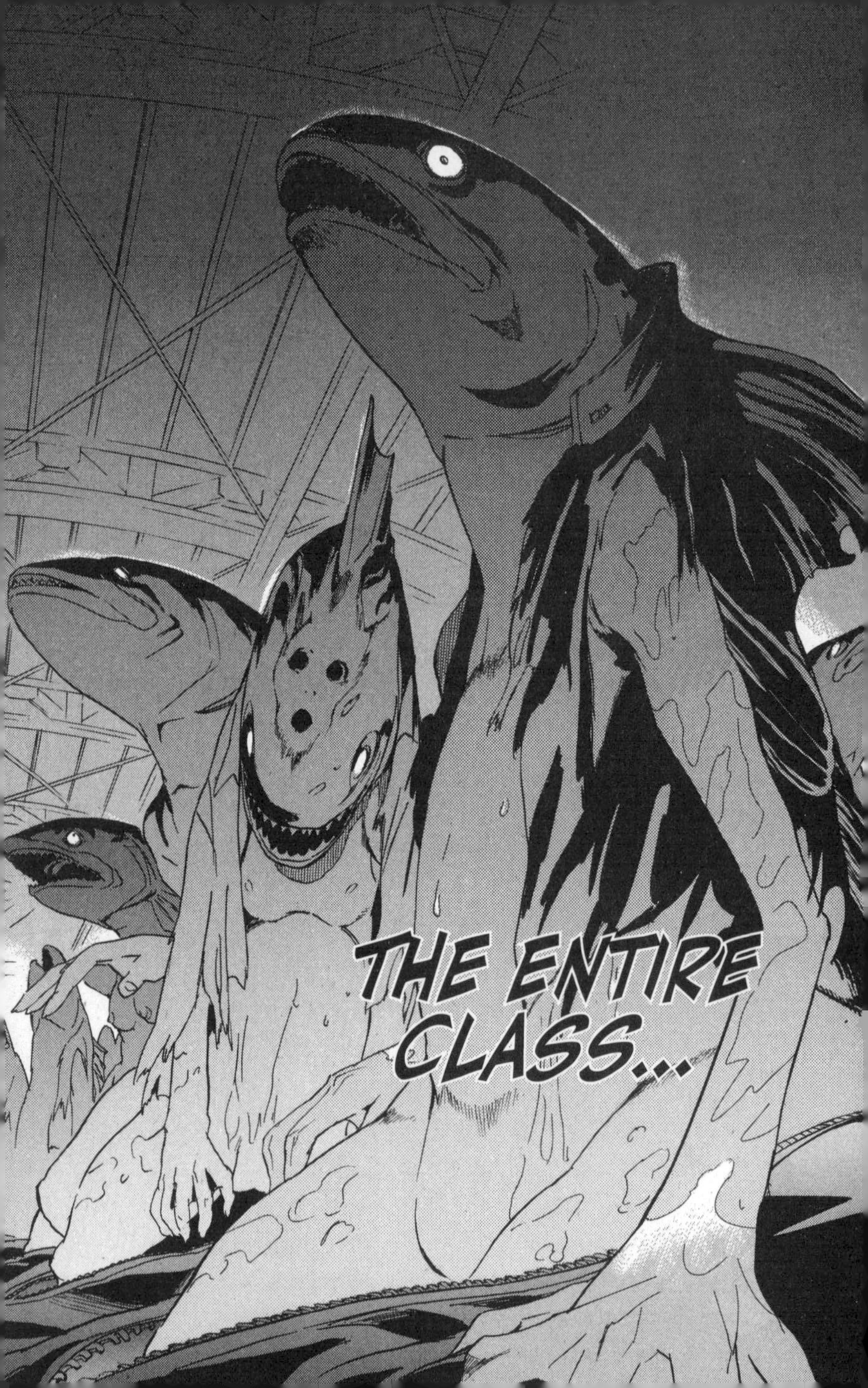
THE ENTIRE CLASS...

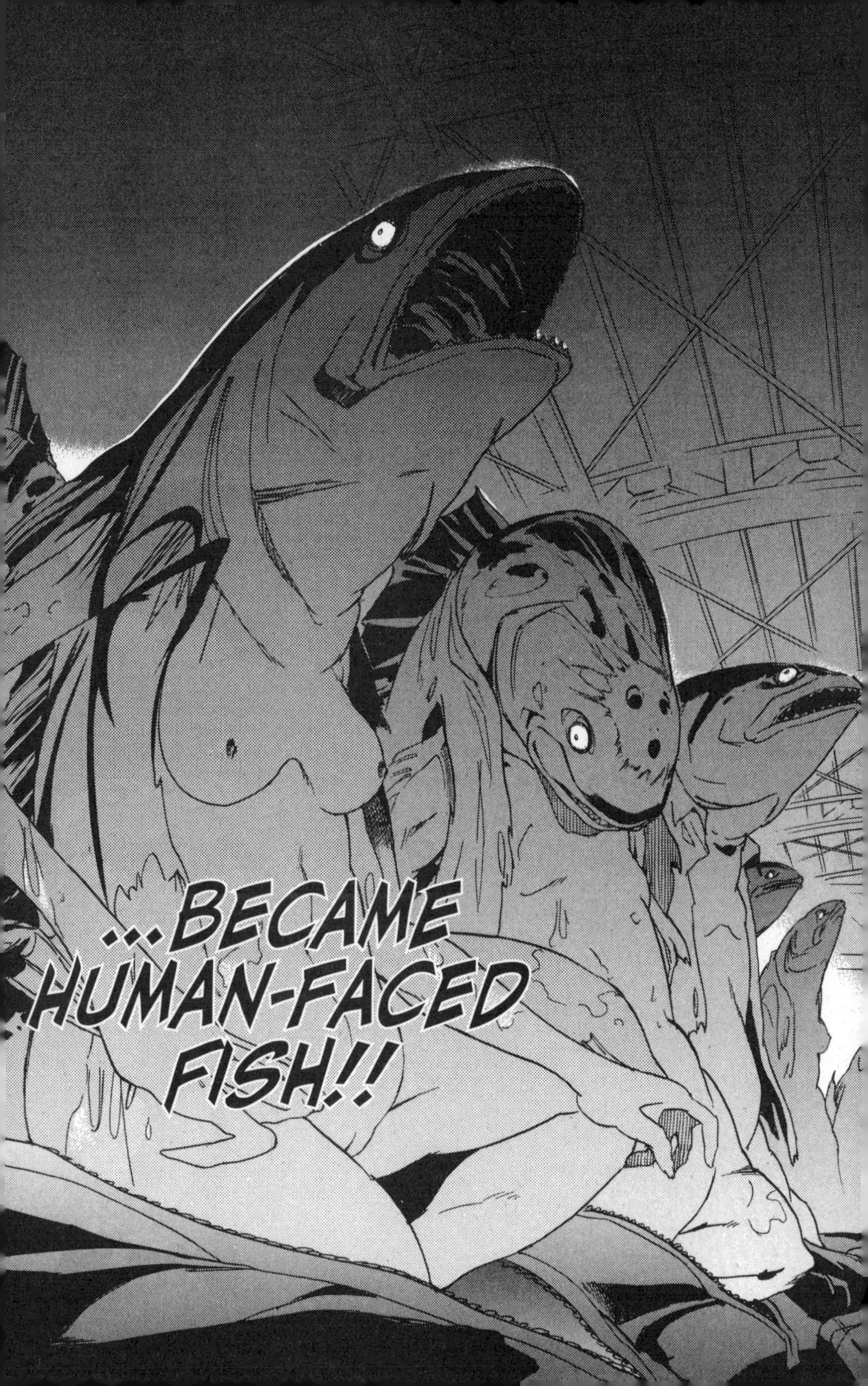
...BECAME HUMAN-FACED FISH!!

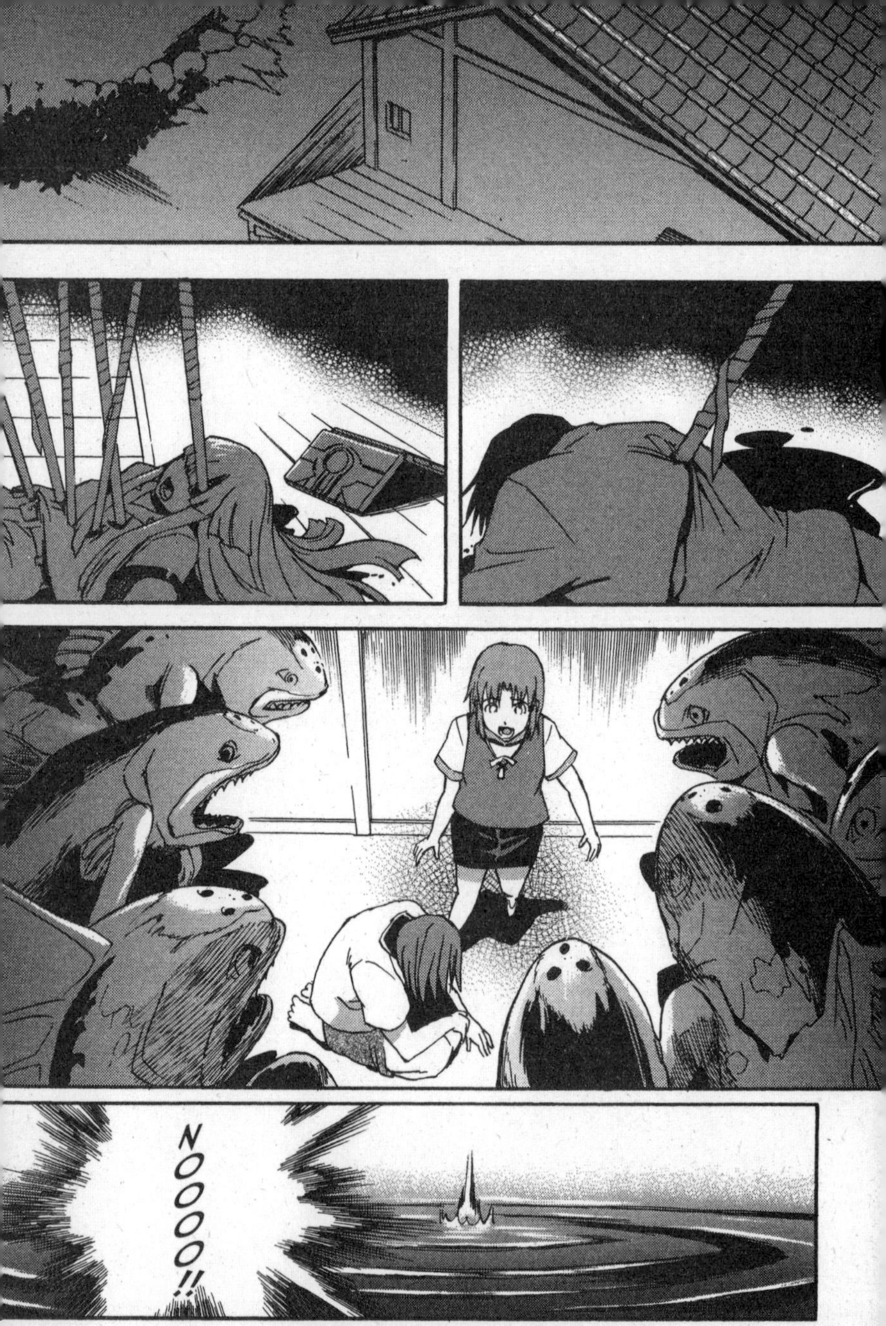
NOOOOO!!

Human-Faced Fish – Part I - End

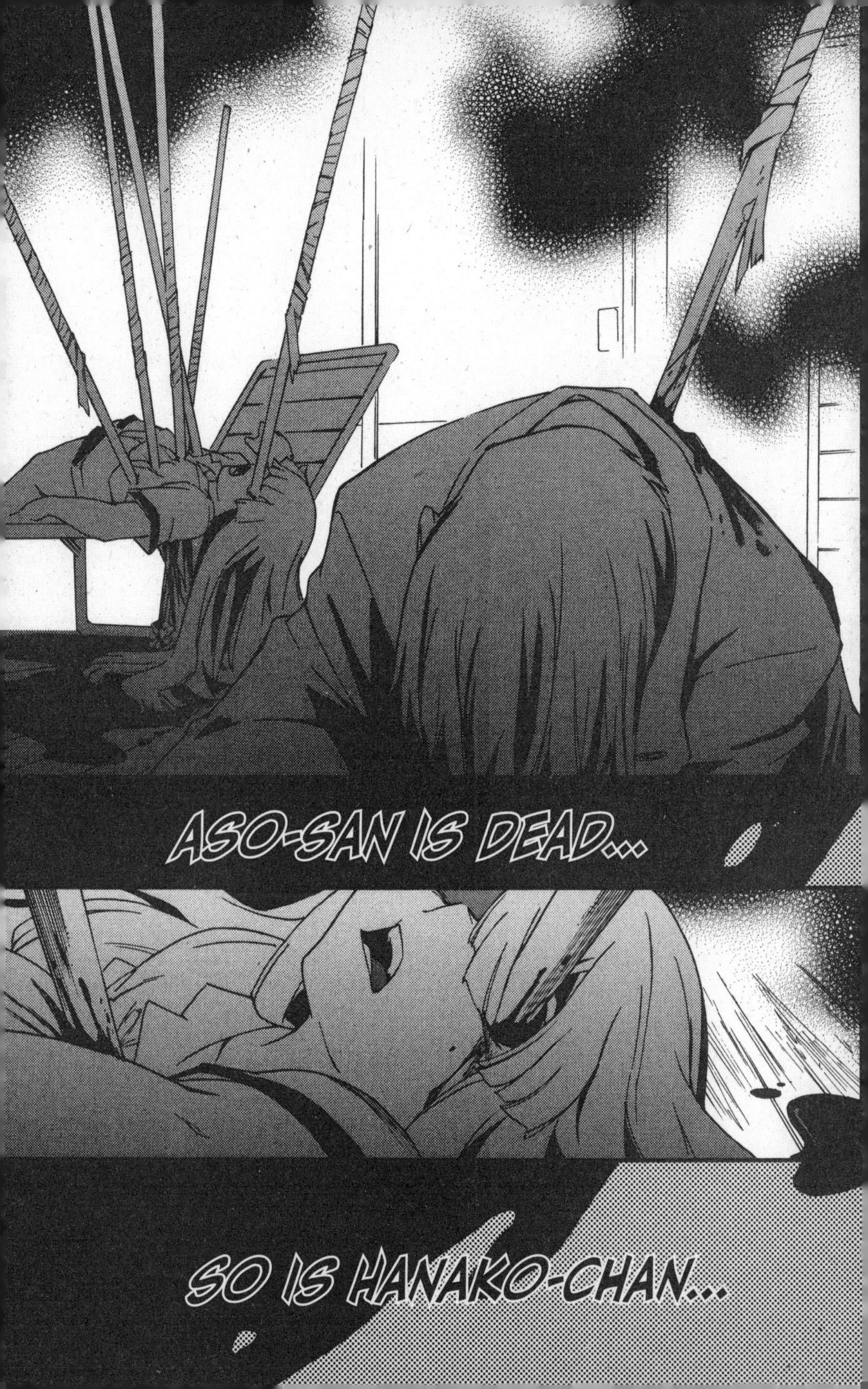
ASO-SAN IS DEAD...
SO IS HANAKO-CHAN...

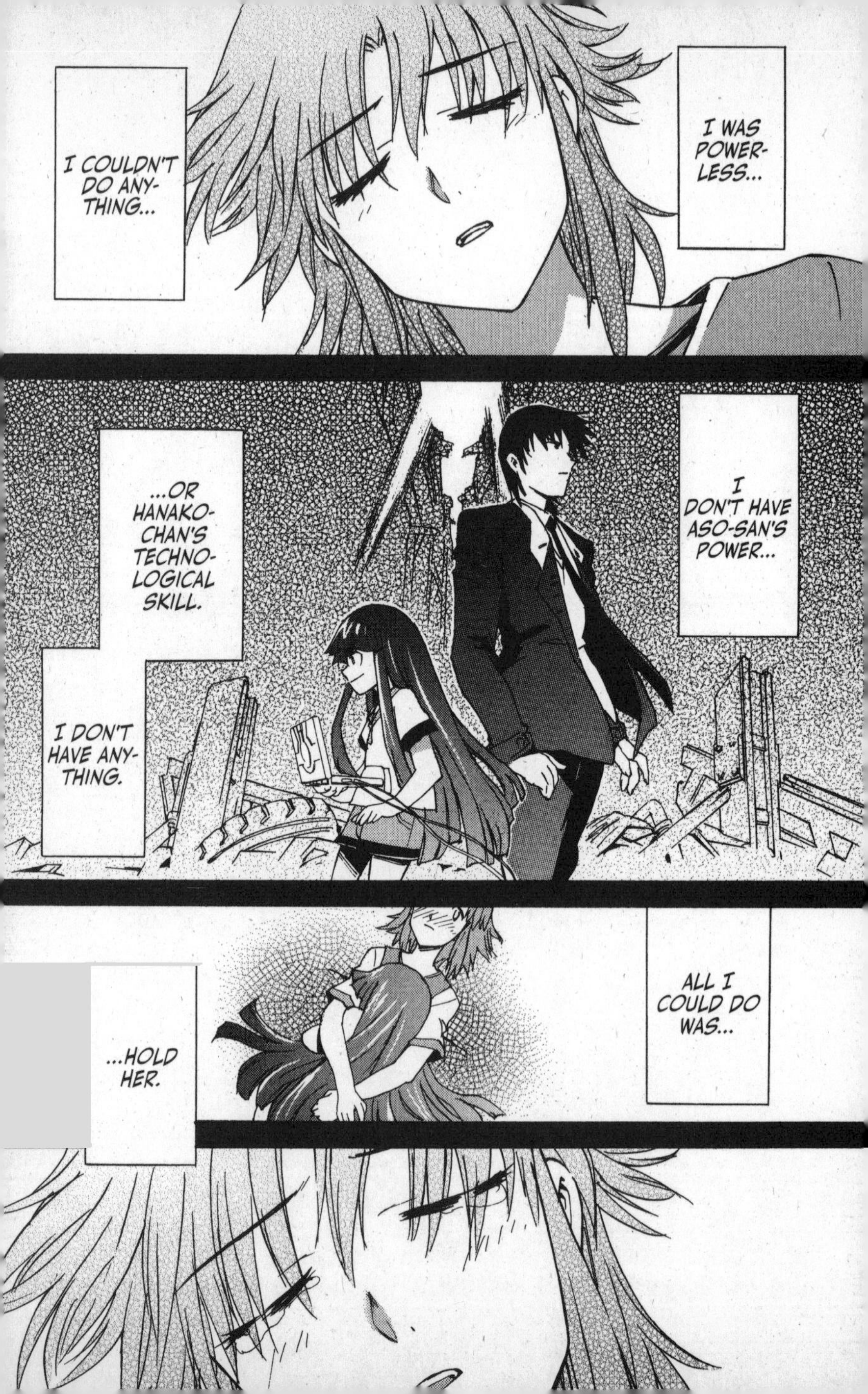
I WAS POWER-LESS...
I COULDN'T DO ANY-THING...
I DON'T HAVE ASO-SAN'S POWER...
...OR HANAKO-CHAN'S TECHNO-LOGICAL SKILL.
I DON'T HAVE ANY-THING.
ALL I COULD DO WAS...
...HOLD HER.

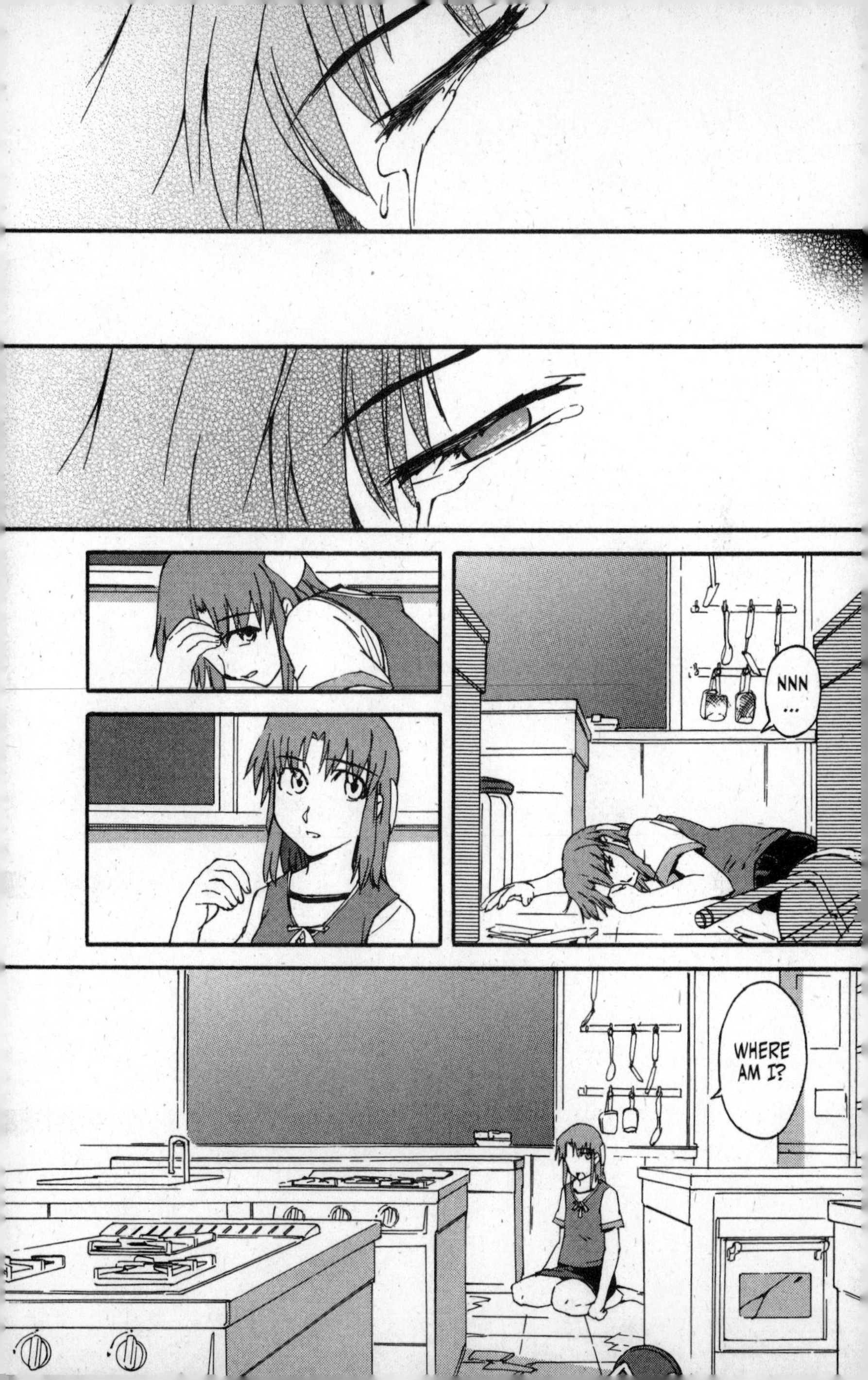
NNN ...
WHERE AM I?

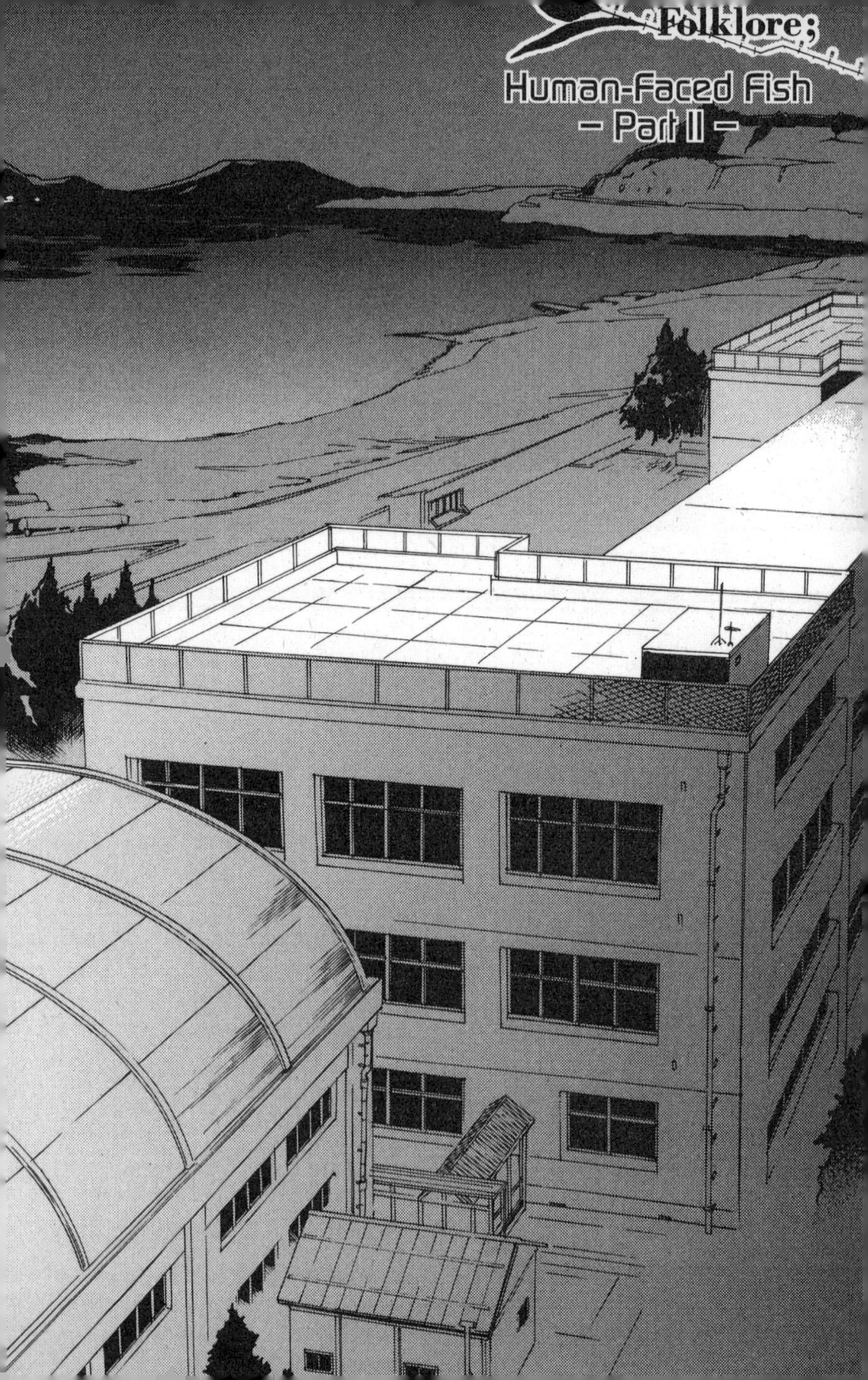
Folklore;
Human-Faced Fish
- Part II -

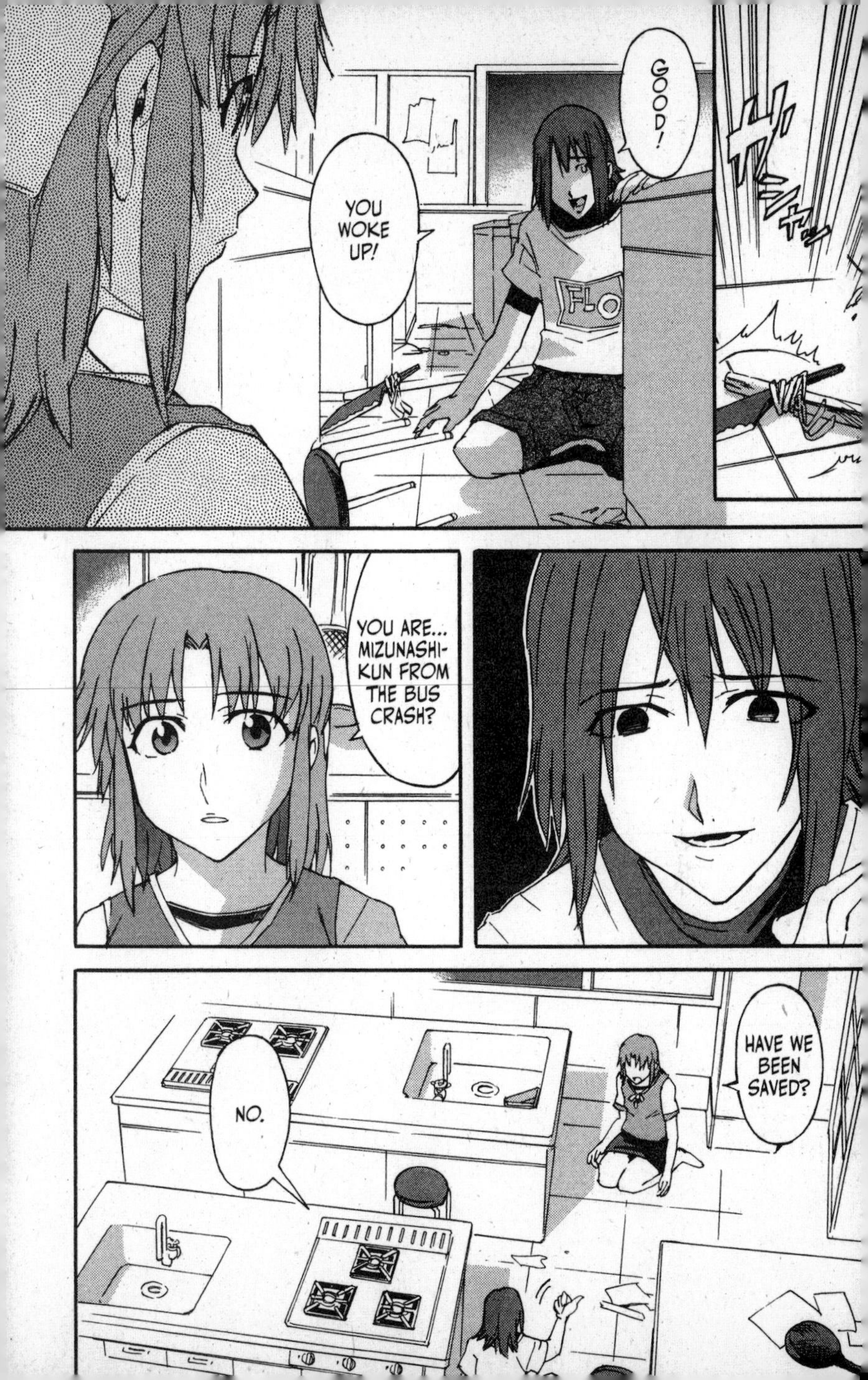
GOOD!
YOU WOKE UP!
YOU ARE... MIZUNASHI-KUN FROM THE BUS CRASH?
HAVE WE BEEN SAVED?
NO.

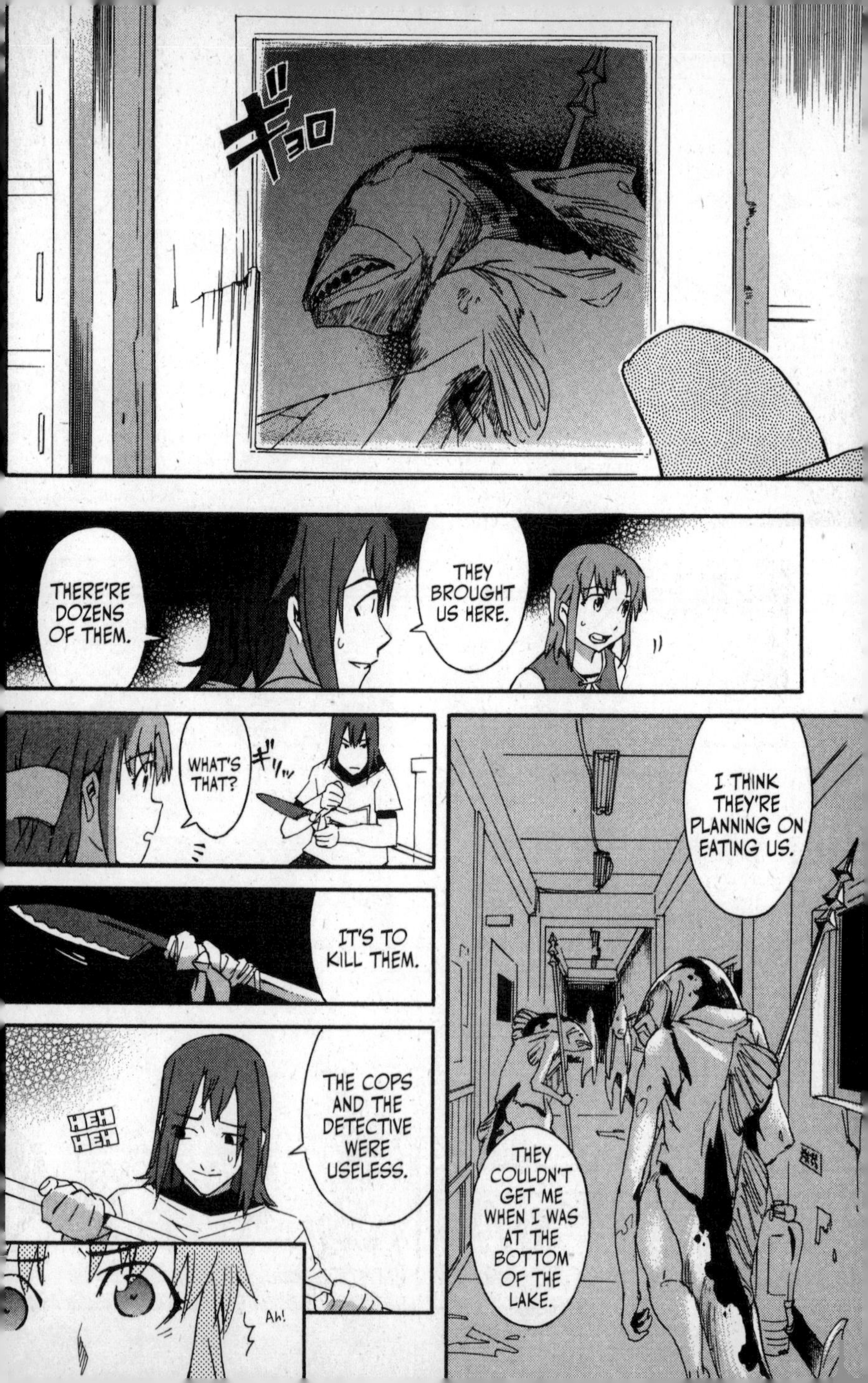
ギョロ
THEY BROUGHT US HERE.
THERE'RE DOZENS OF THEM.
I THINK THEY'RE PLANNING ON EATING US.
THEY COULDN'T GET ME WHEN I WAS AT THE BOTTOM OF THE LAKE.
ギリッ
WHAT'S THAT?
IT'S TO KILL THEM.
THE COPS AND THE DETECTIVE WERE USELESS.
HEH HEH
Ah!

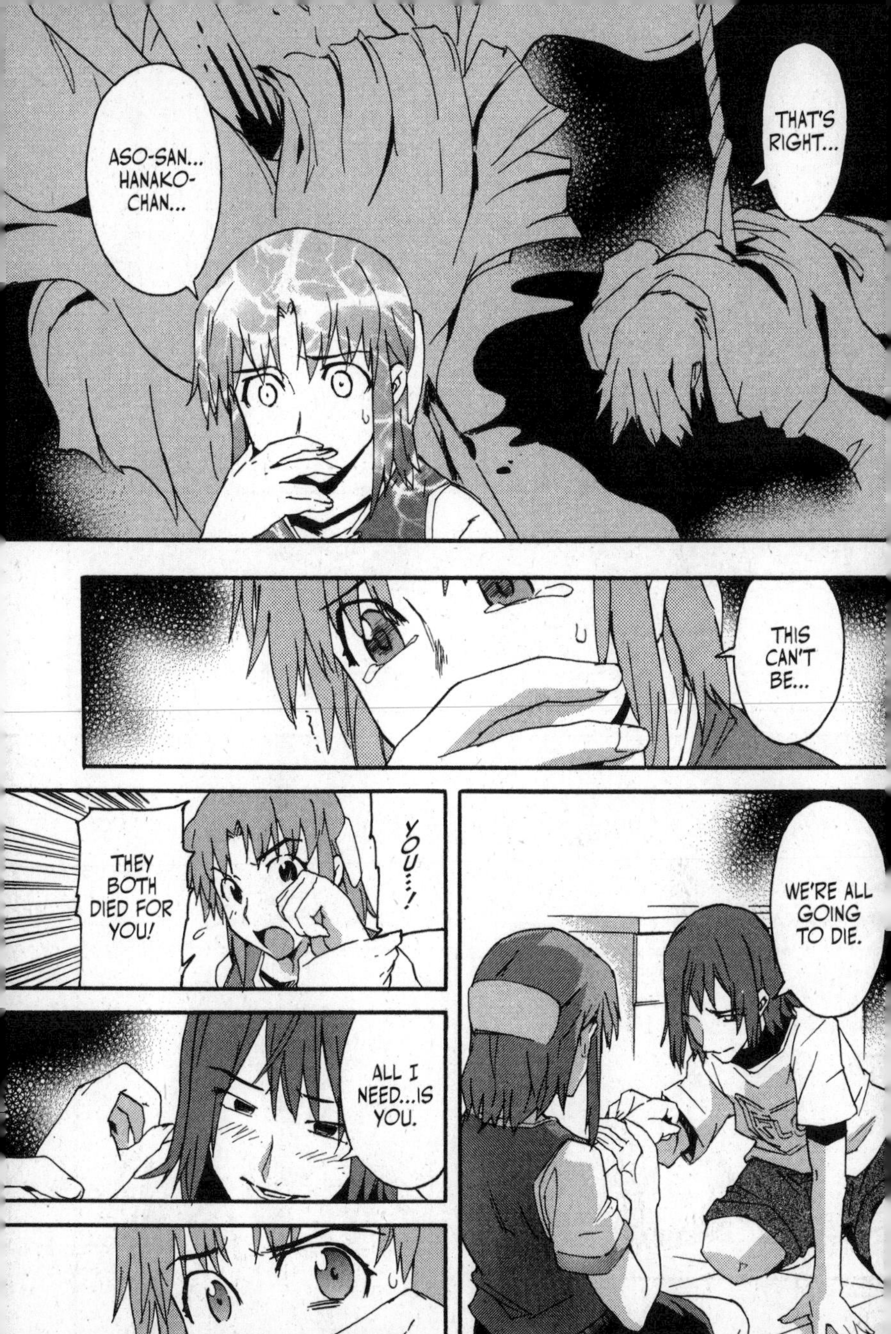
THAT'S RIGHT...
ASO-SAN... HANAKO-CHAN...
THIS CAN'T BE...
WE'RE ALL GOING TO DIE.
YOU...!
THEY BOTH DIED FOR YOU!
ALL I NEED...IS YOU.

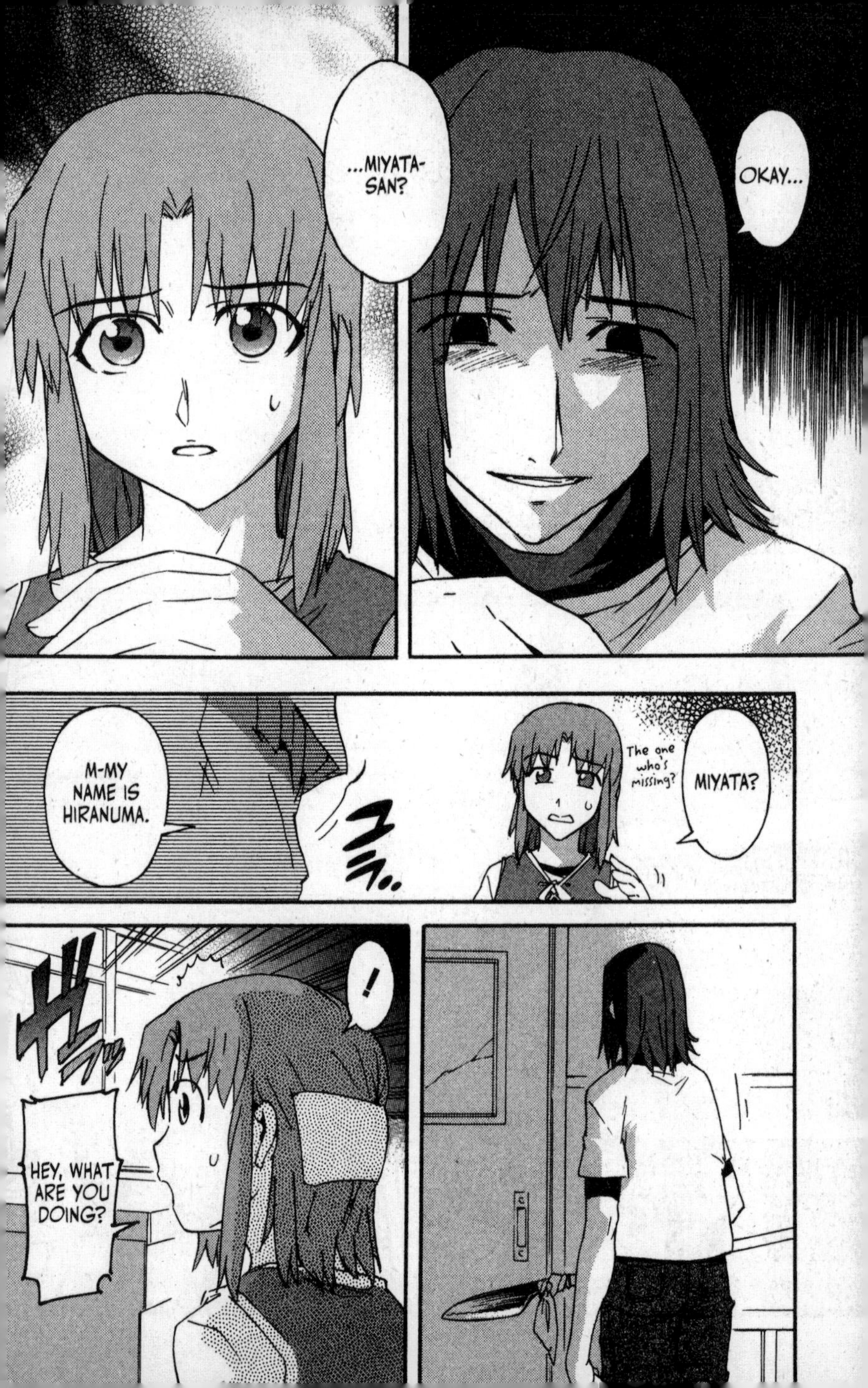
OKAY...
...MIYATA-SAN?
MIYATA?
The one who's missing?
M-MY NAME IS HIRANUMA.
!
HEY, WHAT ARE YOU DOING?

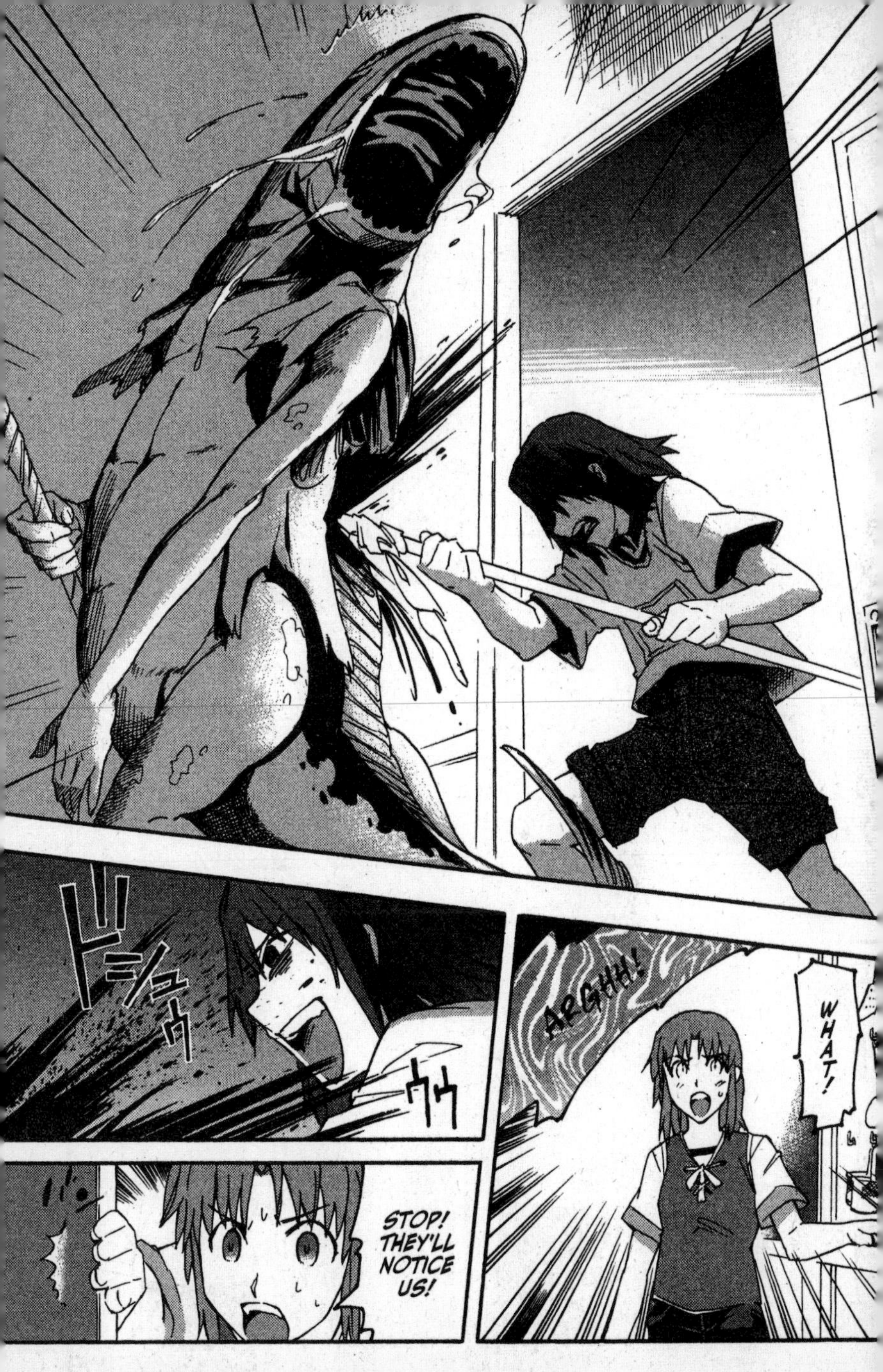
WHAT!
ARGHH!
ドシュウ
ウウ
STOP! THEY'LL NOTICE US!

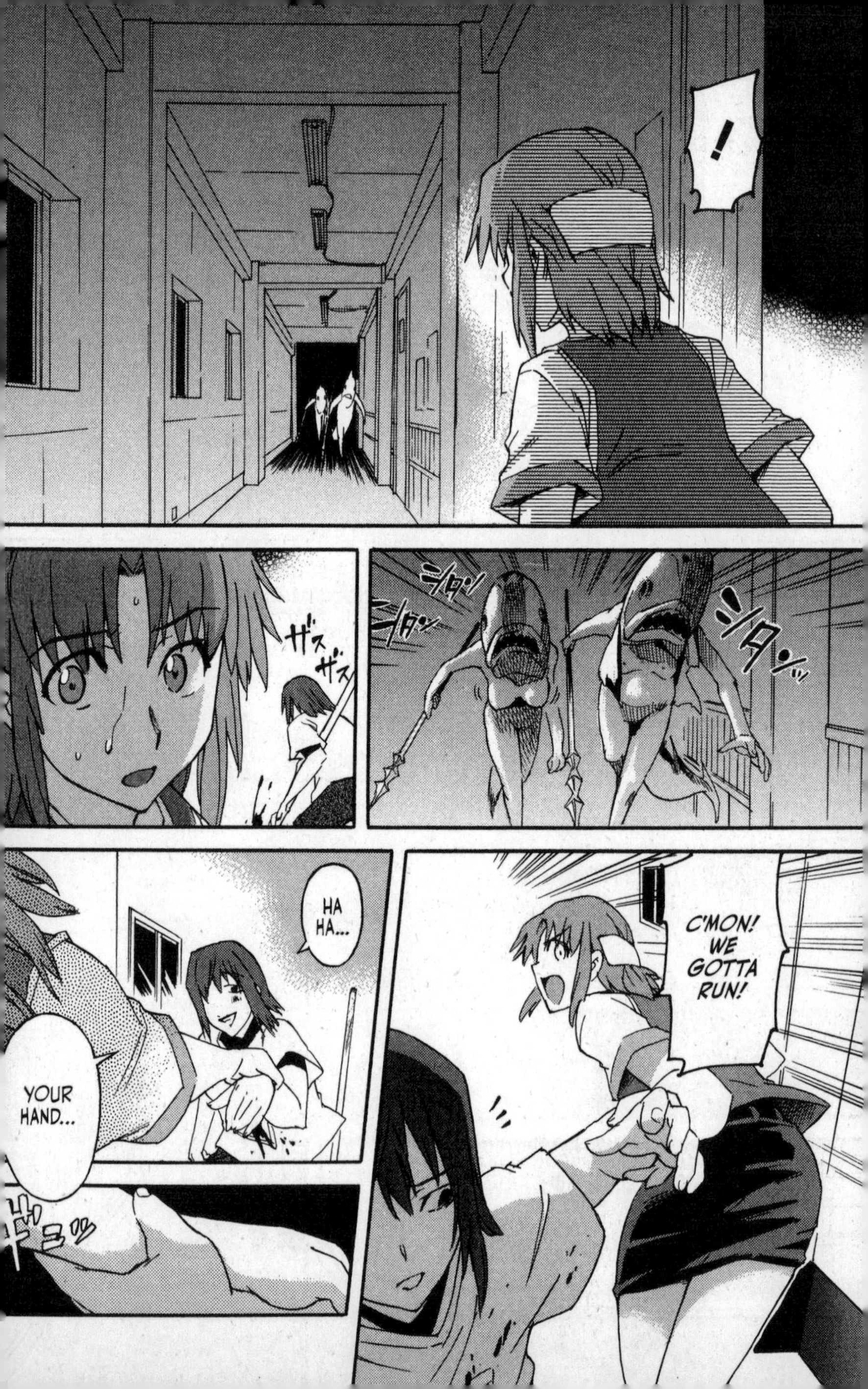
!
ザス
ザス
C'MON! WE GOTTA RUN!
HA HA...
YOUR HAND...

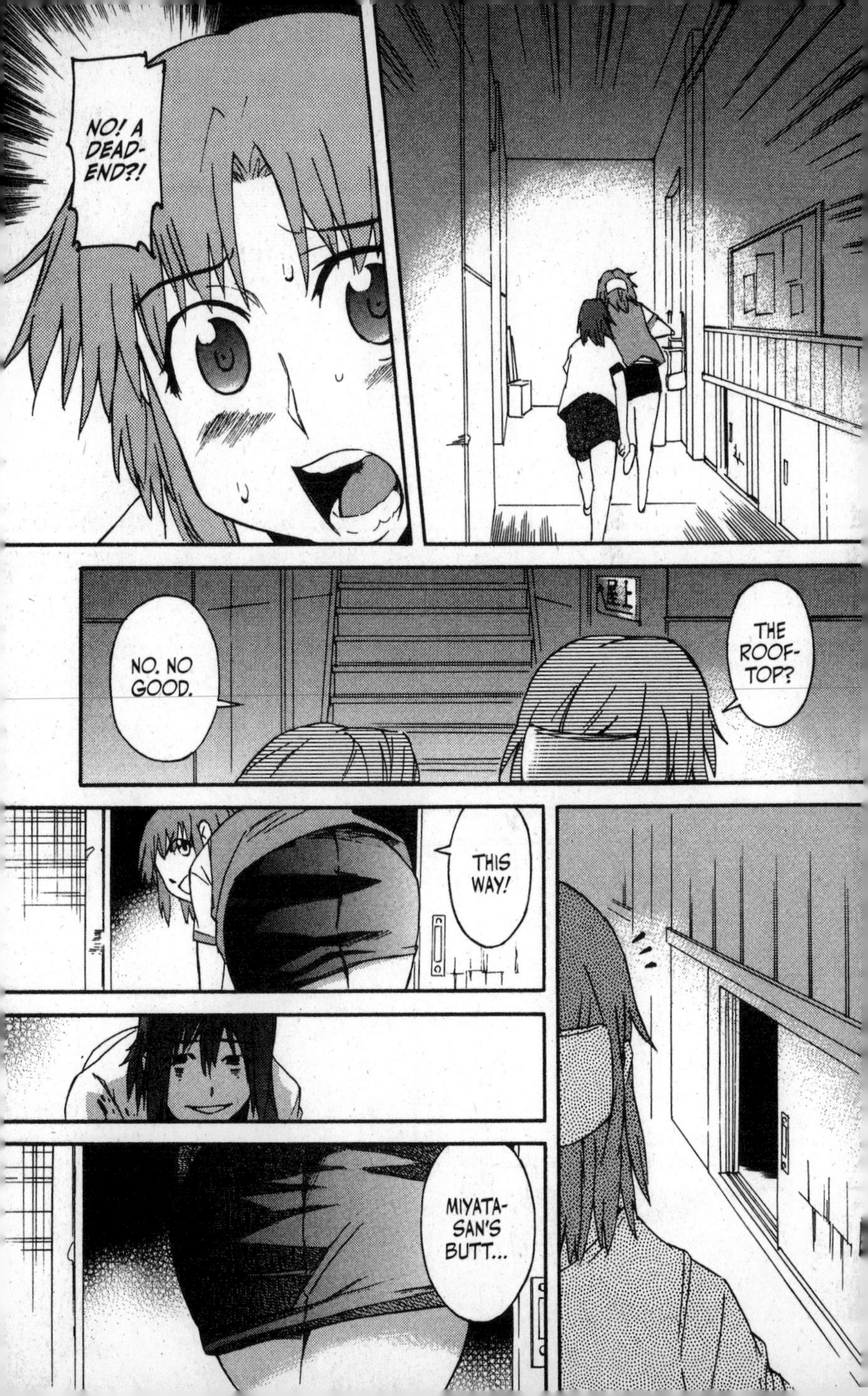
NO! A DEAD-END?!
THE ROOF-TOP?
屋上
NO. NO GOOD.
THIS WAY!
MIYATA-SAN'S BUTT...

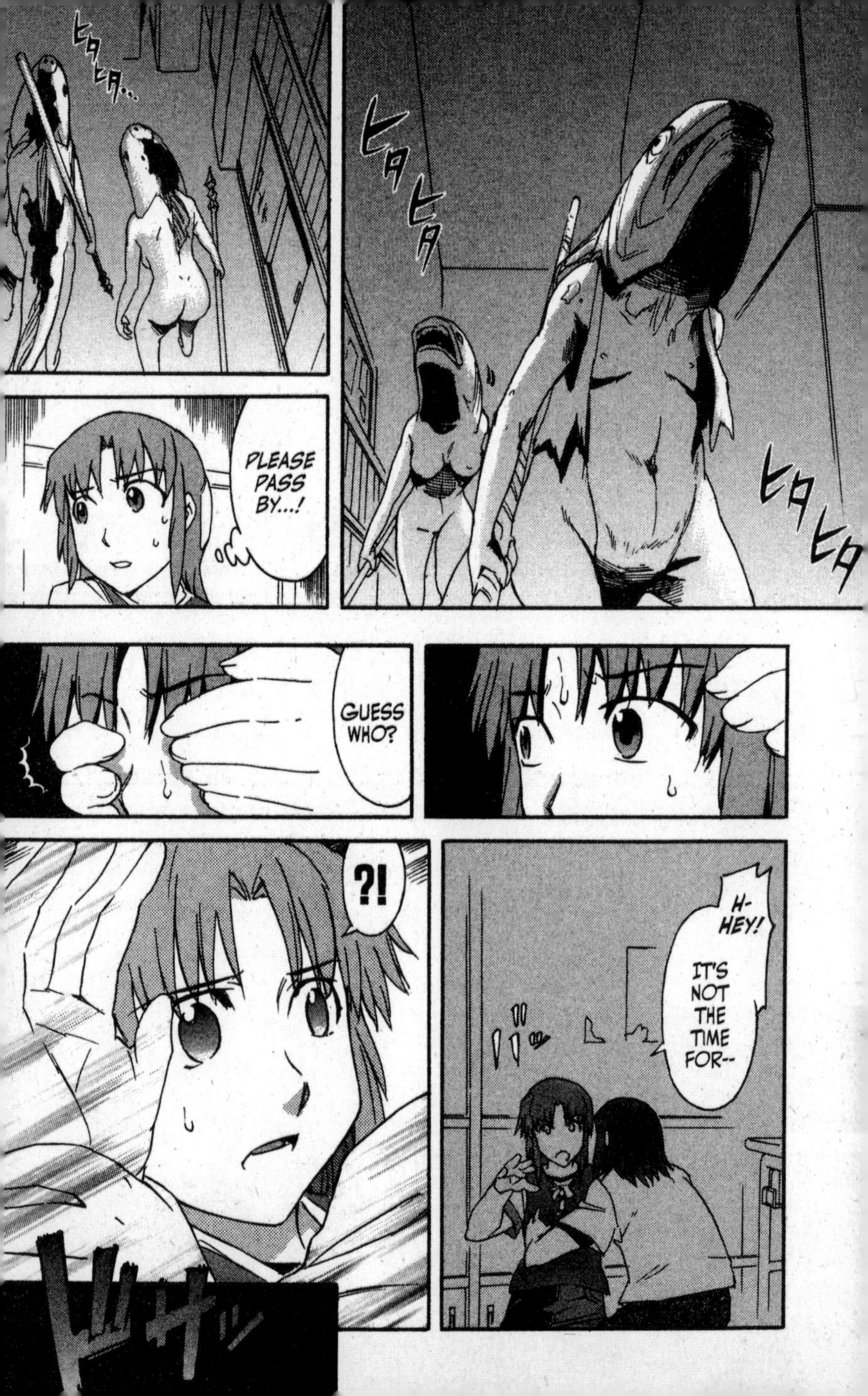
ヒタヒタ
ヒタヒタ
ヒタヒタ...
PLEASE PASS BY...!
GUESS WHO?
H-HEY!
IT'S NOT THE TIME FOR--
?!

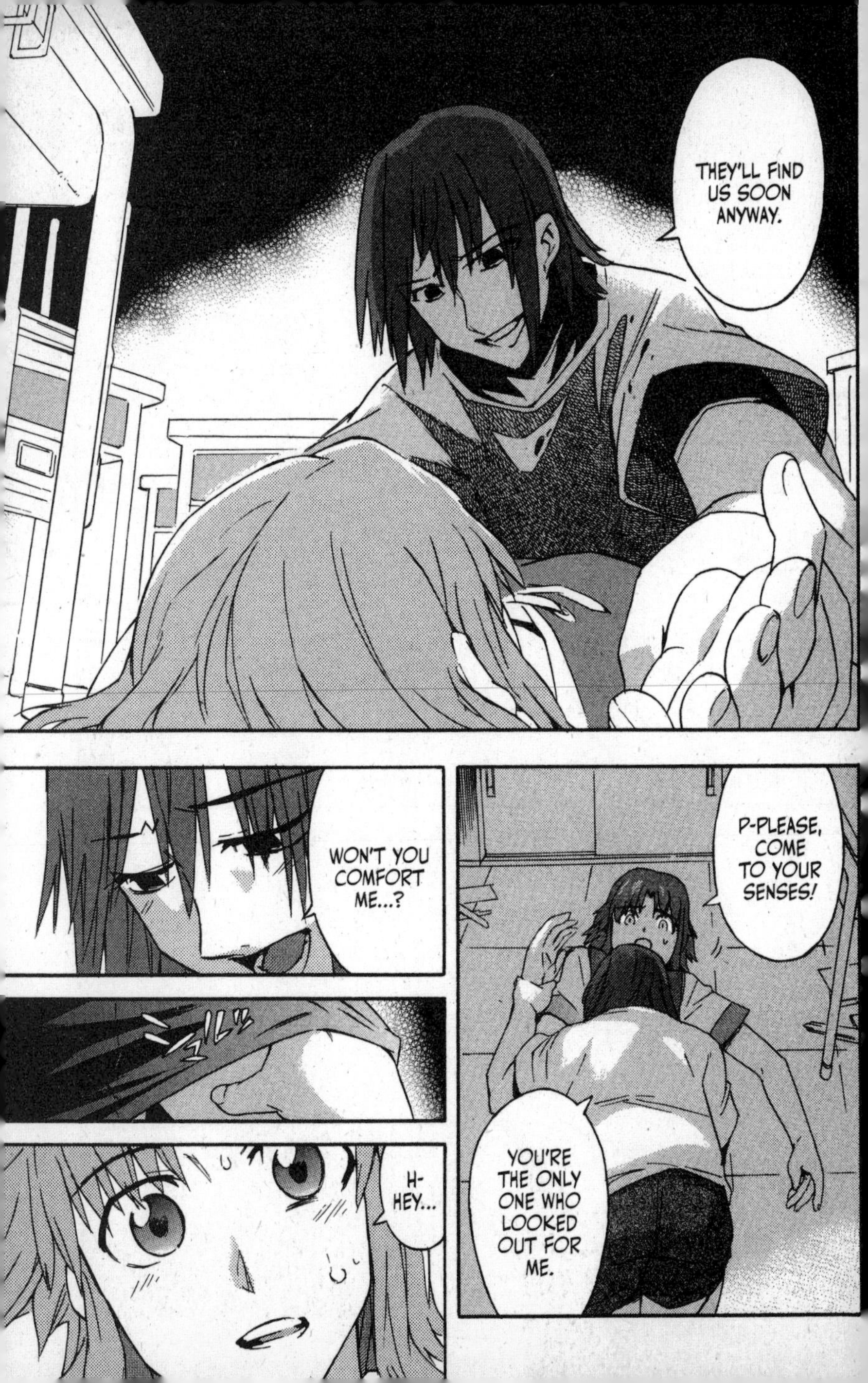
THEY'LL FIND US SOON ANYWAY.
P-PLEASE, COME TO YOUR SENSES!
YOU'RE THE ONLY ONE WHO LOOKED OUT FOR ME.
WON'T YOU COMFORT ME...?
H-HEY...

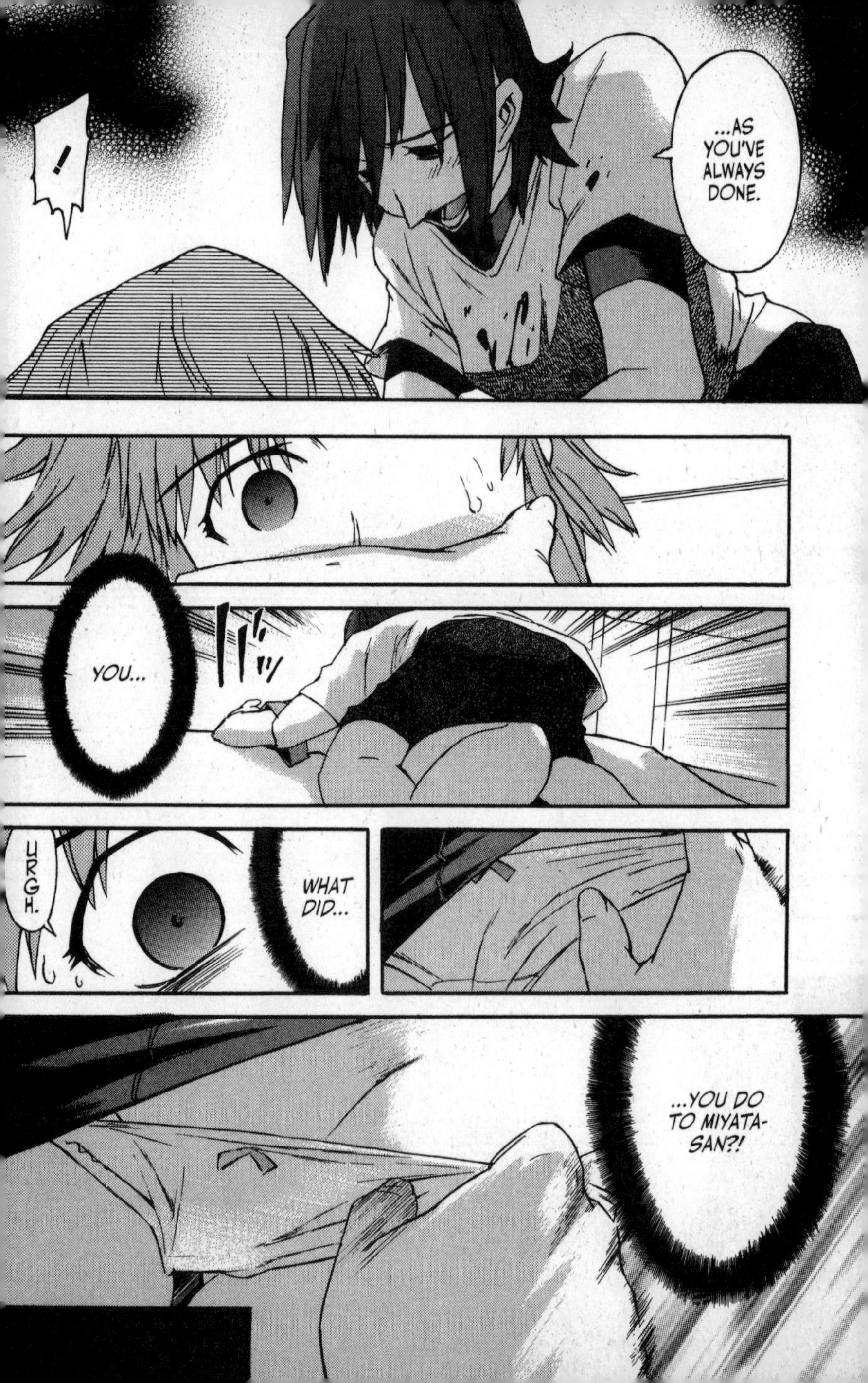
...AS YOU'VE ALWAYS DONE.
!
YOU...
WHAT DID...
URGH.
...YOU DO TO MIYATA-SAN?!

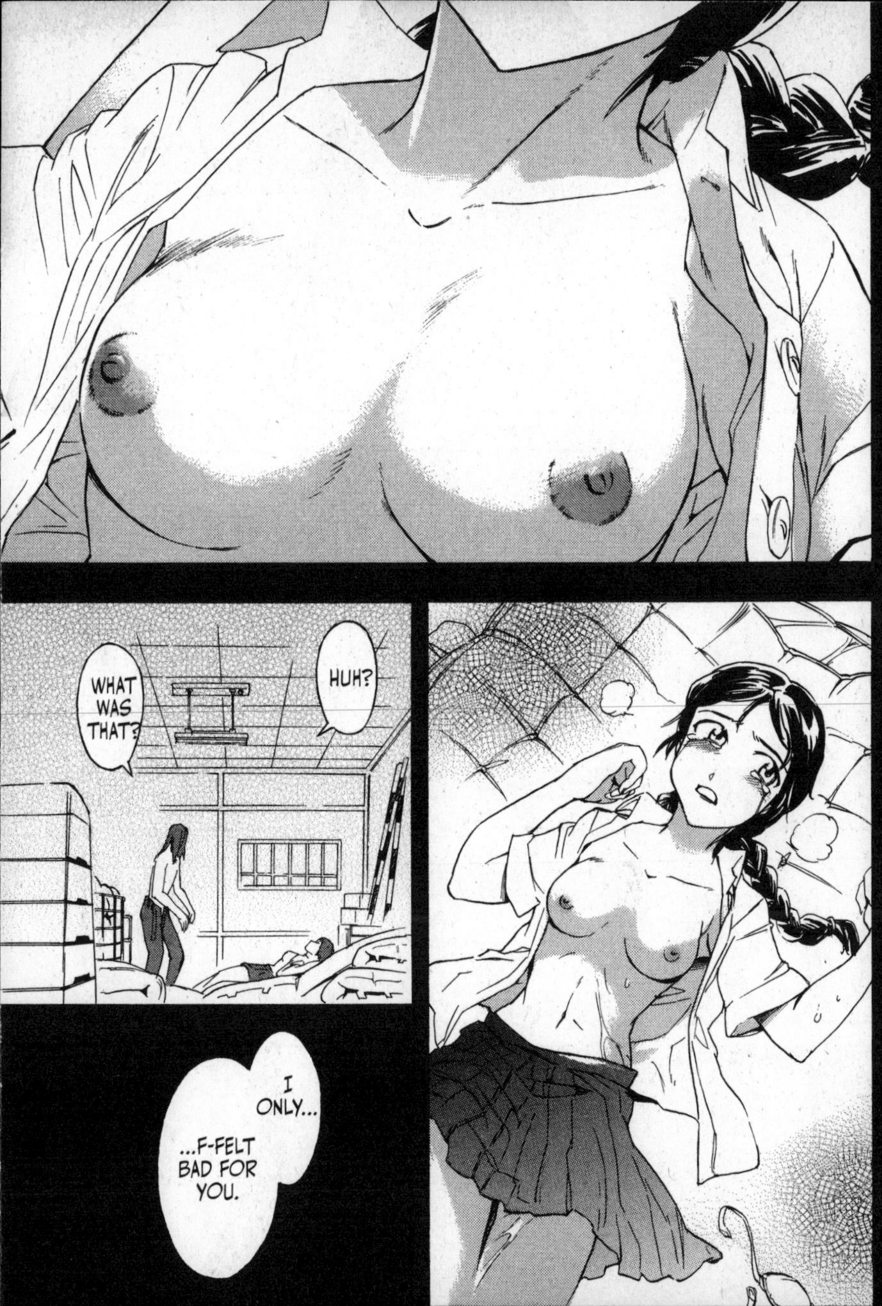
HUH?
WHAT WAS THAT?
I ONLY...
...F-FELT BAD FOR YOU.

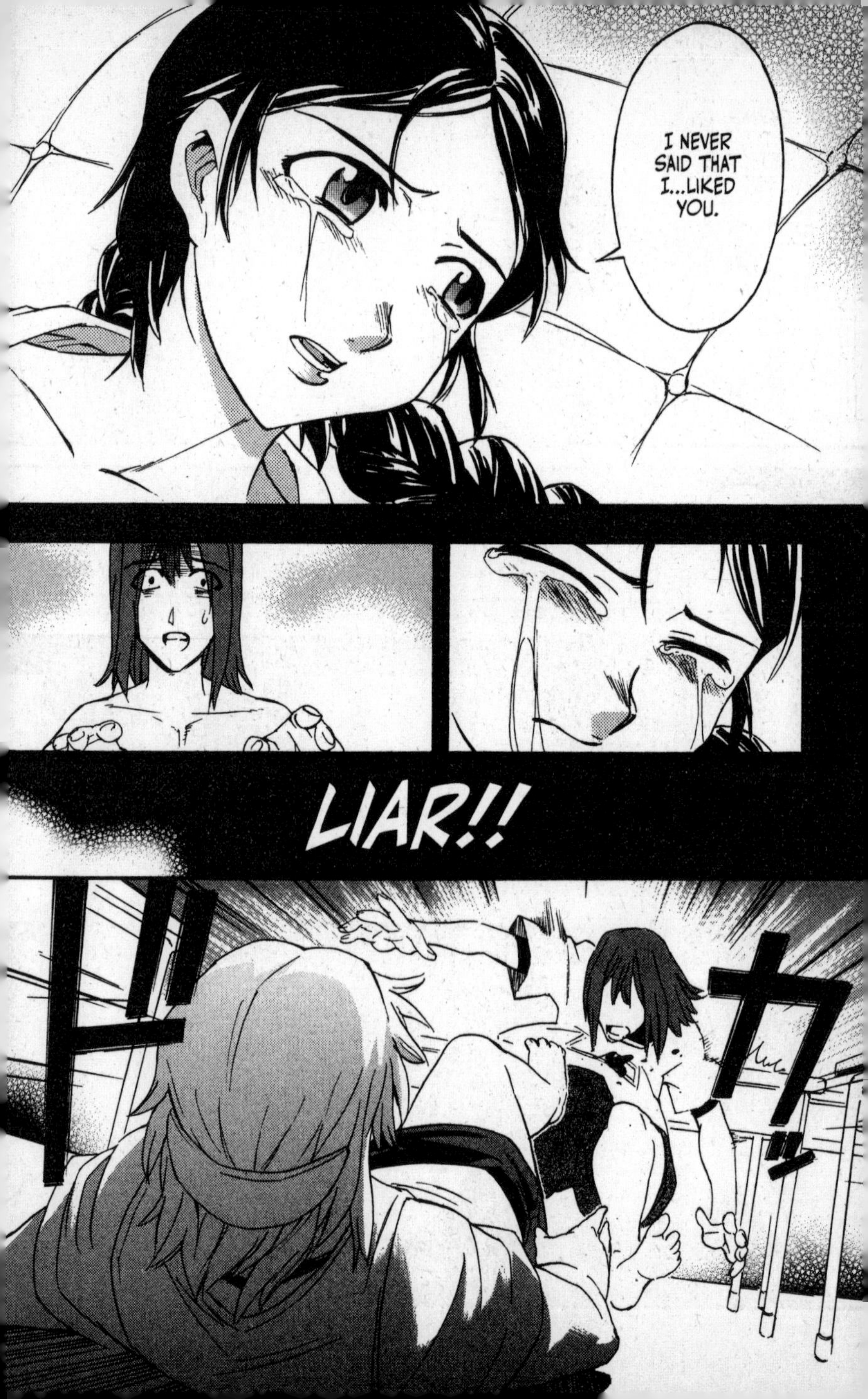
I NEVER SAID THAT I...LIKED YOU.
LIAR!!
ド
カッ

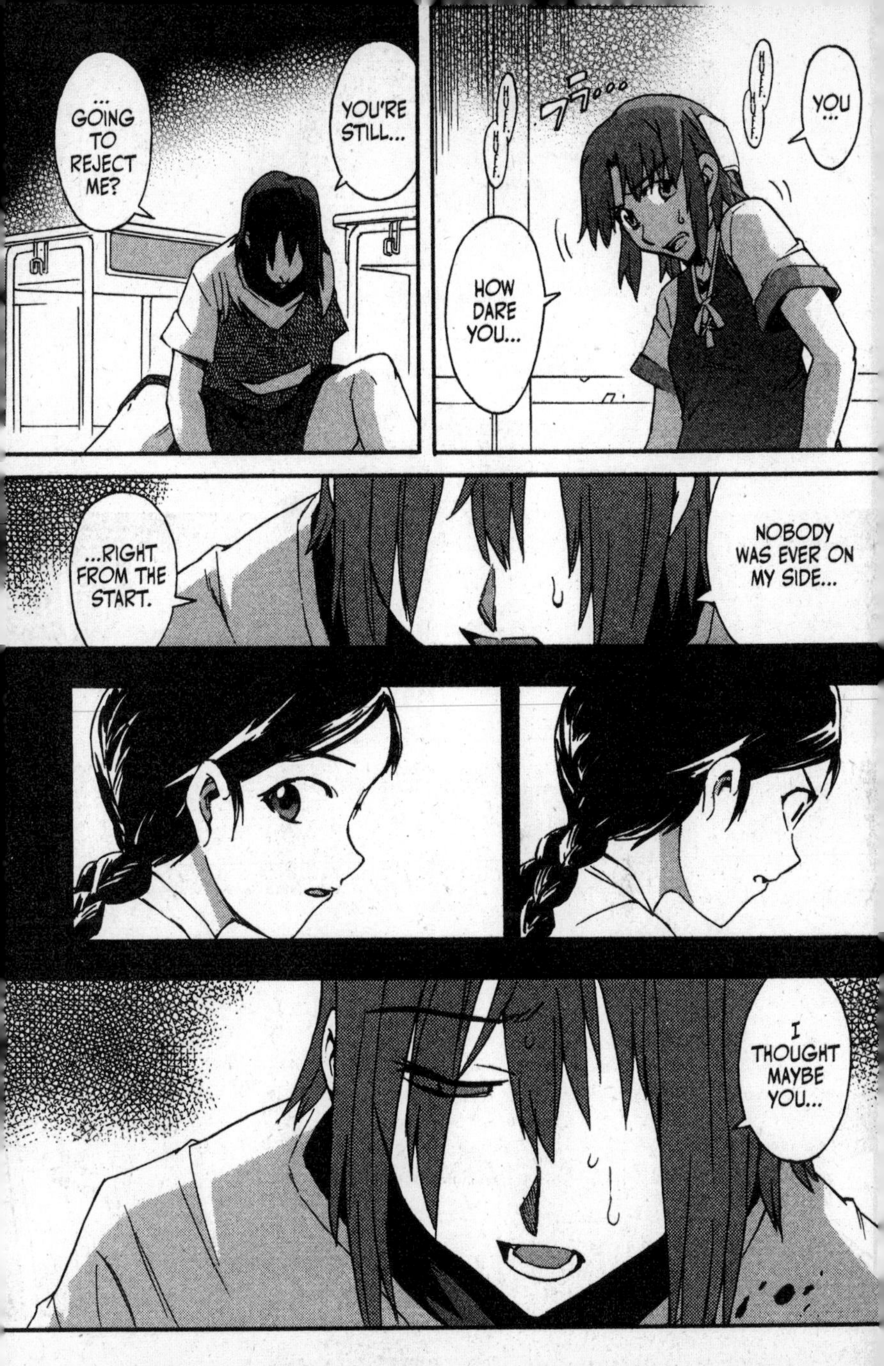
YOU...
HUFF. HUFF.
HUFF. HUFF.
フラ
HOW DARE YOU...
YOU'RE STILL...
...GOING TO REJECT ME?
NOBODY WAS EVER ON MY SIDE...
...RIGHT FROM THE START.
I THOUGHT MAYBE YOU...

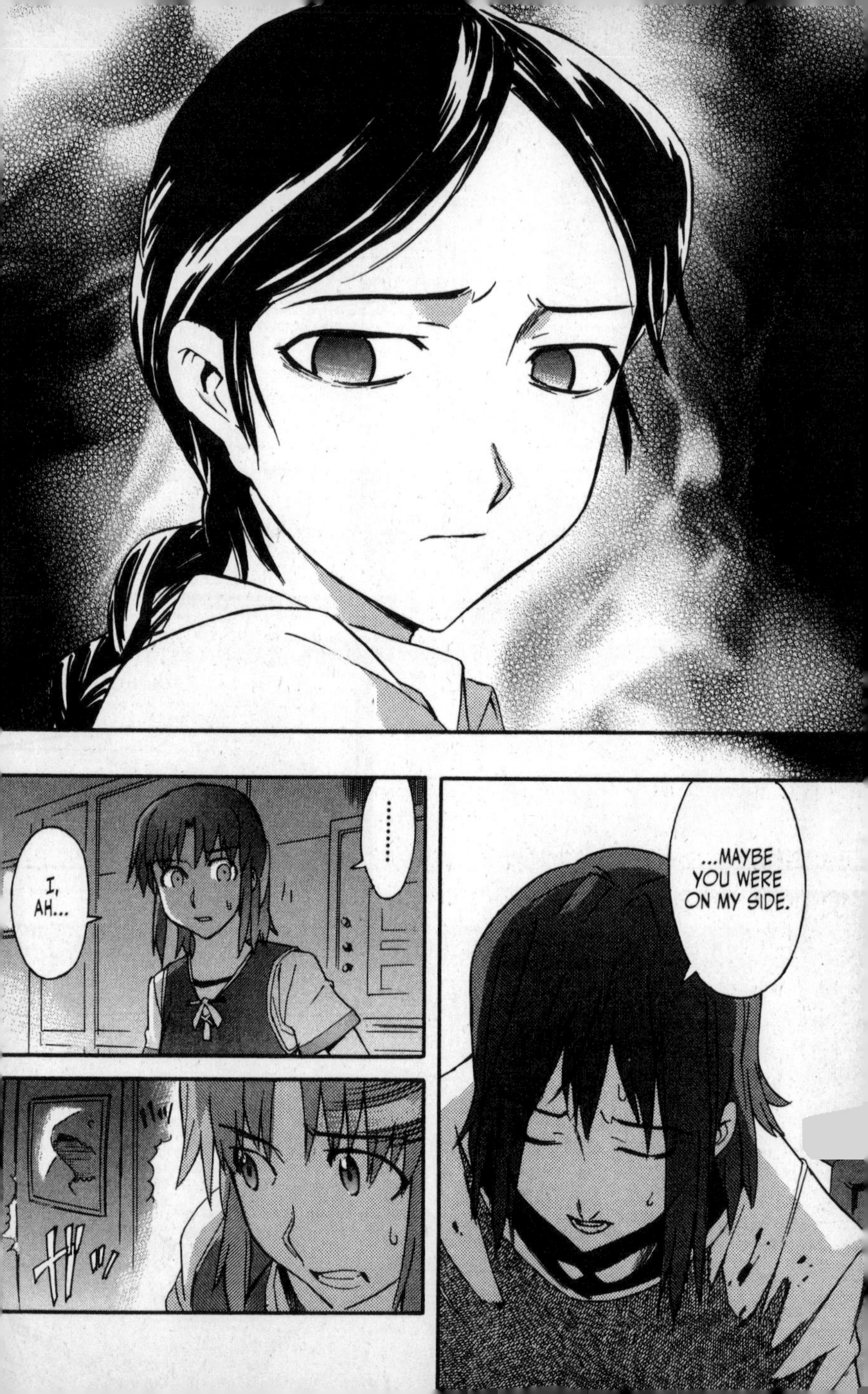
...MAYBE YOU WERE ON MY SIDE.
......
I, AH...

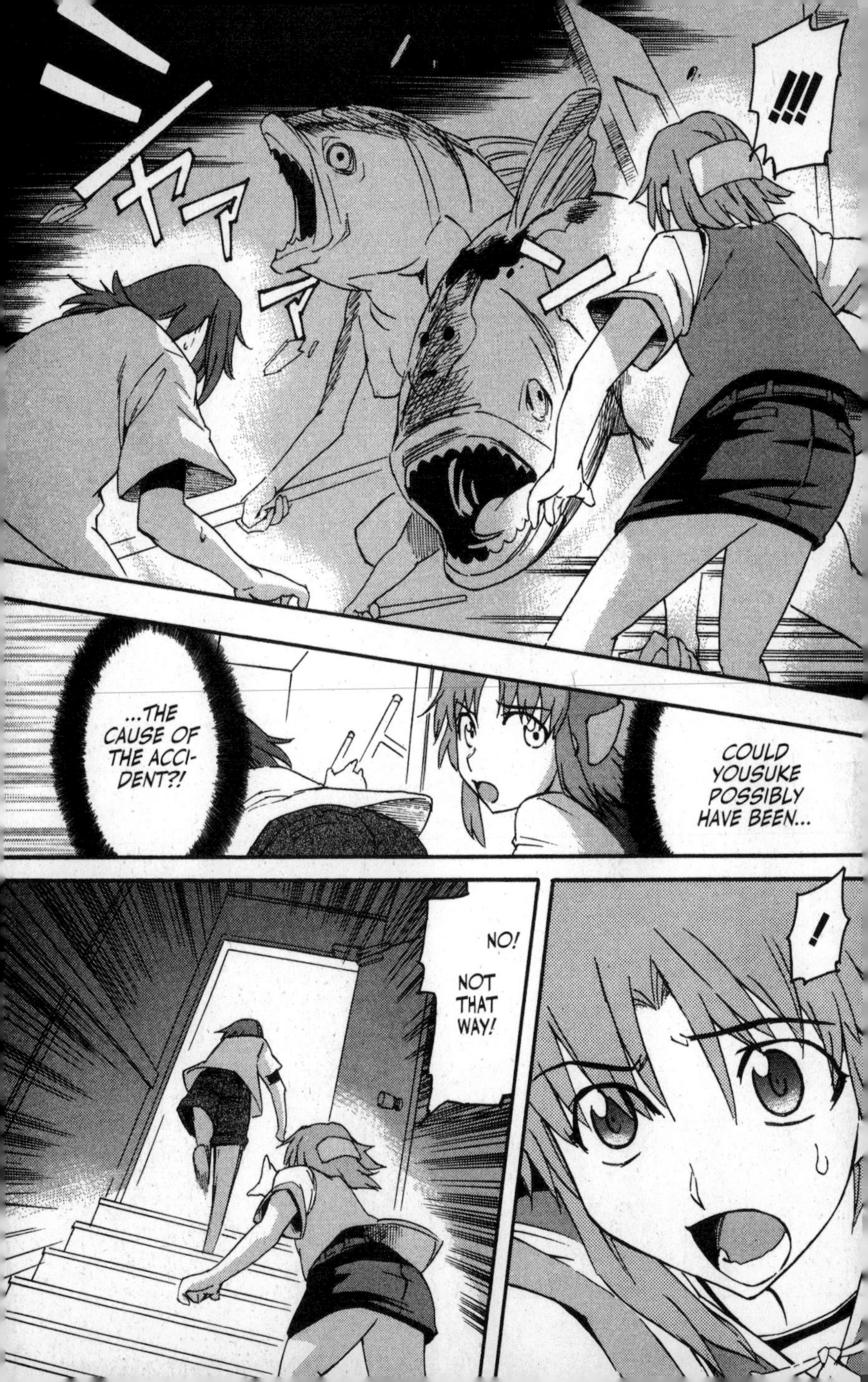
!!!
COULD YOUSUKE POSSIBLY HAVE BEEN...
...THE CAUSE OF THE ACCIDENT?!
!
NO!
NOT THAT WAY!

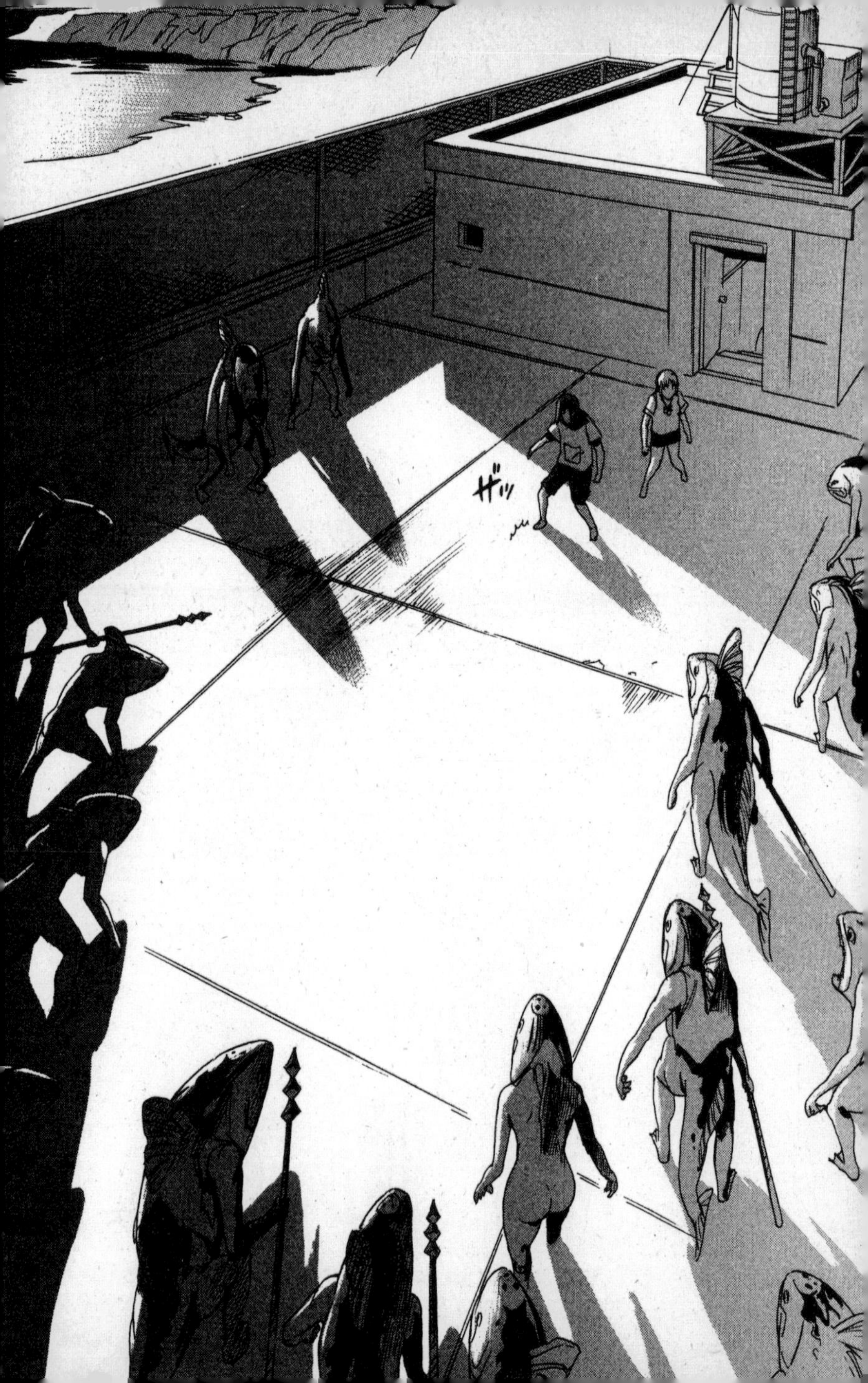
ザッ

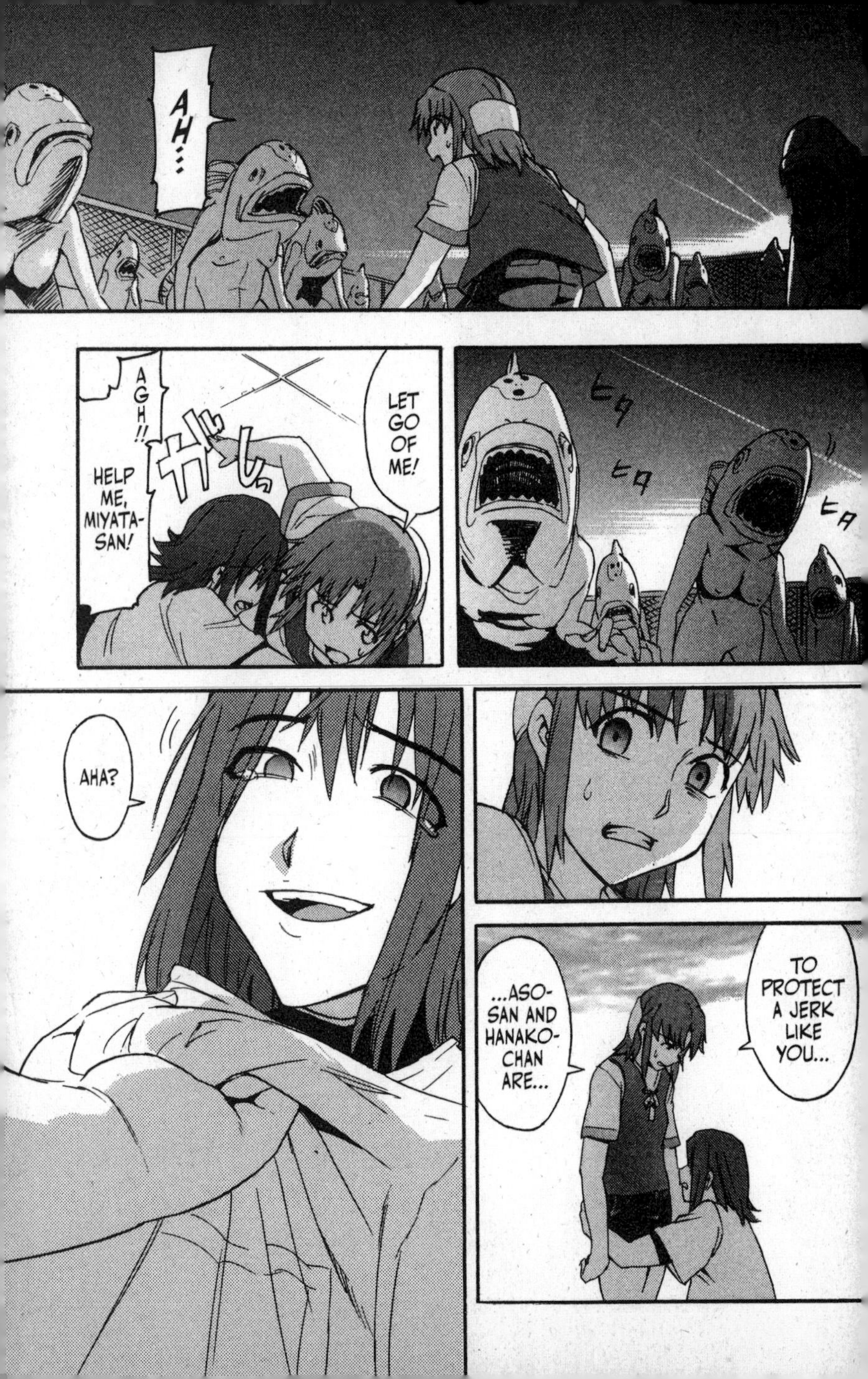
AH...
ヒタ
ヒタ
ヒタ
LET GO OF ME!
ガしっ
AGH!!
HELP ME, MIYATA-SAN!
TO PROTECT A JERK LIKE YOU...
...ASO-SAN AND HANAKO-CHAN ARE...
AHA?

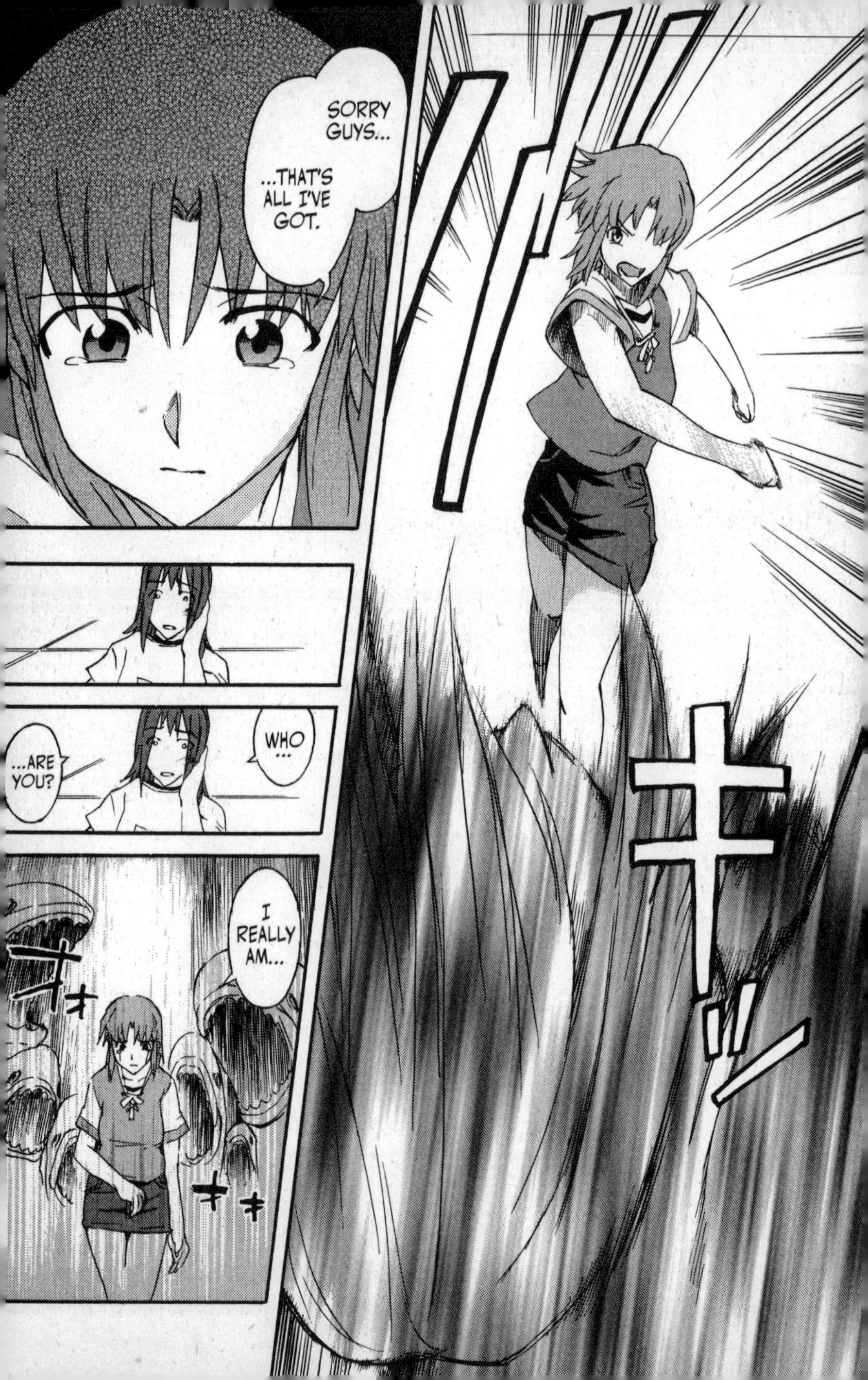
SORRY GUYS...
...THAT'S ALL I'VE GOT.
WHO ...
...ARE YOU?
I REALLY AM...

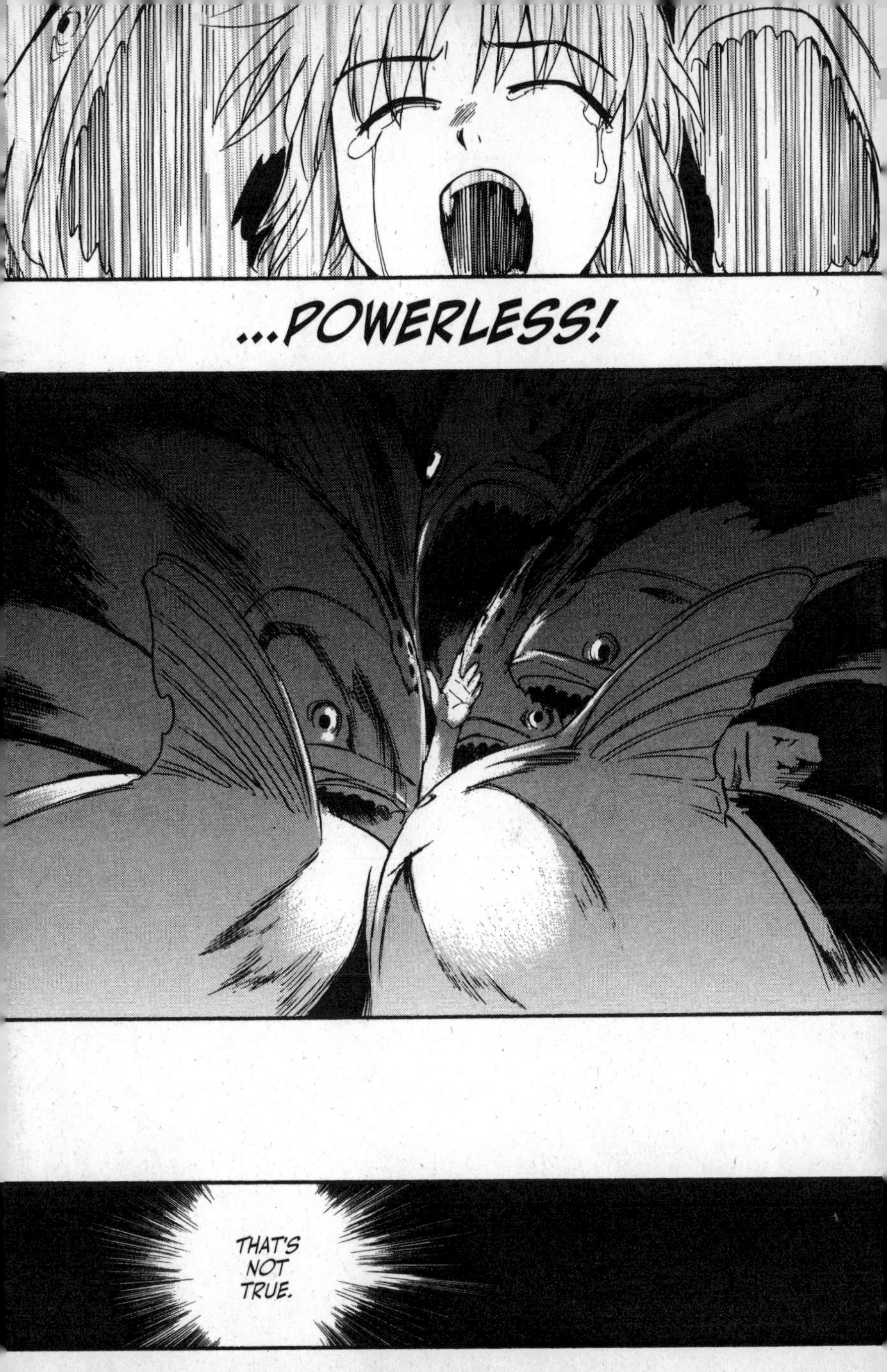
...POWERLESS!
THAT'S NOT TRUE.

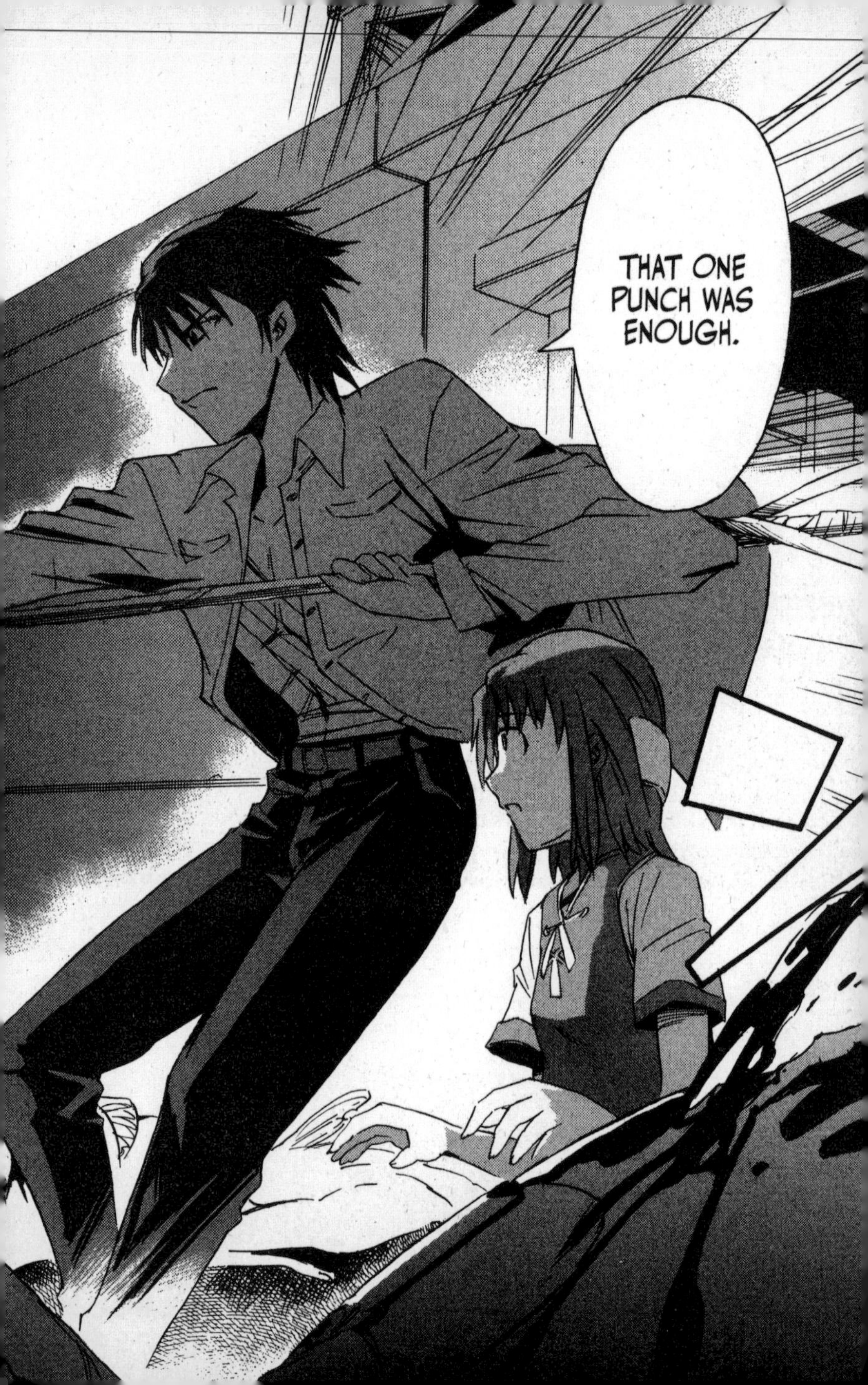
THAT ONE PUNCH WAS ENOUGH.

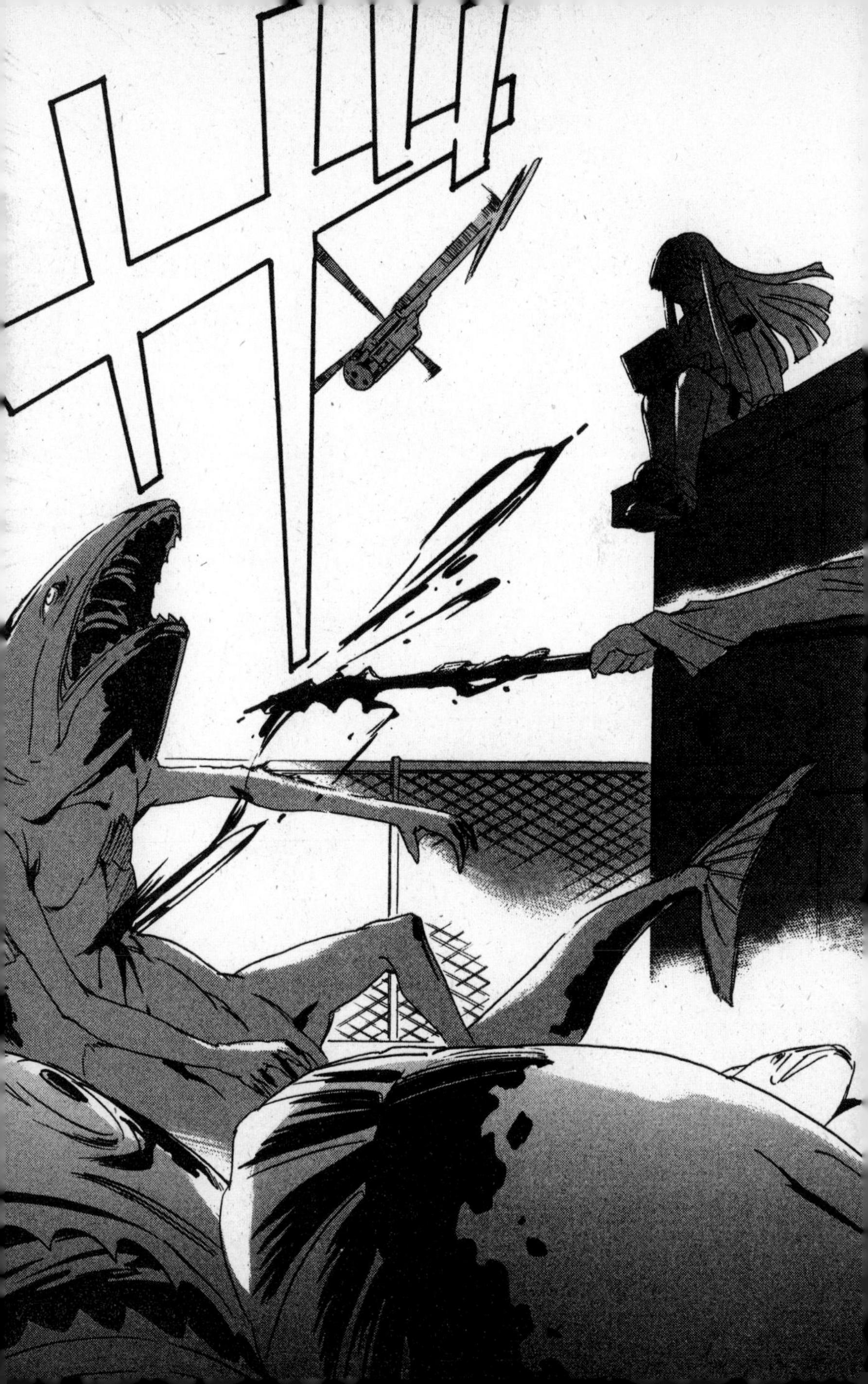

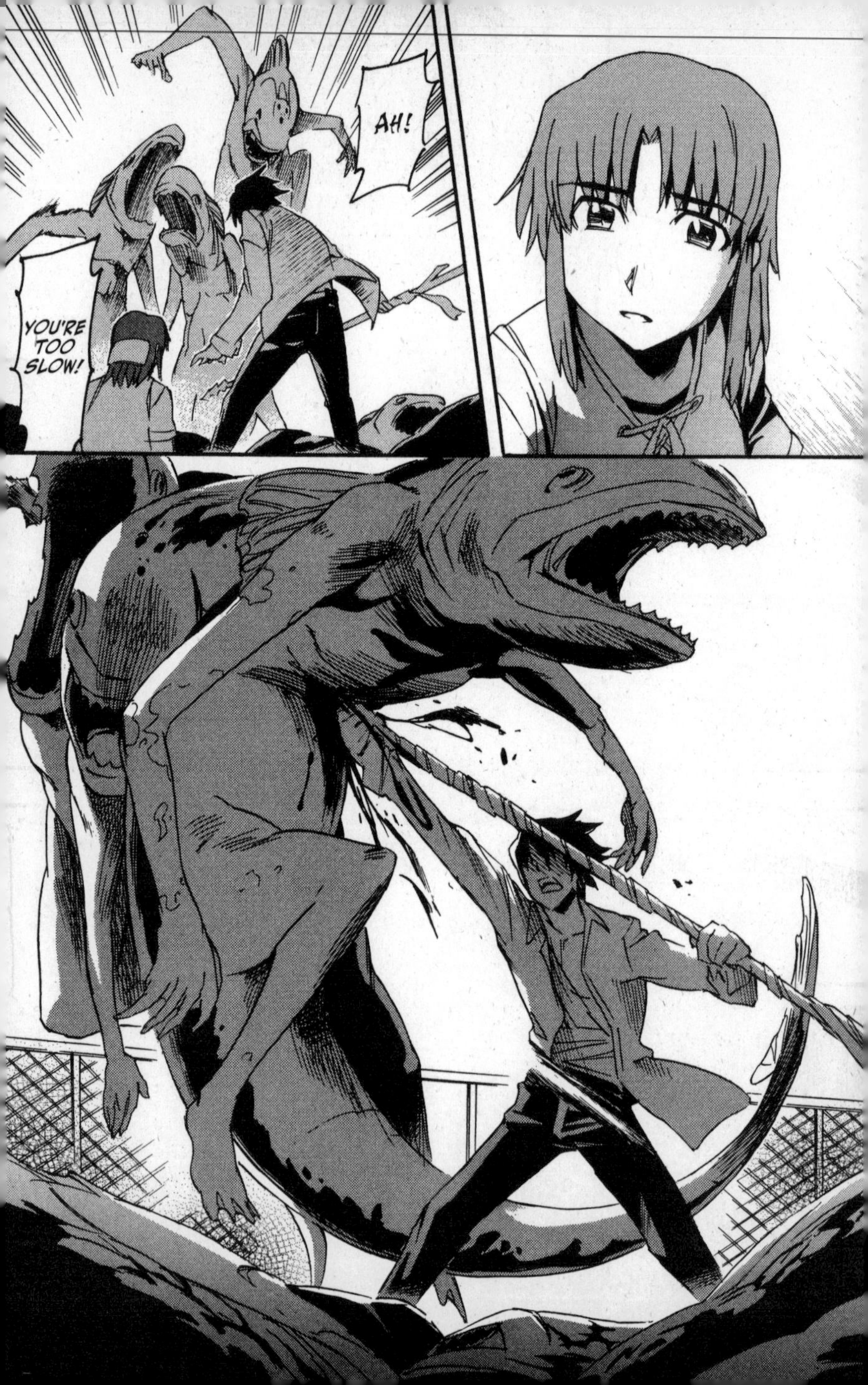
AH!
YOU'RE TOO SLOW!

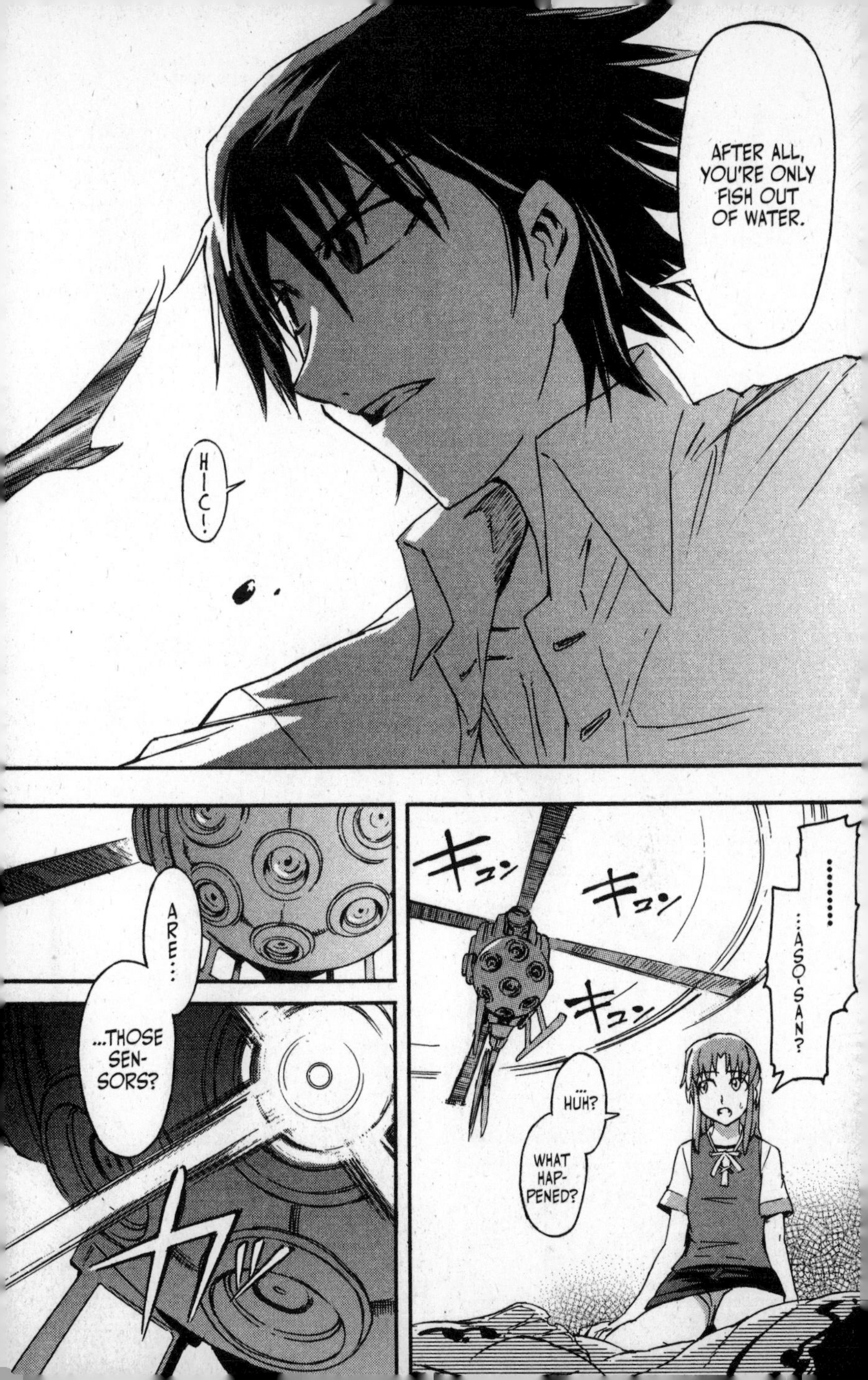
AFTER ALL, YOU'RE ONLY FISH OUT OF WATER.
HIC!
......
...ASO-SAN?
キュン
キュン
キュン
...HUH?
WHAT HAP-PENED?
ARE...
...THOSE SEN-SORS?

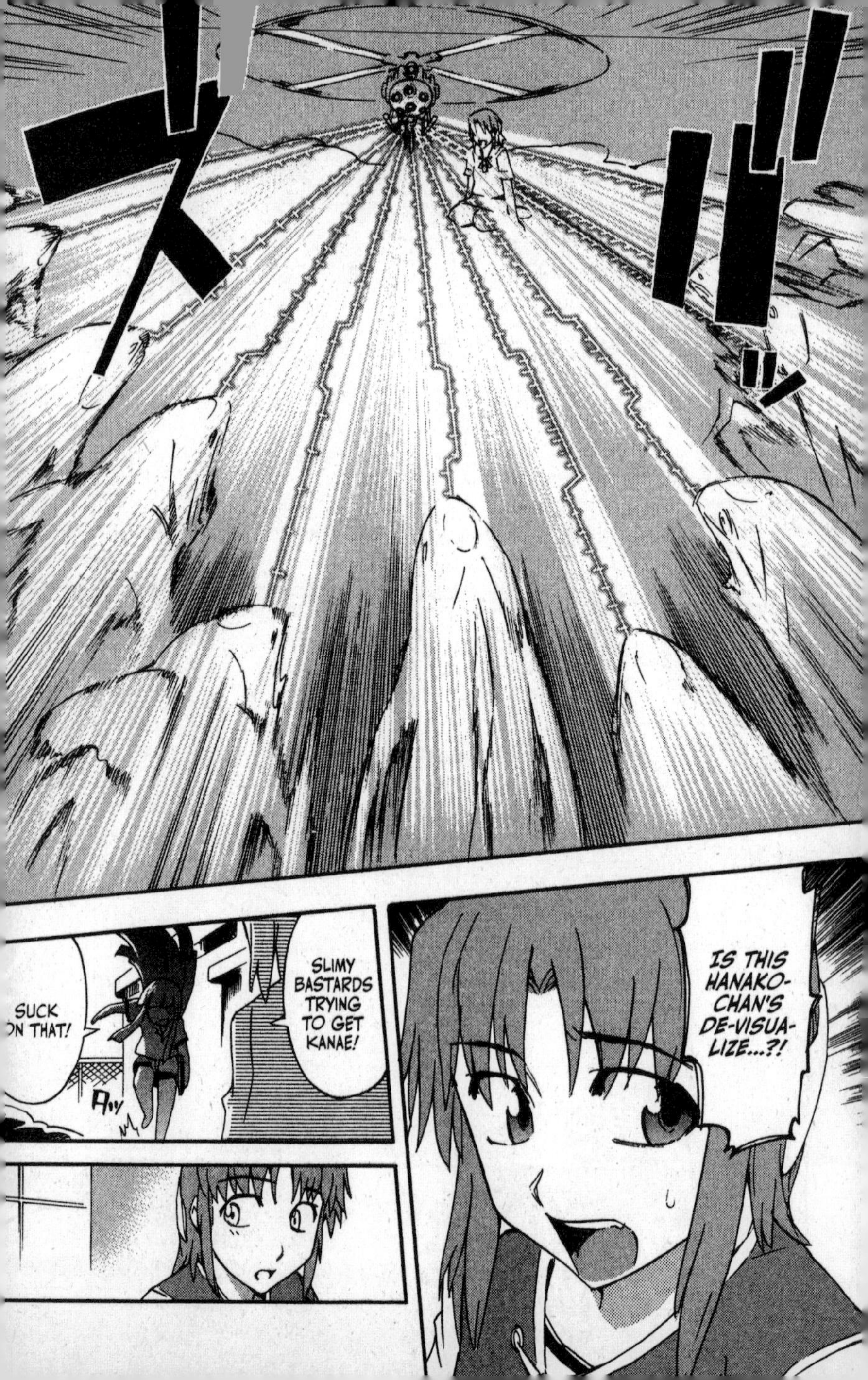
IS THIS HANAKO-CHAN'S DE-VISUALIZE...?!
SLIMY BASTARDS TRYING TO GET KANAE!
SUCK ON THAT!

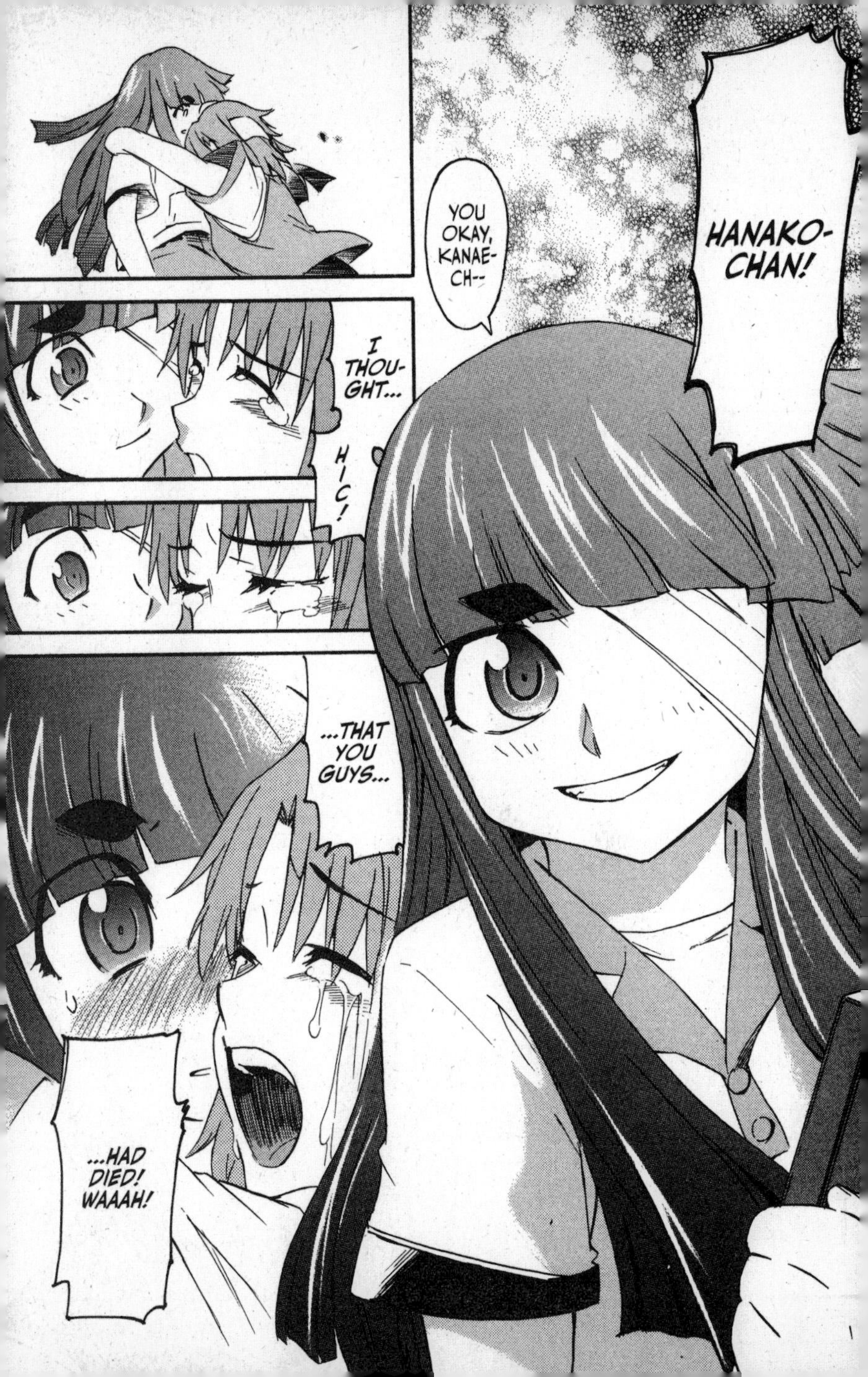
HANAKO-CHAN!
YOU OKAY, KANAE-CH--
I THOUGHT...
HIC!
...THAT YOU GUYS...
...HAD DIED! WAAAH!

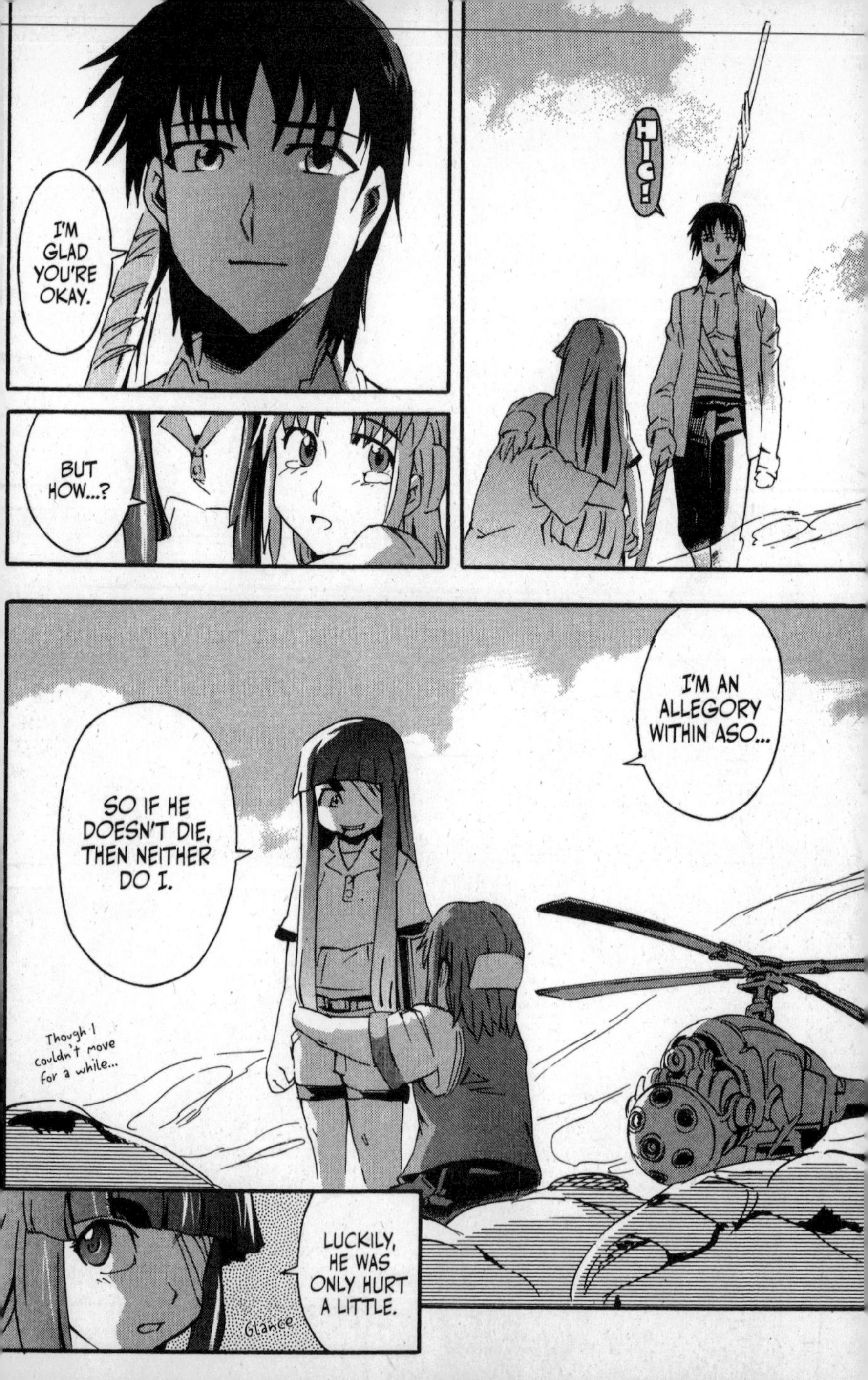
HIC!
I'M GLAD YOU'RE OKAY.
BUT HOW...?
I'M AN ALLEGORY WITHIN ASO...
SO IF HE DOESN'T DIE, THEN NEITHER DO I.
Though I couldn't move for a while...
LUCKILY, HE WAS ONLY HURT A LITTLE.
Glance

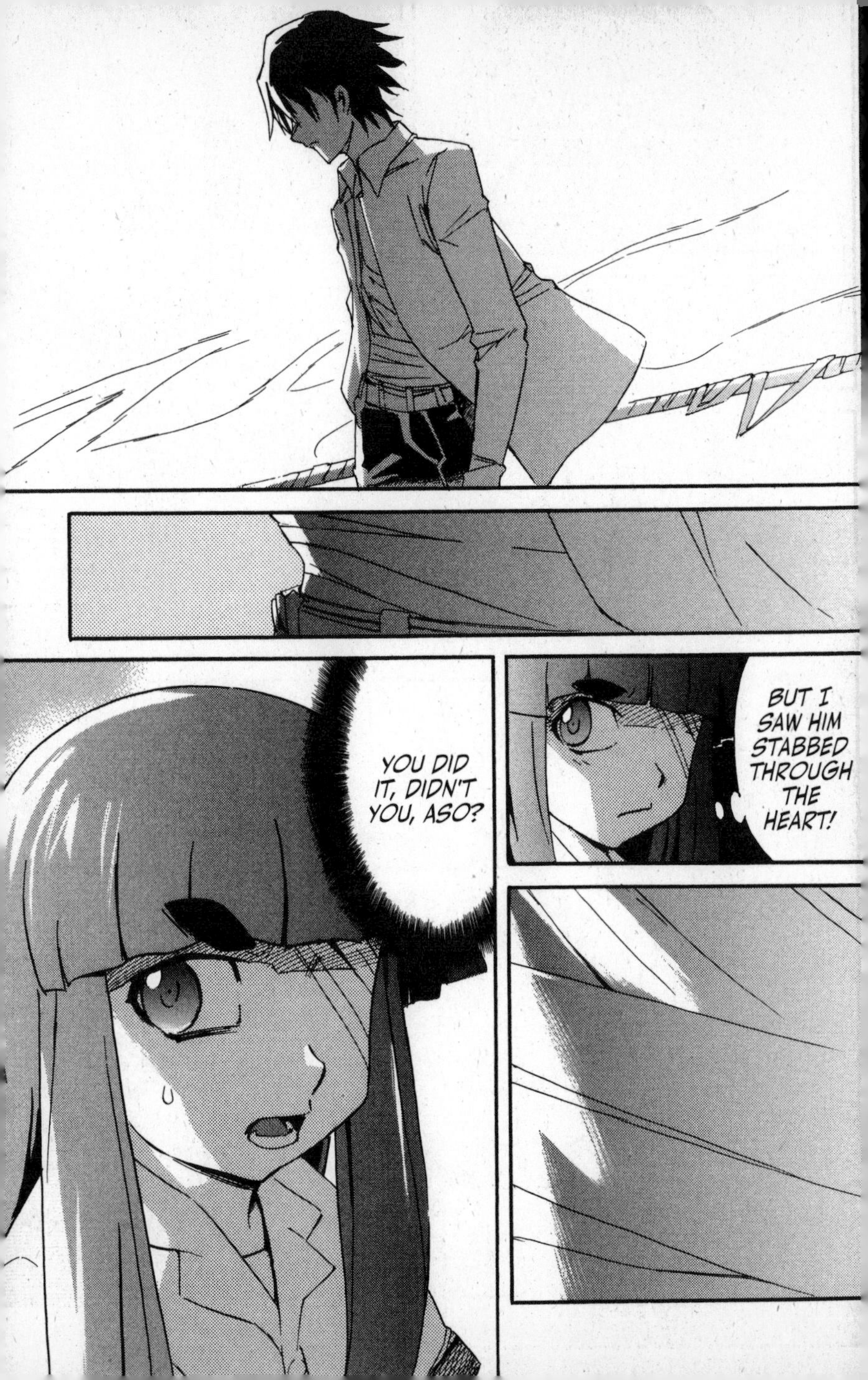
BUT I SAW HIM STABBED THROUGH THE HEART!
YOU DID IT, DIDN'T YOU, ASO?

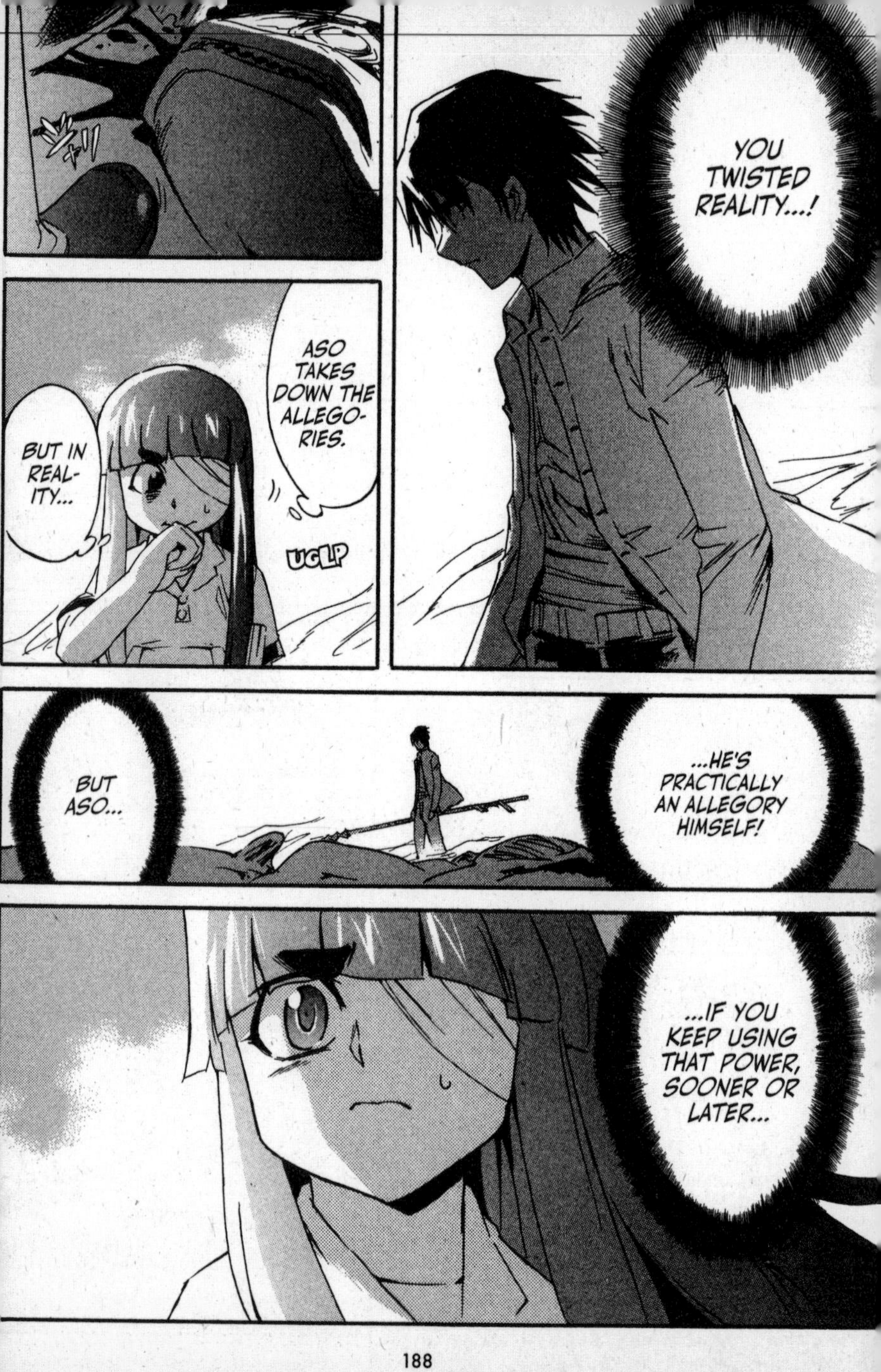
YOU TWISTED REALITY...!
ジャリ
ASO TAKES DOWN THE ALLEGO-RIES.
UGLP
BUT IN REAL-ITY...
...HE'S PRACTICALLY AN ALLEGORY HIMSELF!
BUT ASO...
...IF YOU KEEP USING THAT POWER, SOONER OR LATER...

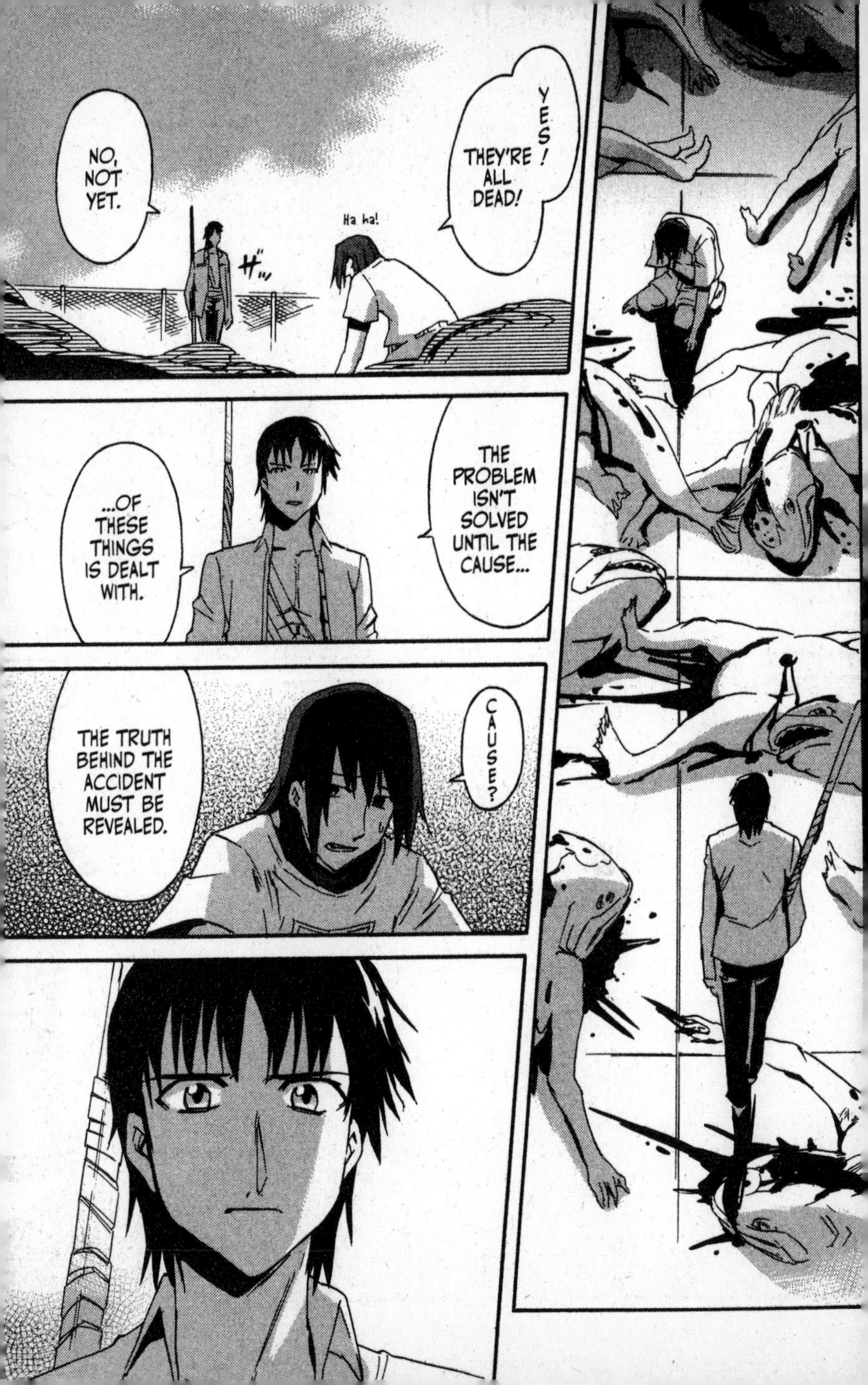
YES! THEY'RE ALL DEAD!
Ha ha!
NO, NOT YET.
THE PROBLEM ISN'T SOLVED UNTIL THE CAUSE...
...OF THESE THINGS IS DEALT WITH.
CAUSE?
THE TRUTH BEHIND THE ACCIDENT MUST BE REVEALED.

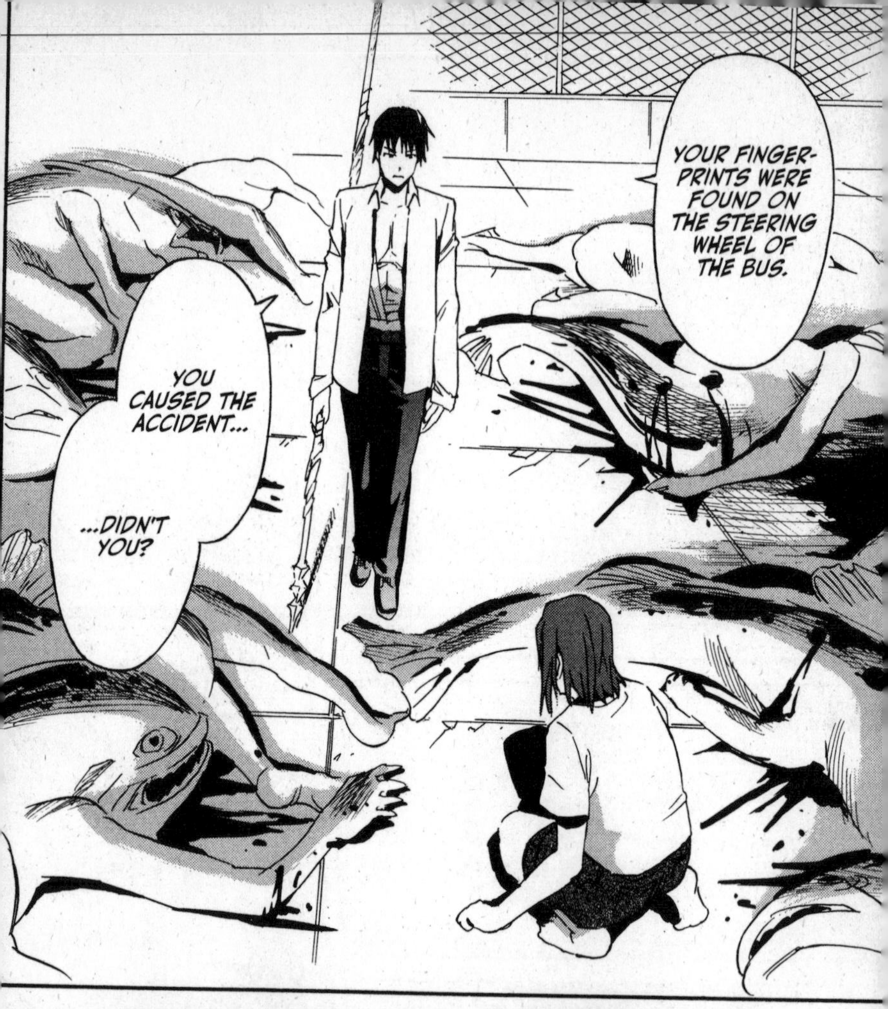
YOUR FINGER-PRINTS WERE FOUND ON THE STEERING WHEEL OF THE BUS.
YOU CAUSED THE ACCIDENT...
...DIDN'T YOU?
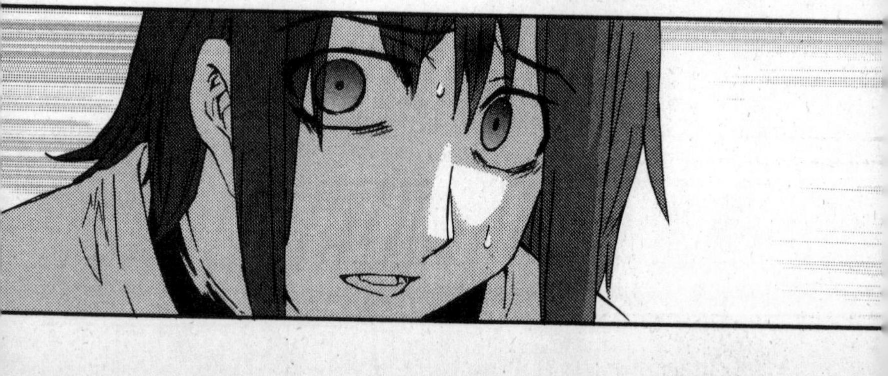

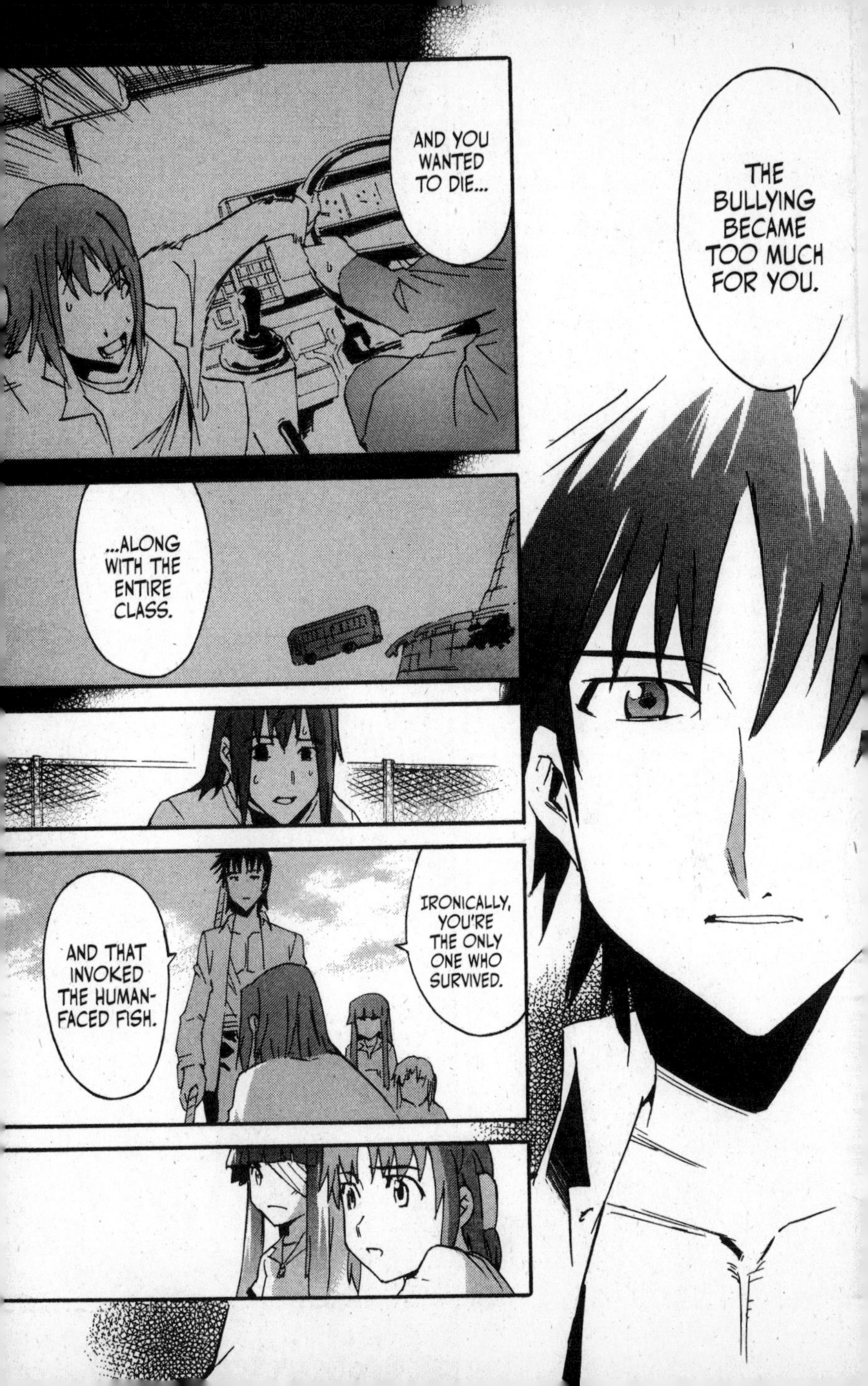
THE BULLYING BECAME TOO MUCH FOR YOU.
AND YOU WANTED TO DIE...
...ALONG WITH THE ENTIRE CLASS.
IRONICALLY, YOU'RE THE ONLY ONE WHO SURVIVED.
AND THAT INVOKED THE HUMAN-FACED FISH.

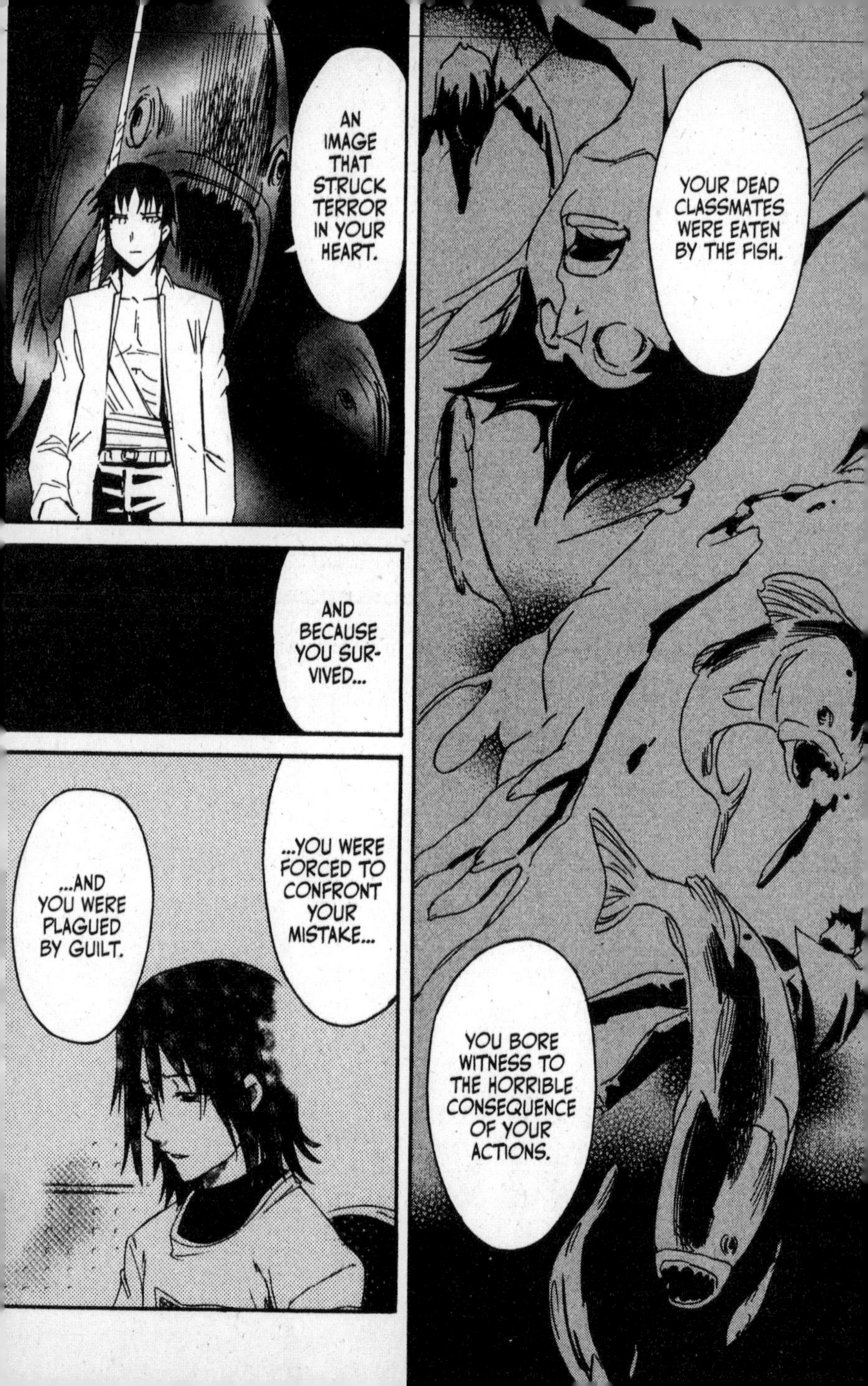
YOUR DEAD CLASSMATES WERE EATEN BY THE FISH.
YOU BORE WITNESS TO THE HORRIBLE CONSEQUENCE OF YOUR ACTIONS.
AN IMAGE THAT STRUCK TERROR IN YOUR HEART.
AND BECAUSE YOU SUR-VIVED...
...YOU WERE FORCED TO CONFRONT YOUR MISTAKE...
...AND YOU WERE PLAGUED BY GUILT.

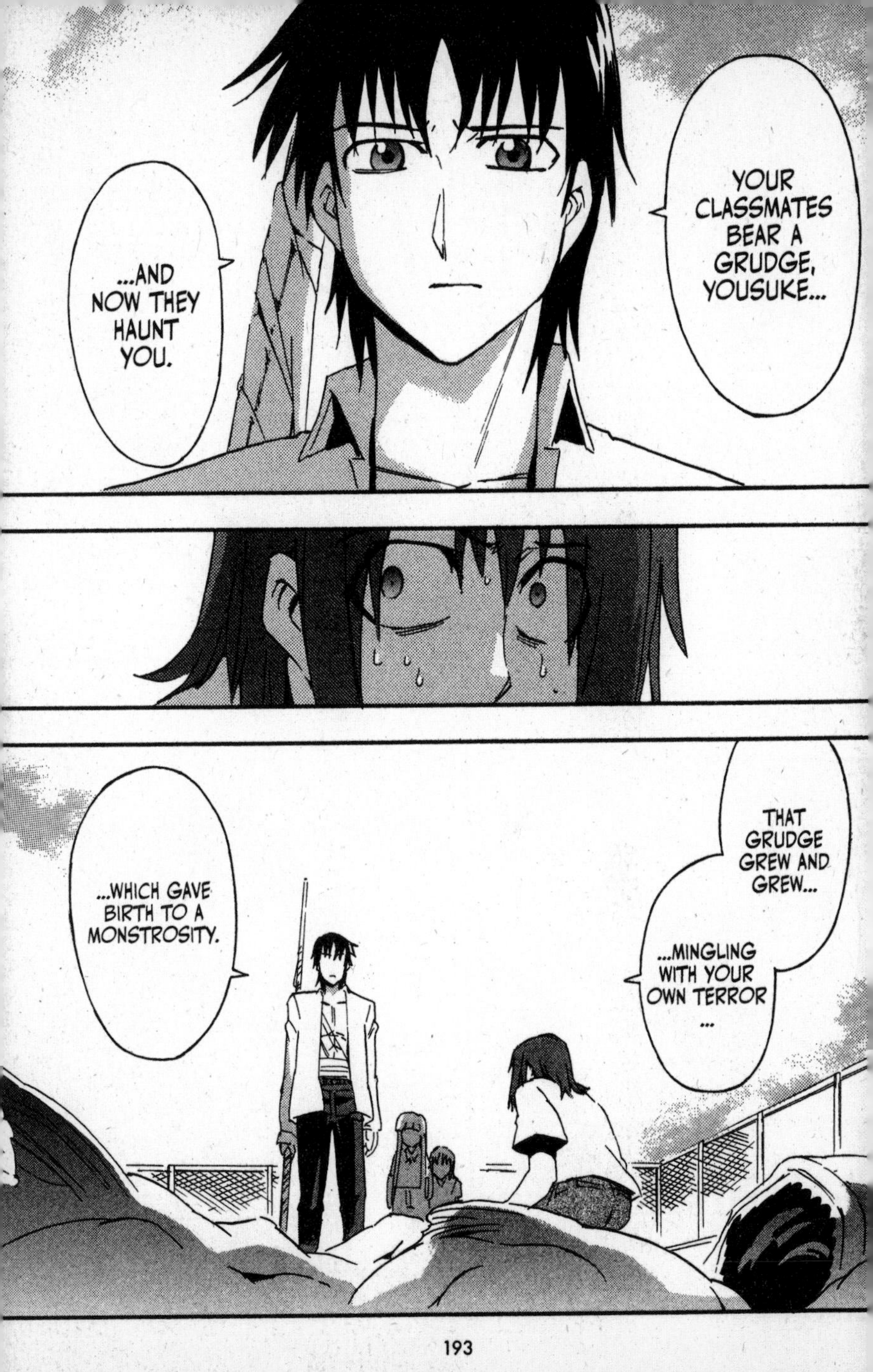
YOUR CLASSMATES BEAR A GRUDGE, YOUSUKE...
...AND NOW THEY HAUNT YOU.
THAT GRUDGE GREW AND GREW...
...MINGLING WITH YOUR OWN TERROR ...
...WHICH GAVE BIRTH TO A MONSTROSITY.

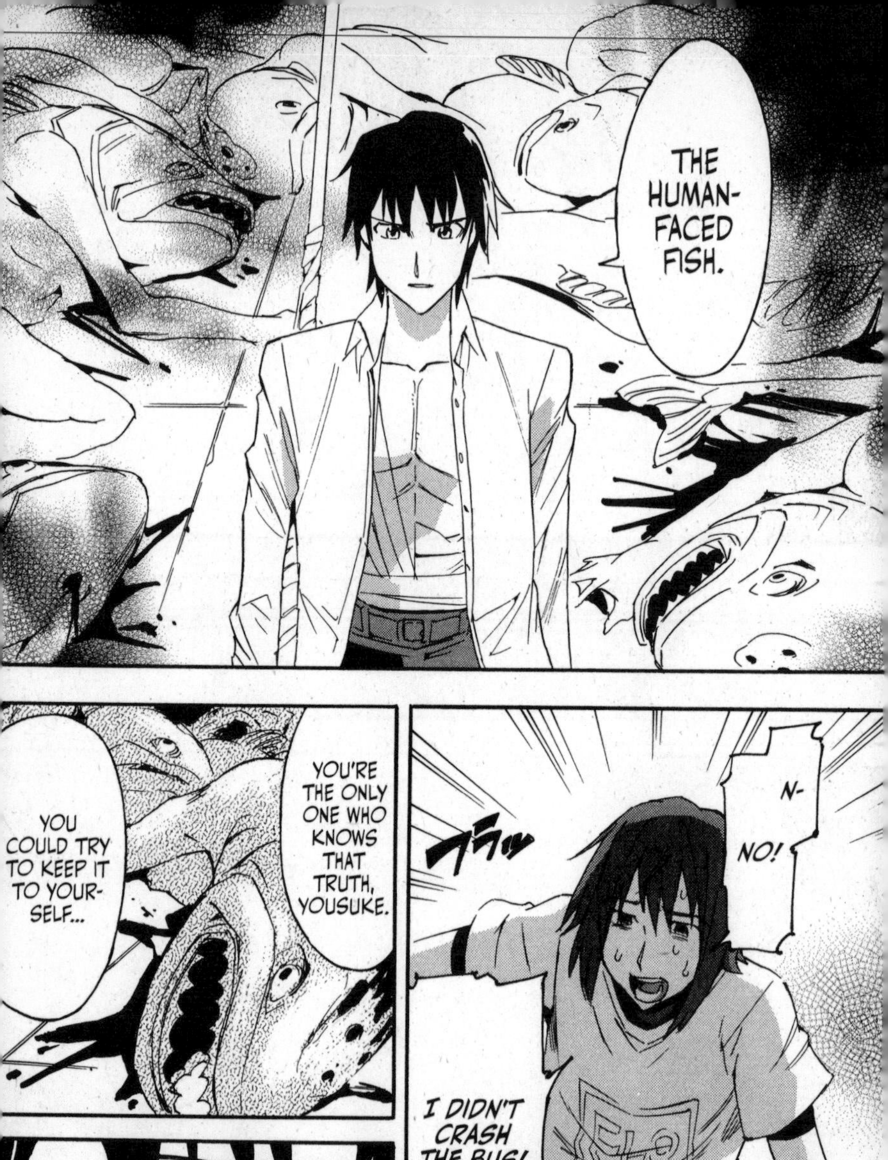
THE HUMAN-FACED FISH.
N-
NO!
フラッ
I DIDN'T CRASH THE BUS!
YOU'RE THE ONLY ONE WHO KNOWS THAT TRUTH, YOUSUKE.
YOU COULD TRY TO KEEP IT TO YOURSELF...
HOW-EVER...

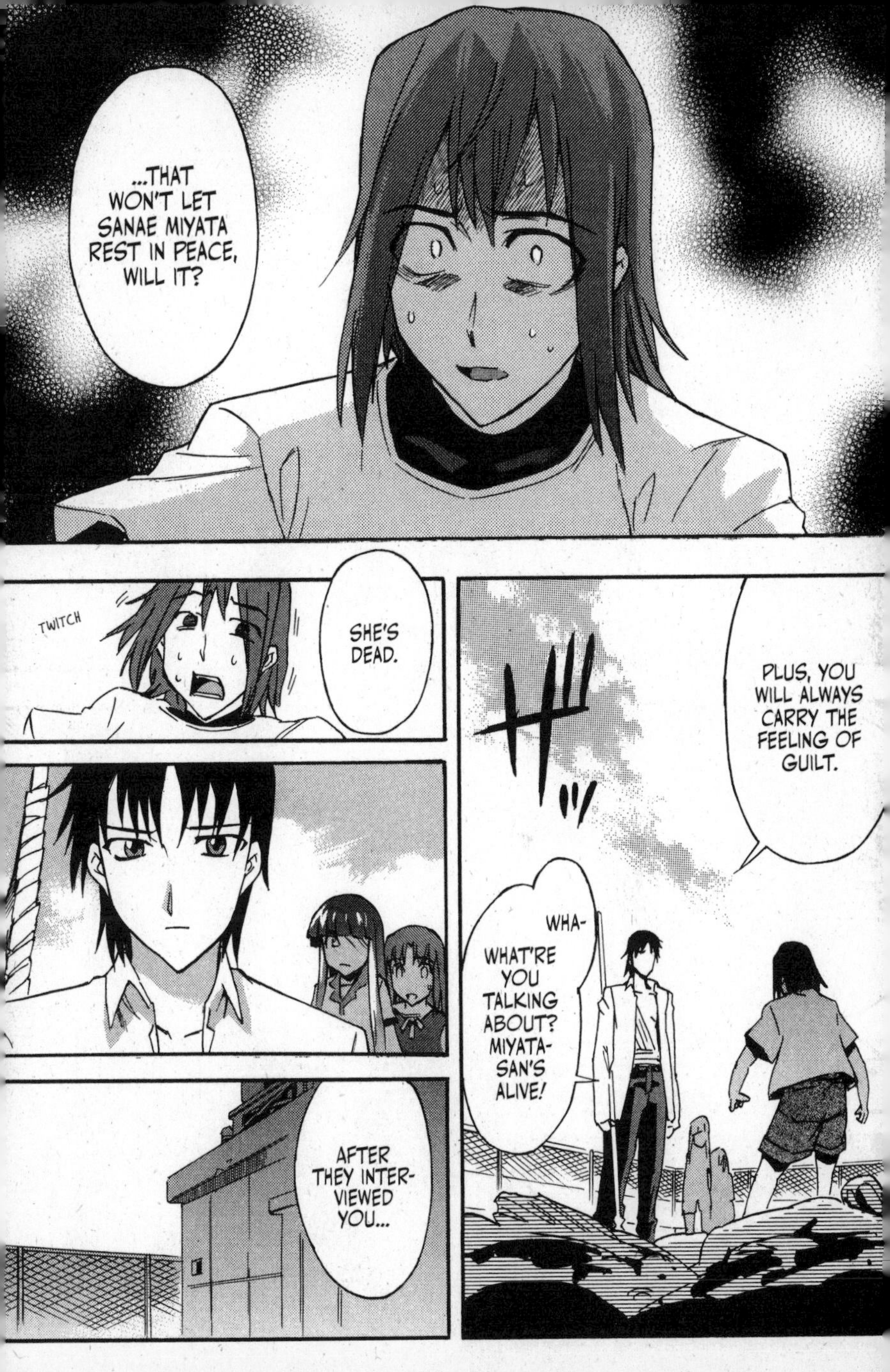
...THAT WON'T LET SANAE MIYATA REST IN PEACE, WILL IT?
PLUS, YOU WILL ALWAYS CARRY THE FEELING OF GUILT.
WHA-
WHAT'RE YOU TALKING ABOUT? MIYATA-SAN'S ALIVE!
TWITCH
SHE'S DEAD.
AFTER THEY INTER-VIEWED YOU...

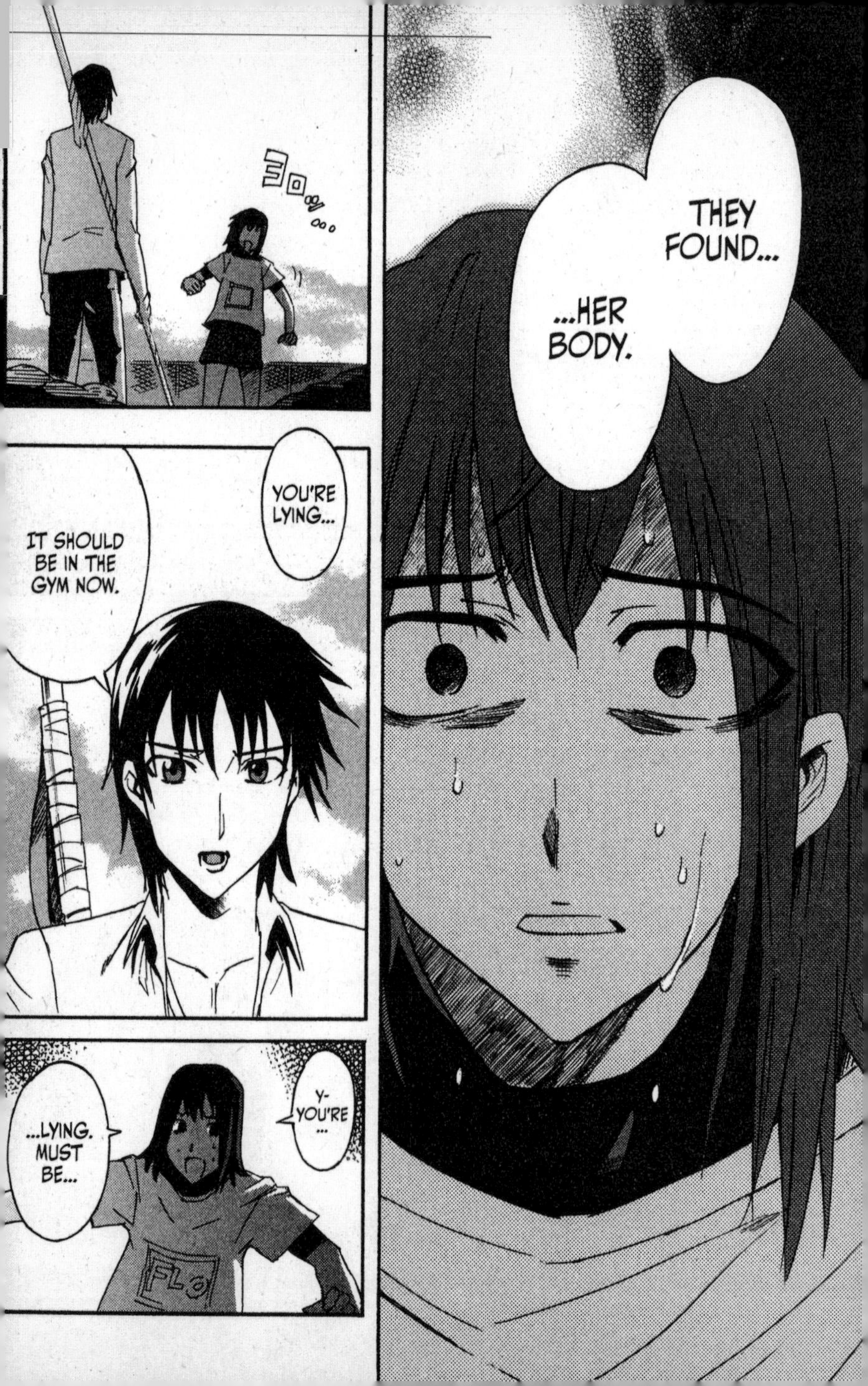
THEY FOUND...
...HER BODY.
ヨロッ
YOU'RE LYING...
IT SHOULD BE IN THE GYM NOW.
Y-YOU'RE ...
...LYING. MUST BE...

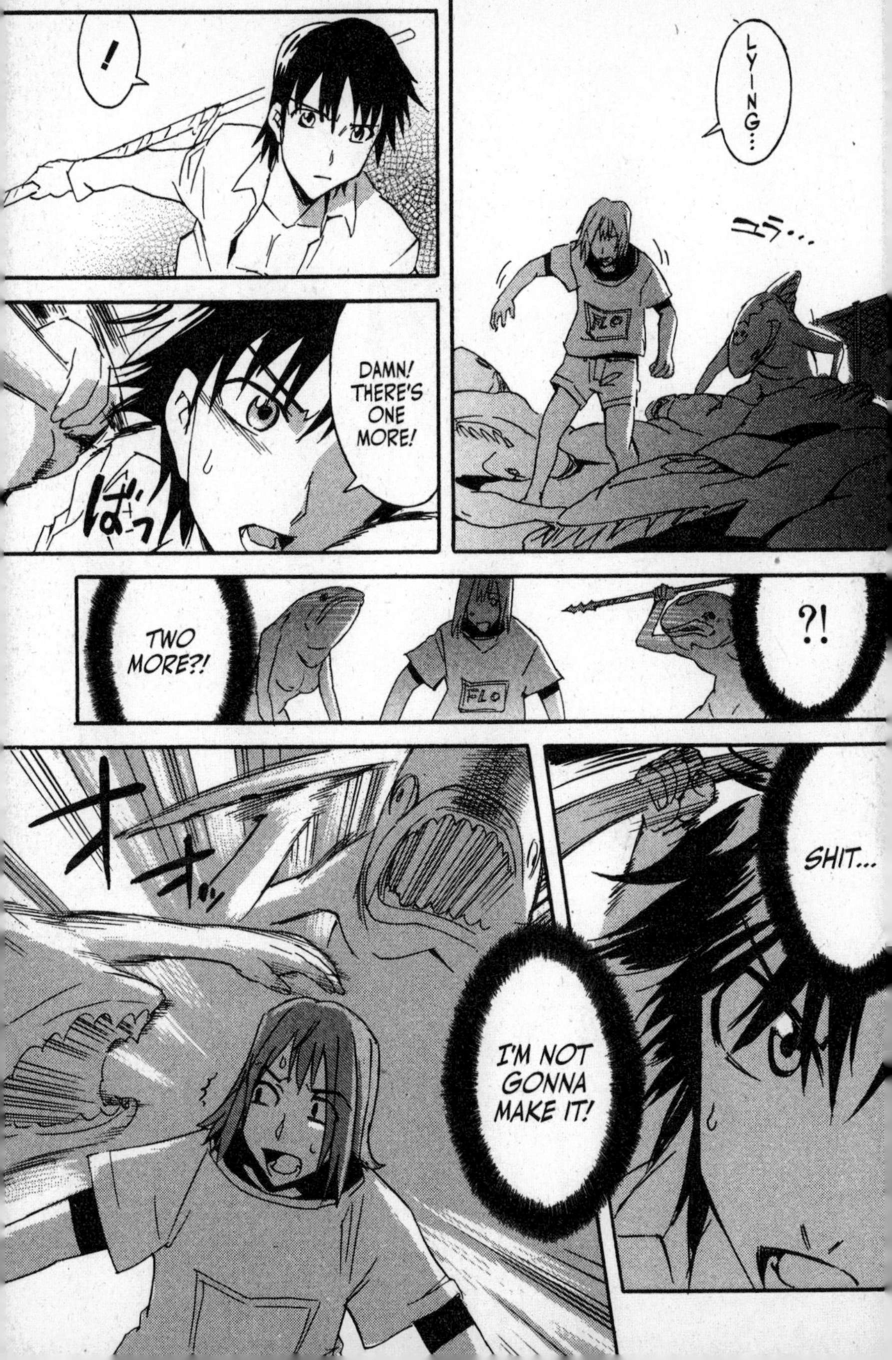
LYING...
ユラ...
!
DAMN! THERE'S ONE MORE!
ばっ
?!
TWO MORE?!
SHIT...
I'M NOT GONNA MAKE IT!
オオッ

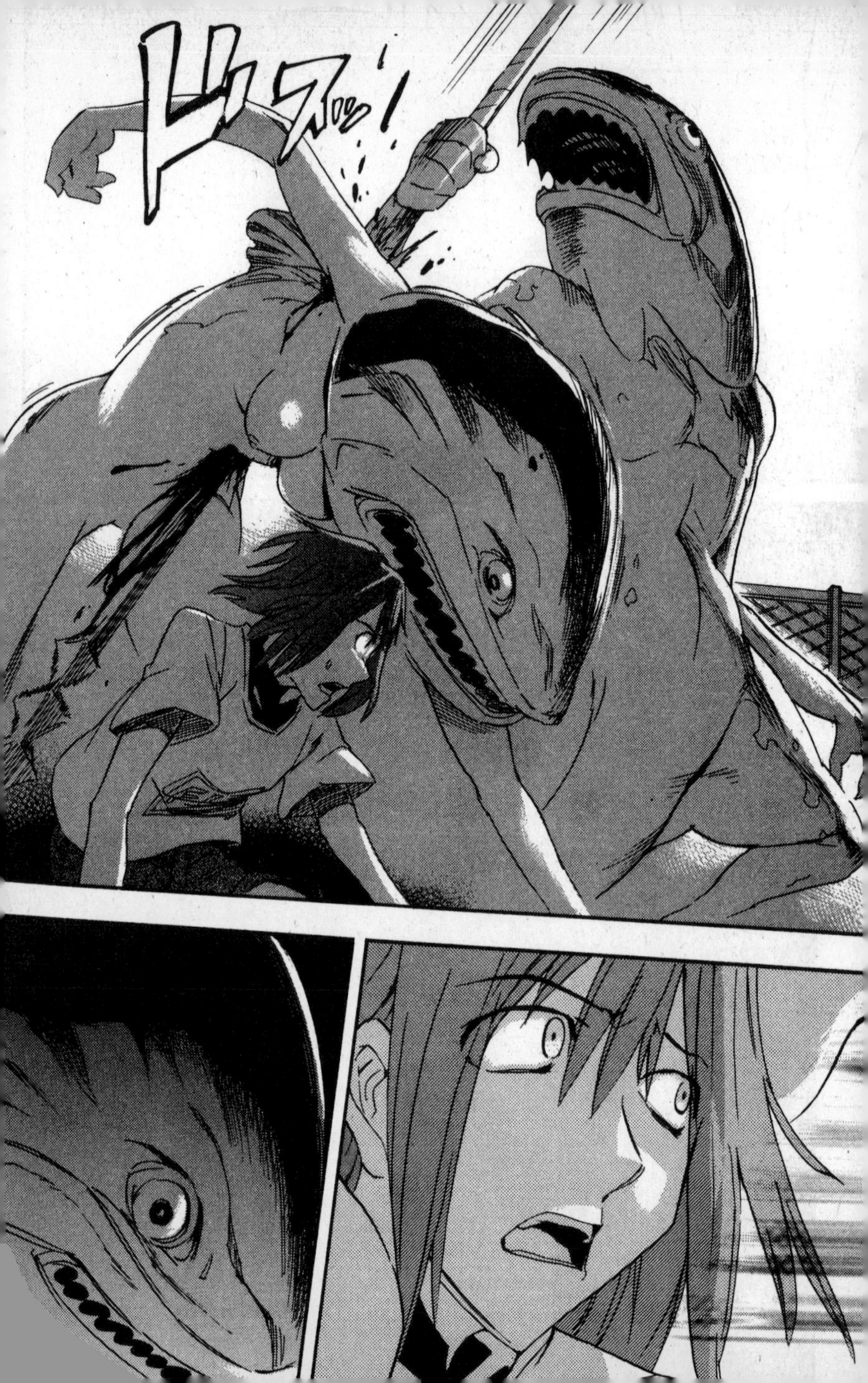

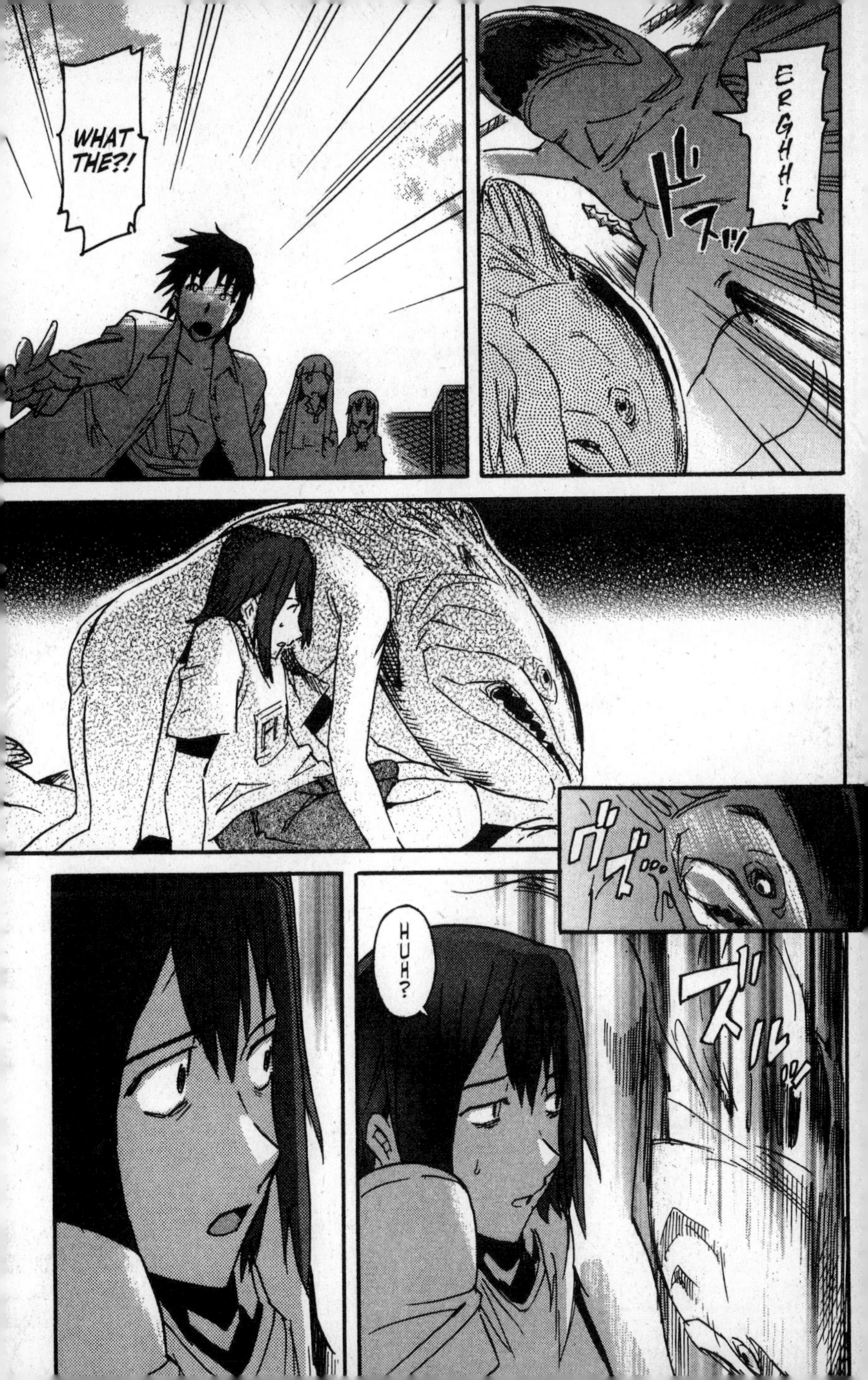
ERGHH!
WHAT THE?!
HUH?

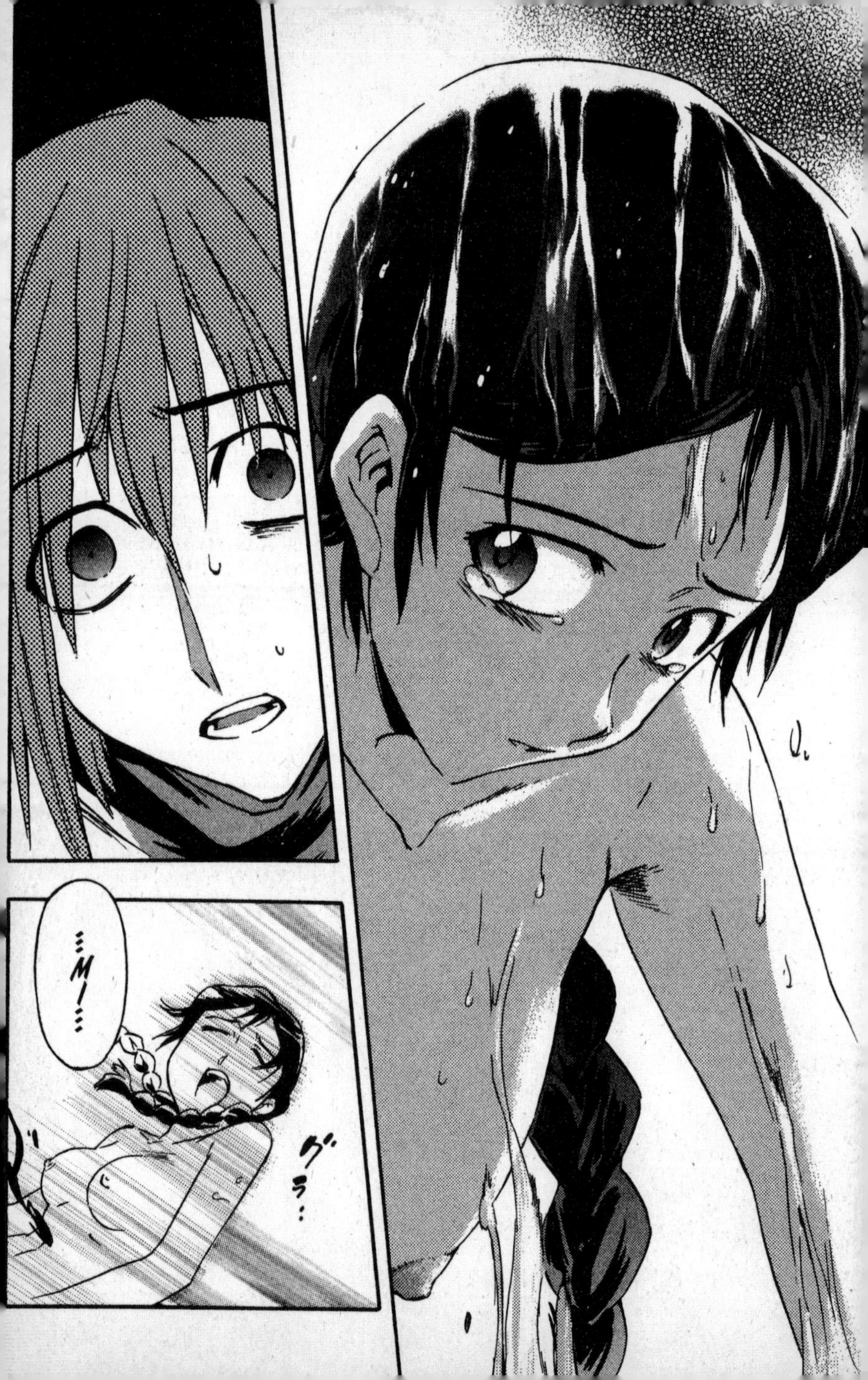
...MI...
グラ‥

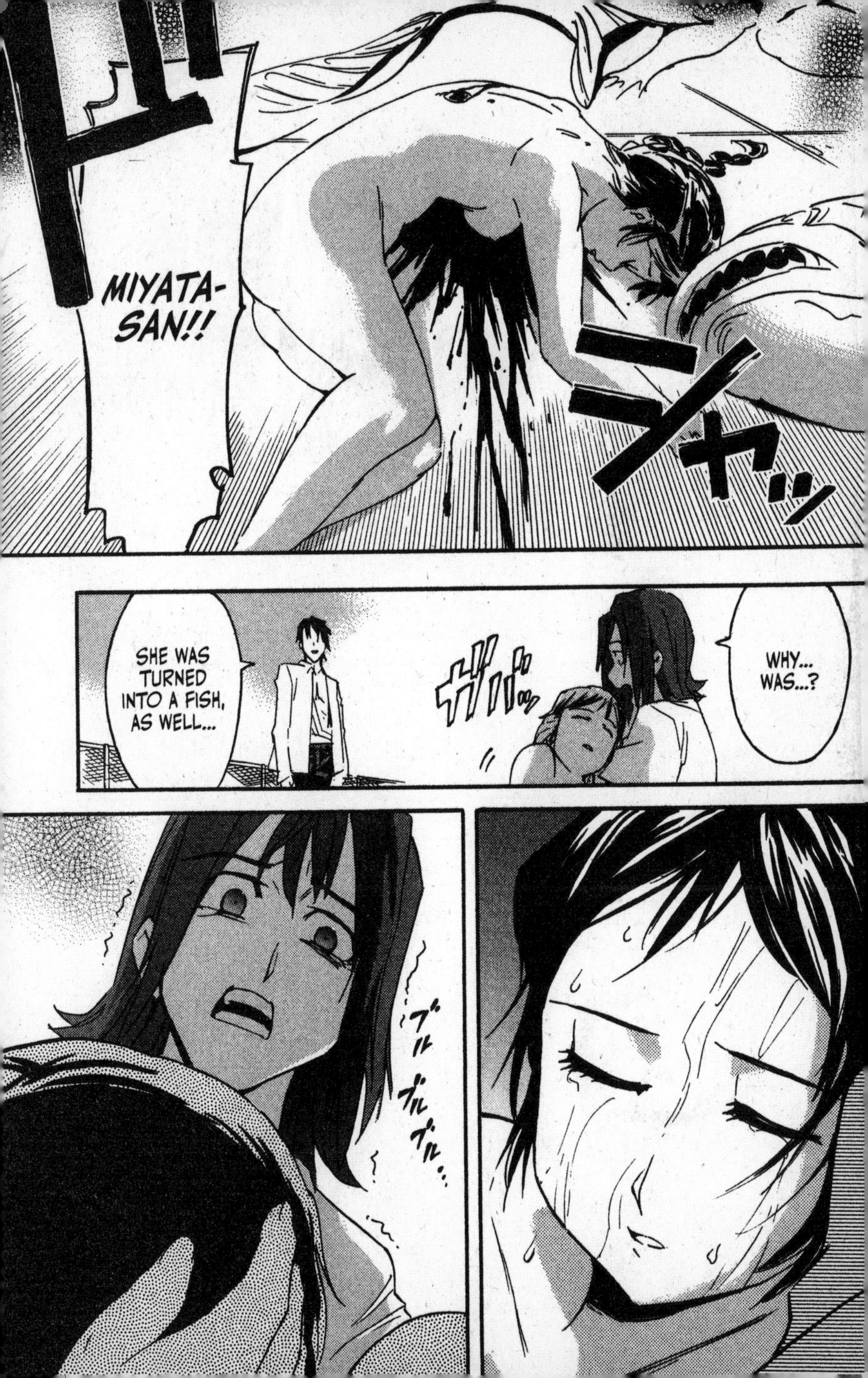
MIYATA-SAN!!
WHY... WAS...?
ガバッ
SHE WAS TURNED INTO A FISH, AS WELL...
ブル
ブルブル...

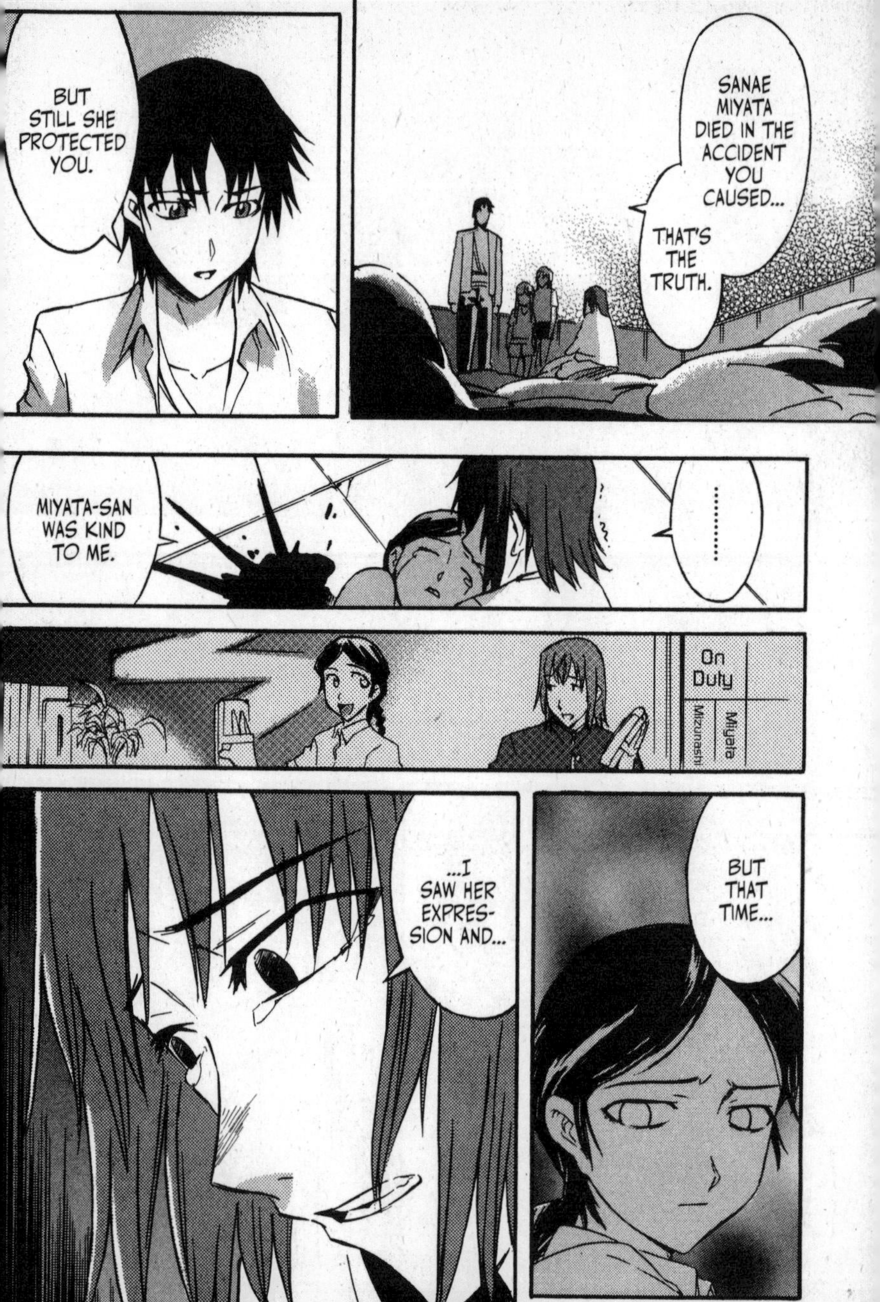
SANAE MIYATA DIED IN THE ACCIDENT YOU CAUSED...
THAT'S THE TRUTH.
BUT STILL SHE PROTECTED YOU.
....
MIYATA-SAN WAS KIND TO ME.
On Duty
Miyata
Mizunashi
BUT THAT TIME...
...I SAW HER EXPRESSION AND...

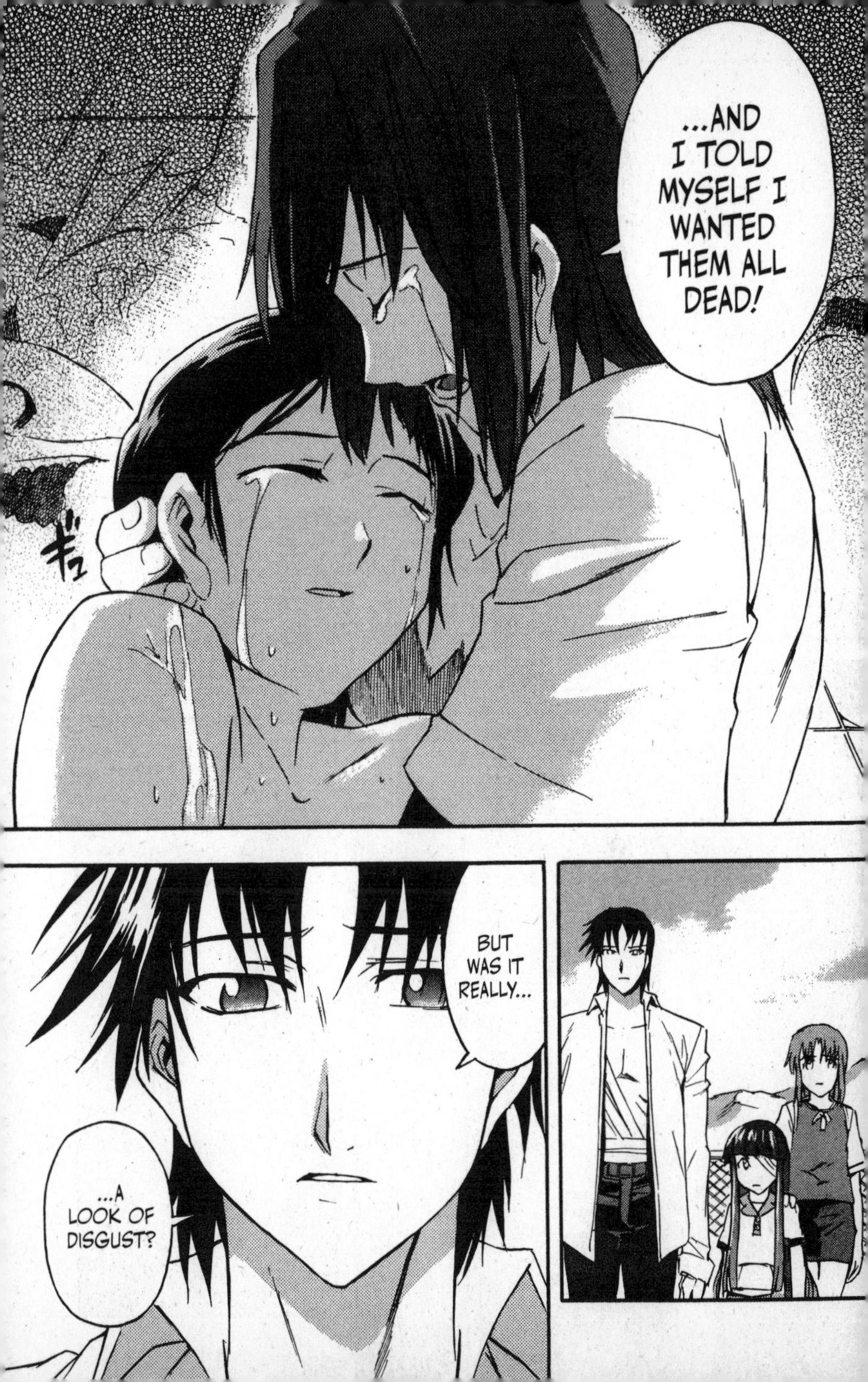
...AND I TOLD MYSELF I WANTED THEM ALL DEAD!
ギュ
BUT WAS IT REALLY...
...A LOOK OF DISGUST?

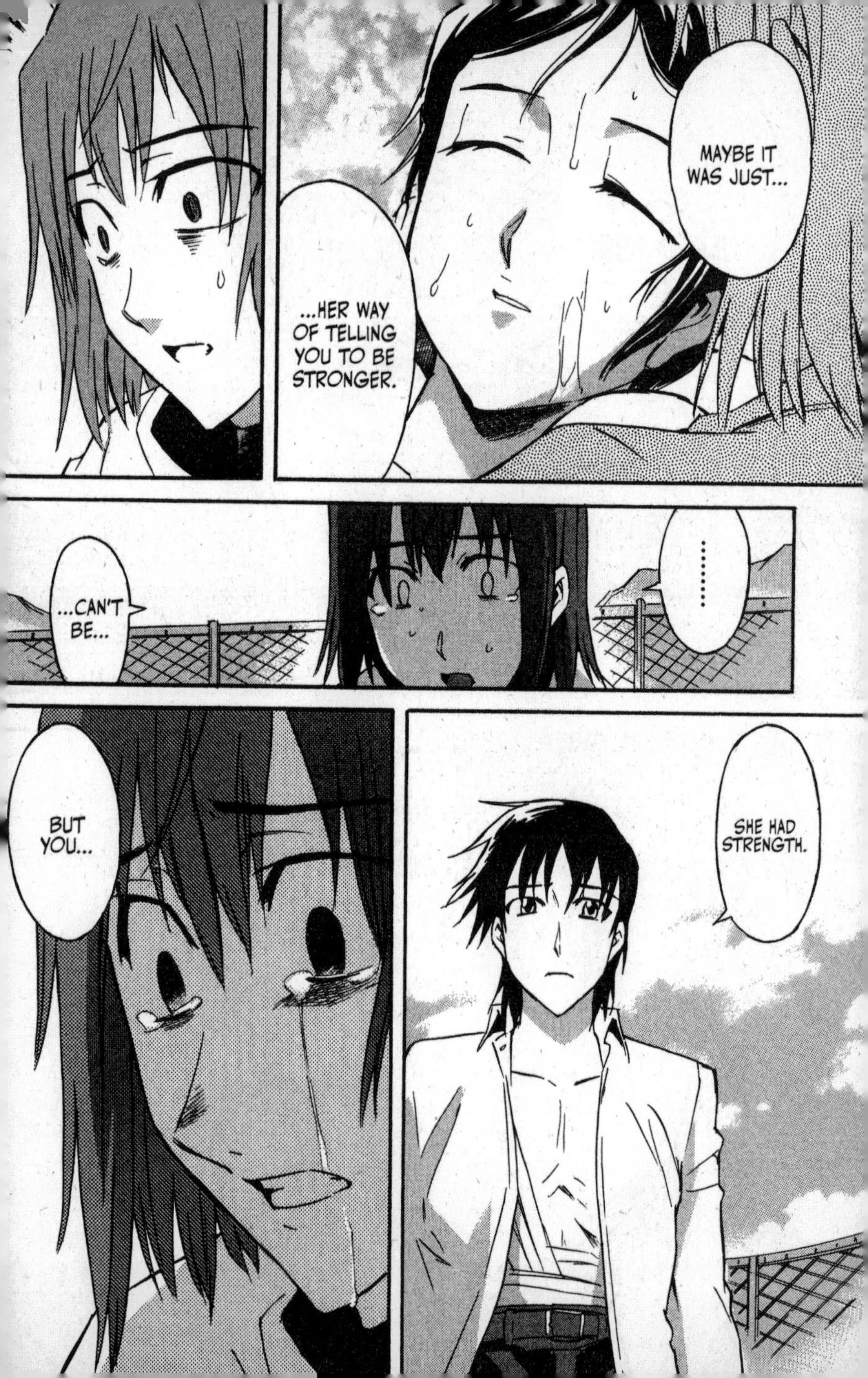
MAYBE IT WAS JUST...
...HER WAY OF TELLING YOU TO BE STRONGER.
......
...CAN'T BE...
SHE HAD STRENGTH.
BUT YOU...

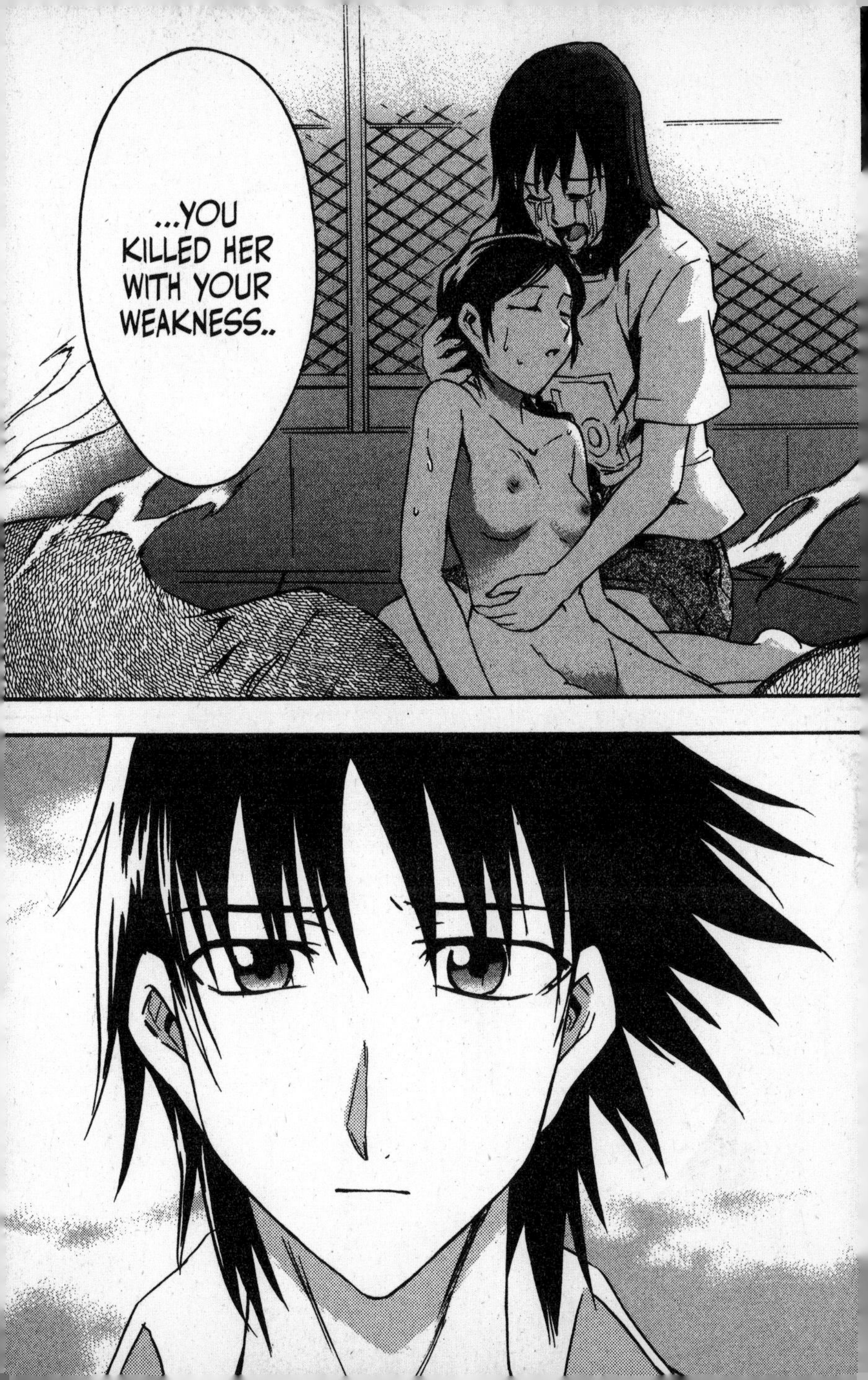
...YOU KILLED HER WITH YOUR WEAKNESS..

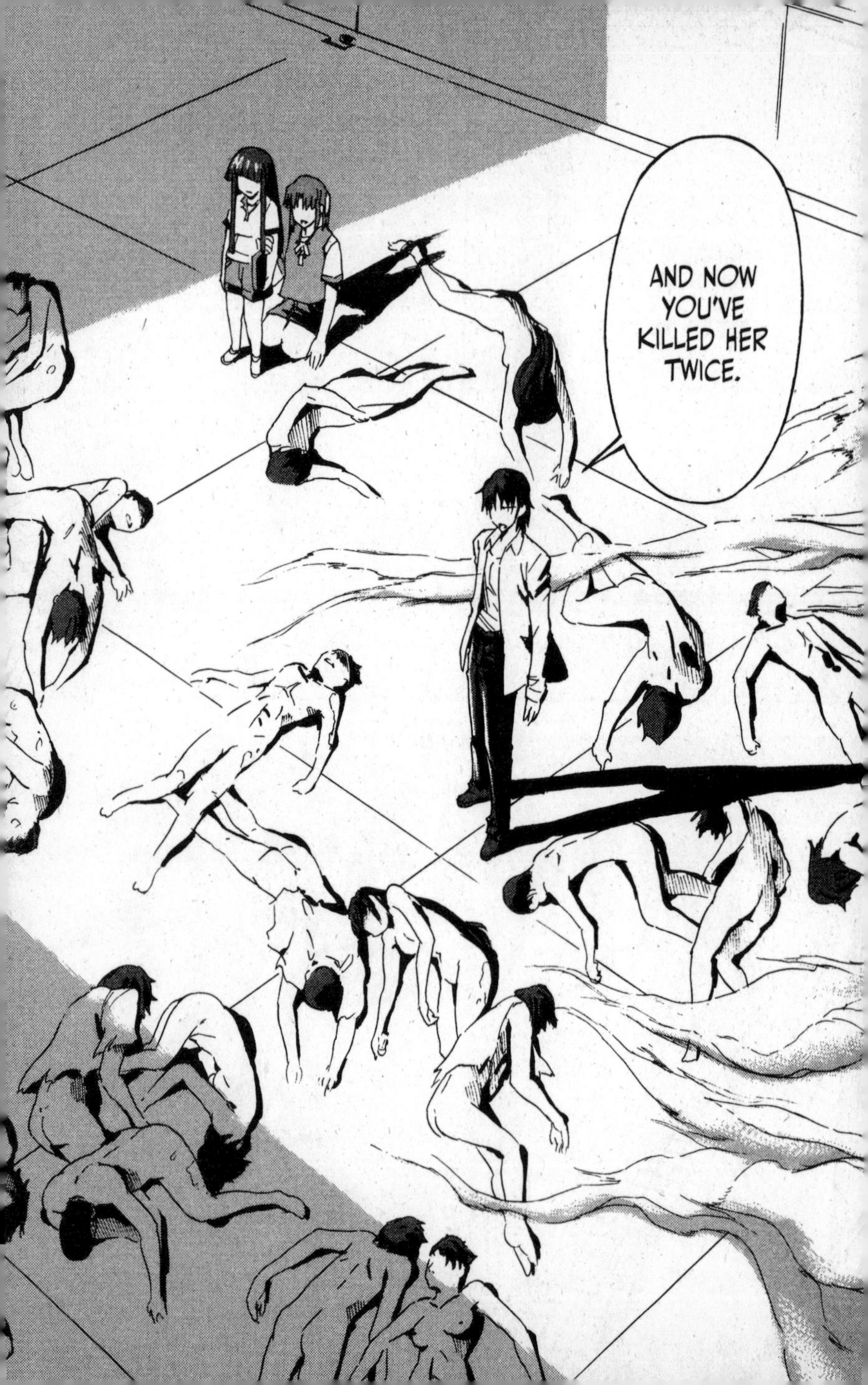
AND NOW YOU'VE KILLED HER TWICE.

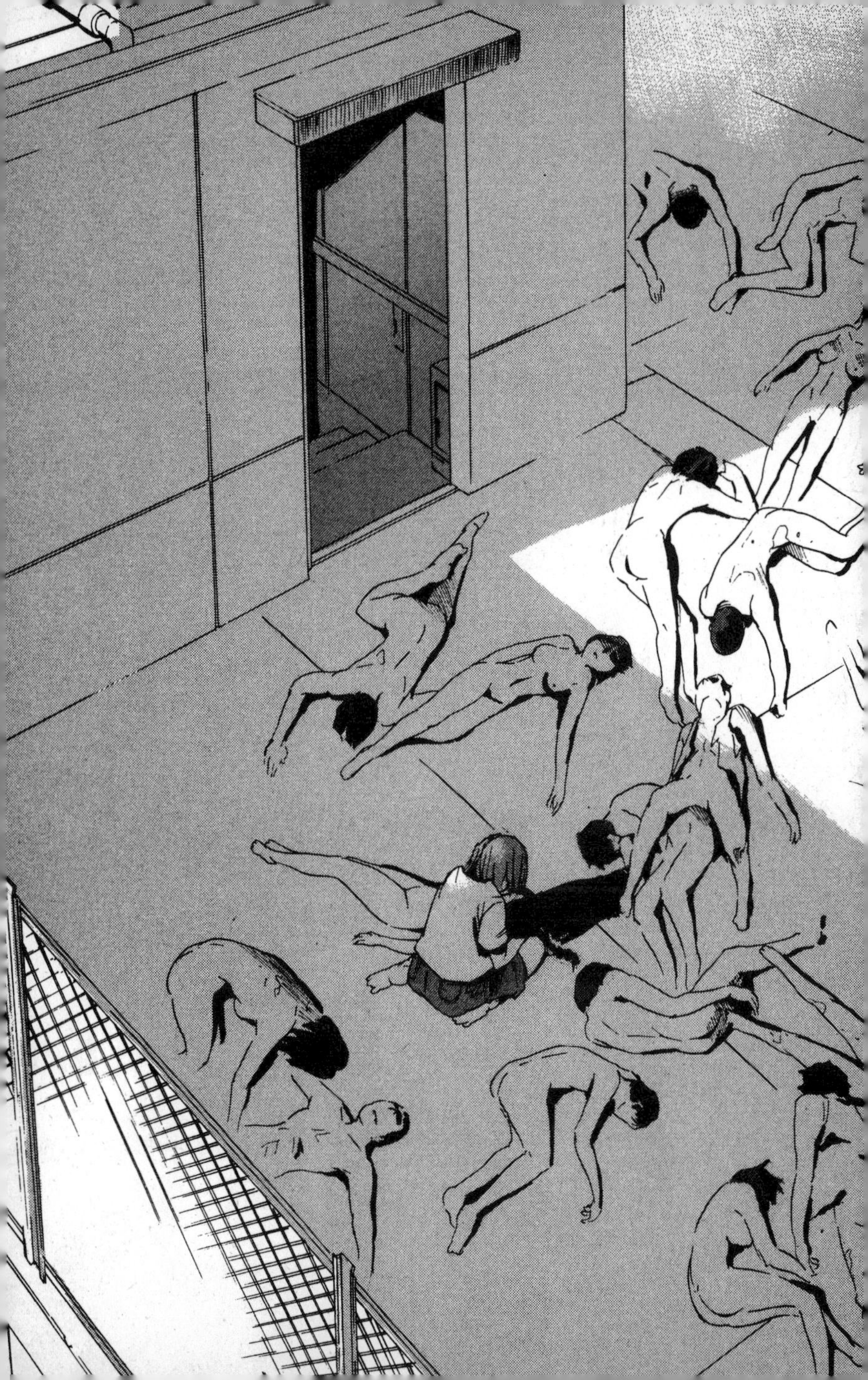

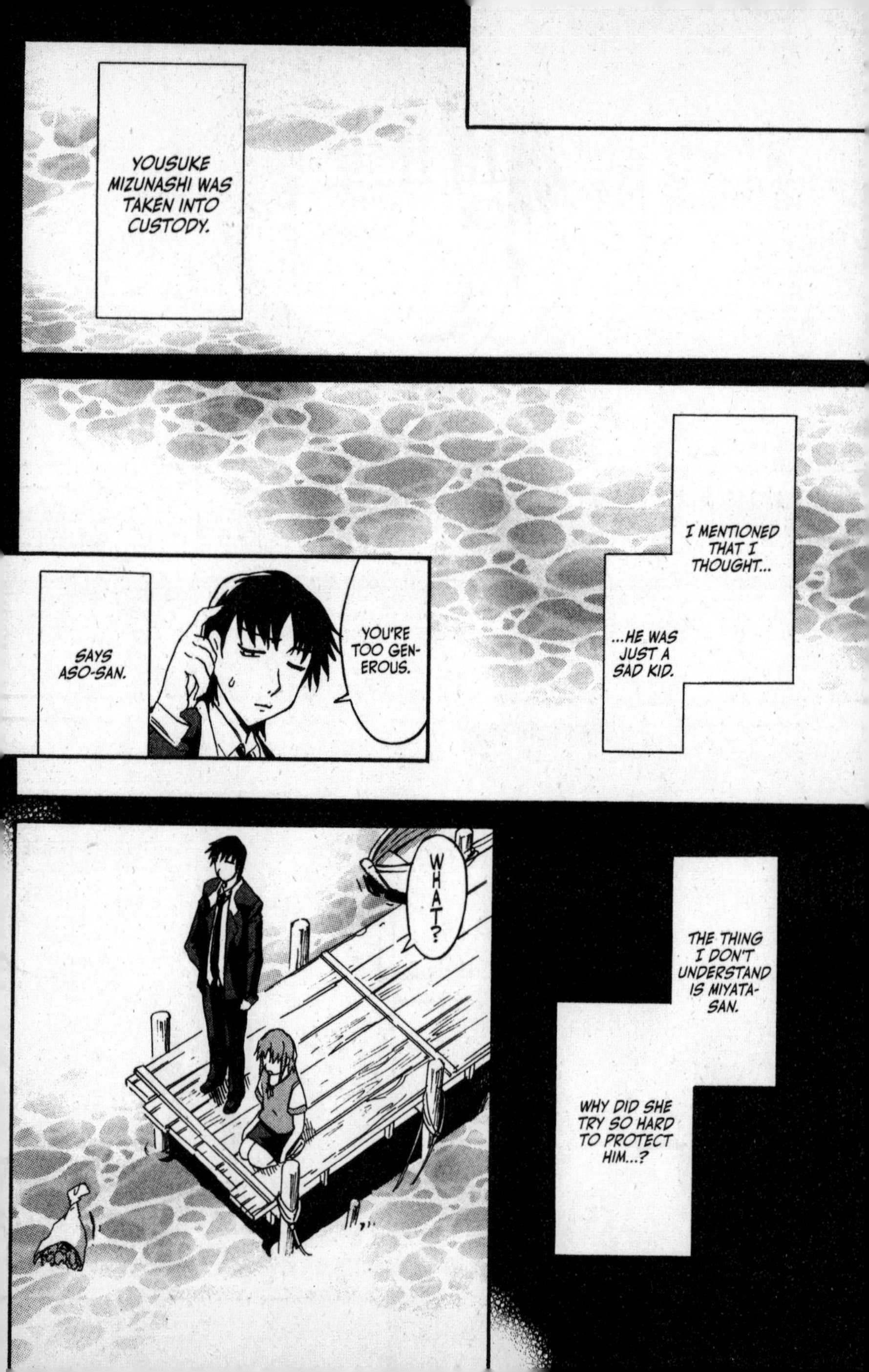
YOUSUKE MIZUNASHI WAS TAKEN INTO CUSTODY.
I MENTIONED THAT I THOUGHT...
...HE WAS JUST A SAD KID.
YOU'RE TOO GEN-EROUS.
SAYS ASO-SAN.
THE THING I DON'T UNDERSTAND IS MIYATA-SAN.
WHY DID SHE TRY SO HARD TO PROTECT HIM...?
WHAT?

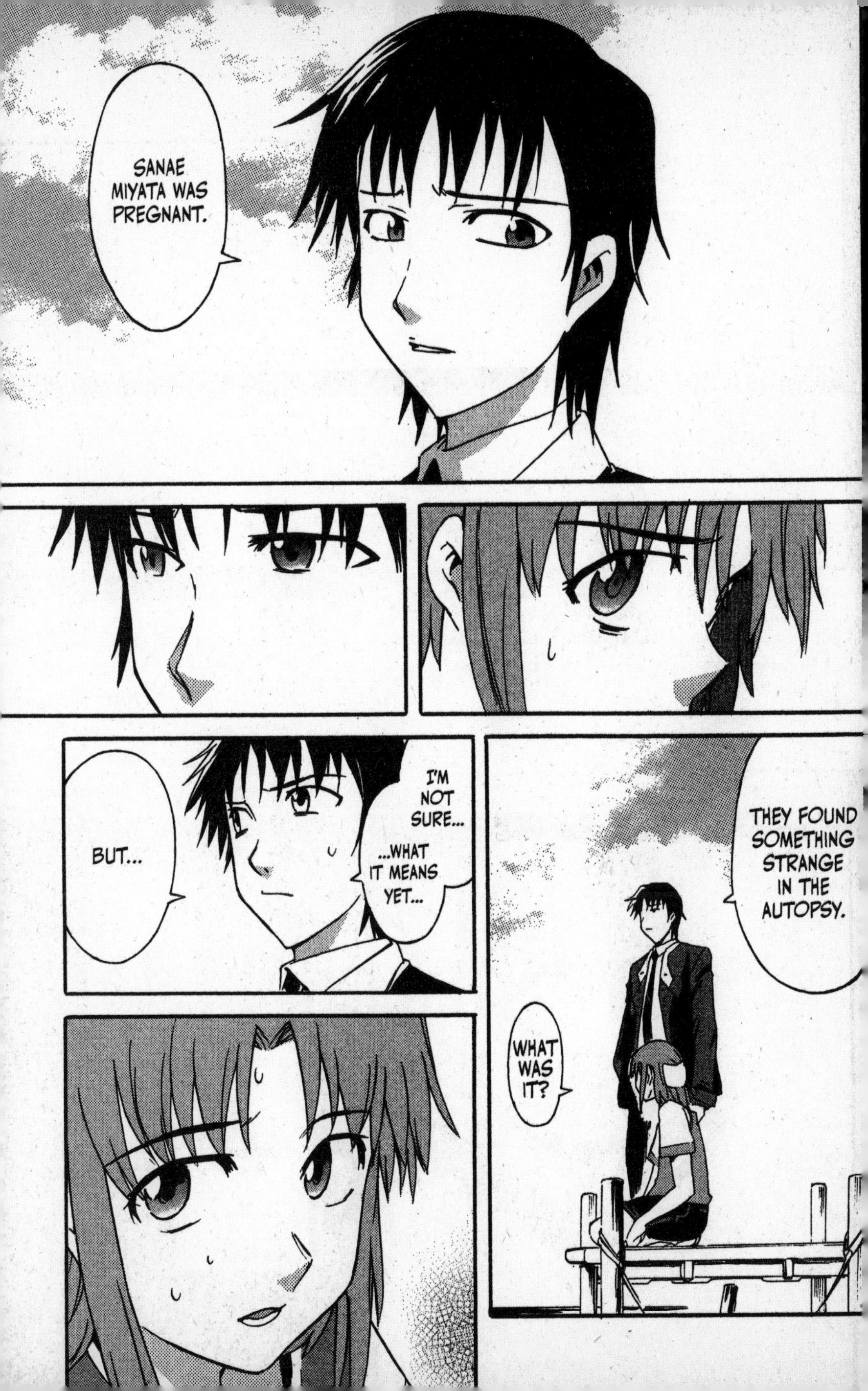
SANAE MIYATA WAS PREGNANT.
THEY FOUND SOMETHING STRANGE IN THE AUTOPSY.
WHAT WAS IT?
I'M NOT SURE...
...WHAT IT MEANS YET...
BUT...

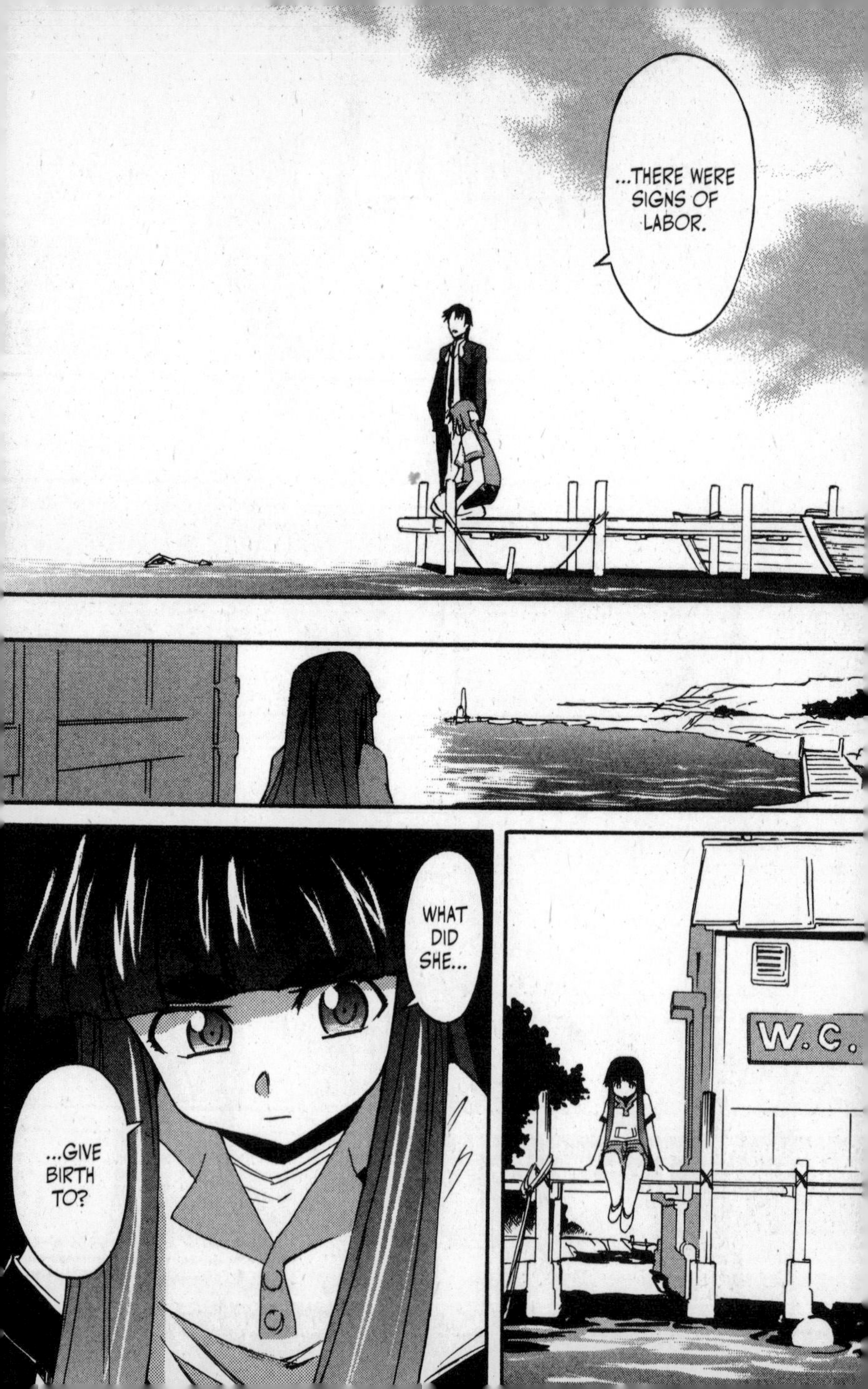
...THERE WERE SIGNS OF LABOR.
W.C.
WHAT DID SHE...
...GIVE BIRTH TO?

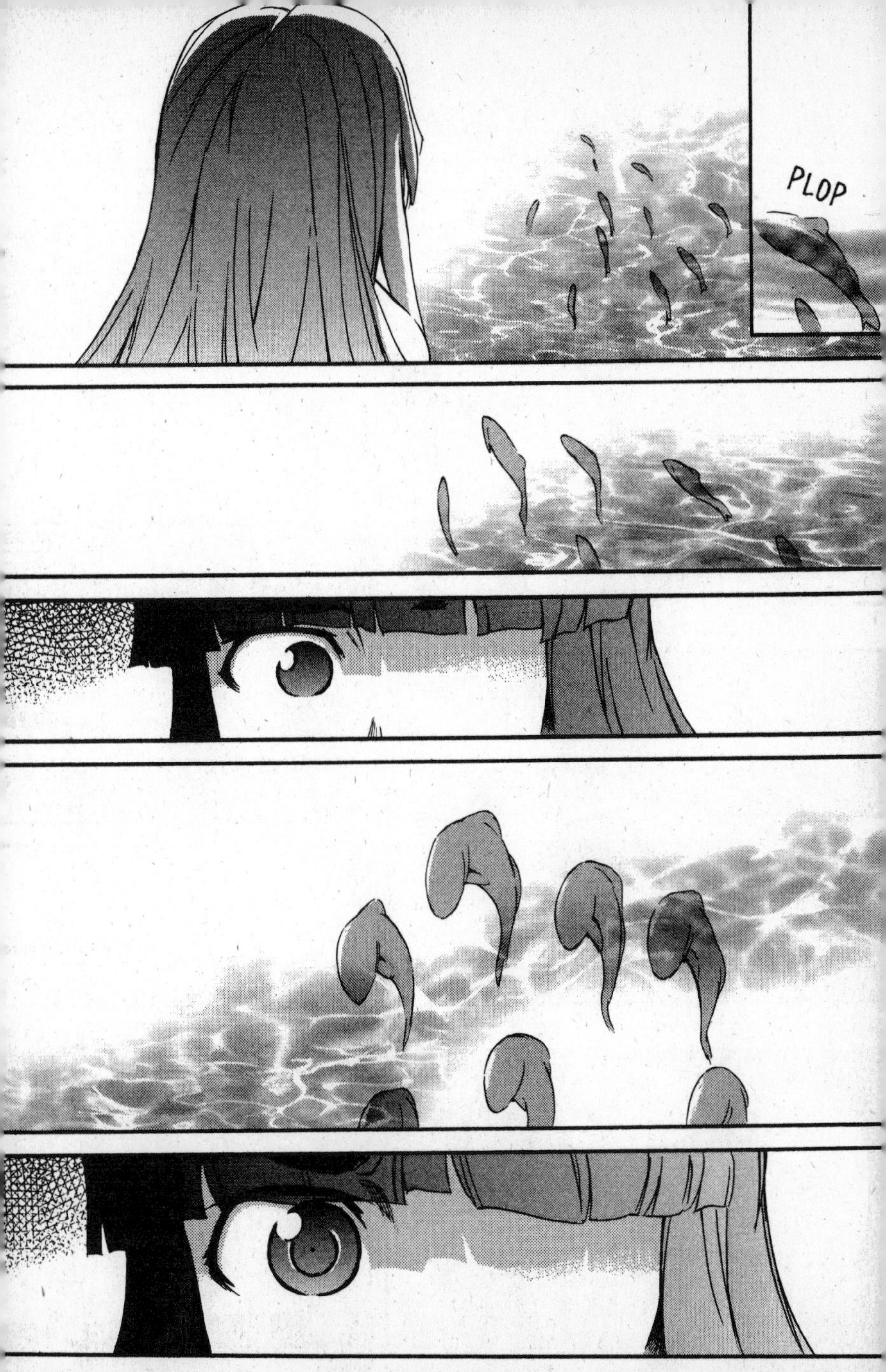
PLOP

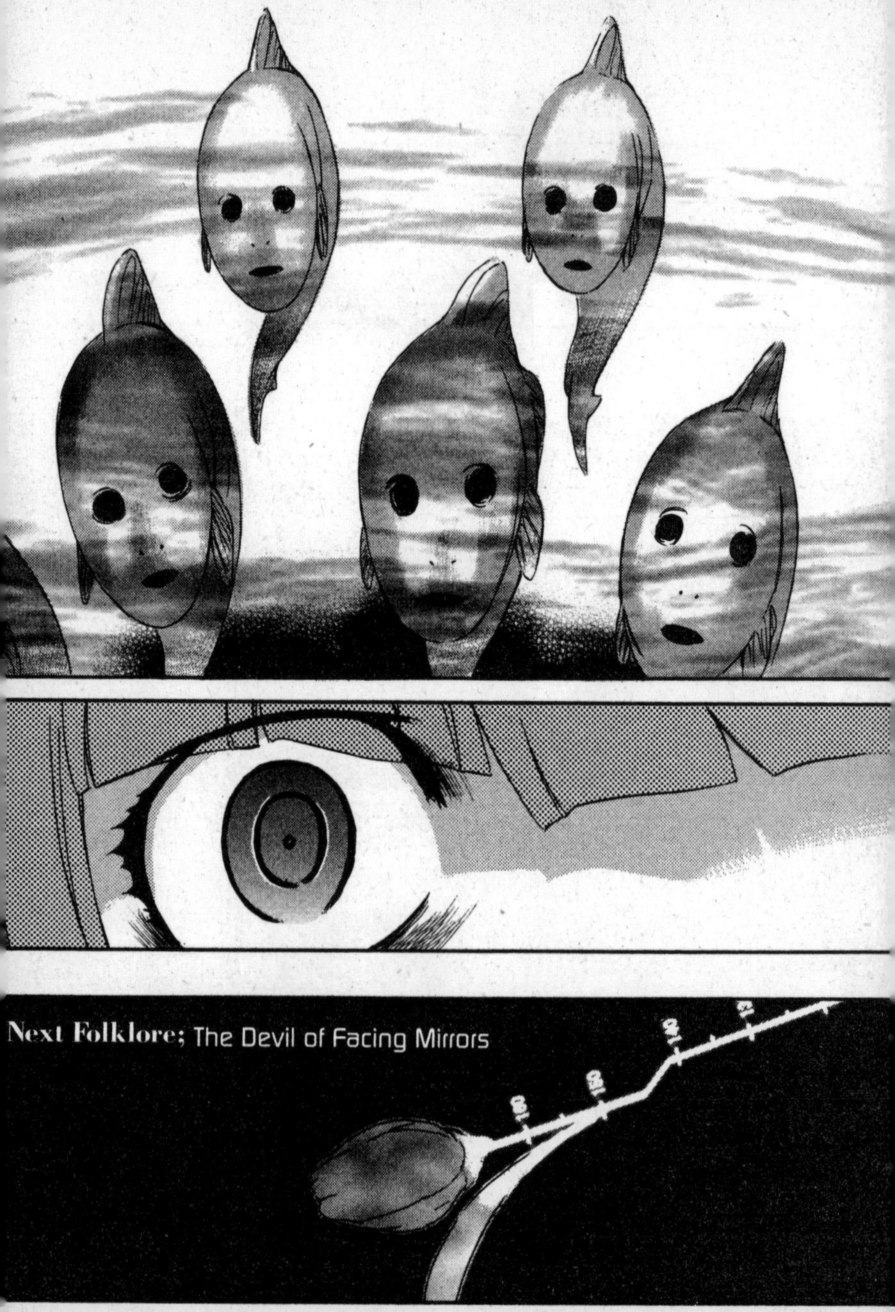
Next Folklore; The Devil of Facing Mirrors

to be continued... File;2

Commentary

The Man Under the Bed

THE STORY ABOUT A STRANGE MAN HIDING UNDER THE BED WITH AN AXE IS A FAIRLY NEW ADDITION TO FOLKLORE.

ONLY RECENTLY HAS THE PROBLEM OF VIOLENT STALKERS BECOME MORE PREVALENT IN JAPAN. IT IS THIS RECENT, ALBEIT UNFORTUNATE, HISTORY THAT LENDS CREDIBILITY TO THIS TALE.

FEELINGS OF FEAR AND TERROR, AND THE CONCEPTS THAT INCITE THOSE FEELINGS ARE SPECIFIC TO THE TIMES WE LIVE IN. FOLKLORE IS A DIRECT REFLECTION OF THOSE TIMES AND THEIR CORRESPONDING SOCIETAL CONDITIONS.

Slit Mouthed Woman

AMONG ALL LEGENDS IN FOLKLORE, THIS IS THE STORY THAT IS SAID TO BE THE MOST WIDELY KNOWN.

IT IS ABOUT A WOMAN, HER MOUTH SLIT FROM EAR-TO-EAR, WEARING A MASK TO COVER THE ATROCITY, HAUNTING PEOPLE WITH A SINGLE QUESTION:

"AM I BEAUTIFUL?"

IF YOU ANSWER NO, SHE WILL SLASH YOU TO DEATH. HOWEVER, IF YOU TELL HER SHE IS, SHE WILL TAKE OFF THE MASK, REVEALING THE HORROR, AND ASK, "HOW ABOUT NOW?"

AFTER WHICH... SHE WILL SLASH YOU TO PIECES. "SO-SO" IS THOUGHT TO BE THE BEST ANSWER, BUT NO ONE'S EVER LIVED TO TELL THE TALE, SO WHO KNOWS.

SHE'S ALSO AMAZINGLY FAST, ABLE TO RUN 100 METERS IN 3 SECONDS.

SHE LOVES SUGAR CANDY AND FEARS MEN WHO USE THE HAIR PRODUCT POMADE, AS WELL AS THE WORD, "POMADE" - ADDING A LITTLE HUMOR TO THE LEGEND.

Human-Faced Fish

AT ONE TIME, THIS WAS ONE OF THE HOTTEST RECURRING NEWS STORIES. BUT THE TRUTH WAS SIMPLY THAT A FISH HAD A PATTERN ON THE TOP OF ITS HEAD THAT VAGUELY RESEMBLED A HUMAN FACE.

IN THE SAME CATEGORY, THERE WAS A HUMAN-FACED DOG THAT WAS MUCH TALKED ABOUT. THE REASON WHY PEOPLE TALK ABOUT THEM WITH SOME LEVEL OF FEAR IS BECAUSE THEY ASSOCIATE THEM WITH A HUMAN'S WILL.

THINGS WITH HUMAN FACES HOUSING A HUMAN'S WILL.

WHAT WOULD THESE ANIMALS THINK ABOUT...?

IN THE NEXT VOLUME OF...

HANAKO 花子
AND THE TERROR OF ALLEGORY

THE SHOCKING TAILS CONTINUE IN VOLUME 2 OF HANAKO AND THE TERROR OF ALLEGORY. WHAT IS LURKING IN THE MIRRORS AT MIDNIGHT, AND WHAT HORROR IS CAUSING THE KILLING SPREE OF HUNDREDS OF SUICIDAL GIRLS? AND AS ASO DELVES INTO THE MIND OF KANAE'S BLIND COUSIN, HE AND HANAKO DISCOVER THE HAUNTING ALLEGORY THAT ENTRAPS HER. AND WHAT WILL HANAKO AND KANAE DO WHEN THEY SEE ASO LYING LIFELESS IN A POOL OF HIS OWN BLOOD?

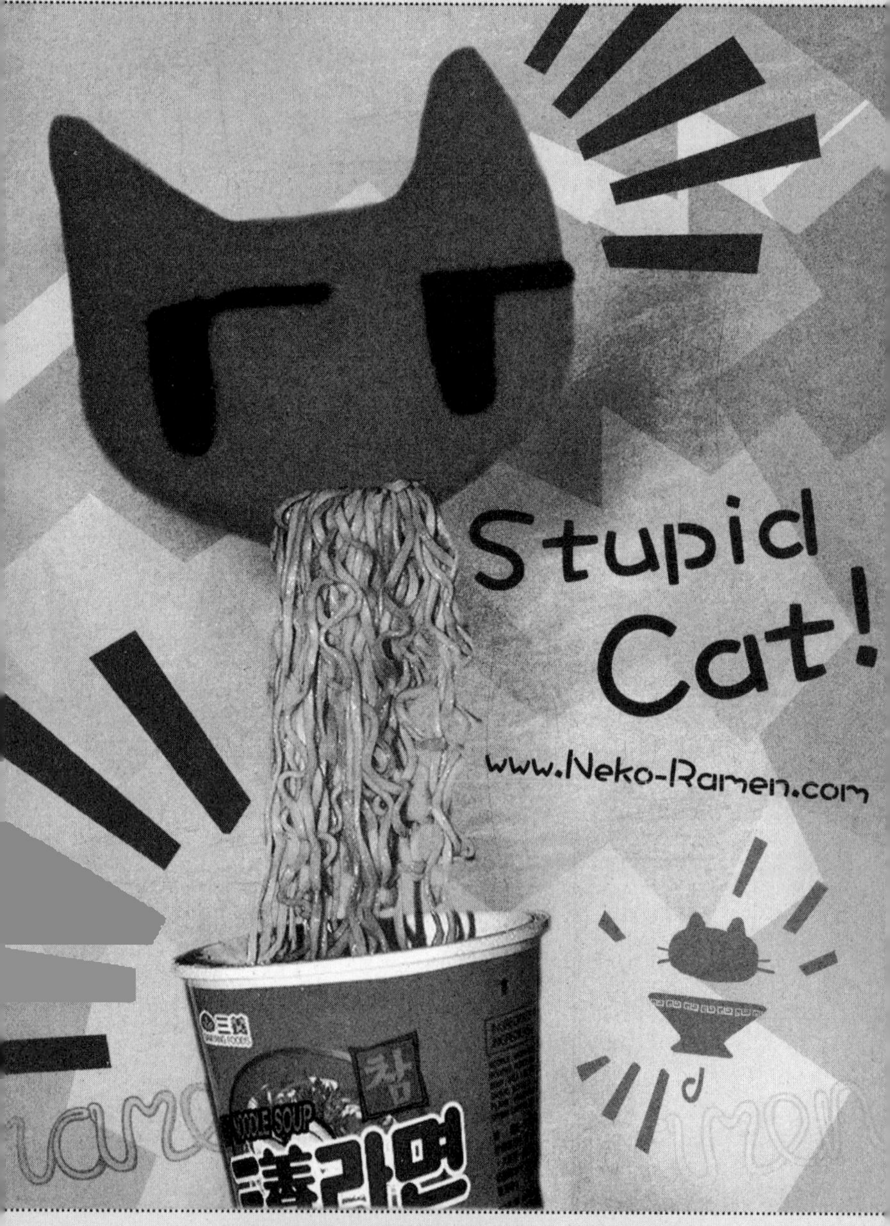
Stupid Cat!
www.Neko-Ramen.com

THE SMALLEST HERO!?

RATMAN

ラットマン

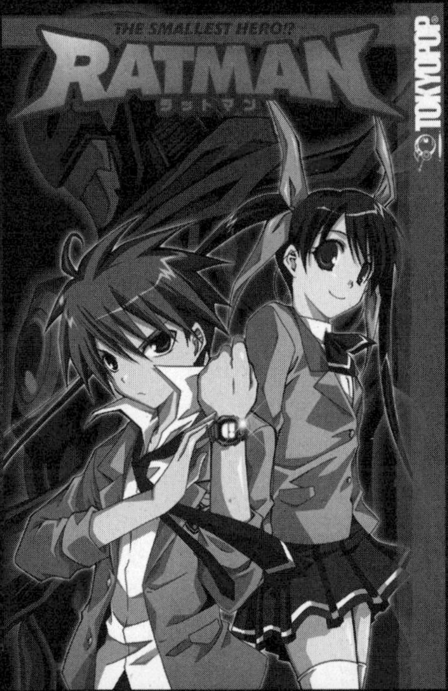
THE SMALLEST HERO!?
RATMAN
ラットマン
TOKYOPOP

Shuto Katsuragi is a shrimp that can't catch a break. He wants to emulate his favorite super hero, Mr. Thunder, but instead he gets teased all the time for his height and he can't win any fights. The one thing that keeps him going is his love for super heroes, which he shares with his classmate Mirea Mizushima. Little does he know that she's about to make his dreams come true by tricking him into participating in her mother's experiments!

ACTION

OT
OLDER TEEN AGE 16+

WWW.TOKYOPOP.COM/SHOP

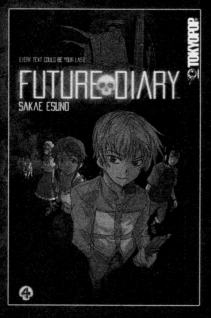

The second epic trilogy continues!

Princess Ai: The Prism of Midnight Dawn

Ai fights to escape the clutches of her mysterious and malevolent captors, not knowing whether Kent, left behind on the Other Side, is even still alive. A frantic rescue mission commences, and in the end, even Ai's magical voice may not be enough to protect her from the trials of the Black Forest.

Dark secrets are revealed, and Ai must use all her strength and courage to face off against the new threat to Ai-Land. But will she ever see Kent again...?

Princess Ai: The Prism of Midnight Dawn

Created by Courtney Love & Stuart "D.J. Milky" Levy
Story by Stuart "D.J. Milky" Levy Written by Christine Boylan Art by Misaho Kujiradou

2

"A very intriguing read that will satisfy old fans and create new fans, too."
– Bookloons

KARAKURI ODETTE

カラクリ オデット

VOL. 2

She's a robot who wants to learn how to be a human... And what she learns will surprise everyone!

Odette is now a sophomore at her high school. She wants to be as close to human as she can, but finds out she still has a long way to go. From wanting to be "cute" by wearing nail polish, to making a "tasty" bento that people would be happy to eat, Odette faces each challenge head-on with the help of her friends Yoko, Chris, the Professor and, of course, Asao!

FROM THE CREATOR OF *AKUMA TO DOLCE*

"A SURPRISINGLY SENSITIVE, FUNNY AND THOUGHT-PROVOKING SCI-FI SHOJO SERIES ... AS GENUINELY CHARMING AND MEMORABLE AS ITS MECHANICAL HEROINE." —ABOUT.COM

TOKYOPOP MANGA SUPPLEMENT

DISCOVER STARCRAFT GHOST ACADEMY

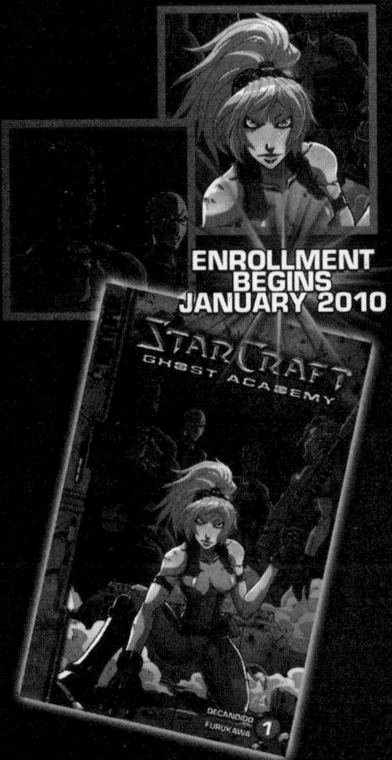
ENROLLMENT BEGINS JANUARY 2010
STARCRAFT
GHOST ACADEMY
DECANDIDO
FURUKAWA
1

Ghosts – The terrans powerful assassins, capable of reading minds and calling nuclear strikes... These ultimate weapons of Emporer Mengsk's arsenal are crafted at a sinister instiution – the Ghost Academy.

In this never-before-seen chapter in ghost prodigy Nova's life, the doors of the Ghost Academy are flung wide open! Join Nova as she navigates the challenges of brutal training, both physical and psychological, along with fellow cadets whose unusual telepathic and telekinetic powers are being twisted to serve the Dominion. But the cadets have no choice other than to endure and overcome, because at this school, failure is not an option.

THE MANGA REVOLUTION · LEADING · 漫画革命

SCI-FI

T TEEN AGE 13+

LICENSED BLIZZARD ENTERTAINMENT PRODUCT

FOR MORE INFORMATION VISIT: WWW.TOKYOPOP.COM/STARCRAFT

STOP!

This is the back of the book. You wouldn't want to spoil a great ending!

This book is printed "manga-style," in the authentic Japanese right-to-left format. Since none of the artwork has been flipped or altered, readers get to experience the story just as the creator intended. You've been asking for it, so TOKYOPOP® delivered: authentic, hot-off-the-press, and far more fun!

DIRECTIONS

If this is your first time reading manga-style, here's a quick guide to help you understand how it works.

It's easy... just start in the top right panel and follow the numbers. Have fun, and look for more 100% authentic manga from TOKYOPOP®!